15

The Poetry of W. H. AUDEN

The Poetry of
W. H. AUDEN

The Disenchanted Island

MONROE K. SPEARS

NEW YORK   OXFORD UNIVERSITY PRESS   1963

Preface

This book is written out of the conviction that Auden's poetry can offer the reader entertainment, instruction, intellectual excitement, and a prodigal variety of aesthetic pleasures, all in a generous abundance that is unique in our time. Its basic aim is to set the facts in order, clear away the obstacles to understanding, and provide the background and context required for a full appreciation of the poetry.

Auden, while vivid in personality, is diffident toward the public, and over the years a considerable body of misinformation about him has accumulated. For example, in his *Auden: An Introductory Essay* (London, 1951) Richard Hoggart stated that in 1950 Auden was appointed Assistant Professor of English at Ann Arbor University, Michigan. This mythical appointment is the only part of Auden's American academic history that seems to have found its way across the Atlantic; it has been solemnly recorded in British—and some American—reference works ever since. The fact is that Auden has had no connection with Michigan since 1942. On the other hand, the impression was widespread in this country that Auden was moving back to England when he accepted the Oxford Professorship of Poetry in 1956. Other persistent bits of misinformation are that Auden drove an ambulance for the Spanish Loyalists in 1937 and that his *For the Time Being* was set to music by Benjamin Britten. In view of the prevalence of such errors, I have taken some pains (and put Mr. Auden to some trouble) to try to make sure that I have the facts straight.

A more serious obstacle to understanding was created un-intentionally by Auden himself when he arranged the *Collected Poetry* of 1945 according to the alphabetical order of first lines. By producing difficulties for the serious reader and making even casual readers curious, this arrangement gave an unnecessary prominence to questions of date, revision, and publishing history—questions that distract from the poetry itself. I have tried to remedy this situation by including as an appendix a first-line index to Auden's poetry, which gives such information in compact form, and by discussing the poetry chronologically within a biographical framework. This framework consists primarily of a tabular chronology prefixed to each section; aside from this, biographical considerations have been introduced only when strictly relevant to the poetry.

I have tried throughout to keep firmly in mind the criterion of usefulness to the reader. Assuming that the reader will have the *Collected Poetry* at hand, I quote frugally from that volume and more liberally from sources that are not readily accessible. I have not dealt extensively with Auden's ideas, because too many previous discussions of Auden's poetry have turned out to be discussions of the sources, merits, and defects of his ideas, and because it seems to me worse than useless to present deceptively simple summaries of such complex thinkers as Freud, Marx, Groddeck, Blake, Lawrence, Kierkegaard, Niebuhr, and Auden himself. Instead, I have kept the emphasis on the poetry. Neither the plays nor the very numerous critical and other prose pieces are treated as fully as they deserve, though I hope I have made clear the great intrinsic interest of *The Dyer's Hand* (1962) as well as its usefulness in interpreting the poetry.

The chronology includes a bibliography of Auden's writings, not pretending to technical completeness but including, I hope, everything of importance. References to Auden's works in the text and notes use the shortest intelligible form; either the chronology or the first-line index will supply full information. A title index is appended also, for cross-reference to the first-line index.

There remains only the pleasure of acknowledging several debts of gratitude. The largest of these I owe Mr. Auden, who has patiently answered numerous questions and has gone out of his way to give me every possible kind of help and co-operation. My friend Daniel G. Hoffman of Swarthmore College gave me invaluable encouragement and assistance. To mention only two of the many others at Swarthmore who helped me, Samuel Hynes made several useful suggestions and Howard Williams put every resource of the library at my disposal. David Posner of the Lockwood Memorial Library at the University of Buffalo sent films of the Auden manuscripts in their collection and gave permission to quote from them. My colleague Brinley Rhys of the University of the South gave me the benefit both of his musical knowledge and of his remarkable collection of phonograph records; he also called my attention to several recent publications I might otherwise have missed. William Harkins and Corinne Burg of the library of the University of the South have been most accommodating in obtaining books and periodicals for me. I am aware of three special obligations to written sources: *The Romantic Survival* by John Bayley (London, 1957) suggested in part my approach to the early poetry, and *The Making of the Auden Canon* by the late Joseph Warren Beach (Minneapolis, 1957), and Edward Callan's "Annotated Checklist of the Works of W. H. Auden" (*Twentieth Century Literature*, April-July 1958) contributed heavily to the first-line index and bibliography.

I am greatly obliged to Random House, Inc., and to Faber and Faber, Ltd., for permission to quote from all the works of W. H. Auden to which they hold copyright, and to Mr. Auden for carte blanche to quote from all his works. Since all the books quoted from are fully described in the chronology, they are not listed separately here.

Sewanee, Tennessee
31 December 1962

M. K. S.

Contents

The Poetry of W. H. AUDEN

1907-1932

1907   Wystan Hugh Auden born on February 21 in York, third son of George Augustus and Constance Rosalie (Bicknell) Auden.

1908   The family moved to Birmingham, where Dr. Auden became Medical Officer and Professor of Public Health in Birmingham University.

1915-20   St. Edmund's School (preparatory). Met Christopher Isherwood, who was three years older and left in 1918.

1920-25   Gresham's School, Holt (Norfolk). Specialized in biology. In an essay in *The Old School* (ed. Graham Greene, London & N.Y., 1934), Auden describes the school with generosity and himself with candor: "The son of book-loving, Anglo-Catholic parents of the professional class, the youngest of three brothers, I was . . . mentally precocious, physically backward, short-sighted, a rabbit at all games, very untidy and grubby, a nail-biter, a physical coward, dishonest, sentimental, with no community sense whatever, in fact a typical little highbrow and difficult child" (p. 9).

1922   Discovery of vocation. "One afternoon in March at half-past three / When walking in a ploughed field with a friend; / . . . he turned to me / And said, 'Tell me, do you write poetry?' / I never had, and said so, but I knew / That very moment what I wished to do" (*Letters from Iceland*, p. 208). The friend was Robert Medley, according to Julian Symons (*The Thirties*, London, 1960, p. 78); Medley became a painter and theatrical designer and was associated with Auden in the Group Theatre.

     First poem published in *Public Schools Verse*, 1924 ("It is a lovely sight and good").

3

1925-28   Christ Church College, Oxford. Went up as Exhibitioner. Influenced by W. P. Ker's essays, J. R. R. Tolkien's reading of Old English.

1926   Discovery of T. S. Eliot's poetry. Auden's tutor, Nevill Coghill of Exeter, describes revolutionary impact in *T. S. Eliot: A Symposium* (ed. R. March & Tambimuttu, London, 1948).
Edited, with Charles Plumb, *Oxford Poetry 1926* (including three poems by Auden).
Edited, with C. Day Lewis, *Oxford Poetry 1927* (with one poem by Auden).

1928   *Poems* (S.H.S.: 1928) hand-printed by Stephen Spender on his press at Oxford; probably fewer than 45 copies printed. (Dedicated to Christopher Isherwood.)

1928-29   Berlin. Auden recalls in a recent *Encounter* (Jan. 1963) that he "fell in love with the German Language," and continues "When I went down from Oxford in 1928, my parents offered me a year abroad. For the generation of intellectuals immediately preceding mine, the only culture that counted was French culture. I was bored with hearing about it, and, therefore, determined that, wherever I might go, it would not be to Paris. Where then? Rome? No; Mussolini and fascism made that impossible. Berlin? That was an idea! Why not? I knew no German and hardly any German literature, but, then, nobody else I knew did either . . . Perhaps, also, I had an unconscious bias in favour of Germany because, when I was a little boy in prep-school during the First World War, if I took an extra slice of bread and margarine, some master was sure to say—'I see, Auden, you want the Huns to win'—thus establishing in my mind an association between Germany and forbidden pleasures . . ."
Influenced by German poetry, cabaret-songs, and theater, especially that of Bertolt Brecht, and by psychological doctrine of John Layard, deriving from Homer Lane, D. H. Lawrence, Gide, and ultimately from Freud and Groddeck.

4

Isherwood abandoned his medical studies and joined Auden in Berlin, March 1929.

1930   *Paid on Both Sides: A Charade* (dedicated to C. Day Lewis) published in *The Criterion* in January.

Poems (dedicated to Christopher Isherwood) published by Faber & Faber in September, containing *Paid* and thirty poems. In the second edition, 1933, seven poems were dropped and seven others (all written before 1931) substituted.

Review in *The Criterion* (April 1930) of *Instinct and Intuition* by G. B. Diblee.

1930-35   Schoolmaster at Larchfield Academy, Helensburgh, Scotland, and at The Downs School, Colwall, near Malvern.

1932   *The Orators* (dedicated to Stephen Spender) published by Faber & Faber.

Review of *The Complete Works of John Skelton* (ed. Philip Henderson) in *The Criterion* (Jan. 1932).

Note on *Edda* and *Saga* by Dame Bertha Phillpotts in *The Criterion* (Jan. 1932).

Review article on several books on education, "Private Pleasure," in *Scrutiny* (May 1932).

Review of *Education and the Social Order* by Bertrand Russell in *New Statesman & Nation* (Oct. 15, 1932).

I

Fantasy and Diagnosis

If I ask myself what single piece of literature gave me greatest pleasure in 1961, it was an article in the *Scientific American* called "Cleaning Shrimps."

W. H. AUDEN IN THE LONDON *Sunday Times*, DEC. 24, 1961

DIAGNOSIS

Auden's interests until his sixteenth year were exclusively scientific. His father was a distinguished physician of broad scientific interests,[1] and his mother had been a nurse; the atmosphere of the home was scientific rather than literary. Auden's great loves were machinery and mines; he intended to be a mining engineer. Isherwood describes him at preparatory school as a "sturdy, podgy little boy" who was "precociously clever, untidy, lazy, and, with the masters, inclined to be insolent. His... playbox was full of thick scientific books on geology and metals and machines, borrowed from his father's library." Since his father was a doctor he knew about sex, and with his "hinted forbidden knowledge and stock of mispronounced scientific words, portentously uttered, he enjoyed among us, his semi-savage credulous schoolfellows, the status of a kind of witch-doctor." [2] At school he specialized in biology, and this interest is prominent in his early verse (most plainly in the images based on evolution, mutation, survival of the fittest, and the like). At Oxford he read widely in psychology and used it to diagnose his friends; Spender, meeting him for the first time in 1928,

The notes are to be found at the end of the section, on page 61.

found him interested not in politics but in "poetry, psycho-analysis, and medicine. . . . At this early age, Auden had already an extensive knowledge of the theories of modern psychology, which he used as a means of understanding himself and dominating his friends." [3] Both Spender and Isherwood describe their relation to Auden as partly that of patient to analyst. Isherwood represents him as saying that the poet's first duty is to be "clinically minded": "Love wasn't exciting or romantic or even disgusting; it was funny. The poet must handle it and similar themes with a wry, bitter smile and a pair of rubber surgical gloves. Poetry must be classic, clinical, and austere." [4] It must concern itself with shapes and volumes: colors and smells were condemned as romantic; form alone was significant. "Auden loathed (and still rather dislikes) the Sea—for the Sea, besides being deplorably wet and sloppy, is formless." [5] Spender remarks, "I think that Cocteau's image in *Orphée* of Death as the surgeon with white coat and rubber gloves was his secret fantasy of the poet." [6] The notion of the poet as clinically detached, diagnosing the sicknesses of a society and its component individuals, and of poetry as a kind of therapy, performing a function somehow analogous to the psychoanalytic, is fundamental in Auden's writing.

Auden as spiritual physician continued to play the role of witch-doctor, however; as Geoffrey Grigson observed perceptively in 1937, "There is something about Auden of the benign wizard casting out devils, but enjoying the devils and the wizardry." [7] He had a strong histrionic bent, and loved assuming roles, mimicking, clowning. Isherwood describes him as fond of wearing peculiar hats, especially one "representing, I think, Weston's conception of himself as a lunatic clergyman; always a favourite role." [8] He delighted in extreme and shocking statements, surprising poses. MacNeice portrays him as "by nature partly a buffoon, and largely a gossip." [9] Day Lewis presents an unforgettable picture of him at Oxford in 1927, taking his favorite walk past the gasworks and the municipal rubbish dump, moving with his phenomenally long, ungainly stride, and talking incessantly, his words tumbling over one another in the hurry to get out, a lock of tow-coloured hair falling over the brow of his rather puffy but wonderfully animated white face. As likely as not, he was carrying a starting-pistol and wearing an extraordinary black, lay-reader's type of frock-coat which came half way down to his knees and had been rescued by him from one of his mother's jumble sales.[10]

Day Lewis was most impressed by his exuberance and vitality: "a vitality so abundant that, overflowing into certain poses and follies and wildly unrealistic notions, it gave these an air of authority, an illusion of rightness, which enticed some of Auden's contemporaries into taking them over-seriously" (*The Buried Day*, p. 176). As lunatic clergyman, witch-doctor, or magician, he could maintain that all disorders are ultimately spiritual, and that the plausible, solemn, normal world is not the real one.

In Berlin, Auden became an enthusiastic convert to the psychological doctrine of John Layard, who was a disciple of the American "healer," Homer Lane.[11] Auden describes it in *Letters from Iceland:* "Part came from Lane, and part from D. H. Lawrence; / Gide, though I didn't know it then, gave part. / They taught me to express my deep abhorrence / If I caught anyone preferring Art / To Life and Love and being Pure-in-Heart / ... The Pure-in-Heart is never ill..." (p. 210). The notion that disease is invariably teleological, a mode of expression of the Id, caused by a sense of guilt—that physical disease is always symptomatic of a psychological cause—was part of this doctrine. (It is also to be found in Freud and Groddeck, whom Auden continues to quote and recommend.) [12] According to Isherwood, his first collaboration with Auden was a play called *The Enemies of a Bishop*, in which the Bishop is an idealized portrait of Homer Lane. He represents sanity and wins out against the pseudo-healers, the willfully ill and the mad (*New Verse*, Nov. 1937, p. 8). Auden, says Isherwood, "assimilated all these ideas with his customary zest and ease, adding to them a touch of extravagance which was peculiarly his own" (*Lions and Shadows*, p. 302). "When people are ill, they're wicked," Auden said; a sore throat means that the sufferer has been lying; cancer means refusal to make use of creative powers; rheumatism means obstinacy, refusal to bend the knee; deafness and short sight are attempts to shut out the exterior world; epilepsy is an attempt to become an angel, and fly. The great attraction for Auden of this kind of diagnosis was that, in interpreting disease as morally symbolic, it made possible a new mode of rendering moral abstractions concrete and vivid. Further, it sanctioned the desire for revolt against the existing system, for a transvaluation of values. Isherwood thus paraphrases a letter from "Barnard" (Layard) to "Weston" (Auden):

> Every disease, Lane had taught, is in itself a cure—if we know how to take it. There is only one sin: disobedience to the inner law of our own nature. The results of this disobedience show themselves in crime or in disease; but the disobedience is never, in the first place, our own fault—it is the fault of those who teach us, as children, to control God (our desires) instead of giving Him room to grow. The whole problem, when dealing with a patient, is to find out which of all the conflicting things inside him is God, and which is the Devil. And the one sure guide is that God always appears unreasonable, while the Devil appears always to be noble and right. God appears unreasonable because He has been put in prison and driven wild. The Devil is conscious control, and is, therefore, reasonable and sane. Conventional education inverts the whole natural system in childhood, turning the child into a spurious adult... So diseases and neuroses come to kill off the offenders or bring them to their senses. Diseases are therefore only warning symptoms of a sickness of the soul; they are manifestations of God—and those who try to "cure" them without first curing the soul are only serving the Devil. (*Lions and Shadows*, p. 300)

"Weston" is, Isherwood says, a "caricature" of Auden, and Isherwood's account of these matters is clearly simplified and theatrically heightened; the impression he gives is that Weston picked up a wildly eccentric gospel of dubious origins and swallowed it uncritically. The truth seems to be that Homer Lane was more saint than mere eccentric, that the basic doctrine is thoroughly respectable, and that Auden had learned it from Freud and, presumably, from Groddeck before he went to Berlin. That Auden is a serious, competent, and responsible student of psychology is apparent in his first review (1930) and is overwhelmingly evident in his important essay of 1935, "Psychology and Art Today." In this piece Auden, in the course of a brilliant interpretation of Freud, attributes this doctrine to him: "Not only what we recognize as sin or crime, but all illness, is purposive. It is an attempt at cure." At the root of all disease and sin is the sense of guilt; the cure consists in removing it. (In the same essay Auden observes that all of Freud is in Blake's "Marriage of Heaven and Hell," and discusses the relation between Freud and Lawrence.)

Both in poetry and in prose, Auden's approach may be said to remain primarily psychological throughout all changes of emphasis and perspective, political or religious, and his knowledge of this and related sciences—particularly biology and anthropology—is extensive and current.

FANTASY

An inclination to fantasy—using the word to mean not merely compensatory wish-fulfillment, but any concern with a level of reality transcending common sense and natural law—is, no doubt, partly a matter of temperament. Perhaps it is not fanciful to say that, as the youngest of three brothers, Auden inhabited a fairy-tale situation; [13] certainly these tales, particularly those of Andersen and the Grimms, have had a compelling influence upon his imagination. The art of the novelist he admires but finds uncongenial; [14] the prose fiction he likes best, such as Kafka, Carroll, Potter, Verne, Macdonald, Firbank, certain detective stories, and most recently J. R. R. Tolkien's *Lord of the Rings*, is all essentially fantasy. "Dream Literature," as Auden defines it in his introduction to the *Visionary Novels of George Macdonald* (1954), deals with mythical characters who are universal in appeal and independent of their histories (e.g., Sherlock Holmes, Mr. Pickwick); it includes detective stories and opera libretti, and it must steer between incoherence and mechanical allegory. Macdonald notably possessed, Auden thinks, the mythopoeic power "to project his inner life into images, events, beings, landscapes which are valid for all." Among Auden's early favorites were Jules Verne's *Child of the Cavern* and Macdonald's *Princess and the Goblin*, because they related to his Sacred Objects, his obsession with caves. His list of those who have written just as he would like to write, in *Letters from Iceland* (p. 202), consists of "Firbank, Potter, Carroll, Lear." In *The Dyer's Hand* (1962), the only prose discussed at any length belongs to this category: Verne, Wodehouse, Nathanael West, *Don Quixote*, and *Pickwick Papers*. As we shall see, the powerful attraction of fantasy is expressed in the Island symbolism of Auden's poetry and in his later preoccupation with the myth of Eden (as distinguished from New Jerusalem), as well as with opera.

The religious and musical influences of his youth must have enriched his inner life and strengthened his inclination to fantasy. Both his grandfathers and four of his uncles were Church of England clergymen; the atmosphere of his home was devoutly Anglo-Catholic. He was a boat-boy at six, and his "first religious memories are of exciting magical rites . . . rather than of listening to sermons." [15] He had a good musical education. sang in his school choirs, and loved to play hymns, chants, and psalms on the piano. (In *Letters from Iceland*, p. 202, he confesses to daydreams of being a concert pianist or opera singer.) By the time he began to write poetry he had ceased to believe in Christianity, but his writing was permeated by its modes of thought, feeling, and language; Isherwood describes him in 1937 as "still much preoccupied with ritual, in all its forms," and continues:

> When we collaborate, I have to keep a sharp eye on him—or down flop the characters on their knees . . . : another constant danger is of choral interruptions by angel-voices. If Auden had his way, he would turn every play into a cross between grand opera and high mass. (*New Verse*)

The plays have, as we shall see, little element of character or everyday reality in them, and what little there is was presumably contributed by Isherwood. His prophecy, by the way, was accurate; Auden did go on alone to write grand opera and an oratorio.

The tendency to fantasy had for Auden and his contemporaries social as well as psychological implications. As Isherwood indicates in describing the elaborate joint fantasies produced over many years by himself and Edward Upward,[16] these imaginary worlds—the Other Town, with its Rats' Hostel, and later the mythical village of Mortmere—served both to provide escape from and to express revolt against the existing order, as, psychologically, they both camouflaged and expressed his feelings about War and The Test. (In his latest novel, *Down There on a Visit*, 1962, Isherwood recalls that his dominant motive at this time was Ancestor Hatred.) The fantastic element in Auden's early work serves the same purposes. While he had little interest in politics until his visit to Berlin, and then tended to add the political dimension to his clinical picture in a manner unsatisfactory to those, such as Spender, who were more ardent politically, the feeling of alienation from society and the need to shock and expose it are plain in his earliest verse. His psychological interests, encouraging the investigation of dreams and the unconscious and a profound suspicion of the rational mind, reinforced his other impulses toward fantasy.

Many of Auden's early poems thus sound like excerpts from a private narrative which goes on indefinitely, creating a fantasy world.

Auden was well aware that fantasy was not enough:

> The psychologist maintains that poetry is a neurotic symptom, an attempt to compensate by phantasy for a failure to meet reality. We must tell him that phantasy is only the beginning of writing; that, on the contrary, like psychology, poetry is a struggle to reconcile the unwilling subject and object; in fact, that since psychological truth depends so largely on context, poetry, the parabolic approach, is the only adequate medium for psychology.
>
> (Introd. to *The Poet's Tongue*, 1935, p. ix)

The parabolic approach he attributes to Freud: "You cannot tell people what to do, you can only tell them parables; and that is what art really is, particular stories of particular people and experiences, from which each according to his immediate and peculiar needs may draw his own conclusions." [17] In the same essay he defines escape art as the other principal type: "there must always be two kinds of art—escape art, for man needs escape as he needs food and deep sleep, and parable art, that art which shall teach man to unlearn hatred and learn love." As John Bayley observes,[18] the dichotomy is crude and is related to the similar dichotomy in Auden's own poetry. The problem in the early verse is to unite the inner, private, emotional, magical, obscure world with the public, rational, social world, to bring together fantasy and diagnosis. The problem is by no means peculiar to Auden: one thinks of Yeats's long quest for "unity of being" and Eliot's formulation of "dissociation of sensibility." But the division is particularly marked in Auden's early verse.

Since Auden is Northern in background, affinities, and tastes, his fantasies were of the North. In childhood, "With northern myths my little brain was laden, / With deeds of Thor and Loki and such scenes; / My favourite tale was Andersen's Ice

Maiden. . . ." [19] Isherwood describes the landscape of the early
poetry:

> The scenery of Auden's early poetry is, almost invariably,
> mountainous. As a boy, he visited Westmorland, the Peak
> District of Derbyshire, and Wales. For urban scenery, he
> preferred the industrial Midlands; particularly in districts
> where an industry is decaying. His romantic travel-wish
> was always towards the North. He could never under-
> stand how anybody could long for the sun, the blue sky,
> the palm-trees of the South. His favourite weather was
> autumnal; high wind and driving rain. He loved indus-
> trial ruins, a disused factory or an abandoned mill; a
> ruined abbey would leave him quite cold. He has always
> had a special feeling for caves and mines. At school, one
> of his favourite books was Jules Verne's Journey to the
> Centre of the Earth.   (*New Verse*, 1937)

Isherwood observes that Auden was brought up on the Icelandic sagas and that his feelings about heroic Norse literature
were his own personal variety of war-fixation. He made Isherwood read the sagas, and Isherwood made the fruitful comment
that they reminded him of their preparatory school:

> The saga-world is a schoolboy world, with its feuds, its
> practical jokes, its dark threats conveyed in puns and
> riddles and understatements: 'I think this day will end
> unluckily for some; but chiefly for those who least expect
> harm.' I once remarked to Auden that the atmosphere of
> Gisli the Outlaw very much reminded me of our school-
> days. He was pleased with the idea: and, soon after this,
> he produced his first play: Paid on Both Sides, in which
> the two worlds are so inextricably confused that it is
> impossible to say whether the characters are really epic
> heroes or only members of a school O.T.C.
>   (*Lions and Shadows*, p. 193)

This school-saga world became for a time a kind of Mortmere
for them, a collaborative fantasy based on their prep-school
lives. Isherwood tried to write a story about it, combining saga-

language and schoolboy slang, but without success. For Auden, the fusion of the two worlds was magical: not only is it the basis of *Paid on Both Sides*, but as an implicit metaphor it underlies much of the early poetry. The persistent image of war is an obvious extension of it, suggesting both that the difference between adult and schoolboy society is less real than apparent and that social conflicts are disguised warfare. British schools emphasized self-government by the boys, and this led often to a tyranny of adolescent values, especially those connected with sports. Team spirit, with its excesses of conformism and brutality, was often exalted into a morality. (The defects of the system were widely recognized; Graham Greene, editing *The Old School* in 1934, assumes that it is doomed and describes the book as a memorial, more funny than tragic.) The fact that Auden was himself a schoolmaster is important, for the politically radical schoolmaster was in a peculiarly ambivalent situation: a bourgeois and a product of the system himself, he is yet dedicated to the overthrow of the moral and social values it supports and is supported by. Hence he must regard himself sometimes as a spy and saboteur.

PAID ON BOTH SIDES

Paid on Both Sides was written late in 1928 and first published in *The Criterion* for January 1930. The dedication to C. Day Lewis may well be related to the fact that when Auden became a schoolmaster in this year he succeeded Day Lewis as English Master at Larchfield Academy.[20] (By an odd coincidence, he succeeded Day Lewis as Professor of Poetry at Oxford many years later.) The subtitle, "A Charade," suggests that the piece is not to be read as a play, that it will have hidden meanings, and that it is intended to be entertaining. The break with naturalistic theater is complete: there is no dramatic illusion, and the reader's interest is not in characters or plot but in what each of these represents. The piece is indeed on one level a guessing game in which tableaux and actions represent, not words, as in most charades, but ideas; and in which the appeal to the interest and challenge of riddles is constant.

The time is Christmas Eve, and the piece has elements of the traditional Christmas pantomime in the farcical and fantastic middle section that begins with the entrance of Father Christmas. (Auden said a few years later, "The music hall, the Christmas pantomime, and the country house charade are the most living drama of today.") [21] The place is both the medieval Iceland of the sagas, with its blood feuds and isolated, fortified farms, and, at the same time, contemporary England. The plot concerns the feud between the Nowers and the Shaws, which after several exchanges is interrupted by the marriage of John Nower (the central character) and Anne Shaw; but Seth Shaw's mother makes him ambush the Nowers at the wedding party, John is killed and the feud is on again.

On one level, the piece presents an image of the essential human condition. By saga-characters, as by Anglo-Saxon warriors or Greek epic heroes, warfare is regarded as man's normal condition and peace as an accidental breathing space. Man constantly faces insecurity and danger; all he can do is to accept his fate bravely. The style helps to convey this meaning: it gives the impression of being stripped down to bedrock as the situation is stripped down to the permanent, unchanging human predicament. Its most striking characteristic is ellipsis, often so extensive as to omit grammatical connectives, so that syntax tends to become parataxis:

> Can speak of trouble, pressure on men
> Born all the time, brought forward into light
> For warm dark moan.
> Though heart fears all heart cries for, rebuffs with mortal beat
> Skyfall, the legs sucked under, adder's bite.

The ambiguity of meaning thus produced contributes to the riddling, oracular effect, which is heightened by frequent understatement and other forms of grim irony. The meter—often a line with four heavy stresses, with much use of alliteration, assonance, and other devices of sound—strongly suggests Old English poetry, with its characteristic tone and attitude. The final chorus, "Though he believe it, no man is strong," renders this meaning of the play explicit.

There is, however, another and very different level of meaning, which may be called the political. In this interpretation, the conditions of existence can be changed: the feudal society must be abandoned, and things will be different in another country (that is, in a new society). Thus Dick emigrates to the Colonies; Anne urges John Nower to join him: "John, I have a car waiting. There is time to join Dick before the boat sails. We sleep in beds where men have died howling." But John refuses, saying merely, "You may be right, but we shall stay." The chorus, "To throw away the key and walk away," is the fullest statement of this meaning (it is reprinted in both the *Collected Poetry* of 1945 and the *Selected Poetry* of 1958). A brief explication will perhaps be useful. The basic metaphor of migration, changing one country for another, means giving allegiance to the Marxist society of the future. The poem argues that once the key has been thrown away—the essential commitment made—instead of leaving the old society abruptly and completely, it is better to follow carefully the frontier between the old and new societies. This close following of the frontier teaches more than any school, and also "makes us well / Without confession of the ill"—i.e., it removes the social causes of neurosis (and, presumably, of physical disease) and renders the psychiatrist unnecessary. The frontier is chronological rather than geographical, as the next part of the poem makes clear; the "future shall fulfil a surer vow," and life in this new society will be unimaginably different and better, though painful at first, like an evolutionary mutation: "Not swooping at the surface still like gulls / But with prolonged drowning shall develop gills." (Probably an allusion is intended here to the "destructive element" passage in Conrad's *Lord Jim*.) The second section of the poem requires no elucidation, with its picture of the traveler increasingly dissatisfied and frustrated in the old country, finally reaching happy oblivion in the new, "Rock shutting out the sky, the old life done." The fact that Dick does this proves that, in terms of the play, it is possible; but the central character, John, cannot leave; and we admire John.

The discovery that the saga-heroes are also schoolboys has a literally mock-heroic effect, which, as usual, works both ways: the saga-heroes are exposed as permanent adolescents . (this effect works at odds with the poetry, which takes them very seriously indeed), and the school athletes are revealed as brutal, harsh, and cruel. (Auden commented in *Letters from Iceland*, p. 129: "I love the sagas, but what a rotten society they describe, a society with only the gangster virtues.") Politically, the thesis is the Marxist one that these are the molding influences that lead to war, that the schools, inculcating the capitalist ethos, psychologically shape their products to be aggressive and brutal.

There is, finally, a psychological level of meaning. Here the chief point is the malignant influence of the mothers, who are the chief bearers of the feud and who, from infancy, instill hatred in their sons. Joan, revealed at the beginning with the corpse of her husband, just slain in the feud, and her child John Nower, makes a speech vowing vengeance, "An unforgiving morning," and rejoices in the thought of the baby carrying on the feud. At the end, Seth Shaw's mother forces him to renew the feud and ambush the wedding party. The final chorus comments, "His mother and her mother won." In the Father Christmas fantasy in the middle, Joan is warder of the Spy and threatens him with a gigantic feeding bottle; the reference here may be to theories of the traumatic effect of weaning, as well as more generally to the Oedipus or Coriolanus complex.[22] The traditional fierceness of tribal old women and modern lady patriots needs no discussion. To some extent, this interpretation fits in with the political: for the new life, tradition of all kinds must be rejected: "By loss of memory we are reborn, / For memory is death...."

The basic ambiguity remains, however: what is responsible for the tragedy is and is not just a corrupt society or mistakes in the raising of children; it is also the unchangeable human condition. The difficulty is that the ambiguity is too radical and involves shifts of tone so great that the piece lacks emotional coherence: the gaps between grim tragedy, schoolboy humor, political satire, psychological jokes (some of which, in the episodes of the Man-Woman and the Mad Surgeon, are very private), and fantastic farce are too great. Nevertheless, the piece is full of entertaining and moving things, and it provides an indispensable context and background for the early poetry.

POEMS 1928

Poems (S.H.S.: 1928), of which only about forty-five copies were hand-printed by Stephen Spender on his press at Oxford, is a collector's rarity, extremely difficult of access, though Xerox reproductions are now available. The book seems not to have been used by any previous critic of Auden and, since it is of exceptional interest in showing the development of his style, I shall consider it in some detail.

The volume contains twenty-six poems, if one counts as separate poems the seven parts of the first, which are headed I(a) to I(g). Only one of these had been published before: I(f), "Consider if you will how lovers stand," had appeared in *Oxford Poetry* 1927. Of the twenty-six poems, fifteen were retained in the 1930 volume: nine in the same form as separate poems and six incorporated into *Paid on Both Sides,* which was published in *The Criterion* for January 1930 and then included in the 1930 volume of *Poems.*

These six poems [23] raise an interesting question, for they sound as if they were excerpted from a work already in existence in some form. Auden, queried on the point, replied that he wrote them first as separate poems. "Then they seemed to be part of something." [24] *Paid*, he continued, was finished in Berlin around Christmas 1928. Several of the poems are based on some such situation as that in *Paid*, most specifically the one that became the final chorus, "Night strives with darkness . . . ," including the line "His mother and her mother won." Without going into speculations about the possible mode of existence of *Paid* in Auden's mind when the poems were written—perhaps unconscious or implicit or potential existence—we may proceed to the important point: that the difference between a separate poem and an excerpt from a longer work is clearly not an absolute one for Auden.

The composite first poem in the 1928 volume is an example of this, for the basis for considering the seven parts as constituting one work is obscure; they appear to be as independent of each other as are the other poems. (This question will be discussed further when we come to consider the pattern of the volume.) In several later instances Auden has published poems separately and then later incorporated them in longer works (see below, pp. 99, 102). Other poets do the same kind of thing, of course: perhaps the most striking modern example is the way various parts of *The Waste Land*, *The Hollow Men*, and "Minor Poems" were shifted about and recombined variously at different times by Eliot, sometimes with Pound's help. [25] In fact, the absolute distinction between a work that is a separate entity and one that is a part of a larger work would seem to be no more than an assumption, useful to critics but not to poets.

Since Auden had read little poetry before his discovery of his vocation in 1922, [26] his mind was a blank tablet for the poets he encountered after that date; and we know with unusual fullness and precision the history of his early tastes. He began in 1922 with de la Mare, W. H. Davies, A.E., and other minor figures whom he enjoyed, but none of whom was what he was seeking. De la Mare's anthology, *Come Hither!* (1923) was an important early influence: in 1939 Auden remarked that it, "more than any book I have read before or since, taught me what poetry is" (review of de la Mare, *Behold This Dreamer, The New Republic,* Dec. 27, 1939). Its range is catholic, and nursery rhymes, songs, ballads, singing-games, incantations and the like are included on equal terms with formal poetry. In the summer of 1923 he discovered his first great master, Thomas Hardy, and read him exclusively until the autumn of 1924; [27] after that, Edward Thomas shared his reign. As one would expect, the poems Auden showed Isherwood in 1925 were strongly imitative of Hardy and Thomas, with perhaps a suggestion also of Frost.[28] The revolutionary impact of the discovery of Eliot in 1926 has been described by Auden's tutor, Nevill Coghill, as well as by Isherwood.[29] Eliot, however, never inspired the exclusive devotion that the first love, Hardy, did; Isherwood describes brief crazes in 1926-27 for, successively, Robinson, Dickinson, Bridges, and Hopkins, all of whom left detectable traces in the early verse.

These are the principal formative influences, though one can see from time to time in the early verse what seem to be definite impressions of numerous other poets, from Wilfred Owen and Lawrence back to Skelton, Langland, and the Anglo-Saxons. (In 1941 Auden cited Dante, Langland, and Pope as the three greatest influences on his work.) [30] Auden is deeply rooted in the whole tradition of English poetry, and his critical writings as well as the anthologies he has edited give evidence of the catholicity of his taste.[31] Once Auden's own style, or styles, had been formed, however, the influences fade into the background; even as early as the 1928 *Poems,* there is nothing derivative or imitative in the manner of the juvenile work. In describing the various styles in this 1928 volume, I shall speak of "influences," but chiefly as a means of describing by comparison, not with any suggestion of close resemblance. Before proceeding to this description, it might be useful to attempt a brief general characterization of Auden's early style, to keep its unique qualities before the reader.

Perhaps the most obvious characteristic is the detached, clinical, objective attitude, with modern and scientific imagery:

> Consider if you will how lovers stand
> In brief adherence, straining to preserve
> Too long the suction of good-bye: others,
> Less clinically-minded, will admire
> An evening like a coloured photograph . . .

A second is the variety in meter and stanza, the technical virtuosity; this will be demonstrated amply when I proceed to analyze the varieties of style. A third is the closeness to dream, riddle, the non-logical, and the subconscious, both in the ellipsis of grammatical and logical connectives (what MacNeice calls the "dream parataxis") [32] and in the images (as in the birth image that opens the second poem: "Bones wrenched, weak whimper, lids wrinkled, first dazzle known . . ."). Fourth and last, and perhaps not really separate from the preceding point, is the frequent obscurity, resulting not only from ellipsis of connectives but from lack of any discoverable connections among images or statements, from excessive privacy of reference or association, from uncertainty as to who is speaking and what is going on.

To proceed now to distinguish some of the different styles in the volume: perhaps the most striking is that already described as characteristic of *Paid on Both Sides*, which might be called, in its fully developed form, the Nordic mask. In his Oxford inaugural lecture of 1956 Auden recalled the impact of hearing Old English poetry read by J. R. R. Tolkien at Oxford, and obviously this poetry was (together with the sagas, of course) the primary influence. Only those poems in the volume that were made part of *Paid* employ the style; the best example is the one that became the final chorus: "Night strives with darkness, right with wrong."

Another style, which is similar in that it is often accentual in meter and laconic and elliptical in language, but differs in that it employs short lines of two or three stresses and emotionally charged abstractions, may be designated the clipped lyric. Anglo-Saxon verse, if the half-line is taken as unit, is in the background here; but a more definite influence is Skelton, with his irregular two- to five-stress tumbling meter and eccentric rhyming.[33] Of modern models, certainly the most important was Hardy, who used this kind of verse very effectively, as in "Rain on a Grave" or "In Tenebris I." The verse of Robert Graves may possibly have had some influence, particularly his impressive early (1920) achievement "Rocky Acres," and possibly also that of Laura Riding, from whom Graves once accused Auden of stealing a passage.[34] But these influences are hard to disentangle, if they are present at all: Graves himself was following Old English and Skeltonic models in returning to accentual meters, and was much influenced by Laura Riding in the handling of abstractions. A more definite source for Auden's bold treatment of abstractions is Emily Dickinson. The best example of this style in the 1928 volume is the one incorporated in *Paid:* "The summer quickens grass," with its severe taut restraint in the contrast between the summer lovers and the future when "we shall choose from ways, / All of them evil, one."

> Look on with stricter brows
> The sacked and burning town,
> The ice-sheet moving down,
> The fall of an old house.

The image of geological change, of the glacier moving, is peculiarly effective: the other kinds of change acquire dignity and inevitability from it.[35] A similar example of the functional effect of the disciplined, strict style is the one beginning:

> I chose this lean country
> For seven day content,
> To satisfy the want
> Of eye and ear, to see
> The slow fastidious line
> That disciplines the fell, . . .[36]

Here, the use of landscape to represent a state of mind is in the same mode as Graves's "Rocky Acres," though completely different in effect. The technique of Moralized Landscape is developed much more elaborately later on.

A third variety of style may be called the colloquial or middle style; the label is self-explanatory. It should be added, however, that this type not only approximates the language of civilized conversation but sometimes suggests the specialized attitudes of particular kinds of civilized persons to produce special effects, as the poem already cited, "Consider if you will how lovers stand" uses language that is clinically flat and academically colorless to produce the effect of a schoolmasterly demonstration. Perhaps the most clear-cut example of the middle style in the volume is this:

> This peace can last no longer than the storm
> Which started it; the shower wet and warm,
> The careless striding through the clinging grass
> Perceiving nothing, these will surely pass
> When heart and ear-drums are no longer dinned
> By shouting air. As surely as the wind
> Will bring a lark song from the cloud, not rain,
> Shall I know the meaning of lust again;
> Nor sunshine on the weir's unconscious roar
> Can change whatever I might be before.
> I know it, yet for this brief hour or so
> I am content, unthinking and aglow;
> Made one with horses and with workmen, all
> Who seek for shelter by a dripping wall,[37]
> Or labour in the fields with mist and cloud
> And slant rain hiding them as in a shroud.

This is cited by Isherwood (*Lions and Shadows*, p. 187) as an example of the influence of Hardy, Thomas, and Frost. In form it suggests the sonnet, though it is in fact eight regular couplets. There is, of course, an ironic point in the use of this thoroughly traditional idiom and form to describe a kind of peace which is merely release from lust; it is not parody, but there is a delicate shock effect. In other poems, the style produces an effect of striving for clarity, with the surface lucidity masking obscurities beneath; for example, "Taller to-day, we remember similar evenings" (which was kept in the later volumes of *Poems*) and the one beginning, mysteriously,

> The four sat on in the bare room
> Together and the fire unlighted,
> And One was speaking;—'she turned the page,
> More quavers on the other side.'

A fourth variety of style may be called high: it is florid, extravagant, elevated, profuse; usually it is written in long lines, and it often exhibits baroque incongruities of diction. The effect is thus frequently mock-heroic, sometimes with specific literary parody. An example in the 1928 volume is:

> Bones wrenched, weak whimper, lids wrinkled, first dazzle known,
> World-wonder hardened as bigness, years, brought knowledge, you,
> Presence a rich mould augured for roots urged, but gone,
> The soul is tetanous: gun-barrel burnishing
> In summer grass, mind lies to tarnish ...

Here the style seems highly imitative of Hopkins, almost to the point of parody, but not merely parody; the imagery is highly modern and scientific, as in the last two lines quoted, and "Life stripped to girders, monochrome" and "Ought passes through points fair plotted...."

Finally, there is the Rilkean sonnet: a sonnet or the recognizable equivalent (often highly irregular in form) in the manner of Rilke's *Sonnets to Orpheus*. The sonnet had, of course, been used with distinction by Hardy, Robinson, Frost, Wilfred Owen, and other writers Auden admired, and plainly he learned from them. But the characteristic device he takes over from Rilke is that of putting unidentified persons, indicated only by pronouns (*he, she, they*), in usually symbolic landscapes, with the sonnet beginning in the middle of an unexplained dramatic situation. At its best, the technique makes possible a fresh union of abstract and concrete, of generalization about life and particular example; at its worst, the oblique and riddling approach which is a necessary part of the technique leads to nothing but hopeless obscurity. The best example in the 1928 volume is "Control of the Passes was, he saw, the key" (retained in 1930 and 1933). Here the dramatic situation is perfectly clear, and "he" is identified as the "trained spy"; but the meaning spreads out from this central core teasingly and fascinatingly. The spy in enemy country symbolizes, to put it crudely, the adolescent in the adult world, the intellectual among Philistines, perhaps the political radical in a bourgeois society [38]—the alienated of all sorts. What gives the sonnet (actually it is unrhymed, but divided on the page into two quatrains and a sestet, so that the form is unmistakable) its tension and power is the representation of the spy as both responsible for his capture (he has "walked into the trap...seduced with the old tricks") and betrayed by his own side ("they ignored his wires. / The bridges were unbuilt and trouble coming"). The "new district" will thus fall to the other side. The diction is restrained and carefully colloquial and neutral, thus adding to the pathos of the doomed individual denied love and caught between impersonal forces: "They would shoot of course, / Parting easily who were never joined." The spy is caught internally as well as externally, of course; his own feelings are mixed, for he likes the street music and the love of the enemy city. The other example of the style in *Poems* 1928 is a regular sonnet beginning:

> On the frontier at dawn getting down,
> Hot eyes were soothed with swallows: ploughs began
> Upon the stunted ridge behind the town,
> And bridles flashed. In the dog days she ran
> Indoors to read her letter. He in love,
> Too curious for the East stiffens to a tower;
> The jaw-bone juts from the ice; wisdom of
> The cooled brain in an irreverent hour.

The diction here is audacious, but the images, after the implicit dramatic situation is abandoned, seem without connection. (In the sestet there is a muted violin which puts cloth and glasses by; "the hour deferred / Peculiar idols nodded." It concludes with a horse neighing and a bird crying at sunset; this balances dawn at the beginning, but no other relation is discernible.) The obscurity here seems impenetrable, and the poem is an example of the dangers of this style. Perhaps it is one of those of which Isherwood said,

> When Auden was younger, he was very lazy. He hated polishing and making corrections. If I didn't like a poem, he threw it away and wrote another. If I liked one line, he would keep it and work it into a new poem. In this way, whole poems were constructed which were simply anthologies of my favourite lines, entirely regardless of grammar or sense. This is the simple explanation of much of Auden's celebrated obscurity. (*New Verse*, 1937)

It has seemed worthwhile to categorize these five different styles, and even to give them labels, in order to make the point that there is no single style that is characteristic of the early poetry; at least these five varieties are present from the beginning. There has been a tendency among critics of Auden to over-emphasize the changes in his style and to draw sharp contrasts between the styles of different periods of his career. The differences between the periods, however, are primarily matters of emphasis; most of the styles that will dominate the later work can be seen plainly in this first volume.

No single style predominates in *Poems* 1928; the poems are divided fairly evenly among the five types described. The poems seem to be arranged in no discernible pattern: they are held together by the recurrent images of War (often fused with the world of school sports), the Spy, the Frontier, and the like, but these do not carry over from one poem to another; that is, there is no continuity. The problem of why the seven poems grouped together as "I" should be put together instead of numbered separately has been mentioned. Certainly there is no obvious reason. My guess is that they are imitations of various styles, "five-finger exercises" in different idioms, but incorporating in each case a shocking or discordantly modern element. The first seems Imagist in technique, but heightened by the two alien medical terms, "vertigo" and "rigid":

> The sprinkler on the lawn
> Weaves a cool vertigo, and stumps are drawn;
> The last boy vanishes,
> A blazer half-on, through the rigid trees.

The second, "Bones wrenched, weak whimper...," we have already discussed; it is Hopkinsonian in aural techniques and tortuousness of syntax, but uses scientific and modern images. The third, "We saw in Spring," seems vaguely Eliotic; there is a vivid anti-poetic image of the "frozen buzzard / Flipped down the weir and carried out to sea"; [39] and at the end a melodramatic image of spring, with the "bulb pillow / Raising the skull, / Thrusting a crocus through clenched teeth." The fourth, "This peace can last no longer than the storm" we have already considered as an exercise in the mode of Hardy and Thomas. The fifth is a traditional lyric, for which Hardy, de la Mare, or numerous others might furnish the model. It begins:

> "Buzzards" I heard you say,
> And both of us stood still
> As they swept down the sky
> Behind the hill.

The unpoetical buzzard again supplies a slight shock. The sixth poem, "Consider if you will...," already cited as an example of Auden's detached, clinical attitude, is an exercise in a different style from the others, but is certainly not imitative in any obvious way. It is, in fact, much the best of the seven, and it seems a pity that Auden chose to discard it.[40] The last seems to be in a nursery-rhyme or folksong mode, but with a scientific image:

> Amoeba in the running water
> Lives afresh in son and daughter
> "The sword above the valley"
> Said the Worm to the Penny.

This riddling, however, is excessively private. The model is perhaps de la Mare, in such poems as "Song of the Mad Prince."

Even if this conjecture about the reason for grouping together the first seven poems is right, it remains true that the arrangement of the rest of the poems seems to be without significance. (The six that were used in *Paid* are grouped together at the end; but two others are within the group: "Control of the Passes . . . ," already discussed, and "Taller to-day, we remember similar evenings.") As we have seen, the general weakness of the poems is obscurity, both in lack of apparent connection among the images and in privacy of reference (as in the mysterious proper names freely used). Some obscurity is necessary to suggest closeness to dream, to the unconscious, the effect of coming from a level deeper than the rational; but when it is essential rather than superficial, the effectiveness of the poem is limited. Many of these poems (most obviously those developed into *Paid*) sound like excerpts from a continued fantasy; they sound compulsive, hallucinatory, and this is their weakness as well as their strength. "I chose this lean country," already quoted as an example of the clipped lyric, is a good example of the virtues and faults typical of these poems. There is first the lean country, cold, harsh, and northern; then there is a valley with crumbling sheds, a waterwheel, and a deserted mine where a mysterious conversation takes place ("Spoke with a poet there / Of Margaret the brazen leech, / And that severe Christopher"); [41] then in the second stanza a dream ("sucked giddy down / The funnel of my dream") of a buried engine-room with a professionally sympathetic listener; finally, in a brown study at the water-logged quarry, a vision of everyman sitting under the abject willow [42] after, presumably, disappointment in love, "Till death shall sponge away / The idiotic sun, / And lead this people to / A mildewed dormitory." At the end the poet identifies himself with the vision and the living dead, "I climb the hill, my corpse / Already wept, and pass / Alive into the house." [43] This is simply a series of favorite images, magical, wonderfully vivid, but unconnected. The strictness of the form has been mentioned earlier; the systematic use of assonance instead of rhyme adds to this effect.

Another poem is especially interesting for its bringing together of images of adolescent rebellion with others suggesting rejection of religion (in the father-image), first experiences of love, rebirth, and perilous adventure. It begins, "Suppose they met, the inevitable procedure":

> Yet, spite of their new heroism they feared
> That doddering Jehovah whom they mocked;
> Enough for him to show them to their rooms—
> —They slept apart, though doors were never locked.

> (The womb began its crucial expulsion.
> The fishermen, aching, drenched to the skin
> The ledge cleared, dragged their boat upon the beach.
> The survivor dropped, the bayonets closing in.)

At the end, the lovers, failing to take warning from "certain curious carvings on the porch," come to a bad end, expressed with the understatement of the briefly assumed Nordic mask: "Down they fell. Sorrow had they after that." Finally, we may look at one more typical fusion of war and biology and school sports. This one begins, "Because sap fell away / Before cold's night attack, we see / A harried vegetation." There is then a picture of a school gymnasium, where we "Open a random locker, sniff with distaste / At a mouldy passion." The second section of the poem presents Love first in the saga-world and then in a powerful (if obscurely related) pair of medical images:

> Love, is this love, that notable forked-one,
> Riding away from the farm, ill word said,
> Fought at the frozen dam? Who prophesied
> Such lethal factors, understood
> The indolent ulcer? Brought in now,
> Love lies at surgical extremity;
> Gauze pressed over the mouth, a breathed surrender.[44]

I have said enough, or perhaps too much, about the weaknesses of these poems; they were mostly written before Auden was twenty-one, and the final impression they leave with one is that of a rich and radically different sensibility together with great technical virtuosity and a wide range of knowledge. Obviously, the task before him is to keep the dreamlike vividness of apprehension while making the structure and relations more accessible to the rational mind. *Poems* 1930 marks a tremendous advance in that direction.

POEMS 1930 (AND 1933)

Poems 1930 was Auden's first volume to be published (the 1928 volume was privately printed) and was the basis of his reputation. It consists of thirty poems, nine of which had appeared in *Poems* 1928,[45] and *Paid on Both Sides*. The nine poems from *Poems* 1928 are not revised significantly. The twenty-one new poems differ from those in *Poems* 1928 chiefly in that they imply more clearly a social-political theme. The feud-war-sports images, the biological-geological metaphors, and the psychology—the feeling that there is something wrong with love—of the earlier poems are all brought into focus and fusion by the implication that they form an analysis of bourgeois society, of capitalist England. This implication is never made fully explicit, and ambiguities and obscurities remain in plenty; but it is enough to pull together the elements that formerly seemed disparate and to provide a structural basis. It brings together fantasy and diagnosis, to put it simply, or gives to the fantasy a diagnostic significance. The first poem establishes the pattern: it addresses, and hence tends to identify the reader with, the Revolutionary—not a ruffian with bombs, but equally alienated, a secret agent in the land of the diseased and perverted:

> Will you turn a deaf ear
> To what they said on the shore,
> Interrogate their poises
> In their rich houses;
>
> Of stork-legged heaven-reachers
> Of the compulsory touchers . . . ?

The secret agent must guard against the death-wish so prevalent in the enemy country; he can expect no protection, recognition, or reward; but the "neutralizing peace" and "average disgrace" at least are not for him, though honorable for "later other." The second poem, "Which of you waking early and watching daybreak," is unusually explicit, using dawn as symbol of the new social-political day; the terms are primarily psychological, but the political significance is plain: the old life must die, the new be welcomed. Isherwood observes (*New Verse*, 1937) that the meter and style show the influence of Bridges's *Testament of Beauty*, which had just been published in 1929; this is true, though it should be added that there is an element of parody in the use of it ("How heroes have fallen into vats and stewed while men / Drink up their beer unknowing and are soon asleep"). The third, "Since you are going to begin to-day," is an address to the doomed bourgeois by Dame Kind, or the Life Force, explaining how and why he is to be superseded. IV, "Watch any day his nonchalant pauses, see" pictures the inner emptiness of the prosperous capitalist. There is no need to continue the analysis; the pattern is obvious enough. Once this basic dramatic situation is established, with its associated themes and images, there is, of course, no narrative sequence nor any clear progression; the poems are apparently arranged according to the principles of variety and contrast. Poem XXIX, "Consider this and in our time," reaffirms the social-political theme explicitly ("Financier, leaving your little room . . . The game is up for you and for the others . . ."), and XXX, "Sir, no man's enemy, forgiving all," is an effective conclusion, since its prayer is political as well as psychological: "look shining at / New styles of architecture, a change of heart."

The changes in the second edition of *Poems*, published in 1933, were relatively minor, and may be described before we proceed to discuss the style of the volume in detail. Seven poems were dropped and seven new ones substituted; the same numbers were used for the new poems, so that there was no change in the order of the old.[46] Five of the discarded poems had been first published in 1928; clearly the intention here was to replace early work with more mature productions. This left only four poems from 1928 in this final form of the volume.[47] It is important to note, however, that the new poems in the 1933 edition were not necessarily written later than those in *Poems* 1930: Auden stated in a prefatory note that the new poems were all written "before 1931," and in the chronologically arranged *Selected Poetry* of 1958 he puts several poems from 1933 ahead of some from 1930. Of the two poems first published in 1930 that were discarded in 1933, the first is "Which of you waking...," discussed a moment ago. It was eliminated perhaps because it was somewhat diffuse and imitative, though it served the useful function of making the social theme of the volume explicit. The poem that replaced it, however, is the magnificent "Doom is dark and deeper than any sea-dingle," which is worth any slight delay in the reader's apprehension of the pattern of the volume. The other poem discarded from 1930 is "To have found a place for nowhere," a clipped lyric in a rather Skeltonic rhythm, hopelessly obscure; it was replaced by another in the same mode, but better, "Between attention and attention."

One final bibliographical remark: the first American edition of Auden's *Poems* (Random House: New York, 1934) reprints *Poems* 1933 without change, including *Paid*; it also includes *The Orators* and *The Dance of Death*, which have always been published in England as separate volumes. Auden has made no change of any kind in any of the later printings of any of these volumes. His treatment of this poetry in the *Collected Poetry* of 1945 and the *Selected Poetry* of 1958 will be discussed at the end of this section.

In discussing the style and dominant images of *Poems*, I shall be referring to the final form (1933) of the volume, unless otherwise indicated. Since, as we have seen, the new poems in this edition were not necessarily written later than those in the 1930 edition, I shall not mention dates. First, a few general-izations about the dominant images (one could say "myths") and ideas. The chief figure—one would call him a *persona* except that he doesn't speak, but is spoken to—is the Spy, the Secret Agent; but the meaning of the new conflict is clearer now than it was in the earlier volume: it is both class war and international war as a symptom of decaying capitalism. But the Spy's feelings are still mixed, because he is himself a bourgeois; hence the war is basically internal, a psychomachia; and the terms of the conflict are much too nebulous to fit the Marxist analysis. The middle class, however, is doomed, not only by the Marxist wave of the future, but also by its own subconscious death-wish (in conflict with its conscious resist-ance) and evolutionary urge toward its own extinction. Hence political, psychological, and biological metaphors can all be used to show the hopeless plight of the poor bourgeois, and the future may be regarded with confidence:

> Yet the dawn of each day is still as a promise to man
> ... truth's assurance of life—that darkness shall die
> Desiring at last the perfect security of death,
> Shall bless the new life and die ...[48]

The arch-rebels, Blake and Lawrence (invoked, with Homer Lane, in "Get there if you can ..."), are frequently in mind as predecessors in this kind of political-psychological analysis, showing the relation between the defects of love and those of society.

In style, the most striking development is the appearance of a new style that we may call popular. In this, the trite and flat language of popular songs and speech is used for satirical effect, and the poem is spoken by a *persona*. In "It's no use raising a shout," the baffled speaker has found out that the "love" of the popular songs is not enough; he doesn't want "any more hugs," and though he has his Honey he doesn't have the expected happy ending. He can only say, "Here am I, here are you: / But what does it mean? What are we going to do?" The poem is not simply parody, for the speaker is capable of self-analysis: he knows that part of his trouble is an unresolved Oedipus complex (he has never found an adequate substitute for his mother) and that evolution has made him obsolete: "In my veins there is a wish, / And a memory of fish." "What's in your mind, my dove, my coney" is an ironic love song, with less of the element of parody than the one just discussed, but clearly based on the mode of the popular song.

Auden's acquaintance with German cabaret and theater songs, especially those of Brecht, developed during his stay in Berlin, must have had something to do with the emergence of this style. His most extended use of it is in *The Dance of Death* (1933), which will be discussed in the next section with his other theater-pieces; in it the commercialized emptiness of the musical-comedy style both reflects and describes the defects of the society. Another variety of popular style is the nursery rhyme or folk ballad; this appeared in 1928 in "Amoeba in the running water" and in the present volume in "The silly fool, the silly fool," with its ironic comment on folk wisdom and the difference between fact and fiction. But the flowering of this variety comes a few years later.

The middle or colloquial style is also notably developed, and is used for satire. (In 1928 he had not had enough detachment, nor enough clarity about "objective" meanings, perhaps, to make satire possible. One indication of the difference is the appearance of *personae* in the 1930 *Poems*.) In "We made all possible preparations" the style characterizes the speaker: here it is a parody of bureaucratic language, and its timid conventionality and over-qualification suggest the defects of the upper civil servant, his government, and his class. In the war (unspecified, but suggesting class war, which the speaker is unwilling to mention, as well as international war) "We" have followed all the customary procedures, but have lost. The speaker speculates with sterile academicism on the explanation: the most that can be hoped for is "a reasonable chance of retaining / Our faculties to the last." The title Auden gave the poem in 1945 is neatly ironical: "Let History Be My Judge."

A more complex example of this style is "Since you are going to begin to-day," which Auden called in 1945 "Venus Will Now Say a Few Words." It is an address by Nature or the evolutionary Life Force to the typical bourgeois, explaining to him, in short, that he is obsolete and that she will "Select another form, perhaps your son; / Though he reject you, join opposing team. . . ." Her speech has the tone and manner of a schoolmaster coldly and objectively analyzing a boy's weaknesses and explaining just what is expected of him. The meter is free pentameter, close to speech rhythms; the form is couplets, but employing double consonance [49] instead of rhyme, and it is perhaps not fanciful to say that the effect of slow inevitable shifting so produced is harmonious with the evolutionary thesis. (The same form is used, with similar effect, in "To throw away the key. . . ," discussed above, p. 17.) Part of the complexity of the poem arises from the fact that the bourgeois is by no means wholly unsympathetic; both the poet and the reader (who are, after all, bourgeois too) recognize many of his characteristics in themselves:

> You are the one whose part it is to lean,
> For whom it is not good to be alone . . .

So, when these apparently harmless symptoms are interpreted as indications of inexorable doom, there is a real pathos. Auden's satire is never pure denunciation, but always partly self-satire, done with mixed feelings; and undoubtedly this fact has much to do with its richness and continuing interest. At the end, Nature explains that there is no escape: "Do not imagine you can abdicate; / Before you reach the frontier you are caught"—the frontier being the metaphorical one we have seen before, both sociological (between the bourgeois and the proletariat) and chronological (between allegiance to the past and to the new society of the future). And awareness of doom makes no difference, for it does not affect the essential rigidity, failure to adapt, which means biological obsolescence: "Holders of one position, wrong for years."

An interesting use of high style for satire is "Get there if you can and see the land you once were proud to own." [50] This employs the meter of Tennyson's "Locksley Hall" and "Locksley Hall Sixty Years After," but makes the diction contrastingly modern and often low; the effect is closer to that of mock-heroic than of parody. Partly because of this quality of the diction—the speaker is a bourgeois intellectual addressing others of his class, but sporadically trying to talk like a working-class revolutionary—and partly because the meter's thumping obviousness seems to lead Auden for once into over-explicitness, the poem is not very successful. (It is one of the two from this volume that Auden omitted from the *Collected Poetry* of 1945.) But this explicitness makes the poem useful as background for the others, since it reveals crudely the ideas that lie behind all of them. The poem begins with an ambivalent vision of a decaying industrial landscape with abandoned mines, representing what capitalism has done to England. "We" have not been aware of this, because we have been seduced away from Life by bourgeois culture, by such philosophers, religious thinkers, and aesthetes as Newman, Plato, Pascal, Baudelaire, Freud, and Flaubert, who lead to a preoccupation with internal and individual problems. But we must rebel against the whole bourgeois tradition, including the family:

Perfect pater. Marvellous mater. Knock the critic down who dares—
Very well, believe it, copy, till your hair is white as theirs.

"Lawrence, Blake and Homer Lane, once healers in our English land" are dead, and the situation is desperate. We had

better quit talking and charming, lecturing on navigation while
the ship is going down, and take action:

Drop those priggish ways for ever, stop behaving like a stone:
Throw the bath-chairs right away, and learn to leave ourselves alone.

If we really want to live, we'd better start at once to try;
If we don't, it doesn't matter, but we'd better start to die.

The striking thing here is that, after the call to action in good
Marxist terms, the action called for is purely moral-psychological; it has political implications, but these are not even
mentioned. As with the three martyred healers, Lawrence,
Blake, and Homer Lane, the revolution that is being preached
is primarily a psychological one.

A somewhat similar stylistic effect is produced in "Look
there! The sunk road winding" by beginning each stanza with
two smooth trimeter lines, the first with feminine ending and
the second without; the reader expects the pattern to be repeated, as, for instance, in Housman, but the third line follows
the pattern of the second rather than of the first. The reader,
after this suspension, is sure that the fourth will return to the
pattern of the first, but it shifts instead to an irregular dimeter. The effect is thus one of cadence unresolved and pattern
shifting in the middle. This, together with the contrast between
the mythical, dream-like images and some brutally colloquial
phrases, embodies the theme of the necessity of breaking patterns of expected behavior and of destroying the existing
society:

> Bitter the blue smoke rises
> From garden bonfires lit,
> To where we burning sit:
> Good, if it's thorough.

The speaker, the familiar doomed bourgeois, although threat-
ened by archetypal terrors (including "glaciers calving"), is
not like the legendary heroic last defenders:

> In legend all were simple,
> And held the straitened spot;
> But we in legend not,
> Are not simple.

For our feelings are mixed.

"Under boughs between our tentative endearments how should we hear" uses long, metrically complex lines, six- or seven-stress with numerous trisyllabic feet and much alliteration. Each stanza consists of two such lines, followed by two short, curt lines (two- or three-stress). The diction of the long lines is traditional, elevated and "poetic," that of the short ones colloquial and modern; and this contrast is itself part of the theme of the poem, which deals with the relation of past to present. A more extended and subtle use of the style is that in "Consider this and in our time" where the histrionic quality of the diction adds to the effect of detachment and of drama. Since this poem has been well discussed by other critics,[51] I shall confine myself to calling attention to this distancing and heightening function of the style, as the final warning to the financier builds up to a kind of clinical baroque:

> ... the prey to fugues,
> Irregular breathing and alternate ascendancies
> After some haunted migratory years
> To disintegrate on an instant in the explosion of mania
> Or lapse for ever into a classic fatigue.

A similar histrionic effect obtains in the last section of "It was Easter as I walked in the public gardens," [52] with its build-up of ominous images of calm before the storm ("the loud madman / Sinks now into a more terrible calm"). Then comes the secret enemy whose triumph is as inevitable as autumn, mould, conformity "with the orthodox bone, / With organized fear, the articulated skeleton." All this lends the kind of distancing required for the wonderfully ambivalent conclusion, that love needs "death, death of the grain, our death, / Death of the old gang" and the final picture of the dead: the "hard bitch and the riding-master" stiff underground (appropriately, since they were also rigid above ground), while the "lolling bridegroom" who was not rigid but attractive has to die too, and "deep in clear lake," still lolling, is "beautiful, there."

The Nordic mask may be seen occasionally in several poems, but forms the stylistic basis for only one. This one is, however, its ultimate triumph: "Doom is dark and deeper than any sea-dingle." When this appeared first in *New Signatures*, 1932, it was called "Chorus from a Play," and in the *Selected Poetry* of 1958 it is again called "Chorus." There is no clue as to what the play was; the obvious conjecture is *Paid on Both Sides*, which the poem resembles in mood and in style, but it may have been some discarded or unfinished play, such as *The Enemies of a Bishop*. The poem contains an element of pastiche, since the first line comes from a Middle English homily [53] and the Old English elegy, "The Wanderer," is imitated in the second stanza, with its contrast between dreams of home and waking to see alien birds and men. (Indeed, in the *Collected Shorter Poems* of 1950, Auden entitled the poem, "The Wanderer.") The kennings ("houses for fishes"), understatement ("undried sea"), ellipsis ("lonely on fell as chat"), generalization ("ever that man goes"), and the mood of stoic resignation to a grim fate—all these produce a stronger flavor of Old English poetry than anything in *Paid*. Essentially, however, the poem is very different from the Old English. The meter of Old English is suggested without being imitated closely; few of Auden's lines actually follow the pattern of four heavy stresses with regular alliteration. (The first line is, in fact, the only one in which there are four alliterating syllables.) Auden's meter is much more varied, ranging from the pentameter norm of the first and last lines to short two-stress lines, and this makes more effective the contrasts which are the structural basis of the poem. When doom falls upon a man, "No cloud-soft hand can hold him, restraint by women; / But ever that man goes," and the long lines contrast with the short as, previously, the long lines describing the promise of spring have contrasted with the short ones announcing the harsh fate. In the last stanza, variation in line length combines with verbal repetition to produce an effect of incantation: "Protect his house, / His anxious house where days are counted / From thunderbolt protect...." There is also in Auden's poem a kind of ambiguity that is wholly foreign to Old English poetry. The Anglo-Saxon Wanderer speaks most of his poem himself, recalling the happy time when he had companions and a lord, and lamenting the necessity of wandering in his present isolated and unattached condition; his misfortune demonstrates the transience of all things earthly, but there is no doubt that he has been peculiarly unfortunate. Auden's Wanderer, however, has not simply lost security through no fault of his own. "Doom" falls upon him, and the word means, etymologically, "judgment," with the connotation of divine and, probably, adverse judgment. But he is singled out, chosen as well as fated, and in response to the call he goes voluntarily on his dangerous mission into alien territory. Like Auden's Quest-figures in general, he is admirable as well as unfortunate; he may not have been exceptional before, but when the inscrutable choice falls on him he accepts his exceptional fate. Auden's poem is more impersonal than the Old English: except for the brief close-up in the second stanza, his Wanderer is seen from a great distance, and the emphasis at the end is not on him but on "His anxious house where days are counted" and the joy with which his return will be greeted. The last stanza, "Save him from hostile capture, / From sudden tiger's spring at corner...," is, of course, a prayer, though addressed to no one in particular, and the exotic tiger suggests a widening of reference from the Nordic. Finally, there is in context a political ambiguity: the wanderer is in one aspect the middle-class intellectual, doomed by his political awareness to leave his intellectual and spiritual home and endure hardship and isolation. In the alien country he wakes from his dream of home to hear "new men making another love"—a line deeply ambiguous, in the political context. Even the last line, with its brilliant kinesthetic image of "leaning dawn," has this connotation as well as the obvious meaning.

The clipped lyric appears frequently and in great variety; there are more poems in this style than in any other. The first poem in the volume, "Will you turn a deaf ear," which we have already discussed for its political theme, is an example. In the *Collected Poetry* Auden gave this the title, "The Questioner Who Sits So Sly," which is a quotation from Blake's "Auguries of Innocence." These lyrics that are both riddling and morally, as well as politically, revolutionary follow Blake's example in the use of obscurity to short-circuit the rational mind. "This lunar beauty," called "Pur" in the *Collected Poetry* and "Like a Dream" in the *Collected Shorter Poems*, is very different: elevated, restrained, abstract, defining the contrast between the "real" daytime world of history and time and the lunar world of timeless immediacy, of dreams and pure beauty which is, however, remote from both love and sorrow. The laconic diction and taut irregularity of meter, the riddling uncertainties of meaning, the systematic assonance instead of rhyme, the bold use of personification at the end:

> Love shall not near
> The sweetness here
> Nor sorrow take
> His endless look

(which is reminiscent of Emily Dickinson, as Isherwood observed) [54] all contribute to its success. On the other hand, the poem that follows it, "Before this loved one," while generally in the same style, is very different indeed. Instead of being taut it is repetitive and incantatory:

> Before this loved one
> Was that one and that one
> A family
> And history
> And ghost's adversity ...

It uses no abstractions, though it generalizes, and its level is the psychological-political: there is a constant ambiguity as to whether the new love is a person or a new form of society, and the point seems to be that it is both, that love and politics are intimately related (as in Blake and Lawrence). Frontiers must be crossed and ghosts [55] defied if there is to be hope of anything other than a "backward love." "Between attention and attention" has a kind of controlled tumbling rhythm that suggests Skelton; the language is extremely abstract, with occasional precise vignettes: the theme is the divided state of modern man, his indecision, self-doubt, distraction. "Love by ambition" is another psychological lyric, defining love by refusing to define it; the basic theme is that negation has no place in love, nor confession nor jealousy nor any form of selfishness. Love "Designs his own unhappiness / Foretells his own death and is faithless." The theme is closely parallel to Blake's definitions of "free" love. In contrast to the foregoing, "On Sunday walks" is a relaxed, anti-traditional poem given a kind of folk flavor by the irregular two-stress accentual meter. "From scars where kestrels hover" is a relatively uncomplicated version in rapid and regular trimeter of the War and Frontier images: the "tall unwounded leader / Of doomed companions . . . ," the fighters "beyond the border," are now outmoded, and true bravery is now in refraining from individual showing off, "resisting the temptations / To skyline operations." But the effect of the poem is still to celebrate romantically the leaders who "must migrate: / 'Leave for Cape Wrath to-night'," in contradiction of the argument. Finally, "To ask the hard question is simple" is a good example of the power of this style to suggest, through repetitive and incantatory effects, levels below the rational.

> Afraid
> To remember what the fish ignored,
> How the bird escaped, or if the sheep obeyed.
>
> Till, losing memory,
> Bird, fish, and sheep are ghostly,
> And ghosts must do again
> What gives them pain.

There is a kind of collectivity of suggestion, as though depths below those of conscious individuality are being plumbed, a kind of Jungian collective unconscious, with an implicit parallel between biological and political evolution.

The last variety of style to be considered is the Rilkean sonnet. The only example of this in the volume (aside from "Control of the passes...," which had appeared in 1928) is the last poem, "Sir, no man's enemy, forgiving all," called "Petition" in the *Collected Poetry*. This is not technically in sonnet form; it consists of seven couplets which employ consonance rather rhyme; but the images fall into the traditional octave-sestet pattern. Since the poem has been analyzed by Brooks and others [56] it can be dealt with briefly here. Its rhetorical mode is that of pouring new wine into old bottles: this is a modern equivalent of the traditional sonnet and prayer. The Deity (addressed in the manner of Hopkins as "Sir") is represented as a kind of supreme healer, or celestial Homer Lane, who will forgive anything but the "negative inversion" of the will. Instead of the conventional petitions, these are all psychological, and traditional terms and images are given a radically (and often subversively) new meaning. Thus the "sovereign touch" is requested to cure not scrofula, but "the intolerable neural itch," further particularized as "The exhaustion of weaning, the liar's quinsy, / And the distortions of ingrown virginity." Those in retreat from life are to be caught as in a searchlight's beam and made to come back: "Cover in time with beams those in retreat / That, spotted, they turn though the reverse were great"; and human healers are to be publicized. Although the terms of the prayer appear to be exclusively psychological, political implications are also present. The first petition is for "power and light," which suggests electricity as well as spiritual qualities, and at the end the Harrowing of Hell is fused with the image of the old civilization as a "house of the dead" (suggesting Dostoevsky's Siberian prison as well as the ghost-haunted, tradition-bound culture depicted in the poems), and

new physical modes of life are given importance equal to that
of the crucial spiritual change:

> Harrow the house of the dead; look shining at
> New styles of architecture, a change of heart.

THE ORATORS

In his Preface to the *Collected Poetry*, Auden cites *The Orators* as his example of "the fair notion fatally injured," and
certainly the piece is damaged by its notorious obscurity. That
this would be a problem was apparent from the beginning. The
dedication to Stephen Spender seems to be an oblique apology
for private references, and perhaps also for differing with
Spender's view of the propaganda function of poetry:

> Private faces in public places
> Are wiser and nicer
> Than public faces in private places.

The obscurity is curiously tantalizing: one feels constantly on
the verge of discovering the key that will make the whole
thing clear. Since thirty years have failed to reveal anything
of the sort, one must conclude that the feeling is illusory; but
the obscurity has been a part of the attraction of the piece,
serving to give it the challenging riddle-interest that is one
of the primitive and legitimate foundations of poetry.[57] The
obscurity is also meaningful in itself, as a way of saying that
the present state of things doesn't make sense, that jokes and
false beards are the only proper reaction; it is a means of expressing revolt against the rational mind and the solemn plausi-
bilities of the world. To say this is not to deny that the
obscurity is so excessive as to constitute a serious defect, but to
try to explain how so radically obscure a work could produce
such intense enthusiasm and admiration, and be regarded by
many as a kind of political manifesto.

Critics have not usually been willing to commit themselves as to just what they think is going on in *The Orators*. At whatever risk of exposure, I propose to do so, in the hope of pushing back the boundaries of obscurity. We can be sure that enough dark corners will remain, even if we succeed in casting light on a considerable part of its territory.

The subtitle, "An English Study," means both that the study deals with England and the English people and that it deals with the study of English composition and literature in the schools. The subject is the public school as both the microcosm of English society and the chief bulwark of the existing order. Perhaps one should eliminate the "public," since the private boarding school which prepared boys (usually from the ages of eight to thirteen) for the public school was essentially the same (having, according to Cyril Connolly, "all the faults of a public school without any of its compensations").[58] It is, in fact, the preparatory or private school that is the subject of George Orwell's "Such, Such Were the Joys"[59] and of Connolly's most impressive description in "A Georgian Boyhood,"[60] and that was the basis of Isherwood and Auden's shared fantasy. Still, the public school was the crown of the system, and the basis of Connolly's Theory of Permanent Adolescence:

> It is the theory that the experiences undergone by boys at the great public schools, their glories and disappointments, are so intense as to dominate their lives and to arrest their development. From these it results that the greater part of the ruling class remains adolescent, school-minded, self-conscious, cowardly, sentimental and in the last analysis homosexual.[61]

It is important to remember that Auden was himself a schoolmaster at this time, and his later writings on the subject show a penetrating and responsible awareness of the virtues and defects of the system.[62]

The point of view in *The Orators* is partly that of the schoolboy, the adolescent with his profound ambivalence to authority and his yearning for heroism and sacrifice, and partly that of the radical schoolmaster, the bourgeois rebel who was formed by the system and is part of it but rejects it and is on the boys' side against it. (Rex Warner and Edward Upward, who are addressed in the last section of the work, were, like Auden, in this position.) The orators I take to be headmasters, teachers, clerics, propounders of false doctrine and defenders of the system generally: the term suggests an ironic parallel between these highly respectable people and the soap-box orators of Hyde Park, who are also sometimes fake prophets and saviors and hero-leaders.

The prologue, called "Adolescence" in the *Collected Poetry*, presents the ideal young man, the boy scout, loyal product of his family and society, going to war or to preach their gospel gladly. Like the protagonists of *Paid on Both Sides* and *The Ascent of F6*, he is driven by his Oedipus complex to heroism, exceptional risks and achievements. (In one speech in *The Dog Beneath the Skin* the "sedentary and learned" are made psychologically responsible for war: we have "skilfully transferred our envy into an image of the universal mother, for which the lad of seventeen whom we have always sent and will send again against our terrors, gladly immolates himself." [63] And yet the young man who has seemed divinely protected (walking among the psalmist's "green pastures" and "still waters") and himself almost divine to the girls who have played Leda to his swan, when he returns from his extraordinary exertions finds himself rejected by his society and by the mother-image:

> And yet this prophet, homing the day is ended,
> Receives odd welcome from the country he so defended:
> The band roars 'Coward, Coward,' in his human fever,
> The giantess shuffles nearer, cries 'Deceiver.' [64]

Why? Perhaps because the average man resents the exceptional, and because prophets are proverbially not honored in their own countries, and returning soldiers are often regarded as a danger; perhaps also he has become while abroad a prophet of revolutionary doctrines. Prior to all of these, however, is the archetypal experience of returning home and finding it changed: "you can't go home again," the lost Eden of child-hood is irrecoverable. The slow, irregular pentameter coup-lets, with their feminine endings, produce an effect of ironic pathos.

Book I, "The Initiates," presents four types of orators, four who have been initiated into capitalist society. "Address for a Prize-Day" (separately published in *The Criterion*, 1931) is in part specific parody: Isherwood quotes Auden as mimicking the headmaster of their school in virtually the same words that begin the "Address" (*Lions and Shadows*, p. 184). In tone and manner, then, it is a parody of such orations, and the remedies proposed go abruptly from schoolboy retribution to fascist violence. Yet the main content—the analysis of "this country of ours where nobody is well," the location of the cause in a failure of love, with the Dantean division into excessive, de-fective, and perverted lovers, and the description of the phys-ical symptoms which manifest these psychic defects—all this seems to be, allowing for the usual "touch of extravagance," intended seriously. Thus the ridiculous framework contains a real sermon; the irony and absurdity are intended to take away the curse of seriousness, and break down one's usual defenses against sermons. One expects the argument to be ironic; but, with double irony, it isn't. The ending, however, returns to satire, fusing the excesses of schoolboy conformism and "team spirit" with the grimmer excesses of wartime patriots persecut-ing slackers or fascists resorting to force. The myth of psycho-somatic disease established by this section recurs throughout the rest of the work; in the "Journal of an Airman," for exam-ple, self-regard is described as a "sex-linked disease" like haemo-philia: "Man is the sufferer, woman the carrier. 'What a wonderful woman she is!' Not so fast: wait till you see her son." [65] (Obviously, this is related to "Prologue" in theme.) Self-regard is defined as "the treating of news as a private poem;

it is the consequence of eavesdropping." Hence the significance attached throughout to eavesdropping. Both the moral diagnosis and the psychosomatic are, of course, partly jokes, the spotting of symptoms and ascribing of dark psychic meanings to trivialities is a game. But games and jokes are also meaningful, as Freud demonstrated, and the whole work is a defiance of the rational.

"Argument," the second part of Book I, deals with the search for a hero, redeemer, savior; and its chief effect is to ridicule both the search for a political leader (and the adolescent hero-worship upon which it is partly based) and the search for a secular savior and redeemer. There is much literary parody and much use of liturgical language: a lengthy litany invokes first detectives and then pub signs as deliverers, winding up with the king. The next part, "Statement," seems to be an ironic portioning out of praise: "To each an award, suitable to his sex, his class and the power." The language is "objective," scientific, emphasizing man's biological nature, with the possibility of rebirth and evolution: "The action of light on dark is to cause it to contract. That brings forth." Finally, there is "Letter to a Wound." This is a parody of a love-letter, and specifically of the kind written by a bourgeois intellectual of sedentary habits. The whole piece is an elaboration of the psychosomatic disease metaphor: the writer loves his wound, wills it, wills his death; and he is typical of his class. The bold application of the love-letter convention to such content produces a macabre and striking effect. The four sections of this first book are probably relevant to the subtitle in another way. They parody four of the common forms of expository prose that English studies would be likely to deal with in school: oration or public speech, argument, statement or scientific exposition, letter or informal style.

From the beginning Auden has mixed verse and prose, and all his longer works employ prose for considerable portions. In contrast to the restrained, detached style of his critical writing, this "creative" prose is extremely varied and audacious:

much of it is highly "poetic" and mannered, with every sort of artifice. *Paid on Both Sides* is full of virtuoso stylistic effects in which the tone of prose speeches is heightened through inversion and ellipsis and then modulated back to the colloquial; there are accurate renderings of schoolboy slang and small-talk, saga characters, cabaret masters of ceremonies (Father Christmas), patriotic speakers, and the like; there are also a few Joycean stream-of-consciousness passages (pp. 81, 84). Cyril Connolly cited passages from *The Orators* as showing "imaginative prose coming to life again" [66] and noted the influence of Rimbaud's prose poems on it. The two middle sections of the first book of *The Orators* I have characterized very briefly; they are also almost an anthology of experimental prose effects, varied and concentrated.

Book II, "Journal of an Airman," presents the initiate on the other side, the outsider, the man dedicated to the overthrow of the society represented by the orator-initiates of the first book. The airman is, however, seen from inside, and he is anything but a simple figure. (It seems likely that one motive in this book and elsewhere in the work is to parody the black-and-white presentations of much politically conscious literature, in which "We" are wholly good and beautiful and healthy and "They" are evil, ugly, and sick.) The airman is far from a pure hero to oppose the villains of Book I; his defects and peculiarities are many, and he is presented with irony and mixed feelings. There is something in him of such romantic and ambiguous heroes as Lawrence of Arabia (Aircraftman Shaw) and Rimbaud.[67] Primarily, however, he is the bourgeois rebel, the middle-class intellectual committed to the Marxist revolution and the overthrow of his class. The metaphor of the airman conveys this nicely: he is the man committed to the new element, breaking with man's traditional bonds to the earth; as once life moved from sea to land, now it will move to the air. (Bird images often have a similar connotation in *Poems:* the "helmeted airman" and the hawk are conjoined in "Consider this..." and the Wanderer is associated with birds in "Doom is dark...": "lonely on fell as chat...a bird stone-haunting, an unquiet bird." He is, then, an evolutionary forerunner, a kind of mutant. But at present, in the old society, he is isolated, uncertain, in danger—both externally and internally, since the same psychological peculiarities that are responsible for his heroism lead him into what seems to be paranoia. (Auden has remained convinced of the necessity of neurosis, and of its relation to art and other exceptional achievements; he has never had much regard for that "Goddess of bossy underlings, Normality." [68]) At any rate, his peculiarities tend to reveal the airman as a sort of permanent adolescent, and thus his "Journal" is related in theme to the rest of the work: the airman is a glorified schoolboy, or alternatively a master who shares the boys' feelings toward authority (the grown-up world and the existing political order).

Although some details remain obscure, most of the "Journal" makes sense when read in this way. Two questions, however, constantly hover in the background; and though the reader is intended to continue speculating about them, the riddling effect [69] being, as we have seen, part of the fun, it will perhaps be useful for me to suggest some lines for profitable speculation.

1) What precisely is the matter with the airman? His pseudo-scientific establishing of his uncle (the wicked bachelor uncle whom his mother hated) as his real ancestor, and then as model and savior ("Uncle, save them all; make me worthy"), suggests homosexuality, which would fit in with the public school theme and explain the airman's extreme sense of guilt and isolation. The allegiance to the wicked uncle may, however, mean no more than the kind of adolescent rebellion against the family and its tradition, so beautifully expressed in the sestina, "We have brought you, they said, a map of the country," which the airman is presumably supposed to have written. In this poem the young man going into a supposedly dangerous new country disregards the careful instructions and protective advice of his loved ones who lived there for years. He "Finds

consummation in the wood / And sees for the first time the country"; his final discovery is, "This is your country and the home of love." Certainly one plausible reading of this is to take the new country as adult life and the map and advice as the misguided attempts of the young man's parents to guide him.[70] Isherwood suggests that the airman is epileptic, noting that the Lane-Layard doctrine pointed out the relation between epilepsy and the idea of flight; psychologically, it is an attempt to become an angel and fly, a form of regression.[71] The mysterious references to the misbehavior of the airman's hands suggest masturbation—and we recall the stern admonitions against this vice that were traditional in the schools—though sometimes kleptomania seems involved. At any rate, the malady must remain uncertain. It is the price he pays for his exceptional gifts, and there is about him a slight flavor of the scapegoat or at least of the *poète maudit*.

2) Who or what precisely is the Enemy? On the simplest level, it is the capitalist, the Establishment—directly attacked in the fine piece of invective against the pro-fascist newspaper peer, for instance:

> Beethameer, Beethameer, bully of Britain,
> With your face as fat as a farmer's bum ...
> Are you sure you're our Saviour? We're certain you smell ...

But beyond this political level, he is psychologically any kind of authority and power (parents, school, state) as against the adolescent. There is in this attitude a strong tinge of romantic anarchism, both Homer Lane's psychological variety and Blake's more profound transvaluation of values: in this sense the enemy is reason, conscious control, denial and negation. Hence the enemy is also internal, and toward the end of the "journal" appears to be completely so; the war for which the airman is preparing becomes more and more clearly psychological. "The enemy's strength lies in the people's disbelief in his existence. If they believed he would be powerless." The beautiful lyric,

"There are some birds in these valleys," called "The Decoys" in *Collected Poetry*, renders this theme: the necessity not to be taken in. The airman's discovery at the end that he has been wrong, that "the power of the enemy is a function of our resistance," and therefore non-resistance and self-destruction is the only way to destroy the enemy, would seem to be ironic: the death-wish has conquered, he is perhaps insane. Certainly his penultimate speech is distanced in tone and sounds as if he has capitulated:

> O understand, darling. God just loves us all, but means to be obeyed; and unaffecting is our solid tear. Thank you for your share in this, but goodbye. Uncle, save them all, make me worthy.

The enemy is, however, also anyone or anything Auden dislikes on personal or purely whimsical grounds. This is partly a parody of the "we" / "they" semantics of wars and conspiracies—and there are some fine parodies of war propaganda in the work (the "terrible rat-courage of the enemy")—and partly practical and sometimes very private joking.

Book III, "Six Odes," might be called the airman's oratory, the public utterances (as odes traditionally are) of the ambivalent bourgeois schoolmaster who is committed to the overthrow of what the school stands for. The first, called in *Collected Poetry* "January 1, 1931," recalls in the form of a dream-vision (like, e.g., *Piers Plowman*) the losses of the old year: Lawrence's death and the poet's simultaneous operation, Spender and Isherwood in distress, the headmaster muttering "Call no man happy"; nothing but "self-regarders" and perversions of love. A savior is needed, but there are only fakes: "all the healers, granny in mittens, the Mop, the white surgeon, / And loony Layard." The dreamer wakes, and the only orator is a beggar in the courtyard; the hero and savior is still to seek. The second is a parody of Hopkins, primarily the *Wreck of the Deutschland*, and returns ironically to the Greek mode of odes in praise of athletes (e.g. Pindar's), since it sings the praises of a Rugby XV. The parody is perhaps funniest in the second stanza, beginning (in recollection of "The Windhover"):

> Success my dears—Ah!
> Rounding the curve of the drive
> Standing up, waving, cheering from car,
>   The time of their life: ...

and in the last, which begins,

> Whether at lathe-work, loading, reading, to resist
> Rather! the torsion, the tension, the list:
> Fellows you well may be proud of, no matter when or where,

and ends, ". . . Joy docked in every duct, we to the right sleep come."

The third ode, called "The Exiles" in *Collected Poetry*, is addressed "To Edward Upward, Schoolmaster." Upward, who was Isherwood's close friend and his collaborator (as "Allen Chalmers") on the Mortmere fantasies, shared Auden's ambiguous situation of being a schoolmaster with radical convictions.[72] The ode, beginning,

> What siren zooming is sounding our coming
> Up frozen fjord forging from freedom . . .

seems to be a rendering of the feeling of being futile, cut off from "real life," through the metaphor of being exiled to a sanitarium in the north, only the "slight despair / At what we are" providing any life at all: "Saying Alas / To less and less." This may be simply a dramatic representation of the doomed bourgeois' feeling of superfluousness and despair; but the dedication suggests that it refers to the particular kind of futility felt by the ambivalent schoolmaster. The exaggerated alliteration and systematic consonance give a fine effect of empty heartiness.

The fourth ode, in contrast, is full of boisterous high spirits.

It is a birthday ode (burlesquing the tradition of complimen-
tary prophecy, as in Virgil's "Pollio" eclogue and Horace's
Carmen Seculare) addressed to the child of another radical
schoolmaster, Rex Warner.[73] Beginning, "Roar Gloucestershire,
do yourself proud," it uses the method of travesty: the style is
low and joyfully vulgar: "It is John, son of Warner, has pulled
my chain" and "England our cow / Once was a lady—is she
now?" The newborn infant is addressed as the Savior who is
going to make everything all right and redeem England. The
politicians can't do it; they are described in the only excerpt
from the ode preserved in *Collected Poetry:* "These had stopped
seeking," and "went to sleep / On the burning heap." [74] Youth
is no help, for "They're most of them dummies who want their
mummies" and their teachers are even worse: "Master Bleak
will speak in Greek, / Master Dim will sing a hymn." In short,
only John, son of Warner, will "take off his coat and get down
with a spanner / To each unhappy Joseph and repressed
Diana, / Say Bo to the invalids and take away their rugs...."
In an extreme example of private reference, some fictional characters from the unpublished Mortmere fantasies of Isherwood
and Upward are introduced toward the end,[75] among well-
known public figures who are satirized. The Envoi is personal,
describing the poet at his Scottish school.

The fifth ode, "To My Pupils," is the most famous of the
six: it was published first in *New Signatures* earlier in 1932 and
is the only one of the odes to be included in the *Selected Poetry*
of 1958; in *Collected Poetry* it is called, "Which Side Am I
Supposed To Be On?" This is the fullest exposition of the ambivalent attitude of the schoolmaster, and is entirely in terms
of the war myth: he addresses his pupils in the guise of an old
soldier giving informal advice and instruction to younger ones.
I take the speech to be in general an ironic exposition of the
view of "we," the capitalists, the existing order or ruling class or
Establishment; "they" are the political rebels (communists, so-
cialists, etc.) but also intellectuals, artists, and others who have
no place in the existing order. (The definition of the enemy is,

however, no simpler here than in "Journal of an Airman," to which this forms an interesting parallel in reverse: i.e. the airman would belong to the forces of "they" in the Ode.) We, in our armed camp, have our legends of innocence and peace, but they are irrelevant; the child is formed for his harsh military life by his family, and questions are useless; the bishop blesses our cause. The enemy have been created by us, both in the sense that the bourgeoisie exploit the proletariat and in the sense that they are internal, inside us (as in the description of wrath, envy, and others of the seven deadly sins). The two senses are related, of course; the external political conflict results from the internal one, from moral defects, it is implied (exactly reversing the Marxist analysis). The end of the ode is a kind of fusion of schoolboy pep talk and military morale-building; like the end of "Address for a Prize-Day," it is a burlesque of such inspirational talks with their moral crudities. The last stanza is a moving and stoical call to battle which is, by implication, hopeless; in tone it recalls the Nordic mask, which has already been used for the other side (their captain has used the language of the Old English *Battle of Maldon*: "Heart and head shall be keener, mood the more / As our might lessens"):

All leave is cancelled to-night; we must say good-bye.
We entrain at once for the North; we shall see in the morning
The headlands we're doomed to attack; snow down to the tide-line:
        Though the bunting signals
'Indoors before it's too late; cut peat for your fires,'
        We shall lie out there.

The last ode, "Not, Father, further do prolong / Our necessary defeat," is a prayer; it is in hymn stanza, and Auden placed it in the section of "Songs and Other Musical Pieces" in the *Collected Poetry*. It is a queer prayer, both because it is partly a burlesque of the inversions and other torturings of syntax that are the vices of hymnody and of its archaic diction, and because it asks for defeat, not victory but peace:

> Be not another than our hope;
>   Expect we routed shall
> Upon your peace; with ray disarm,
>   Illumine, and not kill.

Perhaps the familiar figure of the doomed bourgeois, seeking his own defeat, is to be seen here; but it is primarily a parody of the hymns sung in school. It carries on the themes of the preceding ode where "we" accuse "they" of fighting against God. It is worth noting that *The Orators*, like the volume of *Poems*, ends with a prayer, however heterodox and peculiar.[76]

The "Epilogue" to *The Orators* takes its first line, " 'O where are you going?' said reader to rider," and its rhetorical pattern from the folksong, "The Cutty Wren." [77] Auden put it in the section of "Songs" in *Collected Poetry* and gave it the title "The Three Companions" in *Selected Poetry*. I read it as an adjuration to courage and action. Reader, fearer, and horror point out various mysterious and ominous dangers; but rider, farer, and hearer—a man of action—dismisses these fears and misgivings, leaves them there and goes on. Where is he going? Perhaps to the revolution, to migrate, to get out of the old house and cross the frontier: to break with the old society. Politically, the poem is, I take it, a refusal of compromise and a call to action. But it has this meaning only in context; in isolation its references would be purely moral-psychological. The poem is technically very complex, with its use of double consonance internally (reader/rider, midden/madden) together with alliteration and alternating feminine and masculine end-rhyme; the riddling effect is set off against the histrionic, but effective, images of terror:

> 'O what was that bird,' said horror to hearer,
> 'Did you see that shape in the twisted trees?
> Behind you swiftly the figure comes softly,
> The spot on your skin is a shocking disease?'

Further, the thumping anapaestic rhythm gives a headlong effect of hysteria which is brought up short by the reversal of it in the last stanza. The poem makes an appropriate epilogue because it is, on one level, an address to the reader in the traditional fashion of epilogues: certainly the reader is supposed to recognize himself in the "reader" of the poem. After all the indirection, joking, and obscurity, the reader is given some specific advice—but it is a little parable in the form of a riddle.

RETROSPECT

In the *Collected Poetry* of 1945 Auden did not reprint *Paid on Both Sides*. As a hostile critic put it,

> To prove that he has not kept the faintest understanding of or sympathy for his earlier work, he does worse than leave out *Paid on Both Sides*—he destroys it for good, by following Untermeyer's precedent of printing a few last surviving fragments as lyrics.[78]

There are, in fact, seven excerpts from *Paid* in the volume; like all the other poems, they are given titles and arranged in alphabetical order of first lines. But of the seven, four are among those written first as separate poems and published as such in *Poems* 1928, before *Paid* was written.[79] These can hardly be considered "last surviving fragments." In 1950 Auden reprinted *Paid* complete in the *Collected Shorter Poems* published in London, which is the English equivalent of the American *Collected Poetry*. Perhaps Auden thought *Paid* as a whole somewhat specialized for American tastes, but clearly he had no intention of destroying it for good.

For the *Collected Poetry*, nothing was taken from the earlier versions that does not appear in the 1933 volume of *Poems*. Of the thirty poems in that volume, only two were omitted from *Collected Poetry*: "It's no use raising a shout" and "Get there if you can . . ."; both of these have been discussed in detail above. Both of them seem comparatively obvious and crude in technique, and this is presumably why they were discarded.

From the reader's point of view, this was unfortunate, however, since both provide useful background for the other poetry and both contain brilliant and amusing passages, whatever their ultimate aesthetic status.

As we have seen, Auden cites *The Orators* in his Preface to the *Collected Poetry* as example of "the fair notion fatally injured," and had obviously concluded that it was not worth preserving as a whole. Of all the prose in *The Orators*, the only part retained in *Collected Poetry* is "Letter to a Wound," published as a separate piece. Two poems are salvaged from "Journal of an Airman" ("We have brought you ..." and "There are some birds ..."). All the other verse in *The Orators* is retained (as separate poems in the same alphabetical arrangement with everything else) except Ode II, the Hopkins parody ("Walk on air do we? ..."), presumably discarded as too lightweight, and most of Ode IV ("Roar Gloucestershire ..."), dropped presumably as too crude and topical, as well as diffuse. The *Collected Shorter Poems* has the same contents except that, excluding all prose, it naturally does not contain "Letter to a Wound." If one accepts the premises on which the *Collected Poetry* is based, this treatment of *The Orators* is unexceptionable, but, as I have intimated, the premises seem to me to be unfortunate. To disregard context entirely and place the poems in an arbitrary order is to make things needlessly difficult for the reader who wants to go beyond the most casual acquaintance.

The *Selected Poetry* of 1958 is chronologically arranged and gives the poems sensible and often helpful titles (instead of the facetious ones so prevalent in *Collected Poetry*). The selection is too small for omissions to be significant, but a brief statement of what Auden chose to represent this early poetry may be of interest. From *Paid* there is only one excerpt (actually first published in 1928), "To throw away the key...." This seems an obvious choice, as it is the passage that comes closest to embodying the central meaning of the play and is probably the finest poetically. There are two poems that first appeared

in 1928, "From the very first coming down," a pastoral poem
in accentual tetrameter (perhaps Old Native Meter would be
a more accurate name) about the enigmatic ways of love, and
"Taller to-day, we remember similar evenings," which seems
to be about adolescent love, and has the properties of the Nordic mask (snow, howling dead, a glacier): two stanzas are deleted here from the earlier versions. From the 1930 and 1933
Poems there are five choices: "Doom is dark ..." and "This
lunar beauty," widely held to be the two most outstanding
poems in the volume; "Who will endure," a kind of companion
poem to "Doom is dark ...," describing a place where there is
no quest nor wanderer, no travel nor even communication; and
two fine but different clipped lyrics, "Before this loved one"
and "To ask the hard question. ..." From *The Orators* there
are the ode, "Though aware of our rank ...," the lyric from
the "Journal," "There are some birds ...," here called "The
Decoys," and the epilogue, " 'O where are you going?'...."
Here again, there would probably be general agreement that
these are the three best poems in the work. In short, the representation of the early poetry is responsible and, within its limits, well balanced; some of the poems are improved by minor
revisions.

So much for Auden's later attitude toward this early work.
Perhaps it would be useful to recur to our original formulation
of the problem as that of bringing together the didactic, diagnostic impulse of the rational mind with the deep, magical,
emotional, irrational impulse (or compulsion) to fantasy. The
problem is to keep the power and magic of the fantasy while
making it accessible and meaningful, to make it, in short, diagnostic. In *Paid on Both Sides*, there is a heavy predominance of
fantasy. In the shorter poems there is a definite progress toward
balancing the two; but in *The Orators* they break apart again,
with fantasy out of control. The problem is not solved at the
end of this section, and in our next we shall see the pendulum
swing the other way.

Notes to Section I

1. M.A. (Cantab.), M.D., Ph.D., F.R.C.P., D.P.H. Translator, *Guide for Visitors, the Danish Collection: Prehistoric Period*, National Museum, Copenhagen, 1908; Editor, *A Handbook to York and District*, prepared for the 75th Meeting of the British Association for the Advancement of Science, 1906; etc.

2. Christopher Isherwood, *Lions and Shadows: An Education in the Twenties* (Norfolk, Conn., 1947), p. 182 (first published 1937). In his introduction to Betjeman's *Slick But Not Streamlined* (1947), Auden recalls the titles of his original nursery library: *Icelandic Legends, Machinery for Metalliferous Mines, Eric or Little by Little, Lead and Zinc Ores of Northumberland and Alston Moor, Struwwelpeter, Mrs. Beeton's Book of Household Management* (1869), *The Edinburgh School of Surgery, Hymns Ancient and Modern,* and *Dangers to Health* (a Victorian treatise on plumbing).

3. Stephen Spender, *World Within World* (New York, 1951), pp. 46, 49. Perhaps it is worth noting that Auden's most recent poem, as I write, is called "After Reading a Child's Guide to Modern Physics" (*The New Yorker*, Nov. 17, 1962).

4. *Lions and Shadows*, p. 191.

5. "Some Notes on Auden's Early Poetry," *New Verse*, Nov. 1937, p. 7.

6. "The Life of Literature, II," *Partisan Review*, Nov. 1948, p. 1207.

7. "Auden as a Monster," *New Verse*, Nov. 1937, p. 15.

8. *Lions and Shadows*, p. 189. "Hugh Weston" is the name given to Isherwood's "caricature" of Auden in the book.

9. Louis MacNeice, *Modern Poetry: A Personal Essay* (London, 1938), p. 192.

10. C. Day Lewis, *The Buried Day* (New York, 1960), p. 177.

11. Homer Tyrrell Lane, (1876-1925), born in New Hampshire, ran away at 14 in revolt against his strict Baptist mother. After working in lumber camps and a grocery and acquiring a wife and children, he began teaching manual training. The lectures on psychology he attended in preparation for this teaching were his first acquaintance with the subject. After teaching, doing settlement work, and directing playgrounds, he made a reputation as superintendent of reformatory schools, which he made self-governing, in both the United States and England. He was a lecturer and consulting psychologist in London from 1918 to 1925, when he was forced to leave by the authorities, and died soon after in France. ("Homer Lane was killed in action by the Twickenham Baptist gang"—*Poems 1930*, xxii.) His only book was put together posthumously from his manuscripts and from notes taken on his lectures: *Talks to Parents and Teachers: In-*

sight into the Problems of Childhood. Preface by A. S. Neill; Introduction by Dr. A. A. David, Bishop of Liverpool (New York, 1949). This book contains nothing about psychosomatic disease, but much, by implication, about purity of heart. As Neill says in the preface, Lane wanted to redeem the child by love, whereas authority wants to redeem him by hate; Lane, taking his doctrine partly from Freud and Jung but mainly from his own experience, emphasizes trust, being on the child's side, and encouraging his creative impulses. Punishment and fear are always bad: "The amount of fear involved in the child's education ... will determine the amount of hatred which is to operate as one of life's motives and to destroy capacities to grow and to create" (p. 103).

John Layard (1891–) was an anthropologist who had been Lane's patient and pupil (*Lions and Shadows*, p. 299; he is there called "Barnard"). He wrote an anthropological study, *Stone Men of Malekula* (London, 1942), and a Jungian analysis, *The Lady of the Hare: being a study in the healing power of dreams* (London, 1944). In the latter work he refers to "one of the subtlest illusions of all, namely, the belief that disease of the body is anything other than a disguised disease of the soul" (p. 99) and remarks that disease depends "on spiritual and not physical factors" (p. 83); but there is nothing else recalling the Lane doctrine. Auden mentions "loony Layard" among the visionary healers in Ode I of *The Orators*, dated Jan. 1, 1931, and again in *Letters from Iceland*, p. 254.

12. According to Spender (*World Within World*, p. 56), Auden's "theory that the body is controlled by the mind" and his psychosomatic explanations of disease were already characteristic of him at Oxford in 1928. The Lane-Layard doctrine must merely have confirmed and made more dramatic what Auden had already learned from Freud and Groddeck.

Auden's thorough knowledge of Freud and continuing interest in him are apparent from articles and reviews throughout his career, as well as from his poetry. Georg Groddeck (1866-1934) has been called the only analyst who influenced Freud; he is also the best writer among the major psychologists. His masterpiece, *Das Buch vom Es* (*The Book of the It*, 1923), is available in a popular edition (London, 1949; New York, 1961) with an introduction by Lawrence Durrell, who says:

> To Freud the psyche of man was made up of two halves, the conscious and the unconscious parts; but for Groddeck the whole psyche with its inevitable dualisms seemed merely a function of something else—an unknown quantity—which he chose to discuss under the name of the "It." "The sum total of an individual human being," he says, "physical, mental, and spiritual, the organism with all its forces, the microcosmos, the

universe which is a man, I conceive of as a self unknown and forever unknowable, and I call this the 'It' as the most indefinite term available ... The It-hypothesis I regard not as a truth —for what do any of us know about absolute truth?—but as a useful tool in work and in life ... I assume that man is animated by the It, which directs what he does and what he goes through, and that the assertion 'I live' only expresses a small and superficial part of the total experience 'I am lived by the It.'..."   (p. vi)

Auden recommends Groddeck in his essay of 1935, quotes him in the notes to "New Year Letter" (*The Double Man*, p. 125), recommends him to Stravinsky in 1947 (*Memories and Commentaries*, by I. Stravinsky and R. Craft, N.Y., 1960, p. 148), and quotes him as recently as 1960, in a review in *The New Yorker*. In the poetry Auden states Groddeck's central doctrine in "In Memory of Ernst Toller": "We are lived by powers we pretend to understand..." and in "New Year Letter," ll. 1649-50.

13. "The fairy tale is a dramatic projection in symbolic images of the life of the Psyche" ("Some Notes on Grimm and Andersen," 1952). In "Psychology and Art Today" (1935) Auden suggests a connection between the "youngest son" motif in fairy and folk tales and the childhood pattern of many artists (as well as neurotics and daydreamers) showing psychological stimulation and emotional frustration as a result of the mother's attempt to set up a conscious spiritual relationship with the child (usually the youngest child, traditionally weakest physically and the mother's favorite). In *The Dyer's Hand* (1962) he interprets *Peer Gynt* as revealing the same pattern: "All fabrication is an imitation of motherhood and whenever we have information about the childhood of an artist, it reveals a closer bond with his mother than with his father ..." (p. 440). See also Auden's self-description, quoted in note 26, below.

As to Auden's temperament, Stravinsky thus describes him in 1947:

> I was puzzled at first by what I took to be contradictions in his personality. He would sail on steady rudders of reason and logic, yet profess to curious, if not superstitious, beliefs—in graphology, for instance..., in astrology, in the telepathic powers of cats, in black magic (as it is described in Charles Williams's novels), in categories of temperament..., in preordination, in fate.   (*Memories and Commentaries*, p. 147)

Lest this make Auden appear too eccentric, perhaps it should be added that Stravinsky goes on to note his conscientious discharge of all the duties of citizenship, and after acknowledging that "few people have taught me as much," opines that Auden is even more profound as a moralist than as literary critic (p. 148).

14. *Letters from Iceland*, p. 20. Auden has professed special admiration for Jane Austen, Proust, Henry James, Colette; but he reads few novels (as he stated in the London *Sunday Times*, Dec. 24, 1961, and elsewhere) and seems not much interested in the novelist's level of reality. Similarly, in *Letters from Iceland* Auden remarked, "All Cézanne's apples I would give away / For one small Goya or a Daumier," and again, "caricatures... are really my favourite kind of picture" (pp. 103, 123). In reviewing Faulkner's *The Mansion* (*The Mid-Century*, Jan. 1960), Auden divided novels into three categories: the Fairy Tale (e.g. Faulkner, Scott, Dickens, Firbank, Compton-Burnett), the Feigned History (e.g. Tolstoy), and the Prose Poem (e.g. Joyce, Woolf's *The Waves*, late James). Plainly Auden finds the first of these categories most congenial, and he describes it in terms almost identical to those he uses elsewhere in discussing literal fairy tales: what in the historical world is internal is externalized in the fairy tale; the characters are like caricatures in that they reveal their inner life immediately and exactly, and are good or bad by nature. Faulkner, he says, is not concerned with constructing a perfect verbal object, but with "keeping us enchanted"; he is a very great magician, and his magic is white because it has a moral purpose. Elsewhere Auden remarks that Dickens is one of his favourite authors (*The Mid-Century* #21, Jan. 1961).

15. Auden, untitled essay in *Modern Canterbury Pilgrims*, ed. James A. Pike (New York, 1956). A "boat-boy" carries a bowl of incense to replenish the censers carried by the thurifers.

16. In *Lions and Shadows*, Upward is called "Allen Chalmers," and this pseudonym was also used by Spender in *World Within World* and for the only part of the Mortmere fantasies to be published: "The Railway Accident," in *New Directions 11* (New York, 1949), 84-116, by "Allen Chalmers" with foreword by Isherwood. Spender (p. 92) has an amusing description of the literary hierarchy in 1930: he deferred to Auden, Auden defered to Isherwood, and Isherwood deferred to "Chalmers." The identity of "Chalmers" was first revealed publicly by John Lehmann in *The Whispering Gallery* (London, 1955), p. 244, who remarked that Upward's great gifts were "slowly killed in the Iron Maiden of Marxist dogma." (He became a Communist in 1932, and remained politically rigid and orthodox.) Upward wrote a novel, *Journey to the Border*, and has recently published the first volume of a fictional autobiography, *In the Thirties* (London, 1962), taking up where *Lions and Shadows* ends. Auden dedicated Ode III of *The Orators* to him, and in *Letters from Iceland* appoints him, with Isherwood, his joint literary executor (p. 239).

17. "Psychology and Art Today," 1935.

18. *The Romantic Survival* (London, 1957), p. 140. As I have acknowledged in the preface, I am indebted to Mr. Bayley for suggesting part of my approach to the early poetry; and in another context (p. 240 below) I express my admiration for his work. The best thing in his discussion seems to me to be his correction of the tiresome emphasis on Auden's ideas by stressing his relation to the English literary tradition: "He owes more to Scott and Hardy than to Kierkegaard, and the tradition in which his writing is unconsciously founded is not an intellectual one" (p. 37). I disagree, however, with his contention that for Auden prose, and not poetry, is the moral and responsible medium, a statement which seems to me to take too literally some of Auden's early and casual observations; and, for the same reason, I disagree with his argument about Auden's relation to the art of the novel and to such novelists as Dickens. It seems to me also that he exaggerates the divisions in Auden between poet and citizen, magic and morality, perhaps in order to fit his general thesis, which I think less valid than his specific comments about the poetry.

19. *Letters from Iceland*, p. 205. A good recent poem deals with this theme: "Hammerfest," in *The London Magazine*, March 1962.

20. Day Lewis, *The Buried Day*, p. 194. The book contains a vivid description of Helensburgh and the school.

21. Program note for *The Dance of Death*, as quoted in Julian Symons, *The Thirties* (London, 1960), p. 78.

22. In "Psychology and Art Today" Auden observed that the use of psychoanalytical techniques by the surrealists had been anticipated by the nonsense passages in the Mummers' plays.

23. "To-night when a full storm surrounds the house," "Night strives with darkness, right with wrong," "The spring will come," "The summer quickens grass," "Some say that handsome raider still at large," and "To throw away the key and walk away."

24. Letter to M.K.S., July 21, 1962.

25. See Hugh Kenner, *The Invisible Poet* (New York, 1959).

26. "*The English Hymnal*, the Psalms, *Struwelpeter* and the mnemonic rhymes in *Kennedy's Shorter Latin Primer* are about all I remember" (*The Dyer's Hand*, 1962, p. 34).

27. Auden gives an account of this discipleship in "A Literary Transference," 1940. Until his sixteenth year he read no poetry: "Brought up in a family which was more scientific than literary, I had been the sole autocratic inhabitant of a dream country of lead mines, narrow-gauge tramways, and overshot waterwheels." The poetry-lover, he observes, is usually an introvert, and is unhappy in adolescence because at school he sees the extrovert successful and happy while he is unpopular and neglected. When he grows up "he realizes that the introvert is the lucky one, the best adapted to an industrial civilization, the collective values of

which are so infantile that he alone can grow, who has educated his phantasies and learned how to draw upon the resources of his inner life" (p. 79). But at the time his adolescence is very unpleasant:

> ...unable to imagine a society in which he would feel at home, and warned by some mysterious instinct from running back for consolation to the gracious or terrifying figures of childhood, he turns away from the human to the non-human: homesick he will seek, not his mother, but mountains or autumn woods, friendless he will mutely observe the least shy of the wild animals, and the growing life within him will express itself in a devotion to music and thoughts upon mutability and death. Art for him will be something infinitely precious, pessimistic, and hostile to life. If it speaks of love, it must be love frustrated, for all success seems to him noisy and vulgar; if it moralizes, it must counsel a stoic resignation, for the world he knows is well content with itself and will not change.   (p. 79)

It was Hardy who struck this note for him, Auden recalls, and hence he seemed the archetype of the poetic. In concluding, Auden observes that he values most in Hardy "his hawk's vision, his way of looking at life from a very great height.... To see the individual life related not only to the local social life of its time, but to the whole of human history, life on the earth, the stars, gives one both humility and self-confidence...." (p. 83).

28. In *New Verse*, 1937, Isherwood quotes three of these—"The Carter's Funeral," "Allendale," and "Consider if you will..."; in *Lions and Shadows* he prints four more: "The Traction Engine," "The Engine House," "Rain," and "The Rookery" (pp. 186-8).

29. Coghill's account is in *T. S. Eliot: A Symposium*, ed. R. March and Tambimuttu (London, 1948); Auden dedicates *The Dyer's Hand*, 1962, to Coghill. Isherwood says, "For Eliot's Dante-quotations and classical learning, he substituted oddments of scientific, medical and psychoanalytical jargon: his magpie brain was a hoard of curious and suggestive phrases from Jung, Rivers, Kretschmer and Freud" (*Lions and Shadows*, p. 191). (Isherwood is, we remember at this point, drawing a caricature.) Spender says of him in 1928:

> He used a vocabulary containing words drawn from scientific, psychological and philosophical terminology. At the same time he avoided...jargon.... He used these technical words with a certain effect of mysteriousness which communicated itself excitingly, as Milton uses names of heathen gods, with an

> intellectual awareness of what they signify and yet like a kind
> of abracadabra.   (*World Within World*, p. 51)

30. "Criticism in a Mass Society," 1941, p. 132; Auden was illustrating the modern artist's consciousness of the whole historical past. Two "Case-Histories," published in *The Adelphi* (June 1931), are of interest as abortive experiments in free verse; they sound rather like Lawrence: "I. The Mother had wanted / To be a missionary in Africa, / So the Son's novel / Must be printed in Paris." But any resemblances to Lawrence may be illusory; Auden remarks in *The Dyer's Hand* (p. 278) that at this time he was impressed by Lawrence's message but did not like his poetry; "it offended my notions of what poetry should be."

31. Most notably *The Poet's Tongue*, 1935, the *Oxford Book of Light Verse*, 1938, the five-volume *Poets of the English Language*, 1950, and the recent volume of his own criticism, *The Dyer's Hand*, 1962.

32. *Modern Poetry*, p. 108. "In dreams the hierarchies of life break down," distances are overruled, the particular stands for the general, MacNeice observes (p. 106), pointing out the dream-quality in the poems.

33. C. S. Lewis, in *English Literature in the Sixteenth Century* (Oxford, 1954), remarks: "Mr. Graves, Mr. Auden, and others receive from Skelton principally what they give and in their life ... does Skelton live" (p. 143). Auden's review of 1932 of an edition of Skelton and his 1935 essay on him make plain his intimate knowledge and appreciation of Skelton.

34. Graves says in *The New Republic*, March 5, 1956, that he wrote Auden in 1928 to complain that he had borrowed from Laura Riding's "Love as Love, Death as Death" (reprinted in Graves's *The Crowning Privilege*, London, 1955, p. 151). The passage Graves cites does not in fact seem very close, the resemblance being chiefly in cadence. In the introduction to the *Faber Book of Modern American Verse* (1956), Auden expresses regret that Miss Riding forbade the inclusion of her verse, and he has mentioned Graves favorably from his 1935 "Psychology and Art Today" to the London *Sunday Times* for Dec. 24, 1961. Louis MacNeice suggests that "Sentries against inner and outer" shows the "clear influence" of Graves, and observes that Auden was "fascinated by the subtleties" of Laura Riding and Emily Dickinson at this time (*Modern Poetry*, p. 171).

In reviewing Graves's *Collected Poems* (*The Mid-Century* #28, July 1961), Auden remarks that he first read Graves in the volumes of *Georgian Poetry* when he was a schoolboy, "and ever since he has been one of the very few poets whose volumes I have always bought the moment they appeared." Graves is, he says, a good example but not model, and he praises his integrity both in resisting current fashions and in his revision of his own verse. In use of traditional forms, and relation to ballads, nursery rhymes, and such poets as Skelton, there is an obvious common ground between Auden and Graves; and Auden parallels to a limited extent in his later poetry the Gravesian contrast between the true Muse (the "White Goddess") and the false Muse (Apollo) who inspired Virgil and Milton.

35. It is interesting to see appearing thus early the kind of imagery that Cleanth Brooks considers to be the basis of Auden's best poetry:

> Auden's surest triumphs represent a recovery of the archaic imagery—fells, scarps..., the becks with their pot-holes left by the receding glaciers of the age of ice. His dominant contrast is the contrast between this scene and the modern age of ice: foundries with their fires cold, flooded coal-mines, silted harbors—the debris of the new ice age. The advent of the new age of ice, a "polar peril," supplies the background for his finest poetry.
>
> (*Modern Poetry and the Tradition*, Chapel Hill, 1939, p. 126)

36. The last two lines quoted were used by Auden in "From scars where kestrels hover," in *Poems* 1930.

37. This line was used by Auden in "Which of you waking early and watching daybreak," in *Poems* 1930.

38. Spender places the beginning of Auden's political awareness a little later: "Auden 'arrived at' politics, by way of psychology. His early poems begin by being preoccupied with neurosis in individuals, but this gradually extends (at the time when he had left Oxford and gone to live in Berlin) to an interest in the epoch and capitalistic society" (Oxford to Communism," *New Verse*, Nov. 1937).

39. Auden used this and some other images and phrases from this poem in "It was Easter as I walked in the public gardens," in *Poems* 1930. Since the frozen buzzard is still there in *Collected Poetry* 1945, Spender's recollection of Auden deleting it at Isherwood's suggestion is clearly inaccurate (*World Within World*, p. 93).

40. He used its closing phrase, "wrong for years," in "Since you are going to begin to-day," in *Poems* 1930.

41. "...that severe Christopher" is presumably Isherwood; the poet is probably Day Lewis, who quoted Auden's phrase "brazen leech" in "It is Becoming Now to Declare My Allegiance" (which also contains an amusing description of Auden) and in *The Buried Day*, pp. 149-52, describes the woman Margaret, to whom it refers. She had been trained as a psychiatrist, had been married to a doctor whom she had divorced to marry a professional singer, Douglas Marshall, and lived with him in Surrey. Day Lewis learned about psychology (and about himself) from her and about singing from her husband, and pays affectionate tribute

to them both in his autobiography. Since Day Lewis was their close friend during his last year at Oxford (1926-7), when he began his friendship with Auden, Auden himself must have been well acquainted with them. Since Margaret was a trained psychiatrist and had introduced Day Lewis to Freud, Jung, and Adler, she may well have contributed, therefore, to Auden's knowledge and awareness of modern psychology.

42. This phrase appears in "Underneath the abject willow," 1936.

43. Auden used this in "From scars where kestrels hover," in *Poems* 1930.

44. The first part of this was turned into prose and used in *The Orators:* "Love, that notable forked one, riding away from the farm, the ill wind said, fought at the frozen dam, transforms itself to influenza and guilty rashes...." (*Poems* 1934, p. 106. *Wind* is surely a misprint for *word*.) Another passage from this poem—"Falling in slush, shaking hands / With a snubnosed winner; / Open a random locker, sniff with distaste / At a mouldy passion"—is used in "Between attention and attention" (1933), which also takes a line from "The four sat on in the bare room": "Scraping back chairs for the wrong train" (*Poems* 1928, p. 27). The "indolent ulcer" was used in *The Age of Anxiety*, p. 37.

Among other phrases from these discarded poems that reappear later, "The diver's brilliant bow" from "No trenchant parting this" (*Poems* 1928, p. 13) is used in "As I walked out one evening" (1937).

45. These were: "The crowing of the cock," "Bones wrenched, weak whimper...," "Nor was that final...," "Suppose they met...," "No trenchant parting this," "From the very first coming down," "Who stands, the crux left of the watershed," "Control of the passes...," and "Taller to-day, we remember similar evenings."

46. The first five poems listed in the preceding note were discarded, together with "Which of you waking early..." and "To have found a place for nowhere." The seven new poems in the 1933 edition were: II, "Doom is dark...," VI, "Between attention and attention," IX, "It's no use raising a shout," XIII, "What's in your mind...," XXIII, "Look there! The sunk road winding," XXV, "Who will endure," and XXVII, "To ask the hard question is simple."

47. These are the last four listed in note 45, above; the numbers are V, XI, XV, XXVI.

48. From "Which of you waking early...," discarded in 1933.

49. It seems likely that Auden learned something about the use of consonance, especially double consonance (such as groined / groaned, hall / Hell, years / yours), as a substitute for rhyme from Wilfred Owen, whose "Strange Meeting" and "From My Diary, July 1914," for example, employ it.

50. John Bayley (op. cit. pp. 129ff.) has some excellent comments on this poem.

51. Cleanth Brooks, op. cit. pp. 127-30; John Bayley, op. cit. pp. 158-62.

52. Called "1929" in *Collected Poetry;* discussed by Brooks, pp. 134-5, MacNeice, p. 172.

53. This was first pointed out by M. W. Bloomfield in *Modern Language Notes,* Dec. 1948. The poem is discussed at length by Richard Hoggart, *Auden: An Introductory Essay* (London, 1951), pp. 97-100.

54. *New Verse,* Nov. 1937.

55. MacNeice remarks, "Auden's view of the world encourages him to use certain words in specialized senses. For example, he sometimes seems to use the word 'ghost' to denote either hereditary influence or a man's own slant backwards towards his parents or ancestors. Auden has always been much occupied with the paradoxes of family relationships" (*Modern Poetry,* p. 172).

56. Brooks, op. cit. pp. 1-2; W. C. Brown, D. A. Robertson, W. K. Wimsatt, and H. Smith in *The Explicator,* III (1945), 38, 51.

57. Cf. Northrop Frye, *Anatomy of Criticism* (Princeton, 1957): "Riddle was originally the cognate object of read, and the riddle seems intimately involved with the whole process of reducing language to visible form.... The actual riddle-poems of Old English include some of its finest lyrics, and belong to a culture in which such a phrase as 'curiously inwrought' is a favorite aesthetic judgement. Just as the charm is not far from a sense of magical compulsion, so the curiously wrought object...is not far from a sense of enchantment or magical imprisonment" (p. 280); "The idea of the riddle is descriptive containment: the subject is not described but circumscribed, a circle of words drawn around it.... A slightly more complicated form of riddle is the emblematic vision, probably one of the oldest forms of human communication..." (p. 300). Much of *The Orators* might be described as "emblematic vision."

58. *Enemies of Promise and Other Essays: An Autobiography of Ideas* (New York, 1960), p. 166.

59. In the volume of the same title (New York, 1953).

60. Quoted in note 55, above.

61. Op. cit. p. 260. Connolly adds: "Once again romanticism with its death-wish is to blame, for it lays an emphasis on childhood, on a fall from grace which is not compensated for by any doctrine of future redemption.... Certainly growing up seems a hurdle which most of us are unable to take and the lot of the artist is unpleasant in England because he is one of the few who, bending but not breaking, is able to throw off these early experiences, for maturity is the quality that the English dislike most..." (pp. 260-61).

62. His essay in *The Old School,* ed. Graham Greene (London, 1934), shows a remarkable candor and objectivity, and a refreshing absence of

any inclination to blame the school (see the passage quoted in the Chronology, above). Auden says, rather shockingly in this context, that he was very happy at school and was never bullied or molested; he acknowledges a great debt to the master who taught classics and English (he had a fine bass reading voice) and the music master, who was not only an excellent teacher and organist but Auden's first grown-up friend. Even the prefect who was captain of Auden's house was good (and in the context of this volume this is perhaps the ultimate heresy). Holt, he says, "is a modern school, i.e. it does not teach Greek and concentrates on science, history, etc."; its library and laboratories are excellent. His only serious criticism is of the honor system, which, he argues, leads to neurosis and defective character.

The pamphlet Auden wrote with T. C. Worsley in 1939, *Education Today—and Tomorrow*, is full of shrewd, practical observations plainly based on experience, for example, "Every teacher knows in his heart of hearts that he has not the slightest idea of what effect he is having, that he is working largely in the dark, that on most of his pupils he has no effect at all, and probably a bad effect on half the rest" (pp. 39-40). The pamphlet was quickly rendered obsolete by the arrival of war instead of the socialist government the authors expected; but it is full of sensible and useful comments, such as that the exaltation of adolescent team spirit into a morality is bad, and that it is just as important to encourage individualism in games (pp. 11-16); that the system isn't really arranged to produce leaders but "a pleasant-mannered yes-man with executive ability" (p. 40).

63. *Two Great Plays by W. H. Auden and Christopher Isherwood*, New York, n.d., p. 91. In *Letters from Iceland* Auden remarks that Englishmen "All suffer from an Oedipus fixation" (p. 233).

64. The last line seems to refer to the fairy tale Auden quotes in *Letters from Iceland*, p. 155, as a childhood favorite.

65. *Poems* (New York, 1934), p. 117. References, unless otherwise specified, are to this edition.

66. Op. cit., p. 87.

67. In "A Happy New Year" (*New Country*, ed. Michael Roberts, 1933) Auden represents Lawrence as an airman passing ambiguous judgment on the representatives of modern England satirically assembled; he flies over and throws down a note saying, "I've a devil...I'm ordered elsewhere / God what a crew! But your best are there." Auden wrote about him in 1934 and quotes his definition of happiness in *Letters from Iceland*, p. 21; he is said to have based Ransom in *The Ascent of F6* partly on Lawrence. For Rimbaud, see the sonnet of 1939, "Rimbaud," and "New Year Letter," line 197, where among the masters sits "The adolescent with red hands."

G. S. Fraser, in an interesting reassessment of *The Orators* (*New*

Statesman, Jan. 28, 1956), says that it seems to him now to be the work of a romantic radical of the right, in its leader mystique and emphasis on male solidarity. This seems to me to be an oversimplification in the opposite direction from the early ones.

68. *Letters from Iceland*, p. 206.

69. The riddling effect is most explicit in the "Airman's Alphabet," which consists largely of kennings and suggests both Old English poetry and a child's alphabet, and in the following section, "Of the Enemy," where the enemy is defined in terms of triads, from "Three kinds of enemy walk" to "Three results of an enemy victory—impotence—cancer—paralysis." Daniel G. Hoffman has pointed out to me that in *1000 Years of Irish Poetry*, ed. K. Hoagland (New York, 1947) the parallel is noted between this section and the ninth century "Triads of Ireland," e.g. "Three rude ones of the world: a youngster mocking an old man; a robust person mocking an invalid; a wise man mocking a fool"; "Three signs of a fop: the track of his comb in his hair; the track of his teeth in his food; the track of his stick behind him"; "Three nurses of theft: a wood, a cloak, night. Three false sisters; 'Perhaps,' 'Maybe,' 'I dare say.'" (p. 23). Several Irish triads are given in Auden and Kronenberger's *Viking Book of Aphorisms* (1962), pp. 14, 68, 126; the last of these is the first I have quoted above.

Spender (op. cit., p. 56) quotes Auden as saying, in his last year at Oxford, "'In a revolution, the poet lies on his belly on the top of a roof and shoots across the lines at his best friend who is on a roof-top of the other side ... of course, at heart, the poet's sympathies are always with the enemy,' he added darkly. '... When he is in love the poet always hopes that his loved one will die. He thinks more of the poems which he will write than of the lover....'"

70. F. A. Philbrick, in *The Explicator*, Jan. 1946, reads it in this way and produces an excellent interpretation.

71. *New Verse*, Nov. 1937, and *Lions and Shadows*, p. 303.

72. See note 16, above, on Upward.

73. Auden had known Warner, poet and, later, novelist, at Oxford, where he had been a close friend of Day Lewis. Day Lewis says that Warner "read philosophy to such effect that one day he saw the Absolute walk in at his door, and taking the hint, saved his sanity by having a nervous breakdown, leaving Oxford for a year, and returning to read for a quiet Pass in English" (*The Buried Day*, p. 166). His first novel, *The Wild Goose Chase* (1937) is discussed in the next section.

74. Most of this excerpt was published in *The Adelphi*, Dec. 1931, as the first of three "Cautionary Rhymes."

75. "Bob and Miss Belmairs spooning in Spain, / ... Where is Moxon? Dreaming of nuns."

76. "Nor was that final..." in *Poems* 1928 and 1930 deals with religion as dishonest escape: " 'Wonderful, was that cross, and I full of sin.' / 'Approaching, utterly generous, came one, / For years expected, born only for me.' / Returned from that dishonest country, we / Awake, yet tasting the delicious lie; / ...No, these bones shall live...."

77. Auden prints "The Cutty Wren" as No. 209 in *The Oxford Book of Light Verse* (1938). He probably encountered it first in de la Mare's *Come Hither!*

78. Randall Jarrell, "Freud to Paul: the Stages of Auden's Ideology," *Partisan Review*, XII (1945), 441.

79. See note 23, above, for a list of these; "The Spring will come..." and "Some say that handsome raider..." are the two on the list that are not in *Collected Poetry*. The three that were not first published in 1928 are: "Not from this life...," "Can speak of trouble...," and "The Spring unsettles sleeping partnerships."

1930-35 Schoolmaster at Larchfield Academy, Helensburgh, Scotland, and at The Downs School, Colwall, near Malvern.

1933 *The Dance of Death* (dedicated to Robert Medley and Rupert Doone) published by Faber & Faber in November. Written for the Group Theatre, with which Auden had worked since 1932, and of which Medley was art director and Doone director.

Reviews in *The Criterion* of *The Evolution of Sex*, by Dr. Maranon and *The Biological Tragedy of Women*, by A. Nemilov (Jan. 1933); *Dark Places in Education*, by Dr. Schohaus (April 1933); *The Poems of William Dunbar* (July 1933); *The Book of Talbot*, by V. Clifton (Oct. 1933).

Reviews in *Scrutiny* of *Thoughts and Adventures*, by W. Churchill (March 1933); *Alfred Mond*, by H. Bolitho (Dec. 1933).

1934 *Poems* published by Random House, New York, containing *The Orators* and *The Dance of Death* as well as the 1933 *Poems*.

"The Group Movement and the Middle Classes," in *Oxford and the Groups*, ed. Richard Crossman.

"Honour (Gresham's School, Holt)," in *The Old School*, ed. Graham Greene.

"T. E. Lawrence," in *Now and Then*, Spring 1934.

Reviews in *The Criterion* of *Gerard Manley Hopkins*, by E. E. Phare (April 1934); *English Poetry for Children*, ed. R. L. Mégroz (July 1934).

Reviews in *Scrutiny* of *Lessons from the Varsity of Life*, by Lord Baden-Powell (March 1934); *G. L. Dickinson*, by E. M. Forster (Dec. 1934).

1935 *The Dog Beneath the Skin*, written with Christopher Isherwood and dedicated to Robert Moody, published by Faber & Faber and Random House. The Group Theatre had its first season in London at the Westminster Theatre and first became widely known; both *Dance* and *Dog* produced, with incidental music by Herbert Murrill.

Worked for six months with G.P.O. Film Unit. Collaborated with Benjamin Britten on *Coal-Face* and other films, including *Night Mail*, which has become a documentary classic.

Edited, with John Garrett, *The Poet's Tongue*, an anthology.

"John Skelton," in *The Great Tudors*, ed. K. Garvin.

"The Good Life," in *Christianity and the Social Revolution*, ed. John Lewis.

"Psychology and Art Today," in *The Arts Today*, ed. G. Grigson.

1936 Trip to Iceland, July-September, with Louis MacNeice.

The Ascent of F6 (written with Isherwood and dedicated to John Bicknell Auden, the poet's elder brother and a famous mountaineer) produced in September. Published by Faber & Faber; by Random House in 1937.

Collaborated with Benjamin Britten on *Our Hunting Fathers* for the Norfolk and Norwich Triennial Musical Festival in September.

Look, Stranger! (dedicated to Erika Mann Auden) published by Faber & Faber in October; the Random House edition, called *On This Island*, appeared in 1937. (Auden preferred the latter title.) Earlier in the year Auden had married Erika Mann, whom he had never met, in order to provide her with a passport.

Essay in *Selected Poems by Robert Frost*, Chosen by the Author (London).

"Poetry and the Film," in *Janus*, May 1936.

"Honest Doubt," in *New Verse*, June-July 1936.

Review of *In Defence of Shelley*, by Herbert Read, in *New Verse*, April-May 1936.

1937   Trip to Spain, Jan.-March.

Awarded King's Gold Medal for poetry.

Spain published by Faber & Faber in May; proceeds donated to "Medical Aid for Spain."

Letters from Iceland (written with Louis MacNeice and dedicated to Auden's father) published by Random House in March.

"Pope," in *From Anne to Victoria*, ed. Bonamy Dobrée.

"Impressions of Valencia," in *New Statesmen & Nation* (Jan. 30, 1937).

"In Defence of Gossip," in *The Listener* (Dec. 22, 1937); reprinted in *Living Age*, Feb. 1938.

Review of *Illusion and Reality*, by Christopher Caudwell, in *New Verse* (May 1937).

Review of *Visiting the Caves*, by William Plomer, in *Poetry* (Jan. 1937).

Review of *Bare Knee Days*, by H. Dimmock, in *The Listener*, Dec. 8, 1937.

1938   Trip to China with Christopher Isherwood, Jan.-July, crossing the United States both ways. On the return trip, both decided to return and settle in the United States, according to John Lehmann (*The Whispering Gallery*, London, 1955, p. 308).

In Brussels with Isherwood during latter part of year.

On the Frontier, written with Isherwood and dedicated to Benjamin Britten. Produced in October and published by Faber & Faber and Random House.

Selected Poems published by Faber & Faber in May (Auden did not make the selection).

Edited *The Oxford Book of Light Verse*.

"Living Philosophies: Morality in an Age of Change," in *The Nation*, Dec. 24, 1938.

Review of *A. E. H., A Memoir*, by Lawrence Housman, in *New Verse*, Jan. 1938.

1939-40   Taught at St. Mark's School, Southborough, Massachusetts.

1939   On Jan. 18, left England with Isherwood for permanent move to the United States.

Appointed to American Writers League Writers School Faculty in October.

Journey to a War, written with Isherwood and dedicated to E. M. Forster, published by Faber & Faber in March, by Random House in August.

Education Today—and Tomorrow (with T. C. Worsley). Hogarth Press: Day to Day Pamphlets #40.

Essay in *I Believe*, ed. Clifton Fadiman (expansion of essay in *The Nation*, 1938, listed above).

Lecture, "Democracy's Reply to the Challenge of Dictators," in *New Era*, Jan. 1939.

"The Public vs. the Late Mr. W. B. Yeats," in *Partisan Review*, Spring 1939.

Address, "Effective Democracy," in *Booksellers Quarterly*, May 1939.

"The Outlook for the 'Poetic Drama,' " in *Bulletin de l'Association France-Grand Bretagne*, July-Aug. 1939.

Reviews in *The Nation* of books on Voltaire ("A Great Democrat," March 25, 1939); *The Clue to History*, by John MacMurray ("Christian on the Left," Sept. 9, 1939); *Of Human Freedom*, by Jacques Barzun ("Democracy Is Hard," Oct. 7, 1939); *Shakespeare*, by Mark Van Doren ("The Dyer's Hand," Oct. 21, 1939).

Reviews in *The New Republic* of *Enemies of Promise*, by Cyril Connolly (April 26, 1939); Rilke, *Duino Elegies*, trans. by J. B. Leishman and Stephen Spender ("Rilke in English," Sept. 6, 1939); *Arthur Rimbaud*, by E. Starkie, and *D. H. Lawrence and Susan His Cow*, by W. Y. Tindall ("Heretics," Nov. 1, 1939); *Moment in Peking*, by Lin Yutang ("Inside China," Dec. 6, 1939); *Behold This Dreamer*, by Walter de la Mare ("Jacob and the Angel," Dec. 27, 1939).

1940-41   Taught at the New School for Social Research, New York City.

1940   *Another Time* (dedicated to Chester Kallman) published by Random House (March) and by Faber & Faber.

Some Poems (a selection not made by Auden) published by Faber & Faber in March.

Commencement address at Smith College in June, "Romantic or Free?" (published in *Smith Alumnae Quarterly*, Aug. 1940).

Radio play, *The Dark Valley*, broadcast June 2, 1940, with Dame May Whitty (published in *Best Broadcasts of 1939-40*, ed. Max Wylie, 1940). Incidental music by Benjamin Britten.

"Mimesis and Allegory," in *English Institute Annual*, ed. R. Kirk, 1940.

"A Literary Transference," in *The Southern Review*, Summer 1940. (On Hardy.)

Review of Yeats, *Last Poems and Plays*, in *Saturday Review of Literature*, June 8, 1940.

Reviews in *The Nation* of *The Last Flower*, by James Thurber, and *About People*, by William Steig ("Icon and Portrait," Jan. 13, 1940); *Historian and Scientist*, by G. Salvemini ("What is Culture?", July 6, 1940).

Reviews in *The New Republic* of *The Novel and the Modern World*, by David Daiches ("Tradition and Value," Jan. 15, 1940); *Modern Poetry and the Tradition*, by Cleanth Brooks ("Against Romanticism," Feb. 5, 1950); *The Wartime Letters of R. M. Rilke*, trans. M. D. Herder Norton, and *Fifty Selected Poems of R. M. Rilke*, trans. C. F. MacIntyre ("Poet in Wartime," July 8, 1940).

II

The Thirties

But there waited for me in the summer morning,
Auden, fiercely. I read, shuddered and knew
And all the world's stationary things
In silence moved to take up new positions; . . .
I was disinclined now for the impositions
Of the school ethic; and I listened to no more physicians,
(CHARLES MADGE IN *New Country*, 1933)

Look west, Wystan, lone flyer, birdman, my bully boy! . . .
Gain altitude, Auden, then let the base beware!
Migrate, chaste my kestrel, you need a change of air!
(C. DAY LEWIS IN THE SAME)

Come then, companions. This is the spring of blood,
heart's hey-day, movement of masses, beginning of good.
(REX WARNER IN THE SAME)

POETRY AND POLITICS

As these quotations indicate, Auden's poetry had a tremendous impact, political and moral as well as aesthetic, on his contemporaries. Considering how indirect and obscure the political implications of *Poems* and *The Orators* now seem, it is astonishing that they should have created a politically oriented "movement" in poetry. In part, the explanation is Auden's ability to express, in symbols and language apparently private and eccentric, attitudes and emotions that turned out to be representative of a great many middle-class intellectuals. (There is a parallel here to the reception of Eliot's *Waste Land* ten years

The notes are to be found at the end of the section, on page 157.

earlier: after the initial outcries over its obscurity, it was wid‹
felt to express the "despair of a generation"—an interpretati ...
that seems to us now much too limited.)

The principal reason for the extraordinary political effect of
Auden's verse, however, is certainly historical, and related to
the political, social, and intellectual climate of the early 1930s.
(Some readers may need to be reminded of the great depres-
sion and the very general feeling that capitalism in its existing
form was doomed, and of the rise of the totalitarian dictators,
reaching a climax in Hitler's assumption of power in January
1933.) In this milieu, at this time, to a limited number of writers and intellectuals,[1] the poems were an agent of moral clarification and a call to action.

The "Auden group" or "movement" was an invention of
critics who wanted it to exist. As Day Lewis says,

> ... in the sense of a *concerted* effort by a group of poets
> to impress themselves upon the public, to write differ-
> ently from their predecessors or about different subjects,
> it was not a movement at all. Though Auden, Spender,
> MacNeice and I have all known each other personally
> since the mid-Thirties, each of us had not even met all
> three others till after the publication of *New Signatures*
> in 1932, while it was only in 1947 that Auden, Spender,
> and I found ourselves together for the first time in one
> room. We did not know we were a Movement until the
> critics told us we were.[2]

The book Day Lewis mentions, *New Signatures*, was extremely
influential in creating the impression of a "movement." This
was arranged and organized by John Lehmann [3] and was published in February 1932 by Leonard and Virginia Woolf's
Hogarth Press. Michael Roberts, the editor, observes that
Auden's *Poems* and Day Lewis's *From Feathers to Iron* (1931)
were "the first books in which imagery taken from contemporary life consistently appeared as the natural and spontaneous expression of the poet's thought and feeling," and praises
their technical achievement. Little is said about politics except

by implication; the hope is that poetry "may be again a popular, elegant and contemporary art." Of Auden's three poems in the volume, only one (the Ode, "Though aware of our rank...," which appeared later in *The Orators*) has any political reference, and it is, as we have seen, very ambiguous indeed. (The other two are "Doom is dark..." and "For what as easy....")

New Country (1933), subtitled "Prose and Poetry by the authors of *New Signatures*," and with the same editor and publisher, is very different. Roberts's preface is entirely political, and in fact becomes an explicit argument that intellectuals should work with the English Communist Party. The intellectuals, he argues, see at last that their interests are the same as those of the workers: "In vicarage and golf club as in dockyard and miners' lodge, there are men who, reluctant to commit themselves to a reorientation, a reorganization of their whole lives, still feel that they are helpless units in an organism which is dying." It is time, he urges, "that those who would conserve something which is still valuable in England began to see that only a revolution can save their standards." Addressing the patriotic reader who loves his country, he says, "you see clearly enough the symptoms of her illness. Cannot you see that they are all symptoms of the one disease? And can't you see that the only way to save England is to save the world?" And he appeals to the future to judge "those of us who, writing before the final collapse, made our rough sketches for a new life and delivered satiric judgment on the old." I have quoted this at length because the images in it (but not, of course, the explicit argument) are so close to Auden's poetry that it is hard to tell how much is derived from Auden and how much is an independent and parallel formulation. Not only Roberts but all the writers in the volume quote Auden constantly and his verse obviously haunts their imaginations. It is not a mere paradox to say that Auden creates many of the modes of thought and feeling characteristic of his time; as Symons observes, "in a very real sense Auden's devices of style and habits of feeling *are* the Thirties . . ." [4] A. Alvarez's comment, "Where Eliot transformed the sensibility of his age, Auden caught the tone of his," [5] could hardly be more completely wrong. But the work of these other writers helps to gloss and explain Auden, since they are of course not purely derivative but are responding to experience as well as to his imaginary world, which has taught them how to look at the "real" world.

The most striking example of this is Rex Warner's first novel, *The Wild Goose Chase* (London, 1937), which, aside from its still considerable intrinsic interest, is probably the best single work from which to recapture the intellectual and emotional atmosphere of the times. (On Warner, see note 73 to preceding section.) Virtually every idea and symbol in the book could have come from Auden, and certainly many of them did; but Warner makes them his own and realizes them in fictional terms. The novel is patterned on the Fairy-tale Quest: three brothers go to seek the Wild Goose; the two elder ones, who are, respectively, adventurer and scholar, come to grief, but the third eventually succeeds. There is not only a Quest but a Frontier (more temporal than spatial) to cross; and then there is the City (capitalist society), which is not only corrupt and ineffectual but puts artists and intellectuals in a Convent of complete futility and subjects them to an operation which renders them sexually ambiguous. If Warner does not have in mind Auden's dedicatory poem to *On This Island*, the coincidence is astonishing, for the "surrealist police" and "baroque frontiers" are precisely represented here. The Goose that the City worships in the Anserium turns out to be a stuffed goose; the football game turns into a literal massacre, as machine-guns are brought into use—a fusion of sports and war under capitalism that is precisely parallel to the one Auden suggests in his poetry. The City has a concrete roof over it which completely keeps out the natural light and air; and the revolution will remove it. We are perhaps likely to forget how completely the political revolution was, at this time, fused for most intellectuals with a vaguely Lawrentian moral revolution; with the new life love would come easy, natural sun and light and air would be let in, man would be in harmony with nature. (See Day Lewis, p. 210, on this point.) For instance, George's speech after the climactic battle:

> Comrades, let us think no more of our dead friends, or of the wasted portions of our lives, since we are on the way to create a new civilization, something which has not existed for a long time, if ever.
>
> What our old leaders most respected we chiefly despise —the frantic assertion of an ego, do-nothings, the over-cleanly, deliberate love-making, literary critics, moral philosophers, ballroom dancing, pictures of sunsets, money, the police; and to what they used to despise we attach great value—to comradeship, and to profane love, to hard work, honesty, the sight of the sun, reverence for those who have helped us, animals, flesh and blood.
>
> (p. 440)

Auden's most striking contribution to *New Country* is "A Communist to Others," which had already appeared in *The Twentieth Century* for September 1932. This is a close parallel to Roberts's argument about the need for the liberal intellectual to make common cause with the workers. It is a self-conscious address by such an intellectual to the workers ("We cannot put on airs with you / The fears that hurt you hurt us too . . ."), occasionally suggesting their language and expressing what are presumed to be their attitudes. The bourgeois young men may be handsome and confident, but the future will belong to the proletariat whom they despise: "You're thinking us a nasty sight; / Yes, we are poisoned, you are right, / Not even clean; / We do not know how to behave / We are not beautiful or brave. . . ." The "dare-devil mystic" who advocates religion to the starving is a coward, for what he hopes for in Heaven is "All that the rich can here afford: / Love and music and bed and board / While the world flounders." The wise man, detached and humorous, who holds that the trouble is lack of money, is an enemy; the Cambridge liberals are false friends, whose "mental-healing," obscuring the problem, is even more harmful. There is a fine stanza, reminiscent of Burns at his satirical best, heaping invective upon them:

> Let fever sweat them till they tremble
> Cramp rack their limbs till they resemble
> > Cartoons by Goya:
> Their daughters sterile be in rut,
> May cancer rot their herring gut,
> The circular madness on them shut,
> > Or paranoia.

Finally, in three stanzas dropped from the version published in *On This Island*, the escapist poet "Who fled in horror from all these / To islands in your private seas" is urged to recognize common cause and help. And even in this most directly propagandistic of all Auden's poems there is a religious ending: the comrades are exhorted to "Remember that in each direction / Love outside our own election / Holds us in unseen connection: / O trust that ever." [6]

The tone of *New Country* is militant and revolutionary: among the prose pieces are Day Lewis's "Letter to a Young Revolutionary" and Spender's "Poetry and Revolution," and there is Edward Upward's sketch, "Sunday," ending with explicit propaganda: history, he says, will go to live elsewhere, with the people who destroy the more obvious causes of material misery. "And the man who doesn't prefer suicide or madness to fighting ... will join with those people." He will "go to the small club behind the Geisha Cafe. He will ask whether there is a meeting to-night ..." Spender and Day Lewis have told the story of their relation to Communism; the latter, in what is perhaps the best recent discussion, has pointed out its religious and romantic aspects and has made the just comment,

"There was generosity as well as absurdity in this, for my friends and I did at least make some attempt to imagine the conditions we did not share ... and we were prepared to help destroy a system that perpetuated itself by such hideous human wastage, even though our own pleasant way of life would be destroyed in the process." [7]

Auden, like MacNeice, apparently had no Communist phase, however brief. Spender says that "A Communist to Others" was "an exercise in entering into a point of view not his own," [8] and that Auden was less drawn to Communism than were most of his contemporaries, partly because he refused to believe that political exigency ever justified lying. Auden's own retrospective comment is:

> Looking back, it seems to me that the interest in Marx taken by myself and my friends ... was more psychological than political; we were interested in Marx in the same way that we were interested in Freud, as a technique of unmasking middle class ideologies, not with the intention of repudiating our class, but with the hope of becoming better bourgeois ... [9]

They were, of course, ignorant of what was really going on in Russia (this was Orwell's point in "Inside the Whale" [10]); it was not that they idealized it so much as that they felt it to be irrelevant to Europe. But when they encountered Communist methods in Spain they were shocked. "Nobody I know who went to Spain during the Civil War who was not a dyed-in-the-wool stalinist came back with his illusions intact." [9]

To put it in another way, Auden clearly never believed that political values were ultimate, transcending moral and religious ones; his Marxism, which was always unorthodox, was essentially another dimension added to the psychological analysis, which was itself always potentially religious. The degree of Auden's early political commitment has been much exaggerated by critics who wish to abuse him as turncoat and backslider for his presumed desertion of the cause of politics for that of religion. Temperamentally he has always been an individualist and maverick; as he wrote in 1936, when the pressures to identify with the Popular Front were at their height,

> I hate pompositas and all authority;
>   Its air of injured rightness also sends
> Me shuddering from the cultured smug minority.
>   'Perpetual revolution,' left-wing friends
>   Tell me, 'in counter-revolution ends.
> Your fate will be to linger on outcast
> A selfish pink old Liberal to the last.'
>   (*Letters from Iceland*, p. 203)

Aside from "A Communist to Others," Auden's only real experiment in the writing of propaganda is *The Dance of Death*, which will be discussed in the next sub-section with the other theatrical pieces. It is interesting to observe, however, that the two pieces must have been written at close to the same time, since *Dance* was published in 1933. Auden's other poems in *New Country* are completely without any propaganda element; three of them ("Now from my window-sill ...," "The chimneys are smoking ...," and "O love, the interest itself ... ") are collected (as is "Brothers, who when ...,") in *On This Island*, and will be discussed as part of that volume. The only one not collected is the first part of "A Happy New Year," dedicated to Gerald Heard.[11] (The second part is "Now from my window-sill ...," untitled in *On This Island*.) This is a kind of satirical dream-vision, in which the poet sees the English come like "an army recruited there" to his Scottish plain. There is a motorcyclist who says, "Sporty and speedy is the British style," a troupe of boys and girls in bathing dresses, but whose drawers keep slipping, a brass band, a choir "on ladies' bikes," a jazz band, and then the main bodies, all ashamed, afraid, suspicious, guilty. Lawrence of Arabia swoops overhead in an airplane and throws down a derisive note. (See note 67 to preceding section.) There is a mysterious spy who warns of mysterious conspiracies; generals, statesmen, press lords, fascists,.

financiers are named and satirically described. There is one literary stanza:

> Unhappy Eliot choosing his words
>   And D'Arcy's beautiful head at a glance
> I noticed building a sanctum for birds;
>   Pound had just sent them a wire from France.
>   The Sitwells were giving a private dance
> But Wyndham Lewis disguised as the maid
> Was putting cascara in the still lemonade.

Suddenly a youth breaks away, wounded, and there is a chase after him as a deserter; the ranks begin to riot but the secret police subdue them and they move out to a mysterious attack. The spy says he warned them "of spies in acrostic odes." Finally the poet is left alone to meditate upon "these blurring images / Of the dingy difficult life of our generation." It is easy to see why Auden would not wish to preserve this; though it has some amusing and effective passages, it is an extreme example of satire that is excessively private and fantastic, while at the same time excessively topical and personal.

Auden seems never to have been seriously troubled, as so many others were, by the temptation to confuse art and propaganda. His gestures in that direction, as we have seen, were limited to two,[12] and his aesthetic theory seems always to have been very clear on the point. We have considered earlier his distinction between escape art and parable art, which was made in 1935 (see above, p. 13). Whatever the inadequacies of this definition, it has the great virtue of limiting the function of art to the parabolic and diagnostic, and distinguishing it sharply from propaganda. (In his later work Auden has elaborated and refined this distinction, using instead of "propaganda" the more inclusive term "magic." See below, p. 188.) In another essay of 1935, he says:

> Poetry is not concerned with telling people what to do, but with extending our knowledge of good and evil, perhaps making the necessity for action more urgent and its

nature more clear, but only leading us to the point where
it is possible for us to make a rational and moral choice.
(Introduction to *The Poet's Tongue*)

And this is precisely the kind of political and social meaning
that his poems of the 1930s have; in fact it is almost a statement
of the central thesis of his most famous political poem, "Spain
1937."

This attitude is characteristic also of the two periodicals that
were founded primarily to publish the work of Auden and
those of like mind: Geoffrey Grigson's *New Verse* (1933-39)
and John Lehmann's *New Writing* (1936-39). These were
both distinctly non-Communist, and were bitterly opposed by
the *Left Review* and other party-line organs. Both tended to
create the impression of an "Auden group" which, if it had
existed, would have been united not by any doctrine but by an
intense awareness of and concern with politics, a conviction of
the need for solidarity and the importance of political action:
"no man is an island." It is striking that their respective dates
of founding correspond to the two crucial dates in the intellectual history of the time: 1933, when Hitler came to power,
and 1936, when the Spanish civil war started and the Popular
Front for collective action against war and fascism became a
powerful force.

Auden's political focus was important chiefly for the basis it
provided for a relation both to fellow-artists and to a larger
audience. Awareness of being a spokesman for, or at least in
relation to, a considerable audience is crucially important to
the development of his style in this period. It makes it possible
for him to work out a mode of discourse in which the public
(including the political) and the private can meet, and in 1936
it made possible "Letter to Lord Byron," Auden's most sustained and successful piece of light verse—a historical anomaly,
a unique tour de force, feasible only in this brief moment
when an easy rapport with a large audience could be attained.
But this audience was attracted by his theatrical activities per-

haps more than by his poetry, and it is time now, before returning to a detailed discussion of the poetry, to consider his work
for the theater. This was openly didactic and politically oriented.

THE THEATER

Auden's works for the theater were written out of what Yeats
called the theater's anti-self, in that none of them has much
resemblance to the conventional play: they are remote from
the tradition of dramatic naturalism. On the other hand, they
are equally remote from Yeats's aristocratic, symbolic dance
plays: Auden's plays are all popular, aimed at the widest possible audience, and openly didactic in the political sense, being
intended to "make action urgent and its nature clear." The
plays they most resemble, and those that were unquestionably
the most important influence on them, are those of Bertolt
Brecht. Brecht's plays were popular, political, brought song
and satirical light verse back into the theater, and established
a genuine rapport with a large audience. During his stay in
Berlin in 1928-29 Auden seems to have been greatly impressed
by this achievement (as was Isherwood, Auden's collaborator
in three of his five plays, in his longer stay).[13] Although an
adequate discussion of Brecht would take us too far afield, a
word must be said about the aspects of his work that seem to
have appealed to Auden particularly.

There was, in the first place, the verse, both in the volume
of *Hauspostille* (1927) and in the theater songs. According to
Willett,[14] there was in Germany after the turn of the century
a large group of satirists who produced light verse to be sung
or declaimed in the cabarets, in the tradition of the Paris chan-
sonnier, and this was Brecht's background. Hence his songs
have a local, popular flavor: like Wedekind, he set many of his
early poems to his own tunes and sang them himself, playing
his own guitar accompaniment. The tradition of the folk ballad

was stronger in Germany than anywhere else in Europe, and this is the other principal element in his verse; as H. R. Hays puts it (somewhat melodramatically), "Here was a form which was nonindividualist, a tool originally forged by the people, which could be resharpened and given back to them." [15] Brecht, he goes on to say, "successfully combined the elegance of the older imagery with the realistic bite of contemporary satire." From the early gruesome ballads ("Apfelböck," "Marie Farrar") to the later more political ones, he mingles irony with emotional pathos, toughness and bitterness with melancholy reference to the ideal and with the sadness of humanity behind. The typical sentiment is "Erst kommt das Fressen, dann kommt die Moral," which Auden has translated neatly as, "Grub first, then ethics." [16]

Brecht's theory of "epic theater" also seems to have influenced Auden. In brief, this is distinguished by a refusal to create a dramatic illusion into which the spectator can enter and escape. The dramatist, instead of representing action in the fashion defined by Aristotle, narrates; he deliberately destroys the illusion of a self-contained world of the play by intervening to remind the audience that it is an illusion, and to prevent its identifying with the characters: this is the Verfremdung (alienation) effect. The plays themselves thus are fables, modern morality plays; they are intended to appeal to the minds and not the emotions of the audience, to be educational and politically didactic.

Willett (pp. 220-21) quotes Auden as saying that he was certainly influenced by Brecht's *Hauspostille* poems and by the *Threepenny Opera* (1928) and *Mahagonny* (1929). He has maintained his interest in Brecht (whom he once described as a remarkable writer but a "most unpleasant man"): [17] in 1946 he collaborated with Brecht and H. R. Hays in adapting *The Duchess of Malfi* for Elisabeth Bergner, and at Brecht's request he translated the songs in *The Causasian Chalk Circle*. [18] With Chester Kallman, Auden translated Brecht's ballet cantata, *The Seven Deadly Sins*, performed with great success in 1959, and more recently, the play *Mahagonny*.[19] The debt to Brecht in the ballads and some of the songs in the 1930s is plain, and the plays all follow the Brechtian model in many respects.

In 1932 Auden, together with Rupert Doone, Robert Medley, and others, founded the Group Theatre, and he took a prominent part in its activities for several years. Doone had been trained in ballet and had worked with Diaghilev; he directed most of the productions. Symons, from whom this account is taken, quotes him as saying, "The form we envisaged for our plays is analogous to modern musical comedy, or the premedieval folk play," [20] and describing theatrical art as "an art of the body, presented by living people in action." Medley did the costumes, scenery, and masks; Herbert Murrill, William Alwyn, and Benjamin Britten wrote music for some of the productions. They played to very small audiences for three years, then in 1935 had a season at the Westminster Theatre, London, when Auden's *Dance of Death* and his and Isherwood's *Dog Beneath the Skin* (both with incidental music by Herbert Murrill), as well as Eliot's *Sweeney Agonistes*, were produced and brought them wide acclaim. According to Symons, the influence of Uncle Wiz, as they called Auden, brooded over the whole group.

The Dance of Death (published Nov. 1933, dedicated to Medley and Doone) was written for the Group Theatre, and in the program Auden said:

> Drama began as the act of a whole community. Ideally there would be no spectators. In practice every member of the audience should feel like an understudy.
>
> Drama is essentially an art of the body. The basis of acting is acrobatics, dancing, and all forms of physical skill. The music hall, the Christmas pantomime, and the country house charade are the most living drama of today.
>
> (Symons, p. 79)

This program for involvement of the audience is carried out fully in the play, in which an announcer mediates between stage and audience, actors are planted in the audience, the theater manager and stagehands appear on stage, and so on; the stage is bare, with the actors occasionally pantomiming scenery. The Dancer's role makes ballet prominent, while the parody musical-comedy chorus does other kinds of dancing, with singing. The small jazz orchestra on stage indicates immediately the distance from conventional drama. Like the later plays with Isherwood, it differs from those of Brecht in being much closer to musical comedy, in using a chorus, and in being lighter and funnier in the satirical scenes—to mention only the most obvious points.

Dance, as critics have agreed from the first, is less interesting as poetry than anything Auden had done, though it may be said in its defense that much of it is intended to be sung as parody of musical comedy or popular song and that it is a first experiment in didactic theater. Certainly the language is, however, uncharacteristically thin and unidimensional and, in spite of the absurd entrance of Marx at the end, it is closer to being doctrinaire than anything else Auden has preserved. It has the fault, most unusual for Auden, of being too obvious; in this respect it is the polar opposite of *Paid on Both Sides*, Auden's first dramatic effort. The whole imaginative conception of a "Danse Macabre," [21] however, with the dancer representing the death-wish of a doomed class, is an impressive one. (It recalls both the historical phenomenon, the compulsive dancing-mania, and the theme in art, as in Holbein's famous series representing Death joining the dance.) The Announcer puts the theme explicitly:

> We present to you this evening a picture of the decline of a class, of how its members dream of a new life, but secretly desire the old, for there is death inside them. We show you that death as a dancer.

And the chorus says, "Our death." This is a dramatic rendering of the theme of many poems,[22] and so are the dancer's other metamorphoses, as he becomes savior-hero, daredevil mystic, epileptic fascist and dying scapegoat—though he becomes so many things that the satire gets rather scattered. One of Auden's first and funniest parodies of popular songs occurs early in it: ("old-time Waltz")—

> You were a great Cunarder, I
> Was only a fishing smack
> Once you passed across my bows
> And of course you did not look back
> It was only a single moment yet
> I watch the sea and sigh
> Because my heart can never forget
> The day you passed me by.

There is also one of the funniest to an existing tune, the dancer's will to the tune of "Casey Jones," combining a kind of quasi-Marxist survey of history with topical comments:

> The Greeks were balanced, their art was great
> They thought out in detail the city state
> But a gap to the interior was found at Carcassonne
> So trade moved westward and they were gone.

The contrast between the words and the inappropriate tune is, as often in this genre of ballad-opera since *The Beggars' Opera*, the basis of much of the humor. The piece is endlessly inventive and full of episodes that are still amusing, and it is useful as background for the poetry; its chief defect perhaps is that it is too close in style to what it satirizes, too popular and simple, while at the same time too varied and unfocused as satire, so that what starts out as a macabre and powerful concept winds up as good clean fun. Auden preserved nothing from it in *Collected Poetry* or *Collected Shorter Poems*.

The *Dog Beneath the Skin, or, Where is Francis?* is, in my opinion, by far the most entertaining and rewarding of these plays for readers now. Though it shares the defects of *Dance*, it is more substantial and larger in scope, even livelier, full of high spirits and provocative ideas; and both the choruses and the songs are among Auden's most effective stage verse. Since the symbolism of the play seems not to have been explained by previous commentators, and since, aside from being interesting in itself, it casts light on the poetry, I shall indicate what I take to be its central meaning. The title parodies Eliot's "Whispers of Immortality." Instead of the skull, the vision of death, this will reveal the dog beneath the skin, the qualities and needs man shares with the animals, even the proverbially low dog ("A living dog is better than a dead lion") whose name is the reverse of "god." Groddeck speaks of the "curious role played by dogs in the secret life of man, . . . which throw a bright light on man's pharisaical abhorrence of perverse feelings and practices." [23] The metaphor of the "underdog" is of course also implicit in the title, both in the political sense and in the literal one: the dog's-eye view reveals

> . . . with what a mixture of fear, bullying, and condescend-
> ing kindness you treat those whom you consider your
> inferiors, but on whom you are dependent for your
> pleasures. It's an awful shock to start seeing people from
> underneath.

This is said by Francis, explaining at the end what he has learned while disguised as a dog. Perhaps the plot should be summarized briefly at this point: Alan Norman is chosen by lot to try to find the missing heir to the squire of the village. (This fairy-tale quest situation is carefully given a surface plausibility.) The play deals with his search, accompanied by a large dog, through numerous places and among a variety of people that make up a satirical picture of English society. Finally the missing heir, Sir Francis Crewe, reveals himself to have been masquerading as the dog all along. Together, they return to the village, where a fascist demonstration is now in progress, and Francis makes the speech to the villagers that is quoted above. After describing his adventures as an underdog, he announces his change of allegiance:

> You are units in an immense army: most of you will die
> without ever knowing what your leaders are really fight-

ing for or even that you are fighting at all. Well, I am
going to be a unit in the army of the other side: but the
battlefield is so huge that it's practically certain you will
never see me again.[24]

Alan comes with him, and the other characters take sides. In a
fantastic ending, the animal-fable theme is carried on: the
fascists and all the villagers wear animal masks and make appropriate noises, suggesting that they, in contrast to the dog,
are the really unpleasant animals. (There have earlier been two
amusing scenes in which women are treated as chickens under
capitalism and fascism—dramatizing the metaphor of the *poule
de luxe*, as the title does that of the underdog.) [25] Before leaving
the animal symbolism, a word should be said about the curious
and interesting scene in which the dog's skin itself speaks and
describes its change of allegiance, hoping to be accepted as one
of them (humans) but finding that to them "I was only a skin,
valued for its associations with that very life I had hoped to
abandon." The relevance to the theme of crossing class lines is
plain. Then the skin, in a rather Lawrentian passage, contrasts
the canine and human attitudes to sex: the trouble with people
is that they have too many ideas in their heads (p. 92).

Much more could be said about the play, which seems to me
still very rich and entertaining, but I will confine myself to
two themes that are closely related to the poetry. These are
the themes of psychosomatic illness and of love as escape or as
disguised self-love. (We recall Isherwood's account of his and
Auden's first collaboration, a play called *The Enemies of a
Bishop*, in which the bishop was an idealized Homer Lane; the
best parts of this play, according to Isherwood, were salvaged
for *Dog*. The scenes we are about to discuss would seem likely
to be among those in question.) In II, iii, Alan searches through
Paradise Park, which contains various types of escapists: a precious solipsist poet who believes he is the "only real person in
the whole world," two lovers in "nursery-teapot-Dutch" costumes who are completely self-absorbed and childish; and in-

valids in wheel-chairs, absorbed in their diseases. The final chorus puts it explicitly, describing the hospital:

1600 beds: in each one patient, apparently alone;
One who has forsaken family and friends; to set up house here with
    his hostile shadow.
You who are amorous and active, pause here an instant.
See passion transformed into rheumatism; rebellion into paralysis;
    power into a tumour.
That which was hated, became hateful; that which was creative, a
    stalking destruction; that which was loving, a tormenting flame
For those who reject their gifts: choose here their punishment.

(pp. 64-5)

The following scene satirizes the conventional practice of medicine and surgery. Entering the operating theater, the surgeon, with nurses, students, and others, recites a medical Credo: "I believe in the physical causation of all phenomena, material or mental: and in the germ theory of disease ... And I believe in surgical treatment for duodenal ulcer ... and all forms of endocrine disturbance" (p. 66). This is followed by a burlesque versicles and psalm, all in praise of the surgeon, Sir William Spurgeon, who then proceeds to kill the patient. The theme of love as disguised self-love is brought out in Alan's affair with Miss Lou Vipond, who is a shopwindow dummy, beautifully dressed. "When the dummy is to speak, Alan runs behind it and speaks in falsetto" (p. 89)—a very explicit way of representing narcissism. The most general analysis of the defects of love is made in the chorus ending III, iv, just before the return to the village, which is a picture of Man "divided always and restless always: afraid and unable to forgive":

Unable to forgive his parents, or his first voluptuous rectal sins,
Afraid of the clock, afraid of catching his neighbour's cold, afraid
    of his own body,
Desperately anxious about his health and his position: calling upon
    the Universe to justify his existence,
Slovenly in posture and thinking: the greater part of the will devoted
To warding off pain from the water-logged areas,

An isolated bundle of nerve and desire, suffering alone,
Seeing others only in reference to himself: as a long-lost mother
    or as his ideal self at sixteen.
                    (pp. 97-8)

Hence, the chorus goes on, no simple solution will do, and a catalogue of them is given, together with one of escapes:

Some have adopted an irrefragable system of beliefs or a political
    programme, others have escaped to the ascetic mountains
Or taken refuge in the family circle, among the boys on the bar-
    stools, on the small uncritical islands.

And the warning is to beware of "those with no obvious vices; of the chaste, the non-smoker and drinker, the vegetarian," of those uninterested in making money, because there are "even less innocent forms of power." And finally,

Beware of yourself:
Have you not heard your own heart whisper: "I am the nicest
    person in this room"?
Asking to be introduced to someone "real": someone unlike all those
    people over there?

There is in the play a great variety of songs and other compositions for music; as we have said, the piece is closer to musical comedy than to the conventional play. The beginning is strongly suggestive of Gilbert and Sullivan, when the characters identify themselves and the chorus echoes and comments:

> With troops of scouts for village louts
> And preaching zest he does his best
>   To guard the moral order.

And so is the financier's song (II, ii), justifying himself. There are songs to familiar tunes, like the manager's song, to the tune of "John Peel," as he presents the bill to Alan after his night with Miss Vipond: "Though the pillow be soft and the lady be kind, / Yet the man has to pay in the morning" (p. 92). There are various kinds of parodies of popular songs, such as the journalist-song with the refrain "They're in the racket, too!" (pp. 25-6), the blues-dirge in the "red light district":

> Let us remember in a little song
> Those who were with us but not for long.
> Some were beautiful and some were gay
> But Death's Black Maria took them all away.
>
> (p. 39)

and the burlesque cabaret songs beginning with the patriotic "Rhondda Moon," with its slogan "Love British!" (p. 79). In the operating theater scene there are parodies of liturgical chants and of Wagnerian operatic duets.

Symons says that *Dog*, as performed in 1935, was enormously enjoyable, but "did not merely employ the technique of 'modern musical comedy', it *was* that musical comedy, or something so near to it that the edge of satire was indiscernible." [26] The Destructive Desmond episode, he reports, was removed from the acting version; this seems a pity, since Desmond's act, in the cabaret of the Nineveh Hotel (the luxury hotel being an obvious symbol of decadent capitalism that Auden uses frequently) consists in destroying a Rembrandt or other example of high art and thereby gratifying the resentment and lack of taste of his audience. As showing the influence of capitalism in debasing popular taste, it would seem to be an important part of the satirical effect. But perhaps it wasn't clear enough that capitalism was responsible.

Auden preserved in *Collected Poetry* far more from *Dog* than from any other play: five poems and one prose piece. (Two of the poems and the prose piece had been published separately in periodicals before 1935, thus furnishing a limited parallel to the history of *Paid on Both Sides*.) The first of the poems is the latter part of the opening chorus, beginning, "The young men in Pressan to-night," called in *Collected Poetry* "The Witnesses." All but the first four stanzas were originally published in 1933 as part of a much longer poem with the same title. In its original form it is a burlesque Quest story of a matchless hero who, after all his marvelous deeds, sat down and died in despair.

> What had he done to be treated thus?
> If you want to know, he'd offended us:
>   for yes,
> We guard the wells, we're handy with a gun,
> We've a very special sense of fun,
>   we curse and bless.

In the play the ominous elements have been heightened and the satirical ones toned down, to make the whole an evocation of the archetypal Quest situation. "Enter with him," a chorus from the first scene, is given in *Collected Poetry* the neatly punning title, "I Shall Be Enchanted." It is a very beautiful example of what I have called the clipped lyric. The song of the first mad lady at the beginning of Act II, "Seen when night was silent," based on a sonnet published in 1933,[27] is included in the section of Songs and Other Musical Pieces in *Collected Poetry*. The chorus at the end of II, ii, "Happy the hare at morning, for she cannot read," is called "The Cultural Presupposition" in *Collected Poetry*; in the play it is perhaps the finest passage suggested by the animal-human contrast implicit throughout. Finally, there is the chorus that concludes Act II, "Now through night's caressing grip," perhaps the finest single lyric in the play; this was included among "Songs" in *Collected Poetry* and was later set very beautifully by Benjamin Britten.[28]

The prose passage included in *Collected Poetry* is the vicar's sermon from the last scene; it is given the title "Depravity: A Sermon," and is prefaced by a note interpreting it. This was originally published in 1934 with the title, "Sermon by an Armaments Manufacturer." [29] The vicar in the play has been presented as pro-fascist and as a pathological case (as distinct from his curate, who is a sympathetic character), and his sermon is a brilliantly lunatic one. The British *Collected Shorter Poems*, since it contains no prose, of course does not contain this; but it adds one verse selection to those in *Collected Poetry*: the "Prothalamion" recited by the chorus of waiters when Alan goes to bed with the dummy, "You who return tonight to a narrow bed." This is an ironic celebration of Eros in all its forms, from birds and flowers to all varieties of human sex.

The other plays may be dealt with much more briefly, since they contain less to our purpose. *The Ascent of F6, a Tragedy in Two Acts*, was written with Isherwood and produced in 1936;[30] it is dedicated to Auden's brother, a famous mountaineer. *F6* is much closer than *Dog* to traditional dramatic form, the musical element being slighter. (Benjamin Britten wrote the music, for piano and percussion.) The central action of Ransom and his companions and their attempt to scale F6 resembles that of a conventional play, though the essential action is psychological and takes place inside Ransom, being partially externalized in the exchanges with the Demon and the Mother. Mr. and Mrs. A., with the Announcer, constitute a kind of chorus, mediating between the audience and the central action; most of the verse in the play, aside from the scenes between Ransom and his mother, falls to them.

MacNeice's comment on the psychological aspect of the play is excellent:

> Auden being so interested in the phenomenon of the man of action (for example, in Colonel Lawrence), many of his lyrics contain in condensed form what is worked out at length in the play, *F6*—the tragedy of the man who gets his own way. But Auden, while regarding so many of our neuroses as tragic, so many of our actions as self-deception, yet believes, as I have already said, that neurosis is the cause of an individual's development. Such a psychological dialectic reflects itself in the paradoxes and the tension of his poems.   (*Modern Poetry*, p. 173)

Ransom is (as we have commented in discussing poems with similar themes, as well as *Paid on Both Sides*) the hero, the exceptional man, driven by his Oedipus complex to undertake

Quests, and the play's attitude toward him is ambivalent, as Auden's always is: he is both absurd and admirable. One of the difficulties of the play is that, in spite of the authors' best efforts, there does not seem to be much connection between Ransom's drama, which is psychological and religious, and the rest of the play, which has its caricature villains in the group of public figures led by James, and its victims in Mr. and Mrs. A., who seem excessively dreary. The theme of the corrupting effect of power provides what link there is. The play thus suffers from a radical incoherence, as well as a plethora of ideas and effects; to put it fliply, the Freud and Marx in it don't jell. It contains, however, many fine things: the two preserved in *Collected Poetry* (both in the section of "Songs") are the burlesque Blues dirge for a dead political savior, "Stop all the clocks . . ." and the chorus, "At last the secret is out, as it always must come in the end." There is also a good parody love song, which had been separately published with the title, "Foxtrot from a Play." [31]

On the Frontier, A Melodrama in Three Acts, written with Isherwood and produced in 1938 by the Group Theatre (which had produced *F6* as well as *Dog* and *Dance*), is dedicated to Benjamin Britten, who wrote incidental music for it for piano, percussion, and trumpets. There are a good many sung choruses, and songs of various types, including burlesque martial and soldier songs like those Auden had adapted in Toller's *No More Peace*; [32] but music plays a smaller part in it than in *F6*. The play marks in some respects an advance in technical skill, since it is far more like a conventional drama than either of its predecessors; unlike them, it has characters and a plot in the traditional fashion. But it is a propaganda work, against war and fascism, and utterly without permanent interest: the characters are thin and conventional, indistinguishable from those in dozens of other anti-war and anti-fascism works; the ideas and references are dated, with the sentiments; the language is impoverished and near cliché. If the other plays are overly complex and tended to incoherence, this one is altogether too simple, in every respect. The only innovation in mediating between audience and stage is to use the device of the radio in a different way: the stage represents the "Ostnia-Westland Room," that is, a room in the house of each of the two families on either side of the border, each containing a radio; thus the impact of public events on private lives can be represented and also the reactions of the two families can be paralleled and contrasted. The chorus represents various groups—workers, prisoners, soldiers—in interludes between the scenes. Auden preserved nothing from this play in *Collected Poetry*.

Frontier was Auden's farewell to the legitimate theater; since that time his only works for the stage have been operas. But he wrote one more dramatic work, and in view of the prominence of radios and their announcers and audiences in all his plays (Box and Cox and the Announcer in *Dance*, the portrait-loudspeaker in the lunatic asylum in *Dog*, Mr. and Mrs. A. and the Announcer in *F6*, the radios dominating the stage in *Frontier*) it is appropriate that it should have been a radio play. At the invitation of the Columbia Workshop, he wrote a half-hour monologue, broadcast on June 2, 1940 by Dame May Whitty.[33] Auden's title for it was, "The Psychological Experiences and Sensations of the Woman Who Killed the Goose that Laid the Golden Egg"; the Columbia Workshop changed this to "The Dark Valley." It is a complex kind of parable, based on Auden's earlier cabaret sketch, "Alfred," [34] and written in an elaborate poetic prose, highly metaphorical and alliterative. Benjamin Britten composed incidental music for it. The director, Brewster Morgan, describes it thus:

> Here, in a Gothic landscape of crags and crevices and waterfalls and abandoned mining shafts, lives a lonely woman and her goose. The twisted old soul is about to take the final step across the threshold of solitude. She is going to kill the goose. As she goes about the task, all the circumstances that have thrust her toward solitude buzz about in her mind. . . . But this is only half the problem. The old woman looks down upon the world with the unclouded vision of bitter solitude. She tells the goose what she sees, and it is not pleasant. Here the actress becomes

a kind of oracle, discoursing philosophically on the fate of this world—a fate which fuses in the alchemy of poetry with the fate of the goose.

A few typical passages may be quoted, since the piece is inaccessible. The woman laments the death of her father (who is, naturally, the archetypal father-image, as well as the object of her Electra complex):

> When father spoke the monsters grew mild in the sea, and the roses opened and the eagle hung spellbound over the spellbound lamb. When he smiled it was the shining spaces of summer, but when he frowned it was ages of ice, his anger ended the earth. Oh, but *he* is ended, ended his life, lost, away, a no one, a nothing, as if he never were, his body broken by a blast in the earth.... He was a stag among sheep, a star among tapers, alone with fools in a foul field.

She talks about the modern young people who think love disgusting: "To read about it and photograph it, to talk and titter is one thing; but to touch a real live person—ugh! Only soap and bath salts...can make it bearable." And she contrasts this with her youth, when father was alive. It is Sunday evening, and she ridicules the respectable modern church:

> The minister is modern and well mannered and mild and well read in evolution and the latest theories of physics and astronomy and is tolerance itself. The flames of hell are an old-fashioned idea, for his God is a mathematician and much like a man and understands perfectly and expects little. For business is business, and boys will be boys, and lust is a natural need like eating, and the search for the gold of grace is a grueling voyage.

This leads into the ending, with the killing of the goose (named Nana):

> For the All-Father is proud of his pretty world and takes her on his knees, Nana, as I take you now, and strokes her back, smiling . . . and she looks into his eyes and is ever

so happy for the sunset is beautiful and the bells are ring-
ing, though she wonders a little why his loving hands are
gripping so tightly that she gasps for air . . . Father, don't
you remember, I'm the world you made. Father, I'm so
young and white, I don't want to die. Father. . . .

The interesting thing about this, in relation to the other
plays, is that it is about as remote from propaganda as it is
possible to get. Fantasy is heavily predominant over diagnosis—
though there is some conflict between them: the director commented that not even May Whitty could always "ride with
the furies of deep feeling and at the same time pause to make
footnotes on the state of the world," and that Auden worked
in rehearsal to make the dichotomy less apparent. But the
landscape, with its abandoned mines, waterfalls, and mountains
is Auden's dream one,[35] and the whole play is as close to fantasy as *Paid on Both Sides*—further, if anything, from the rational, discursive level. The mad old woman makes no sense
on that level (naturally), but she is a chillingly effective embodiment of nightmare terrors. The fairy-tale—or fairy-tale
gone wrong—atmosphere is heightened by the two songs, both
of which are included in *Collected Poetry:* "Eyes look into the
well" [36] and "Lady, weeping at the crossroads."

SONGS

To begin with a dictum: Auden is supreme among modern
poets as a writer of songs. His songs are his most distinctive
accomplishment and his most popular; in them he achieves the
rapport with a large audience and the quality of lightness that
he strives for with varying success in his other works. Sometimes he parodies the popular genres or treats them ironically,
and sometimes he deepens and enriches them, using them seriously but without losing the popular appeal. Both of his anthologies of this period, *The Poet's Tongue* (with John Garrett,
1935) and *The Oxford Anthology of Light Verse* (1938),

show his deep interest in folk and popular verse—and as someone has observed, only verse intended to be sung is truly
popular; both contain far more verse intended to be sung (car-
ols, ballads, sea shanties, nursery rhymes, blues, spirituals, singing games, riddles, counting-out rhymes, and songs of all kinds)
than conventional poetry. The quality of lightness is memor-
ably defined in the introduction to the *Oxford Book* in terms
of the relation between the poet and his audience: it is possible
only when they are close together in interests and perceptions.
The shared political interest lies behind Auden's achievement
of this quality, though few of the songs have any political content, and the quality persists, in some measure, after the collapse of the brief political rapprochement. The theatrical
experience, too, was essential. We have seen how large a part
choruses and songs play in all those pieces, and no doubt working closely with the Group Theatre helped increase his sense of
rapport with the audience.

Rather than attempt a rigorous or elaborate definition, I shall
define "song" broadly as any poem that suggests clearly that
it is intended to be performed to music. The section of "Songs
and Other Musical Pieces" in *Collected Poetry* is not, as one
might expect, made up of pieces written to be set to music
or actually so set. Only about a third of the pieces in the section are known to have been set, and we happen to know
that at least two poems in it were written without thought of
music.[37] On the other hand, at least four pieces that had been
set by Benjamin Britten [38] were placed in the section of "Poems";
and some of these are known to have been written specifically
to be set. Auden's criterion seems to have been whether or not
the piece sounded like a song, quite apart from the existence of
any actual musical setting. We will follow this definition, but
expand it to include everything that has actually been set and
everything (whether included by Auden among "Songs" or
not) that strongly suggests an association with music.

Auden's songs may be divided into two types, which may be
called popular songs and art songs. Popular songs are those

written either to fit an existing tune or to suggest a specific kind of music (blues, waltz, ballad); they have nothing to do with commercialized "popular" songs, but to call them folk songs would be even more misleading. Art songs are written with the intention of being suitable for musical setting of whatever sort the composer chooses, or produce the impression of special suitability for musical setting. There is of course no ready and easy way to separate art songs from lyric in general, though popular songs are recognizable immediately.

Popular Songs. Virtually all the songs in the plays belong to this type, which obviously owes something to Brecht's example. There is generalized parody of the language of popular songs in *Poems* 1933 (e.g., "It's no use raising a shout"), but the technique first appears extensively in Auden's own theatrical pieces, after which it appears in the poems. The most obvious effect is straight parody through exaggeration, as in "You were a great Cunarder, I," in *Dance*. "Foxtrot from a Play" ("The soldier loves his rifle"), published in 1936 and, partially, in *F6*, catalogues the varied objects of "love," concluding each stanza with, "But you're my cup of tea." There is an element of parody of "The British Grenadiers," which begins, "Some talk of Alexander, and some of Hercules, ... But of all the world's brave heroes, there's none that can compare, ... to the British Grenadiers." [39] Auden's second stanza begins, "Some talk of Alexander / And some of Fred Astaire / Some like their heroes hairy / Some like them debonair ..." The implicit contrast of the rousing patriotic march to the foxtrot adds a further dimension of irony to the parody love song. The final chorus begins, "The blackbird loves the earthworm / The adder loves the sun," and ends, "And dogs love most an old lamp-post / But you're my cup of tea." The cabaret songs for Miss Hedli Anderson [40] in *Another Time* are all parodies of popular songs of various types. The first of these, "Stop all the clocks, cut off the telephone," appeared in *F6* as a burlesque lament for a secular savior; but in the cabaret version (reprinted in *Collected Poetry*) it is entitled "Funeral Blues," and exaggerates the customary blues sentiment in lamenting a dead lover. The blues rhythm and syncopation are expertly suggested. The other one of these cabaret songs to be reprinted in *Collected Poetry* [41] is "O the valley in the summer," which seems to be a parody of popular love songs without reference to any particular rhythm or mode, using marvelously trite images to describe the inscrutably uncooperative lover: " 'Squeeze me tighter, dear Johnny, let's dance till it's day': / But he frowned like thunder and he went away."

These parodies, however, are never pure parodies: that is, the form is enjoyed at the same time it is exaggerated and ridiculed. In many other poems the popular form is used perfectly seriously, for example, "Refugee Blues" (1939), in which the blues form increases the pathos, fusing the generalized hopeless lament that is traditional in the form with the topical plight of the German Jews. There is here no element of parody whatever; the blues style, which is carefully underplayed, is an element essential to the meaning. There is in most cases, however, some degree of irony in the treatment of the popular form, and this can lead to very subtle effects. The ballads provide the most striking examples of this.

"Let me tell you a little story," to the tune of "St. James' Infirmary," and "Victor was a little baby," to the tune of "Frankie and Johnny," both 1937, employ extremely trite language and style; they are not only full of the stereotypes of the folk ballad but are as full of clichés as any modern "ballad" produced by Tin Pan Alley. But this produces a kind of double irony: the reader condescends to the form, is amused by its flatness and triteness, and then finds himself moved nevertheless. Both of these modern horror tales are very much in the Brechtian vein (as in "Jakob Apfelböck," "Marie Farrar"), with the same combination of irony and pathos. "Miss Gee" has been censured for cruelty; but this is, of course, exactly the point: it is a gruesome exaggeration and reversal of the moral fable, like Hilaire Belloc's *Cautionary Tales*.[42] On this level, both ballads are mock-warnings against virginity and religion. "Victor" is more horrifying and less funny; I should say that it is about as close as it is possible to come to a modern equivalent of the genuine ballad. The third ballad in *Another Time*, "James Honeyman," is about a man who made poison gas which is finally used on his own family; like the other two, it is a horror story, a cautionary tale; but it is topical and dated, and wisely not included in the *Collected Poetry*.

The two finest ballads of all do not specify tunes and do not mock the popular form, but use it to give collective significance to deeply felt emotions. "O what is that sound which so thrills the ear" (first published in 1934, and called "The Quarry" in the 1958 *Selected Poetry*) uses the question and answer pattern that occurs so frequently in the ballads, and presents a situation of ballad-like drama and simplicity. But the meter is more complex and expressive than that of any folk ballad; in fact it suggests musical effects so strongly that it could hardly be set to music successfully, having its own music already built in, so to speak. The language, too, is more complex and varied than that of the ballads, though carefully kept unobtrusively so. Both meter and diction are contrasted in the question-answer pattern: the girl's rapid anapaests, slowing down to a repeated phrase with feminine ending produce an effect of terror modulating into horrified speculation; the man's answers are trite and casual evasions, very much in the modern idiom, and metrically shorter, ending in a curt dimeter line:

> O where are you going? Stay with me here!
>   Were the vows you swore deceiving, deceiving?
> No, I promised to love you, dear,
>   But I must be leaving.

The repetition of this pattern, with the man's tone counterpointing the woman's as the situation gradually becomes clearer, allows a building up to a very powerful climax; it is an effect analogous to a musical crescendo. The evocation of terror is very effective: in 1934 and succeeding years there were special reasons for the nightmare image of soldiers coming, of (as MacNeice put it) waiting until "the gunbutt raps upon the door." No doubt, in that context, the poem was a parable showing the inadequacy of romantic love, or private life in general, as a refuge or escape from public events. But it has also an archetypal quality, representing the ultimate fears of betrayal and of being the object of hostility and malice. And this horror story is not distanced by irony, as are "Miss Gee" and "Victor."

> O it's broken the lock and splintered the door,
>   O it's the gate where they're turning, turning;
> Their boots are heavy on the floor
>   And their eyes are burning.

Perhaps the best of all the ballads is "As I walked out one evening," first published in 1938. Auden has never called this a ballad: the title was "Song" on first publication, and in *Another Time* it was placed, not with the ballads, but among "People and Places." In a public reading he described it, deprecatingly, as a "pastiche of folksong."[43] It is certainly less specifically suggestive of the ballad than are "Miss Gee" and "Victor," but is rather more so than the poem just discussed, since the quatrain is one associated with ballads, and so are such features as the lover's extravagant promise and the stereotyped quality of much of the imagery. But whether or not it should be called a ballad, the important point is that it is close to folk poetry of various types; the first line echoes a ballad, and two phrases have been identified as coming from a folksong.[44] Although there is an element of parody of folk sentiment and imagery in the lover's trite and extravagant protestation, as Brooks and Warren observe, the parody is functional, preparing for the equally extravagant reply of the clocks: "The world of reality, the clocks are saying, is as baffling and topsy-turvy as the factitious world of the lover's song." Against the lover's traditionally sentimental vows of love that will outlast time, the clocks set the vision of reality (as Brooks and Warren point out, the curse is taken off the moralism by the extravagance of the images), of time's triumph, of defeat both petty and spectacular:

> In headaches and in worry
>   Vaguely life leaks away,
> And Time will have his fancy
>   Tomorrow or today.
>
> Into many a green valley
>   Drifts the appalling snow;
> Time breaks the threaded dances
>   And the diver's brilliant bow.

The first line of this last stanza has, it has been observed,[45] a strong suggestion of Housman; but the next line uses Blake's ambiguous word "appall" for a more audacious image; the last line is salvaged from one of Auden's 1928 poems.[46] The important point, however, is not the provenance of particular lines and phrases but the triumph of style; one is tempted to explicate at length how the everyday and commonplace is fused constantly with the ultimate and fundamental. In the last two lines above, there is the common image of breaking a string of beads, while at the same time the line works with the last one to suggest Time's destruction of both the average and the exceptional, the collective and the individual, the social and the personal. It has often been observed that the famous stanza,

> The glacier knocks in the cupboard,
>   The desert sighs in the bed,
> And the crack in the tea-cup opens
>   A lane to the land of the dead.

suggests, as in Eliot (though the styles could hardly be more different), the interpenetration of the everyday and the eternal, the intrusion of fundamental threats into the domestic refuge. The "land of the dead" is—as in much of Eliot—the "real" world seen as it really is: it is the place where all expectations are reversed, where folk wisdom proves useless, the fairy tales all false: "... the Giant is enchanting to Jack ..., And Jill goes down on her back." But the clocks command, nevertheless, in a fashion that Auden was later to call, in the Kierkegaardian sense, "absurd," that "You shall love your crooked neighbor / With your crooked heart." At the end the lovers have disappeared, but the deep river—inevitably suggesting Time—runs on; this fulfills the anticipatory image in the first stanza, where the crowds have been seen as "fields of harvest wheat," ready for Time's reaping.

I have used this very well-known poem as my example of the popular style at its best because its popularity demonstrates its effectiveness. The style, as we have seen, uses the conventions of ballad and folksong to provide a basis for collective emotion, against which individual reversals and variations can then be counterpointed. Although music plays no direct part in it—in fact the poem, like "O what is that sound ...," has so strong and varied a music of its own that it would probably not set well—the folksong style upon which it is based was of course developed for singing to a fixed or strophic accompaniment; and the convention of being written for singing to such accompaniment is essential to the style of this poem.

One final type of popular song may be mentioned: the song for children, or perhaps it would be more accurate to say the song evoking the world of childhood. These are simple in form, recalling the nursery rhyme, the hymn, traditional verses for children. The technique consists, in brief, of reversing the expected associations and fusing the secure ordered world of the nursery and the terror and disorder of the adult world. The technique is like that of Blake in the *Songs of Experience* and elsewhere, one of charging an innocent form with a violently contrasting content. "Now the leaves are falling fast" is in part an example of this, but since it was set by Britten we will consider it in conjunction with Auden's art songs. "O who can ever praise enough" (1936) is more an explicit statement of the contrast between the innocent fantasy world of child-hood and the real world than an embodiment of it. "Lady, weeping at the crossroads" (1940) is a good example of the type, for it evokes the fairy-tale world in depth and then negates it. To meet her love, to arrive at the happy ending, she must perform impossible tasks; but when she succeeds in doing this (according to the convention) she will see herself in the mirror at last, and when she does she will "Find the pen-knife there and plunge it / Into your false heart." The form is the ballad stanza, but trochaic in meter; the language is sim-ple but powerful. The total effect is remote from parody; it is that of producing a complex and continued contrast between the expectations aroused by the form and the developing con-tent.

Art Songs. Art songs are, as we have said, those written with the intention of being suitable for musical setting (of whatever sort the composer chooses), or those which produce the im-pression, or illusion, of special suitability for musical setting.

Auden had a good musical education, played the piano com-petently, sang in all his school choirs (both as pupil and mas-ter), and entertained himself by playing and singing hymns. Day Lewis, who had a good voice, describes singing hymns with him at Oxford, and Auden's efforts to improve his (Day Lewis's) musical taste and teach him the songs of Wolf and Brahms, especially the *Ernste Gesänge.* "In the teeth of his loud, confident but wonderfully inaccurate piano accompani-ment I finally mastered these sombre songs. . . ." [47] He also de-scribes singing (at Auden's instigation) two Auden poems that were set by Lennox Berkeley; though nothing more is known of these settings, it is significant that poems of Auden were being set and sung publicly as early as 1928.

Auden has written a good deal, in the last decade or so, about the relation between poetry and music. Before we begin the detailed discussion of his songs, it may be useful to consider some of these critical formulations, so that we can use them as points of reference. First, much good poetry is not suitable for musical setting: complicated successions of images and metaphors will not work, nor will ideas that take time to understand; "since music is essentially immediate and dynamic, those elements in language, like metaphor, which require reflection in order to grasp them, are dangerous." [48] Similarly, verses which express mixed or ambiguous feelings are ill adapted to setting; music, "generally speaking, can express only one thing at a time," and therefore is best suited to poems "which either express one emotional state or successively contrast two states." Finally, since words take much longer to sing than to speak, poems intended for songs must be short. The song-writer cannot be prolix or private or preachy or obscure; he must strive for graceful ease and conciseness. Conversely, poetry does not have to be first-rate as poetry in order to set well:

> ... conventional properties can be very serviceable to a composer, precisely because, being conventional, they are instantly recognizable. A composer welcomes a poem which expresses either a single state of feeling or an obvious contrast of states and a diction centered round the dynamic elements of language, interjections, imperatives, verbs of motions, etc.[49]

The intention of writing for music, Auden suggests, sometimes produces new and beautiful kinds of poetry; for example, some of the Elizabethan madrigals, which would never have been written except for the musical purpose, yet are poems "at once beautiful and strange." [50] "If the lyrics of the Elizabethan poets are rhythmically more interesting than those of other periods, it is difficult to escape the conclusion that the close association of poets with musicians of high caliber was largely responsible." [51] Citing some examples of metrical unconventionality, he observes that the lines "when spoken have their own vocal music, but their authors would not have found it, had they not been writing songs." [52] The same observation may, I believe, be made of Auden himself.

Most of Auden's writing for music in his earlier career—roughly 1935-42—was done in association with the composer, Benjamin Britten. Britten, six years Auden's junior, attended the same public school that Auden had. They first met in 1935 when they worked together on documentary films for the G.P.O. Film Unit, and their first collaboration was the film, *Coal-Face*. This contained "O lurcher-loving collier, black as night," which Britten set for female voices. (In *Another Time* and *Selected Poetry* Auden gave this the title "Madrigal," pointing up the ironic contrast with an earlier day implicit in this miner's pastoral.) It is notable that this first example follows to a remarkable degree Auden's later precepts for song-writing: a succession of clear and simple images subordinated to one mood, in economical and graceful diction. *Night Mail*, the second film on which Auden and Britten collaborated, has become a documentary classic; according to White [53] the only other film they did together was *The Way to the Sea*, 1937, describing the electrification of the Portsmouth railway line.

In 1936 Britten was invited to compose a work for the Norfolk and Norwich Triennial Musical Festival and asked Auden to devise a libretto. "Auden chose man's relations to animals as his subject, selecting three poems to illustrate animals as pests, pets and prey,[54] and framed them with an original prologue and epilogue. The title of this symphonic cycle for soprano solo and orchestra (Britten's Opus 8) was taken from the beginning of the epilogue, "Our Hunting Fathers." [55] The first performance at Norwich on Sept. 25, 1936, according to Scott Goddard (quoted by White, *loc. cit.*) amused the sophisticated, scandalized those among the gentry who caught Auden's words, and dazzled musicians. The prologue ("They are our past . . .") and epilogue are of course separated by the alphabetical arrangement of *Collected Poetry*, which is a pity, because they make more sense together (and neither is in the section of "Songs and Other Musical Pieces.") The prologue, called "The Creatures" in *Collected Poetry*, is in prose, somewhat oracular and riddling, but providing in each sentence an image or theme which can be rendered in musical terms. The second part, "Rats Away!", is a prayer or exorcism, modernized by Auden from a medieval source, against rats; it begins, "I command all the rats that are hereabout. . . ." The third, "Messalina," a lament for the death of a pet monkey, is called anonymous in the musical score but is attributed to Thomas Weelkes in the *Oxford Book of Light Verse* (p. 118); it begins, "Ay me, alas, heigh ho, heigh ho!" The fourth part, "Dance of Death," is Thomas Ravenscroft's "Hawking for the Partridge," beginning, "Whurret! Quando, Duty, Jew, Travel, Hey dogs hey!" (Auden included this also in the *Oxford Book of Light Verse*, p. 119). The suitability of all three of these pieces for music is obvious: they are full of interjections and imitative sounds, and each represents a simple, clear-cut and strongly marked emotional attitude. The epilogue, however ("Our hunting fathers . . ."), is a different matter. Since it had been published in 1934, it was not written for this occasion and presumably not for musical setting. It is a fine poem, but notably subtle and difficult, full of the kind of tension and ambiguity that cannot well be expressed in music.[56] There is, however, in the contrast of the two stanzas—the first describing, with some nostalgia, the older, self-assured tradition which pitied the animals for their lack of reason; the second the modern situation in which the goal of love must be the imitation of animal qualities, but without the essential one, their innocence —an opportunity for effective musical contrast.

In 1937 Britten published a song cycle, *On This Island* (Opus 11), consisting of settings of four songs from Auden's volume of that name and one from *The Dog Beneath the Skin*. The settings are dedicated to Christopher Isherwood and contain French translations by Maurice Pourchet.[57] The first is "Let the florid music praise." Since this begins by describing a musical effect, it seems to call for music; and the language and formal structure, with the two stanzas contrasting in mood, are well adapted to it. Britten sets the first stanza *maestoso*, in a majestic, florid style suggestive of Handel. The second, dealing with the unloved and the triumph of time, he sets *piu lento— grazioso e rubato,* in a contrasting pathetic style reminiscent of Purcell, and especially of Dido's Lament.[58] The music thus makes its own allusion (more homage than parody) to England's two greatest composers. The setting is, in general, very attractive and effective. There are, however, certain ambiguities in the poem, such as the highly ironic attitude toward beauty in the first stanza and the obscure transaction in the middle of the second, which music cannot express.

The second poem is "Now the leaves are falling fast," and the setting seems to me a triumph. The poem itself is one of those evoking the secure and ordered world of childhood, of nursery rhymes, fairy tales, simple moral and religious verses. By representing England as a nursery, Auden not only suggests satirically the willed regression and escapism of the bourgeoisie, but also expresses universally the archetypal lost childhood, and lost Eden. In *Selected Poetry* he calls it "Autumn Song," and this is the mood of the first stanza, especially; the last three stanzas show the nursery invaded by nightmare. The picture of England as an abandoned nursery, with no one in charge and the prams rolling on unguided and untended, is heightened by the nightmare picture of the living dead following the prams with arms "raised stiffly to reprove / In false attitudes of love." (There is a reference here to the Nazi salute and false authoritarianism, but also, more broadly, to all adults as seen from the child's point of view.) The trolls threaten, but there are no supernatural interventions or happy endings as in childhood stories; the nightingale is dumb and the angel will not come. The mountain goal is impossible, unattainable; the quest will not succed.

The setting is *lento,* and is in part strophic, the repeated pattern in the first three stanzas suggesting rigidity, stiffness, foreboding. The final two stanzas form a separate section, and the last section breaks the pattern with an extremely effective high note on "Cold," then returns to it with a slow *diminuendo* at the end. The union between setting and poem seems to me one of those rare and magical ones, as in Schubert's finest lieder, in which the music is, in a sense, an interpretation of the poem but in no sense a distraction from it or a rival; rather, the music seems to realize fully and inevitably what is implicit in the words, and is, therefore, a fulfillment and completion of the poem. Once heard, this kind of setting becomes inseparable from the poem.

The third poem, "Look, stranger, on this island now," is given the apt title, "Seascape," in the score. This is a conspicuously musical poem, full of complex and delicate effects of sound, with a highly irregular meter and stanza structure based on devices analogous to suspension and delayed resolution in music. Most of the imagery is aural—the "swaying sound of the sea," the "pluck / And knock of the tide," the "shingle scrambles after the suck- / ing surf"—except for the visual images of movement which readily suggest musical equivalents. Yet Britten's setting is disappointing; I should call it much the poorest of the five, and perhaps the weakest of any Britten setting of Auden. Why is this? It seems, again, a clear case of a poem's having a verbal music of its own that is too strong, so to speak, too musical in its own right and its own way, for it to be translatable into musical terms. The setting (the first two stanzas *allegro molto*, the third *molto tranquillo*) does not deepen or strengthen it, but seems extraneous.

The fourth poem is "Now through night's caressing grip" from *The Dog Beneath the Skin;* in the score this is given the appropriate title, "Nocturne." With clear visual images, a relatively simple and unified emotional tone embodied in a tripartite structure, and language and meter without undue complications, this is well adapted to setting. The tempo is *andante piacevole* and both the simple, ascending and descending melodic pattern and the pattern of sound intensity, each time beginning *pianissimo*, building up to *forte*, and returning, *diminuendo*, to *pianissimo*, are repeated three times. At the end there is a *parlante* section, appropriately, for "Unpursued by hostile force / Traction engine bull or horse." The effect is incantatory, hypnotic, with the unvarying tempo, the simple melody rising and falling, and the repeated pattern of dynamics; the music seems an intensification and realization of the poem.

Finally, there is "As it is, plenty," a satirical piece, very different from the others. This is an ironic adjuration to the complacent bourgeois who has achieved "success" to rejoice, lest he see his real situation: "The loss as major / And final, final." The setting, *allegretto ritmico*, is in the style of popular music or light jazz, with much syncopation and vamping. It is funny in itself, and it adds to the poem's satire its own element of parody of bourgeois music. The end is a fine anticlimax, a "whimper" not a "bang"; "final" is repeated *forte* five times, and then one last time *pianissimo* and rapidly.

In the same year, 1937, Britten set two other songs by Auden, both from *On This Island*. "Fish in the unruffled lakes" is another treatment of the human versus animal theme and a love song; it has a symmetrical tripartite structure which is basically simple. There is the description, first, of the beauty, perfection, and completeness of non-human creation: lion, fish, and swan; then, in contrast, of human selfconsciousness, guilt, freedom, and imperfection, with awareness of time; finally, of the union of both in the lover who has "All gifts that to the swan / Impulsive Nature gave" and has added "voluntary love." The setting is delicate, rippling, impressionistic, *durchkomponiert* rather than strophic. The other song is "Underneath the abject willow," a lighter piece, also contrasting man and the creatures, but with a totally different effect. It is a kind of modern "Why so pale and wan, fond lover," and is gently satirical in tone: the absurd human lover is urged to behave like the creatures, to follow nature. The poem is open in texture, uncomplicated in image and mood and well adapted for setting. Britten set it as a duet, and it is one of his most melodious and attractive settings.[59] The tempo is *allegretto* except for the last stanza, which is *vivace*. Bell sounds are suggested in the second stanza, and flying for the geese at the beginning of the third. The piece has throughout an irresistible vivacity and lightness.

In 1938 Britten wrote the music for Auden's text of a B.B.C. feature called *Hadrian's Wall*. In 1939 he wrote *Ballad of Heroes* (Op. 14) for the Festival of Music for the People on April 5th, to honor the men of the British Battalion, International Brigade, who had fallen in Spain. As second movement of this (scherzo, Dance of Death) Britten set Auden's "Danse Macabre," which had been published in 1937 with the title, "Song for the New Year" (first line, "It's farewell to the drawing-room's civilized cry").[60] The first movement, "Funeral March," had words by Randall Swingler, and the third movement, "Recitative and Choral," has words by Swingler and Auden, though it is not clear whether Auden, who had been in the United States since January, had any part in it beyond allowing part of the final chorus of *On the Frontier* to be used. Finally, there is an epilogue, repeating part of Swingler's first section. The part written by Swingler is the worst kind of propaganda art, full of easy nobility, patriotic posturing, and condescension; Auden's violent revulsion against this kind of thing possibly stems in part from his connections with it on a few such occasions as this.

Britten came to the United States in the early summer of 1939, following the example of Auden and Isherwood, and intending, like them, to settle here. His collaboration with Auden on the choral operetta *Paul Bunyan* in 1941 will be discussed in the last section, together with the other operas. In 1942 he decided to return to England, and soon after his return he composed "Hymn to St. Cecilia" (Op. 27), with words by Auden, intended to restore the custom of celebrating her feast on November 22, which happens also to be Britten's birthday. (In *Collected Poetry* Auden uses the title "Song for St. Cecilia's Day," following Dryden's precedent.) It was first performed on November 22, 1942, by the B.B.C. Singers, with great success.[61] The music is still available, and several recordings are extant.[62] (The setting is dedicated to Elizabeth Mayer, whom Auden addresses in *New Year Letter* and to whom he dedicates that poem.[63]) Since this is the last collaboration between Auden and Britten, and since the poem itself deals with the nature of music, a brief analysis will be appropriate.

Auden follows the tradition of Dryden by telling once more the legend of St. Cecilia's invention of the pipe-organ, but he does so in a baroque and ironic diction that, with the anapaestic four-stress meter and internal rhyme, gives distance to this first part of the poem.[64] In the second stanza there is a Botticellian picture of Aphrodite delighted by the sound (the erotic aspect of music) and an equally emblematic one of the angels drawn back into time and the damned given surcease. After these two somewhat facetious stanzas there is a serious invocation to Cecilia as patroness and muse of musicians. Britten sets this section *tranquillo e comodo*, with an opening melody that recurs as a refrain in the invocation; it is generally harmonious and somewhat languid. The second section, beginning "I cannot grow," is written in choriambic meter, and is a definition of music, with implied analogies to sainthood and to natural creatures. Music cannot grow because it has achieved pure form. For the same reason, it has no shadow (darkness of the unconscious, ambiguity); it is detached, innocent, pure playfulness. (There is a definite resemblance to the Ariel of *The Sea and the Mirror*.) Britten sets this as a scherzo, *vivace*, with a light broken movement and the voices entering separately. The last section (in regular pentameter) is a prayer to Music, to "Restore our fallen day; O re-arrange." [65] The stanza in italics I take to be spoken by Music, in pity and sympathy for man's intellectual difficulties ("O dear white children casual as birds, / Playing among the ruined languages"), for his guilt, for which she urges repentance ("O weep, child, weep, O weep away the stain"), and for acceptance of the human condition ("O bless the freedom that you never chose ... O wear your tribulation like a rose"). Britten's setting is *andante comodo*, with "O dear white children ..." as a very beautiful soprano solo. The last stanza, following the tradition of Dryden, provides opportunities for the imitation of various instruments, and Britten takes advantage of this, with cadenzas suggesting violin, drum, flute, and trumpets.

Britten's last setting of words by Auden occurs in his Spring Symphony (Op. 44), written in 1949. In this choral symphony four stanzas of "Out on the lawn I lie in bed" (the second poem in *On This Island*, and called "A Summer Night 1933" in *Collected Poetry*) are set for alto and mixed chorus.

> The wordless chorus frames the verses, each verse having its own instrumentation: woodwinds predominate for the first three, and for the fourth the brass fanfares stir up the violence in the words, which quickly fades away to a return of the opening. This closely organized, emotionally moving piece gives weight and seriousness to the central point of the symphony.[66]

The stanzas chosen are the first, fifth, seventh, and eighth (in the *Collected Poetry* version; Britten uses the unrevised text, however), and these embody a single, relatively simple mood of temporary tranquility, detached foreboding, which is rendered beautifully in the setting. It comes, appropriately, at the end of the second movement, the slow movement of the symphony.

The only other settings of Auden poems known to me[67] are by Lennox Berkeley, who has been mentioned earlier as having set at least two as early as 1928. The settings I speak of seem to be recent, however; the record on which they are excellently sung by Thomas Hemsley, baritone, was made in 1960,[68] and one of the songs is "Lauds," which was not published until 1955. Since the other four songs are from the period we are considering, we will discuss them all together. Three of the songs, oddly enough, had been set by Britten, though the settings were not published and Berkeley may well not have known about them: "O lurcher-loving collier..." from *Night Mail*, "Eyes look into the well" from *The Dark*

Valley, and "Carry her over the water" from *Paul Bunyan*. All these, with the other poem set, "What's in your mind, my dove, my coney" from *Poems* 1933, are in the "Songs" section of *Collected Poetry*. The settings are all pleasant and attractive, especially "Carry her over the water," but they are strikingly inferior to Britten's. There have been few composers since Schubert who combine, as Britten does, literary sensitivity and understanding with musical genius.

So much for the songs actually set to music. The experience of writing sometimes explicitly for music, in collaboration with a composer, and often with the possibility of musical setting in mind ("words for music perhaps," in Yeats's phrase) or with the conventions of song-writing deliberately suggested (words "as if" for music) had a profound influence on Auden's poetry in general. The types of song I have labeled "popular" and "art" are the two extremes; some of the qualities of both enter into numerous other songs and inform much of the other poetry of the period. Discussion of this topic must be postponed, however, until Auden's styles and ideas of the thirties have been considered.

As we shall see, Auden has maintained his interest in the relations of music and poetry, and has in the last decade edited, with Chester Kallman and Noah Greenberg, *An Elizabethan Song Book* and recorded, with the New York Pro Musica, *An Evening of Elizabethan Verse and its Music*. He has also written numerous critical pieces on the subject.[69] But his own writing for music has since the war taken the specialized form of opera libretti. The great difference between this and song writing is that, while the poet is usually dominant in song writing (the composer striving to realize the poetry or translate it into musical terms),[70] the librettist's aim must be to provide the composer with the maximum musical opportunities. Auden has done much to rehabilitate the art of libretto-writing, but he has always begun from the clear-cut position that the libretto must be subordinate to the music.

FROM ON THIS ISLAND THROUGH THE DOUBLE MAN

On This Island, published in London in October, 1936, as *Look, Stranger!*, consists of thirty-two poems. Twenty-two of these had already appeared in periodicals or anthologies: two in 1932, seven in 1933, five in 1934 and again in 1935, and three in 1936. As the title suggests (and Auden chose the American, not the English title), it is the image of England in crisis that unifies the volume. The first poem, "O love, the interest itself in thoughtless Heaven," called "Prologue" also when first published in 1932, makes this explicit, with its picture of England as fortress and "mole between all Europe and the exile-crowded sea," [71] as does the title poem, "Look, stranger, at this island now." The poet speaks frequently in his own person, locating himself specifically in time and place (as in "Out on the lawn I lie in bed"; "Now from my window-sill I watch the night"); this gives solidity to the larger vision of England in her relations to geography and history. The "island" of the title is symbolic as well as literal, however, suggesting all forms of selfish isolation and escapism; the beautiful sestina called in *Collected Poetry* "Paysage Moralisé" ("Hearing of harvests rotting in the valleys") concludes with the hope that we may "rebuild our cities, not dream of islands." The two principal kinds of escapism described are religion and romantic love. In regarding these as forms of selfish escape Auden agrees with the Marxists, but the central theme of the volume could hardly be further from Marxism: it is the analysis of both social and personal ills as the result of a failure of love. Learning love and unlearning hatred is proposed as a remedy in almost every poem.

In the early verse, love or Eros is conceived of generally in Freudian terms as including both ego- and object-love, the urge to self-preservation and preservation of the species, as well as sexual love; Eros opposes (but sometimes combines with) the other basic drive, Thanatos, the death-wish or the destructive instinct. This concept is interpreted according to the Lane-Layard anarchistic teaching described in Section I: "The disease of the soul is the belief in moral control: the Tree of the Knowledge of Good and Evil, as against the Tree of Life"; "There is only one sin: disobedience to the inner law of our own nature." Eros is therefore good, and the "pure in heart" obey Eros. The perversions of Eros are the main theme of the early poems, satirically portraying "England, this country of ours where nobody is well." "They" are invalids in bathchairs, with Oedipus complexes, incapable even of sexual love, "self-regarders" dominated by Thanatos. Only by reversing Their instructions can We find "the home of love."

In *On This Island* there is a fairly consistent distinction between Eros, now seen as selfish, crooked, and bad, and love which is unselfish and social, not natural but the result of effort and discipline. "O for doors to be open . . ." shows the hatred, envy, and self-love of the natural man; "Our hunting fathers . . ." contrasts the "intricate ways of guilt" in human love with animal innocence. "Here on the cropped grass . . ." describes "the womb's utter peace before / The cell, dividing, multiplied desire" and comments explicitly that "the disciplined love which alone could have employed these engines / seemed far too difficult and dull, and when hatred promised / An immediate dividend, all of us hated." "The earth turns over . . ." uses a similar contrast: "Gone from the map the shore where childhood played, / Tight-fisted as a peasant, eating love; / Lost in my wake the archipelago, / Islands of self through which I sailed all day." Christmas challenges these "shifts of Love," and the speaker hopes some day to celebrate the "birth of natural order and true love." Generally, however, the unselfish love contrasted with Eros and set forth as an ideal has no religious associations; it is secular, produces social consciousness, aims at the "really better world" to be achieved through political action. It is emphatically distinct from sexual love, which is an illusory "whisper in the double bed," a form of isolation and selfish escape. It may be consciously chosen; at the conclusion of "Easily, my dear, you move..." it is put thus: "Yours is the choice... / Crooked to move as a money-bug or a cancer / Or straight as a dove."

On This Island is a profoundly pessimistic volume. In the penultimate poem, "August for the people...," addressed to Isherwood and first published in 1935, Auden recalls the history of their shared ideas: how in 1926 they were without social awareness, indulging in fantasies of "the spies' career,"

> Prizing the glasses and the old felt hat,
> And all the secrets we discovered were
> Extraordinary and false: ...

Then five years later "the word is love":

> Surely one fearless kiss would cure
> The million fevers, a stroking brush
> The insensitive refuse from the burning core.
> Was there a dragon who had closed the works
> While the starved city fed it with the Jews?
> Then love would tame it with his trainer's look.

The next stanza asks pardon for all these vain beliefs, for "private joking in a panelled room," for believing "the whisper in the double bed"—"Pardon for these and every flabby fancy." It is not that he has a better answer now, but that at least he knows these to be inadequate, and he urges Isherwood "in this hour of crisis and dismay" through his writing to reveal things as they are, "Make action urgent and its nature clear." The last poem, "Epilogue," beginning "Certainly our city...," describing "our city," asks "where now are They / Who without reproaches shewed us what our vanity has chosen... had unlearnt / Our hatred, and towards the really better / World had turned their face?" (The stanzas naming them were omitted from *Collected Poetry*, perhaps because of the oddly miscellaneous beginning, with Nansen, Schweitzer, and Lenin; but the rest of the list is significant: Freud and Groddeck, Lawrence, Kafka; and Proust "on the self-regard.") The last stanza asks, "Can / Hate so securely bind? Are They dead here?" and answers "Yes."

Letters from Iceland, on the other hand, is full of high spirits and vitality, if not hope. Written in the summer of 1936, it is the product of the brief and transitory period when Auden could feel both an easy rapport with a large audience and a significant relation to the world of public events. Julian Symons calls 1936 the "heart of the Thirties dream"—the year *New Writing* and the Left Book Club were founded, the Spanish civil war began and the Popular Front for collective action against war and fascism became a powerful force.[72] While Auden entertained this "Thirties dream" only briefly and sporadically, he shared the feelings and attitudes upon which it was based, and he could assume that there were certain fundamentals with which all men of good will were in agreement. Hence he could with confidence report to his audience as journalist; he could amuse and entertain them as well as write serious poems for them. (Symons points out that the sale of *Look, Stranger!* was three or four times larger than that of any of Auden's earlier volumes.) [73] *Letters* is a remarkably attractive volume, full of odd and entertaining information about Iceland and, extensively, about Auden and MacNeice. There is a kind of holiday spirit in the notion that they are temporarily escaping from Europe and its problems; as the title poem puts it, "For Europe is absent. This is an island and therefore / Unreal." But in fact there is a constant contrast and comparison of Iceland with Europe, which is never forgotten. The great monument of the volume is Auden's "Letter to Lord Byron," a unique accomplishment in sustained and highly successful light verse. In a prose letter to his wife, Auden describes the inception of the plan:

> I brought a Byron with me to Iceland, and I suddenly thought I might write him a chatty letter in light verse about anything I could think of, Europe, literature, my-

> self. He's the right person I think, because he was a townee, a European, and disliked Wordsworth and that kind of approach to nature, and I find that very sympathetic. This letter in itself will have very little to do with Iceland, but will be rather a description of an effect of travelling in distant places which is to make one reflect on one's past and one's culture from the outside. But it will form a central thread on which I shall hang other letters to different people more directly about Iceland. (p. 141)

Byron is "the master of the airy manner," which Auden captures perfectly, though with apologies for not using Ottava Rima: "Rhyme-royal's difficult enough to play." (Like Byron, Auden gets much entertainment out of the form itself, with much joking about the difficulty of finding rhymes while displaying a fine inventiveness and humor in finding new and surprising ones.) The Byronic mask gives Auden a focus, a point of departure for discursive comment on modern life and literature; and it relieves him of the burden of seriousness. Byron is congenial also as a political radical, defier of social convention, and shocker of the bourgeois, though this aspect of the mask is not much in evidence.[74] "Light verse, poor girl, is under a sad weather," Auden says, and he will try to rehabilitate it: "Parnassus after all is not a mountain, / Reserved for A.1. climbers such as you"; he will be satisfied to "pasture my few silly sheep with Dyer / And picnic on the lower slopes with Prior" (p. 22). The poem continues in this vein, easily and unaffectedly personal, light but not trivial, as Auden explains to Byron what has happened since his death, what is likely to happen, and what he thinks about it. Since the volume has long been out of print, and Auden has, strangely, never reprinted the "Letter," I will offer a few more quotations. Part II is about politics and society, with a fine diatribe against modern design in architecture, furniture, the antiseptic future, even central heating: "It may be D. H. Lawrence hocus-pocus, / But I prefer a room that's got a focus." "Preserve me from the Shape of Things to Be," he concludes, and proceeds

to some jaundiced remarks on democracy: its universal education ("There is no lie our children cannot read"), social mo-
bility ("we've got no snobbish feeling / Against the more
efficient modes of stealing"), and new type of common man
("Begot on Hire-Purchase by Insurance"), who worships security. "Byron, thou should'st be living at this hour!", says
Auden, and considers what Byron's politics would be if he
were: he rejects the idea that he might have fascist leanings,
and concludes that, since he hated injustice and was never an
isolationist, he might "Have walked in the United Front with
Gide." Part III deals with poetry, and begins by praising Byron:
"I like your muse because she's gay and witty, / Because she's
neither prostitute nor frump," and arguing that comedy and
light verse are important parts of literature: "The pious fable
and the dirty story / Share in the total literary glory." There
is then a fine attack on Wordsworth and Wordsworthians, and
a highly suggestive historical sketch of the predicament of the
modern artist:

> Art, if it doesn't start there, at least ends,
>   Whether aesthetics like the thought or not,
> In an attempt to entertain our friends;
>   And our first problem is to realize what
>   Peculiar friends the modern artist's got . . .
>   (p. 103)

Until the Industrial Revolution, the artist "had to please or go
without his food": "He had to keep his technique to himself /
Or find no joint upon his larder shelf." But then the artists
strove for independence, losing responsibilities and friends:

> So started what I'll call the Poet's Party:
>   (Most of the guests were painters, never mind)—
> The first few hours the atmosphere was hearty,
>   With fireworks, fun, and games of every kind . . .

Poets felt isolated, superior to the common herd; they made
brilliant technical advances, but now the consequences have
become apparent:

To-day, alas, that happy crowded floor
  Looks very different: many are in tears:
Some have retired to bed and locked the door;
  And some swing madly from the chandeliers;
  Some have passed out entirely in the rears;
Some have been sick in corners; the sobering few
Are trying hard to think of something new.

(p. 106)

This analysis is parallel to that in Auden's introduction to the *Oxford Book of Light Verse* (1938), which is similarly concerned with the poet's relation to his audience. Light verse, he says, is produced only when the poet's interests and perceptions are much the same as those of his audience. Yet, when the artist is close to everyday life, though it is easier for him to communicate with his audience, it is harder for him to see honestly and truthfully; "light verse tends to be conventional, to accept the attitudes of the society in which it is written." Conversely, when the poet is more remote from his audience, he finds it easier to see clearly, but harder to communicate. The greatest poetry was written in periods like the Elizabethan, when the artist

> was still sufficiently rooted in the life of his age to feel in common with his audience, and at the same time society was in a sufficient state of flux for the age-long beliefs and attitudes to be no longer compulsive on the artist's vision.

As we have seen, this problem has been a central one for Auden throughout his career. It is significant that he should have formulated it most clearly in this brief period when there seemed to be a real possibility of sharing interests and beliefs with a large audience.

Part IV is autobiographical, and maintains the light tone faultlessly; autobiographical writing with this blend of detachment, candor, and wit is rare indeed. It begins with complaints about his appearance: "My head looks like an egg upon a plate; / ... I have no proper eyebrows, and my eyes / Are far too close

together to look nice" and "I can't think what my It had on
It's mind, / To give me flat feet and a big behind" (p. 202).
There follows an account of his background, family, education, and career to date, all admirably precise, well rounded,
and free from defensiveness and self-justification. It is also un-
failingly entertaining. At the end he states his skeptical position
that "no man by himself has life's solution," and sums up what
he knows:

> That what is done is done, that no past dies,
> That what we see depends on who's observing,
>   And what we think on our activities.
>   That envy warps the virgin as she dries
> But 'Post coitum, homo tristis' means
> The lover must go carefully with the greens.
>   (p. 211)

The last part, written after his return to England, is a short
epilogue reflecting on the state of the country and deciding to
address Byron in Hell rather than Heaven, "For Heaven gets
all the lookers for her pains, / But Hell, I think, gets nearly all
the brains." Those in heaven had well-adjusted childhoods, and
are "happy, lovely, but not overbright. / For no one thinks
unless a complex makes him, / Or till financial ruin overtakes
him" (p. 234). Neither a psychological "Utopia, free of all
complexes" nor a "Withered State" is possible or desirable,
since in eliminating "Complex or Poverty; in short The Trap"
they would eliminate thinkers and artists. The poem closes
with an amusing glimpse of an alternative Poets' Heaven: "I
don't see any books. / Shakespeare is lounging grandly at the
bar,/ . . . Chaucer is buried in the latest Sayers. / Lord Alfred
rags with Arthur on the floor, / Housman, all scholarship forgot at last, / Sips up the stolen waters through a straw. . . ."

  Journey to a War (1938), the other travel book, written
with Isherwood about the war in China, could hardly be more
different from *Letters* in tone. By now the political situation
seems hopeless: the Spanish war is lost, the popular front is an

obvious failure, and it is plain that a general war is coming. When the timeless problems of the East, its confusions and suffering, are seen in such a context, with its war as a foretaste of what is going to happen in Europe, the tone of the reporter is likely to be grim. Isherwood's prose commentary ends thus:

> And the well-meaning tourist, the liberal and humanitarian intellectual, can only wring his hands over all this and exclaim: 'Oh dear, things are so awful here—so complicated. One doesn't know where to start.'   (p. 253)

(In his recent novel, *Down There on a Visit*, Isherwood describes his despairing mood at this time and says that his attitude was so bitterly anti-religious that Auden predicted an early conversion to Roman Catholicism for him.) Auden's part consists of two sections; "London to Hongkong," an introductory poem, "The Voyage," followed by five sonnets; and "In Time of War," a sonnet sequence with a verse commentary. The "Commentary" is of special interest as an explicit statement of Auden's ideas in this transitional period. It is very wide-ranging, beginning with the galaxy and the growth of the forebrain, certainly a biological success; but "liberty to be and weep has never been sufficient." This particular war calls up all human failures, which are all, essentially, failures to achieve the truly human. We are, says Auden in a brilliant capsule survey of history, in the epoch of the third great disappointment: the first was Classical civilization; the second, the Middle Ages; and the third our own dualism between mind and body, isolation of the self in an indifferent universe:

> Never before was the Intelligence so fertile,
> The Heart more stunted. The human field became
> Hostile to brotherhood and feeling like a forest.

Machines made it worse, as did capitalism; now we are afraid and guilty, and the base and violent make their seductive offer: "Man can have Unity if Man will give up Freedom. / The State is real, the Individual is wicked / Violence shall synchronize your movements like a tune, / ... Leave Truth to the police and us; we know the Good; / We build the Perfect City time shall never alter ..." But the truly good and wise (unnamed because humble) have their advice, which begins by denying natural goodness and perfectibility: "Men are not innocent as beasts and never can be, / Man can improve himself but never will be perfect," and testifies to the value and interrelatedness of freedom, truth, and justice. The poem concludes with a secular prayer in which the voice of Man asks, "O teach me to outgrow my madness" and with melted heart and clear head, hopes to rally the "lost and trembling forces of the will, / ... Till they construct at last a human justice, / The contribution of our star...." This kind of eclectic humanism is characteristic of Auden's next two volumes, *Another Time* and *The Double Man.*

Another Time (1940) gives titles to most of the poems and groups them in three categories: People and Places, Lighter Poems, including ballads, cabaret songs, etc., and Occasional Poems (the elegies on Yeats, Freud, and Toller, "Spain 1937," "September 1, 1939," and "Epithalamion"). This is Auden's most topical and discursive volume. It is held together, first, by the theme of man's relation to time and history, as in the title poem ("For us like any other fugitive"), which describes the temptation of escaping into past or future and warns of the need for living in our own time, confronting the present; and, secondly, by the gospel of eclectic humanism. This is put most plainly at the end of "Epithalamion,"

> Vowing to redeem the State,
> Now let every girl and boy
> To the heaven of the Great
> All their prayers and praises lift:

Mozart, Goethe, Blake, Tolstoi, Hölderlin, Wagner, "Looking down upon us, all / Wish us joy." Many poems celebrate these secular saints or substitute gods—Yeats, Freud, Voltaire, Matthew Arnold, Lear, Pascal, Montaigne, Rimbaud, Melville,

Luther—a tendency reaching its height in "New Year Letter," in *The Double Man* (1941).

The Double Man (*New Year Letter*, in the English edition) consists of a prologue, called in *Collected Poetry* "Spring 1940," "New Year Letter," dated January 1, 1940, with extensive notes in prose and verse, the sonnet sequence, "The Quest," and an epilogue, called in *Collected Poetry* "Autumn 1940." The title points to the ambiguity of the whole volume, which vacillates between eclectic humanism which venerates religiously the great Masters and a specifically Christian interpretation. The title not only points to this, but is itself an example of it: it is ostensibly based on the epigraph from Montaigne, but both title and epigraph were taken from Charles Williams's *The Descent of the Dove*.[75] (As we shall see—pp. 177, 242-3 below— Williams both personally and through his writings played an important part in Auden's return to Christianity.) In general, one may say that "New Year Letter" hesitates on the edge of belief in Christianity, as in the beautiful concluding prayer to a deity who has been demonstrated to be a necessary cultural and philosophical hypothesis, "O Unicorn among the cedars...." The sonnet sequence, "The Quest," shows the influence of Kierkegaard (as does "New Year Letter") and, though full of shifting perspectives, often assumes a Christian framework. The epilogue to the volume, however, seems no longer tentative but fully committed:

> That the orgulous spirit may while it can
> Conform to its temporal focus with praise,
>   Acknowledging the attributes of
>   One immortal one infinite Substance,
>
> And the shabby structure of indolent flesh
> Give a resonant echo to the Word which was
>   From the beginning, and the shining
>   Light be comprehended by the darkness.

The volume exhibits, then, a kind of spiritual progression, which seems to correspond generally to the change in Auden's own beliefs. Further discussion of the religious change must, however, be postponed (see p. 171 below); we have here to consider briefly some of the chief features of style and idea in 1936-41.

Symbolic Patterns: Eros, Agape, Logos. To return to the matter of love, in *Another Time* and *The Double Man* Auden carries further the tendency seen in *On This Island* to reverse the "pure in heart" concept in the direction of orthodoxy: nobody is pure in heart, because the law of our own nature is corrupt; Eros, being selfish, tends toward evil. In "September 1, 1939," as the war begins and "the clever hopes expire / Of a low dishonest decade," the poet reflects on the historical, psychological, and political meaning of what is happening; [76] the basic fault, he concludes, is one of love:

> The windiest militant trash
> Important Persons shout
> Is not so crude as our wish:
> What mad Nijinsky wrote
> About Diaghilev
> Is true of the normal heart;
> For the error bred in the bone
> Of each woman and each man
> Craves what it cannot have,
> Not universal love
> But to be loved alone . . .

Even the just are composed "Of Eros and of dust." "Eros Paidagogos / Weeps on his virginal bed" because "he is Eros and must hate what most he loves; / And she is of Nature; Nature / Can only love herself" ("Oxford"). "The Capital" is a "restaurant where the lovers eat each other"; more corrupt than the animals', man's "lust in action to destroy" is "the refined / Creation of machines and mind" ("New Year Letter").

As Auden moves closer to Christianity, the other two members of his symbolic trilogy make their first serious appearance: Agape (selfless Christian love, divine as opposed to human) and

Logos (the incarnate word; eternity as opposed to time; law; authority).[77] Since Auden during this period is entertaining various ideas as possibilities, however, the concepts symbolized and the relations between them are inconsistent and shifting. Thus there is frequently a contrast between selfish and unselfish love, foreshadowing the later clear distinction between Eros and Agape: Melville, arriving at Agape, compares himself with Hawthorne:

> —Nathaniel had been shy because his love was selfish—
> But now he cried in exultation and surrender
> "The Godhead is broken like bread. We are the pieces"

But the elegy on Freud celebrates the Freudian Eros, in terms of Auden's earlier attitudes: Freud "showed us what evil is: not as we thought / Deeds that must be punished, but our lack of faith, / Our dishonest mood of denial, / The concupiscence of the oppressor"; at his death "Sad is Eros, builder of cities." "Sharp and silent in the . . ." meditates on the strange mutations of love, which "like Matter is much / Odder than we thought"; it is based on mutual need: "I believed for years that / Love was the conjunction / Of two oppositions; / That was all untrue." But, though moving hesitantly away from it, this is still Eros; "Bless you, darling, I have / Found myself in you." "New Year Letter" similarly hesitates between Agape and Eros: "We need to love all since we are / Each a unique particular . . . We can love each because we know / All, all of us, that this is so." In a biological metaphor, the mutation of Eros by Logos is described: "The rays of Logos take effect, / But not as theory would expect, / For, sterile and diseased by doubt, / The dwarf mutations are thrown out / From Eros' weaving centrosome." But there are other passages in which Eros is presented favorably: it is desirable that we should "fulfill / Eros's legislative will," thus giving effect to "love's volition"; the trouble is that instead we are dominated by the Ego, self-love. In contrast, Auden later concludes that the political myth of Eros is the source of most of our troubles; similarly, the theme, as in "Crisis," that our political difficulties are the revenge of the Unconscious for our sense of guilt and failure of love shifts later to the conviction that Faith alone, not better psychology, can set our love in order.

A complementary image is that of the Clock. In "The Witnesses" (first published in 1933, then used in *Dog*, then reconverted into a separate poem in *Collected Poetry*) the speakers say, "You are the town and We are the clock. / We are the guardians of the gate in the rock. / The Two." This association of the clock with authority, denial, fear, is clarified by the scene in which the Dog's skin speaks to the clock, explaining that he represents the animal part of man, or perhaps the Id as against the Clock as Superego:

> If it wasn't for me, this young man of mine would never be able to get a good night's rest: and if it wasn't for you he'd never wake up. And look what we do to the audience! When I come on, they start sighing, thinking of spring, meadows and goodness knows what else: While you make them demand a tragic ending, with you they associate an immensely complicated system of awards and punishments. (p. 92)

Earlier in the play, Mildred Luce has protested to her watch the loss of her two sons in the war: "O Ticker, Ticker, they are dead . . . Say something, Ticker" (p. 19). In "Now from my window-sill . . . ," the "church clock's yellow face, the green pier light" are associated with the "influential quiet twins / From whom all property begins," the "Lords of limit" who set taboos—the resemblance to "the two" of the earlier poem is plain—the possessive and separating instincts symbolized by a dream of gamekeepers, to whose "discipline the heart / Submits when we have fallen apart / Into the isolated personal life." In the song, "Dear, though the night . . ." the lovers are happy while "Our whisper woke no clocks," and in "Fish in the unruffled lakes" humans must "weep and sing / Duty's conscious

wrong, / The devil in the clock . . ." In "Out on the lawn . . ."
the evenings are happy when "Fear gave his watch no look."
In "As I walked out . . ." it is the clocks who reply to the lover
and explain that "You cannot conquer Time." On the other
hand, in "New Year Letter" the deity at the end is addressed
as, among many other titles, "O Clock and Keeper of the
Years," a kind of reconciliation with authority; and in the later
poetry the clock no longer tends to be opposed to love but is
absorbed into the Logos symbol.[78]

The Quest. The symbolic pattern of the Quest appears, as we
have seen, in Auden's early poetry: the individual is singled out
for a terrifying responsibility, is required to leave his comfortable life for a dangerous mission (as in "Doom is dark . . .").
In the early verse, this pattern has no very definite conceptual
meaning. The individual chosen has no special qualifications,
is not a Hero; no distinction between the Average and the Exceptional is implied. The sonnet sequence, "The Quest" (included in *The Double Man*, 1941), is Auden's fullest exploration of the rich complex of meanings in this pattern. When first
published in *The New Republic* (Nov. 25, 1940) it was pre-
ceded by the following note:

> The theme of the Quest occurs in fairy tales, legends like
> the Golden Fleece and The Holy Grail, boys' adventure
> stories and detective novels. These poems are reflections
> upon certain features common to them all. The "He" and
> "They" referred to should be regarded as both objective
> and subjective.

The interpretation is primarily in terms of Freudian psychology, with a Kierkegaardian religious analysis tentatively appearing from time to time. "The Door" of the first sonnet is the
threshold between the conscious and the unconscious mind—
"Out of it steps the future of the poor"—and the theme is,
roughly, that most of our troubles, political and personal, stem
from the unconscious. The theme is made explicit in the sec-

ond sonnet: "In theory they were sound on Expectation / Had there been situations to be in; / Unluckily they were their situation. . . ." The religious, or semi-religious, contrast between self-love and unselfish love (in this context, social consciousness, altruism) is the basis of "The City" and of the three following sonnets, describing the temptations which seduce exceptional individuals from the quest and which end in egoism and isolation. The next group presents the theme of the exceptional versus the average: the Freudian interpretation of genius as compensation for maladjustment or physical defects is put explicitly. "The Tower" (exceptional achievement) is "an architecture for the odd"; the danger is that it may become an ivory tower of isolation, since the genius is tempted to avoid commitment to belief: "Those who see all" may "become invisible," the magician may be caught in his own spell. "The Presumptuous" describes average, well-adjusted people who, not noticing that the virgin is ugly, the hero had a "peculiar boyhood," presumptuously "set forth alone / On what, for them, was not compulsory," and either fail or abandon the quest. In the next, an average man, driven by his parents' egoistic illusion that he is exceptional, undertakes the quest: "He saw the shadow of an Average Man / Attempting the Exceptional, and ran." "Vocation," a variation on the same theme, presents a situation reminiscent of Kafka: the bureaucratic official rejects the application of the individual to suffer, and, forced to become a tempter instead of a martyr, he ends as a worldly ironist. Conversely, in "The Useful," those who succumb to temptations become instruments to aid others on the quest. "The Way" is an interesting contrast to Auden's later religious views (such as the Kierkegaardian notion of the Wholly Other): parodying the fairy-tale and grail quests, it observes that the way to salvation in them "is got / By observing oneself and then just inserting a Not" (the piece has an unmistakable Ogden Nash flavor). "The Lucky" considers the questions of destiny, free will, and grace; the failure wonders: " 'Was I doomed in any case, / Or would I not have failed had I believed in Grace?' "

"The Hero," in the next, is unchanged externally by his success, and his only apparent difference from the average is his remarkable humility. Here Auden is very close to a religious point of view; the slightest shift of perspective would make this hero Kierkegaard's knight of faith. The following sonnets, however, show that he is still far from commitment to Christianity. "The Adventurers" describes the desert saints, the mystics who go "the Negative Way toward the Dry"; this is the same representation of mystics as spiritually reckless, as daredevils, that Auden habitually gives in the earlier verse (e.g., the Dancer's flight "from the alone to the Alone" in *The Dance of Death*). "The Waters" deals with human longing for belief, love of illusion, the implication being that the saints of the preceding sonnet cling to "rafts of frail assumption." The last sonnet, "The Garden," describes the condition of innocence, escape from guilt, which, no matter what the apparent object of the quest, is always its ultimate goal; before it, real or illusory, the great blushed "And felt their center of volition shifted."

In recent years Auden has written a number of prose analyses of the various types of quests and heroes, taken as indexes to the political, moral, and religious presuppositions of the cultures they represent.[79] But these concepts have found little expression in his poetry. Part of the explanation, certainly, is the shift in perspective caused by his commitment to Christianity. For, as Simeon says in *For the Time Being*, Christianity negates the distinction between the exceptional and the average:

> The tragic conflict of Virtue with Necessity is no longer confined to the Exceptional Hero; for disaster is not the impact of a curse upon a few great families, but issues continually from the hubris of every tainted will. Every invalid is Roland defending the narrow pass against hopeless odds . . .
>
> Nor is the Ridiculous a species any longer of the Ugly; for since of themselves all men are without merit, all are ironically assisted to their comic bewilderment by the

Grace of God. Every Cabinet Minister is the woodcutter's simple-minded son ... Nor is there any situation which is essentially more or less interesting than another ...

This religious perspective confirms the social analysis which led Auden to conclude that the atomism of modern society has made every man the isolated individual responsible alone for his destiny, made the Kafka hero universal; in "New Year Letter" he says that the machine has compelled all to the admission that

> Aloneness is man's real condition,
> That each must travel forth alone
> In search of the Essential Stone, ...
> Each salesman now is the polite
> Adventurer, the landless knight
> GAWAINE-QUIXOTE, ...

Returning thus to the position implied in his early poems—that there is no ultimate distinction between the exceptional and the average—Auden tends henceforth to use the quest symbolism only incidentally; though it plays an important part in *The Age of Anxiety*.

Paysage Moralisé. A third symbolic pattern that appears with particular clarity in this period is Paysage Moralisé (to use the title that Auden gave in *Collected Poetry* to "Hearing of harvests ...," one of the finest examples of it); it might also be called psychic geography. The technique derives, at least in part, from Rilke; we have seen that it is characteristic of the Rilkean sonnet. Auden observes in a review that Rilke had the first fresh solution since the seventeenth century to the problem of expressing abstract ideas in concrete terms. Rilke's method, he says, is the opposite of the Elizabethans' (anthropomorphic identification); but like them, and unlike the Metaphysicals, who used intellectual ingenuity, wit, Rilke thinks in physical rather than intellectual terms.

> While Shakespeare, for example, thought of the non-human world in terms of the human, Rilke thinks of the human in terms of the non-human, of what he calls Things (Dinge).... Thus one of Rilke's more characteristic devices is the expression of human life in terms of landscape.[80]

For Auden, as for Rilke, the distinction between inner and outer worlds is tenuous and interpenetration is constant. The landscape of the early poems we have already described; its symbolism is largely natural. In the period we are now considering it becomes more conscious and explicit. One type consists in developing the natural symbolism in which landscape represents emotional states or situations. Thus very clearly in "Paysage Moralisé," and in numerous other poems, islands stand for escape, selfish isolation; cities for society, civilization; water for belief, potentiality; valleys for passiveness, innocence; and mountains for effort, decision. The last sonnet of "In Time of War" ("Wandering lost upon the mountains of our choice") is a highly successful use of the last of these. Mountains here represent the human situation, intensified in our time: though we dream of innocence, in which desire and duty are one; though we take refuge in an illusory past or uncertain future, and long for authority and certainty; we must live in the strenuous present, making our difficult choices in dreadful freedom, striving for truth in spite of our imperfections. The surface reference here is topical and political—democracy versus totalitarianism—but the theme is very close to Auden's later Christian version of "redeem the time." In "New Year Letter" there is a long passage describing human nature in terms of English landscape:

> I see the nature of my kind
> As a locality I love
> Those limestone moors that stretch from BROUGH
> To HEXHAM and the ROMAN WALL,
> There is my symbol of us all.

Towns, shops, localities symbolize shoddy thinking, denial of reason or heart, sloth; myth and art are "enormous cones"; "turning states to strata," he sees how "basalt long oppressed broke out / In wild revolt ..."; the derelict mill is "lost belief," with its chimney pointing a question. Mines are associated with a childhood psychological experience (presumably, in Freudian terms, the emergence of the Superego): they made him aware of "Self and Not-Self, Death and Dread," and of guilt.

Another type consists of symbolizing an individual's mind, his character and beliefs, and sometimes his body, through landscape. "There are two atlases," he says in "New Year Letter"; one is public,

> The other is the inner space
> Of private ownership, the place
> That each of us is forced to own,
> Like his own life from which it's grown,
> The landscape of his will and need
> Where he is sovereign indeed,
> The state created by his acts ...

And in "Letter to Lord Byron" he describes the "map of all my youth," with its "mental mountains and the psychic creeks / The towns of which the master never speaks." Matthew Arnold is "a dark disordered city"; Edward Lear "became a land" to which children swarmed like settlers. At Yeats's death, the "provinces of his body revolted, / The squares of his mind were empty, / Silence invaded the suburbs, ..." Later in the poem, the technique is generalized: poetry "survives / In the valley of its saying ... it flows south / From ranches of isolation and the busy griefs / Raw towns that we believe and die in"; it is used climactically at the end: "the seas of pity lie / Locked and frozen in each eye," and the poet prays, "With the farming of a verse / Make a vineyard of the curse / ... In the deserts of the heart / Let the healing fountain start. ..."

A third type might be called moralized anatomy, as in "Sentries against inner and outer," in which the features are interpreted in the manner of the bestiary, and the mouth fixed on as the distinctively human feature, capable of speech and therefore of lying and treachery, vulnerable and erotic. This type is important in *The Age of Anxiety* and in numerous recent poems.

A related type of symbolism, involving the interpenetration and convertibility of inner and outer, is that exhibited most clearly in "Crisis" ("Where do They come from? Those whom we so much dread"). As we have seen, in his early poetry Auden interpreted the enemy as self-created, the result of our spiritual failures (as in "Though aware of our rank . . ."). Similarly, in his later poetry Auden interprets the real wars of our time in psychological terms; these "Nightmares that are intentional and real" arise from our sense of guilt; the unconscious has its revenge. "Crisis" is a good example. When first published in September 1939 it had an epigraph from Dante (*Purgatorio* XIV, 85-7) which is pertinent and shows the relation to the analysis of love: "Of my sowing such straw I reap. O human folk, why set the heart there where exclusion of partnership is necessary?" The answer is that "we conjured them here like a lying map"; "the crooked that dreads to be straight / Cannot alter its prayer but summons / Out of the dark a horrible rector." [81] In his commencement address given at Smith in June 1940, Auden put this explicitly: "Jung hardly went far enough when he said, 'Hitler is the unconscious of every German'; he comes uncomfortably near being the unconscious of most of us." [82] Auden continues, "The shock of discovering through Freud and Marx that when we thought we were being perfectly responsible, logical, and loving we were nothing of the kind, has led us to believe that responsibility and logic and love are meaningless words; instead of bringing us to repentance, it has brought us to a nihilistic despair." By nature we are all bad; it is only by art we become good: "to become civilized one must be reborn." We must accept aloneness as our real condition: "Alone we choose, alone we are responsible"; but "in the last analysis we do not live our lives, but are lived.

[margin note: we don't go w/ what we believe]

What we call I, our little conscious ego, is an instrument of power outside itself. But it is a conscious instrument. To reason and obey logical necessity are its functions." [83] I have not been able to resist quoting this passage, at some cost to logical continuity, because it exemplifies so perfectly the ambiguity of Auden's thought at this transitional stage, the mixture of cultural and religious terms. The psychological analysis I have been quoting comes at the end of the address, most of which, like much of Auden's writing in this period, is an analysis, in terms primarily metaphysical (though calling also on history, psychology, and anthropology), of the causes of the war. (We have already looked at "September 1, 1939," a good example, as is "New Year Letter.") In the Smith address, as in other prose pieces,[84] he finds the basic cause to be Romanticism, a rejection of the paradoxical, dialectic nature of freedom, which has led us to fail to make the completely open society possible and has led others to try to return to the closed type. The open society requires a grasp of the distinction between absolute presuppositions, which are necessary, and propositions; when this is understood, the relation between freedom and necessity becomes clear. The analysis is a brilliant one, full of suggestive and shrewd comments; but there is somehow a fundamental implausibility in the location of the cause of the war in a metaphysical failure; the gospel of distinguishing between open and closed societies, absolute presuppositions and contingent propositions, does not seem adequate to lead to any sort of salvation. As we shall see in the next section, Auden's full acceptance of Christianity soon gives him a solid foundation for his metaphysical analysis, and a larger context in which to place it.

Style. Finally, we may make a few generalizations about stylistic developments in this period. The most striking is the extension of the popular style both in the theater and in many songs, in which it is not parodied but taken seriously enough to use the wide appeal of the medium to convey serious and complex emotions. John Lehmann, speaking primarily of these songs, gives this testimony as to their contemporary impact:

> In that full-flowering moment, feeling, thought, and technical mastery were, it seems to me, in perfect balance; before his passion for rhetorical personification of abstractions... began to devour his invention, and the transplantation to America dried up the sensuous sap and made his utterances for a time seem more like the delphic riddling of a disembodied mind. Each of these astonishing poems was a new discovery about the world we lived in, and seemed to illuminate whole stretches of experience that had lain in a kind of twilight confusion before; disturbing, as all good poetry must be, to accepted ideas and habitual sentiments, by the unexpectedness of its psychological insight... and the images it brought together to act as symbols for that insight.[85]

In addition to the songs already discussed, there are numerous others having a less explicit relation to music that are just as good. "O who can ever gaze his fill," in *Letters from Iceland*, illustrates a fine, unselfconscious use of popular style and swinging rhythm; "O for doors to be open and an invite with gilded edges" uses the popular idiom ironically and effectively—in a form suggesting, with its refrain in each stanza, the ballad—to expose the hatred, envy, and malice that lie behind the apparently harmless and absurd daydreams of the common man. The refrain has a Yeatsian quality, but the rest of the poem is like no one but Auden, with its witty sensationalism and combination of magic and vulgarity.

"May with its light behaving" [86] is a good example of the art song written "as if" for music, i.e. it suggests the conventions of song-writing but is not really suitable for setting. The first two lines are full of the kind of double meaning that music can do nothing with: "May with its light behaving / Stirs vessel, eye, and limb. . . ." The surface meaning is conventional: springtime changes of light and breezes moving boats. But "light" as an adjective suggests moral levity and pulls "vessel" into the

Biblical sense of sexual organ, while retaining also the botani-
cal and anatomical sense. The result is a witty and slightly
shocking ambiguity between the aesthetic and the sexual meanings. In the next two lines, "The singular and sad / Are willing
to recover," "singular" seems at first to mean merely "single,"
but the next line adds the connotation of oddness, maladjustment, neurotics who have chosen their illness. The verbal music
of the poem is so intricate and complex as probably to defeat
any attempt at actual setting: seven-line stanzas using consonance instead of rime, in the pattern *abcddbc*, with trimeter as
a metrical basis, lengthening occasionally to tetrameter and employing frequent feminine endings. The total effect is almost
that of using the traditional spontaneous simplicities of the
spring song as a mask for subtleties in both music and meaning.
The first stanza closes with three lines evoking springtime delights in thoroughly traditional images: "And to the swan-
delighting river / The careless picnics come, / The living white
and red." The next stanza, however, defines the real subject of
the poem: the predicament of the moderns for whom the dead
are "remote and hooded" (that is, the tradition of the past is
meaningless) and who have lost both the innocence of children
and belief in the supernatural (both symbolized by the "vague
woods" from which they have broken). We are mature, responsible, and fallen: "We stand with shaded eye, / The dangerous apple taken." The "real world" which lies before us is
not, however, either that of *Paradise Lost* or that of the clear-
eyed moderns who believe in salvation by science or politics;
it is a sad place, dominated by animality, the death wish, neurosis, and injustice. The last stanza deals with the saddest fact of
all about man, that love, which he shares with the other animals, is for him alone unsatisfactory: "How insufficient is /
The endearment and the look."

"Wrapped in a yielding air" is another song in the same
mode. The imagery and tone are somewhat less complicated,
as man's pretensions are ironically exposed and the human condition is compared with that of plants and animals. The repeti-

tion of word and phrase that is conventional in songs is here employed with excellent ironic effect: man picks his way aggressively past "stronger beasts and fairer," confident in his equipment ("gun and lens and bible"); he is "The essayist, the able, / Able at times to cry." He is oppressed by family relationships, and his psychological history is thus described:

> For mother's fading hopes become
>   Dull wives to his dull spirits
> Soon dulled by nurse's moral thumb,
>   That dullard fond betrayer,
>   And, childish, he inherits,
> So soon by legal father tricked,
>   The tall impressive tower,
>   Impressive, yes, but locked.

In the latter part of the poem the tone changes to a kind of detached pity for the deluded creature who, nevertheless, has grandiose visions of love and reconciliation. And the end is hopeful: though constantly betrayed, "To fresh defeats he still must move, / To further griefs and greater, / And the defeat of grief."

The Rilkean sonnet becomes one of the dominant forms of the period. In *On This Island* "Just as his dream foretold, he met them all" uses the fairy-tale quest archetype effectively; "Fleeing the short-haired mad executives" and "To settle in this village of the heart" both are based on moralized landscape, and "To lie flat on the back with the knees flexed" on moralized anatomy. "A shilling life will give you all the facts" and "Love had him fast, but though he fought for breath" [87] are riddling and enigmatic. In *Journey to a War* the form is used very extensively. The dedicatory sonnet to E. M. Forster is one of the "portrait" type that soon became very prominent: the characteristic theme and significance of a writer's work are summed up within a biographical framework. Of the five "London to Hongkong" sonnets, the first, "The Sphinx," recalls the unicorn sonnets of Rilke; "The Ship" and "The Traveller" are generalized "characters" and travel essays, highly concentrated; the last two are portraits of places, "Macao" and "Hongkong." All these foreshadow the "People and Places" section of *Another Time*, in which a great many of the "portraits" are in sonnet form. To return to *Journey*, however: "In Time of War" consists of 28 sonnets in this mode, wonderfully rich and varied, and deserving more attention than they have received. The Rilkean abrupt beginning, unfixed pronouns and imagery from mythology and legend serve to counteract what would otherwise be almost too explicit a presentation of ideas and of war reporting. "And the age ended, and the last deliverer died" puts the anti-millennial theme, the revenge of the dark gods, the subconscious, on the rational and enlightened modern world, entirely in terms of fairy-tale and mythological images. "Yes, we are going to suffer, now; the sky," like many others, presents a chastened view of human nature and accepts suffering as inevitable. This is the same device we have observed (as in "Crisis") of interpreting war as objectification of inner phenomena, a sort of moralized psyche: the sky "throbs like a feverish forehead"; the enemy "take us by surprise / Like ugly long-forgotten memories, / And like a conscience all the guns resist." We have already looked at the last one, "Wandering lost upon the mountains of our choice," as an example of moralized landscape; in context, it is a return to a more specifically Rilkean mode of imagery and a kind of reconciliation to the human condition, summing up the various aspects of it defined in earlier sonnets. Though we dream of escape to the past or the future, to lost innocence or future certainty, we are doomed to choose, never being sure and always tending to error; we will never be innocent or perfect; but that is what our nature is, we are "A mountain people dwelling among mountains." In *Another Time* "The hour-glass whispers to the lion's paw" is a regular sonnet, dealing with abstractions through emblematic images, and expressing a similar theme: the human proneness to escape through time to past or future, instead of confronting the present; all this is contrasted with the immediacy and incapacity to err of the other creatures, animals and plants. Finally, there is, in *The Double Man*, the sonnet sequence, "The Quest," which we have already discussed as an example of that symbolic pattern. The sonnets in it are perhaps closer to the Rilkean mode than those in "In Time of War," though the forms are varied, one having twenty-one irregularly rhymed lines and one being in couplets.

The great effort and accomplishment of the period is the perfecting of the colloquial or middle style as a flexible instrument for rational discourse and statement that can be public without falsity or loss of integrity. We have looked at "Letter to Lord Byron," certainly Auden's finest achievement in one kind of colloquial verse, and obviously related to the circumstance that in this brief time Auden could feel his reputation firmly established, men of good will united on the Popular Front as well as on more fundamental matters, before the divisions and perplexities began so soon to appear. At the other extreme is "September 1, 1939," with its bitter colloquialism and Yeatsian combination of disabused candor and dignified restraint, in which the meaning of the "low, dishonest decade" is summed up. A part of the style is the ability to be unselfconsciously personal; and this seems to be achieved through his awareness of being the spokesman for, or representative of, many people. "Out on the lawn I lie in bed" is a good example of the personal poem which is also topical and historical-political; [88] as are "Here on the cropped grass of the narrow ridge I stand," "Now from my window-sill I watch the night," and "Musée des Beaux Arts." [89] One advantage of the style is that it can easily be heightened and intensified, as at the end of "August for the people and their favorite islands":

> . . . In the houses
> The little pianos are closed, and a clock strikes.
> And all sway forward on the dangerous flood
> Of history, that never sleeps or dies,
> And, held one moment, burns the hand.

"Easily, my dear, you move, easily your head" (called in *Collected Poetry* "A Bride in the 30's") begins in this style, but becomes ironic and histrionic at many points. On the other hand, "The Unknown Citizen" uses the low colloquial—clichés and bureaucratic speech—to excellent satirical effect: "He was found by the Bureau of Statistics to be / One against whom there was no official complaint, / . . . Our researchers into Public Opinion are content / That he held the proper opinions for the time of year; / When there was peace, he was for peace; when there was war, he went." (There is a distinct flavor of Ogden Nash in the versification.) The great monument of the middle style is of course "New Year Letter," and from the point of view of style alone it is a remarkable tour de force—more than 1700 lines in regular octosyllabic couplets, without the slightest monotony or constraint. The predecessors to whom Auden seems most indebted in the handling of the couplet are perhaps Yeats and Swift, as models of dignity and restraint; there is no crude humor or playing with the form in the manner of Butler. Of course Dryden, the "master of the Middle Style" (as Auden calls him in the poem) and of arguing in verse, with his greater pupil Pope, stands massively in the background. But it is not too much to say, I think, that Auden's octosyllabics are easier, more rapid, and more varied than those of any preceding poet. The genre of the epistle and the use of the couplet give the poem a slightly old-fashioned flavor, or perhaps it would be better to say that they put it very obviously in the tradition; at any rate, they provide enough detachment, enough of a mask, so that Auden can be easily personal. The beginning and the end are remarkable fusions of the personal tribute to a cultivated and affectionate woman and the impersonal celebration of what she stands for or what speaks through her.

In contrast to this, is the style we earlier designated high—the one using normally a long, packed line with elevated diction, often with baroque contrasts of tone; a style that is usually self-consciously and often ironically public, an equivalent of the ode. The prologue to *On This Island*, "O Love, the interest...," is an example, a somewhat histrionic prayer to love, with ironic overtones, with a deliberate arachaic flavor in the elaborate similes and the dactylic movement giving it also an epic detachment: "As when *Merlin*, tamer of horses, and his lords... the *Pillars* passed,"

> And into the undared ocean swung north their prow,
> Drives through the night and star-concealing dawn
> For the virgin roadsteads of our hearts an unwavering keel.

"Casino" is similar in style, though simpler and without archaism; two short lines regularly alternate with the two long ones in each stanza, and all the other effects are muted to give prominence to the brilliant and pathetic image of the gambling casino as the age's substitute for religion: "To the last feast of isolation self-invited / They flock, and in the rite of disbelief are joined." The epilogue, "Certainly our city...," employs the same stanza and style, and the exaggerated melodramatic quality gives detachment to counterbalance the topicality:

> ...For the wicked card is dealt and
> The sinister tall-hatted botanist stoops at the spring
> With his insignificant phial and looses
> The plague on the ignorant town.

"Journey to Iceland," in *Letters*, is another example, with a particularly brilliant melodramatic close:

> Tears fall in all the rivers. Again the driver
> Pulls on his gloves and in a blinding snowstorm starts
> Upon his deadly journey, and again the writer
> Runs howling to his art.

The elegies on Yeats, Freud, and Toller are to some extent in this category, as public utterances with baroque features and irony to take off the curse of solemnity; and "Spain 1937" is a very clear and full-blown example. I have already discussed "Crisis," perhaps the finest poem in this style. In it the histrionic, exaggerated quality is functional, evoking literal nightmares and subconscious terrors; but it is less extreme than in some of the others, and the elevation is less obvious: "Our money sang like streams on the aloof peaks / Of our thinking that beckoned them on like girls"; "For a future of marriage nevertheless / The bed is prepared; though all our whiteness shrinks / From the hairy and clumsy bridegroom. . . ."

Finally, the style we labeled the Nordic mask does not appear at all, and the clipped lyric hardly. Two lyrics already discussed, "Enter with him" and "As it is, plenty," might be considered examples of the latter, since they are in accentual dimeter; but there is no ellipsis and the language is more colloquial, the intensity lower, than in the true clipped lyric.

SELECTIONS AND COLLECTIONS

Since Auden had nothing to do with the choice of poems for *Selected Poems* of 1938 or *Some Poems* of 1940,[90] these are of interest only in illustrating the history of his reputation. The first of these is the larger selection, having 128 pages to 80 for the later. The 1938 volume contains *Paid* complete; 1940 abridges it into incomprehensibility, while preserving most of the best passages. The 1938 contains, from *Poems* 1933, "Doom is dark . . . ," "Watch any day . . . ," "It was Easter . . . ," "Sir, no man's enemy . . . ," "Since you are going to . . . ," "What's in your mind . . . ," and "To ask the hard question. . . ." The 1940 volume omits the last three. From *The Orators*, 1938 has the prologue, epilogue, and two odes: "What siren zooming . . ." and "Though aware of our rank . . ."; 1940 has only the epilogue. The 1938 has four passages from *The Dog Beneath the Skin*, and two from *The Ascent of F6*; the 1940 has two and one. From *On This Island* the 1938 takes exactly half, 16 poems; the 1940 takes 12. Both have "Journey to Iceland" from *Letters from Iceland*, and the 1938 has also "O who can ever gaze...." The 1940 has three sonnets from *Journey to a War*, and the conclusion of the verse Commentary to "In Time of War."

Collected Poetry, 1945. The copy of *On This Island* that Auden used as printer's copy for *Collected Poetry* is preserved in the Swarthmore College library, with his revision, deletions, and other markings. He discarded six of the thirty-two poems, and by the first of these, "Brothers, who when the sirens roar," he wrote in the Swarthmore copy the heartfelt comment, "O God, what rubbish." As we have seen, in this experiment in propaganda poetry, both thought and technique are crude; Auden's reaction is understandable. "The sun shines down..." was rejected presumably as over-simple, a not very successful exercise in the popular idiom: "Gosh, to look at we're no great catch; / History seems to have struck a bad patch." "Night covers up the rigid land" has a brilliant first stanza, and thereafter is perhaps less successful; there seems to be no other reason for its rejection. Finally, there are three that are deleted here but restored in the *Collected Shorter Poems* of 1950: "The chimneys are smoking...," "Here on the cropped grass...," and "August for the people...." The first two of these perhaps relate political and amorous themes somewhat facilely, and the last might have been thought excessively personal in its account of the shared ideas of Auden and Isherwood; but they are certainly all three worth keeping.[91] The selections from the plays need no comment: there are five from *The Dog Beneath the Skin* (to which, as we saw earlier, *Collected Shorter Poems* adds one more) and two from *The Ascent of F6*, as well as two songs from *The Dark Valley* and three from *Paul Bunyan*.

From *Journey to a War*, "In Time of War" is reprinted complete and unchanged, but the verse Commentary is significantly revised: two stanzas are omitted, and the last is changed from its humanist invocation ("Rally the lost and trembling forces of the will, ... Till they construct at last a human justice, / The contribution of our star ...") to a Christian one, in which justice is not human but divine ("Till, as the contribution of our star, we follow / The clear instructions of that Justice ...").

From *Another Time*, the only omissions are the dedicatory poem to Chester Kallman (a new dedicatory poem, first published in the notes to "New Year Letter," is substituted), the sonnet on A. E. Housman, and three lighter poems (the ballad "James Honeyman," the cabaret song beginning "Some say that Love's ...," and "Calypso") that presumably seemed too light. From "September 1, 1939" Auden omitted the famous stanza ending, "We must love one another or die," presumably because it seemed too explicit and facile.[92]

From *The Double Man*, "The Quest" is unchanged except for the title of one sonnet, and "New Year Letter" is unrevised; but ten of the poems published in the notes to it have been given titles and published as separate poems, while the notes have been discarded. The prologue and epilogue to the volume have been retitled and put in the alphabetical sequence of *Collected Poetry;* the new titles date them, which is useful, but they gain in significance from being read in context with "New Year Letter."

As we saw at the end of Section I, the *Selected Poetry* of 1958 is too small in scope for exclusions to be significant; but it is interesting to see what Auden chooses to represent his earlier work. From *The Dog Beneath the Skin* he takes only the lyric "Enter with him," which is certainly the finest single passage. From *On This Island* there are six pieces, all songs: three of those set by Britten, two of the popular type, and one I have not discussed, "Dear, though the night is gone." [93] From *Another Time* there is a large selection, consisting almost entirely of songs and ballads, with a few poems from the "People and Places" section and the elegies on Freud and Yeats. From *Journey to a War* there are seven sonnets, and from *The Double Man* there are seven sonnets from "The Quest." For the purposes of this volume, certainly, Auden seems to think the songs his most lasting achievement of the period; and collected in this way they reveal their great variety and richness.

I have kept this section as short as possible because this is the part of Auden's work that is best known and that has been most fully explained and commented on. This is also the period when his ideas and beliefs were in transition, and to some extent his style too; too much concentration on this period leads to a distorted picture of the poetry as based on ideas which are in constant flux. In the first place, the best poetry of the period is, to make a crude dichotomy, in the songs rather than in the ideological verse; in the second place, the changes of belief and attitude are all consistent and in one direction (and, for that matter, by no means peculiar or eccentric, but representing dominant trends in the intellectual climate). Once Auden has arrived at his destination in his full acceptance of Christianity, there is no more fundamental change. And this is not a reversal nor a denial of most of his earlier ideas, but a fulfillment, a placing of them in a new perspective and on a new basis. The sense of relation to a large audience could not last; and Auden's migration, based on the conviction that "aloneness is man's real condition," was the final element in destroying it. With the deterioration of this sense, the kind of lightness that lies behind the songs and the poems of the middle style becomes difficult to attain; the vice of over-facility, of making tricks of style mechanical (as in "They carry terror with them like a purse, / And flinch from the horizon like a gun"), is no longer a problem, but the older and more fundamental problem arises again, that of uniting outer and inner, public and private, statement and magic. The early poetry had tended to the private, to fantasy; that of the later thirties had tended to the public, the discursive, the explicitly diagnostic. The problem has to be solved all over again, another stasis worked out, after the basic religious change to be discussed in the next section.

Notes to Section II

1. Julian Symons (*The Thirties*, pp. 21-2) shows how small the actual numbers were: of *Poems* 1930 probably 1000 copies were printed, and of the second edition (1933) the same number; in Sept. 1934 there was a re-printing of 1500 copies, and no more until 1937. The first printing of *The Orators* consisted of 1000 copies, and the second (Sept. 1934) of the same number.

2. *The Buried Day*, pp. 216-7. The oldest of the "group," Day Lewis, left Oxford in 1927 just before the youngest, Spender, arrived: the four were thus never together at Oxford, and there is only one year when the three older ones were all there (1926-7).

3. Lehmann's account may be found in *The Whispering Gallery* (London, 1955).

4. Julian Symons, *The Thirties* (London, 1960), p. 162.

5. A. Alvarez, *Stewards of Excellence* (New York, 1958), pp. 87-8. Cf. Lehmann, op. cit., p. 255, "The vision of his generation was, in fact, largely formed by him."

6. When this poem was collected as XIV in *On This Island*, the title and six stanzas were deleted and the first word changed from "Comrades" to "Brothers."

7. Day Lewis, *The Buried Day*, p. 210.

8. Spender, *World Within World*, p. 225.

9. "Authority in America," *The Griffin*, March 1955.

10. George Orwell, "Inside the Whale," in *Such, Such Were the Joys* (New York, 1953). Orwell says, "They can swallow totalitarianism *because* they have no experience of anything except liberalism" (p. 184). His criticism of the "necessary murder" passage in Auden's *Spain* (1937), however, was "densely unjust," as Auden has remarked: "I was *not* excusing totalitarian crimes but only trying to say what, surely, every decent person thinks if he finds himself unable to adopt the absolute pacifist position. (1) To kill another human being is always murder and should never be called anything else. (2) In a war, the members of two rival groups try to murder their opponents. (3) *If* there is such a thing as a just war, then murder can be necessary for the sake of justice" (letter to M.K.S., May 11, 1963).

11. Gerald Heard, b. 1889, son of a clergyman, studied history at Cambridge and was at this time a commentator on science for the B.B.C. (1930-4). In 1937 he came to the United States and settled in California, where he still lives. He has long been associated with Aldous Huxley and Christopher Isherwood in the study of Vedanta, and both have represented him (very favorably) in their novels. Among his numerous books are: *The Ascent of Humanity: An Essay on the Evolution of Civilization*

from Group Consciousness through Individuality to Super-consciousness
(1929), *Doppelgangers: An Episode of the Fourth, the Psychological,
Revolution* (1947), *Is God in History?* (1949), *Is Another World Watching?* (1951—about flying saucers). Under his original name of H. F. Heard
he has written excellent mysteries and scientific thrillers: *A Taste for
Honey* (1941), *Reply Paid* (1942), *The Great Fog* (1944), *The Lost
Cavern* (1948), *The Notched Hairpin* (1949).

J. W. Beach, in his *The Making of the Auden Canon* (Minneapolis,
1957), argues at length (pp. 23, 36, 118-9) that Auden was greatly influenced by Heard's doctrine of psychological evolution, with the emergence of a higher consciousness that will transcend individualism. Love,
Beach suggests, in Auden's earlier verse really means Heard's "higher
consciousness." Beach offers nothing to substantiate this thesis, which
seems to me quite unfounded; his motive seems to be to deny any religious element in Auden's early verse, so as to represent the division
between it and the later Christian work as absolute. Heard's doctrine, he
says, "may be the key to passages in the earlier poems which some recent
critics would interpret in terms of Christian theology. And a reading of
Heard, to whom Auden addressed his 'Happy New Year,' may help to
keep these early poems where they belong, within the framework of a
secular humanism later repudiated" (p. 119). (Beach's book is discussed
below, pp. 202-3.)

12. There are, of course, other pieces with some propaganda element:
"Benthameer, Benthameer..." in *The Orators* (discussed above, p. 52);
the song, "I have a handsome profile," of 1933, which Auden has never
reprinted (discussed very fully by Beach, op. cit., pp. 112-5); and the
last play Auden did with Isherwood, *On the Frontier* (1938). "The
Sportsmen: A Parable," in *New Verse*, Autumn 1938, is a prose parable
dealing with the relation between the poet and the citizen; the emphasis
is on the dangers of poetic isolationism, but the implication is that the
poet should take seriously his responsibilities as citizen, not that he should
use his poetry to bring about political ends. In terms of the parable, trees
have to be cut down before duck-shooting is possible, and the suggestion
is that the sportsmen (poets) should help the villagers clear the trees
(improve society); but they are not to try to combine shooting and tree-
felling, which remain quite separate occupations.

13. Isherwood translated, with D. Vesey, Brecht's *Dreigroschenroman*
(published as *A Penny for the Poor*, London, 1937; reprinted as *Threepenny Novel*, New York, 1956 and London, 1958); Isherwood's versions
of the songs were the basis of Eric Bentley's in his translation of the
Dreigroschenoper (*Threepenny Opera*) in *The Modern Theatre*, Vol. I
(New York, 1955).

14. John Willett, *The Theatre of Bertolt Brecht* (London, 1959), pp. 88-9.

15. H. R. Hays, Introduction to Brecht, *Selected Poems* (New York, 1959), p. 8.

16. *The Dyer's Hand* (New York, 1962), p. 87.

17. Interview with Auden by M. S. Handler, *New York Times*, Nov. 2, 1958; Auden was finishing his translation of Brecht's *Seven Deadly Sins* at the time.

18. Act V appeared in the *Kenyon Review* in 1946; the whole play, trans. by James and Tania Stern with Auden, was included in Brecht's *Plays*, Vol. I (Methuen: London, 1961).

19. The translation of the *Seven Deadly Sins* appeared in the *Tulane Drama Review*, Autumn 1961; that of *Mahagonny* has not yet been published. Kurt Weill's music for these, as for the *Threepenny Opera*, was, of course, responsible for much of their success.

20. Julian Symons, *The Thirties* (London, 1960), p. 78.

21. Used again in 1937 in the poem of that title: "It's farewell to the drawing-room's civilised cry...."

22. See, for example, "Since you are going to begin today," "Consider this...," "It's no use raising a shout," "Watch any day...," "I have a handsome profile."

23. *The Book of the It*, New York, 1961, p. 16. (This is the same translation Auden quotes in the notes to "New Year Letter.")

24. *Two Great Plays by W. H. Auden and Christopher Isherwood* (New York, n.d.), p. 108.

25. Ibid., pp. 43, 81.

26. *The Thirties*, p. 79.

27. Beach, op. cit., pp. 132-5 and 157; the discarded sonnet, one of five published in *New Verse*, 1933, began: "I see it often since you've been away."

28. Discussed, pp. 118-19.

29. In *Life and Letters*, May 1934.

30. On Feb. 26, 1937, it was produced at the Mercury Theatre by Ashley Dukes in association with the Group Theatre. The full cast is given in the Faber paperback edition (1958, with *On the Frontier*).

31. Discussed, p. 107.

32. Pp. 145, 172 in the Faber paperback edition (1958, published with *F6*). Auden's "In Memory of Ernst Toller" was written after Toller's suicide in 1939. Toller, a German playwright and socialist, had been a refugee in England for some years. *No More Peace!* was translated by Edward Crankshaw, lyrics adapted by Auden, with music by Herbert Murrill; it was published in 1937 (London and New York). Many of the

lyrics in this "thoughtful comedy" are amusing and broadly satirical: the peace song which is readily convertible to a war song, the dictator's song, spy song, and others.

33. Published in *Best Broadcasts of 1939-40*, ed. Max Wylie (New York, 1940), pp. 30-43.

34. "Alfred (A Cabaret Sketch. For Therese Giehse)," in *New Writing* (ed. John Lehmann), II, London, Autumn 1936.

35. See above, p. 14, and below, pp. 305, 311-12.

36. There is an additional stanza, dropped from the version in *Collected Poetry:* "The palace servants sing. / The ships put out to sea. / The form that pleased a king / Swings on the elder tree."

37. "O who can ever gaze his fill" and "O who can ever praise enough"; we know the circumstances of their composition from *Letters from Iceland*, pp. 227, 143, respectively.

38. "As it is, plenty," "It's farewell to the drawing-room's civilised cry," "Our hunting fathers told the story," "They are our past and our future...."

39. I am indebted to an excellent analysis by William Power in *The Explicator*, March 1958. Auden includes "The British Grenadier" in the *Oxford Book of Light Verse*, #152.

40. She was one of the singers in the Group Theatre production of *F6*. Since 1942 she has been Mrs. Louis MacNeice.

41. The two not collected are "Calypso and "O Tell Me the Truth about Love."

42. Auden praises the *Cautionary Tales* in *Letters from Iceland* (p. 22) as among the few examples of good contemporary light verse.

43. Philadelphia, YM-YWHA, Feb. 13, 1962.

44. See the excellent analysis by Cleanth Brooks and R. P. Warren, *Understanding Poetry*, 3rd ed. (New York, 1960), pp. 332-5. The ballad is #202 and the folksong #104 in Auden's *Oxford Book of Light Verse*.

45. By Hoggart, op. cit., p. 225 (note to p. 14).

46. Cf. Blake's "London"; for the 1928 poem, see above, I, note 44.

47. Op. cit., p. 185.

48. Jacket notes to *An Evening of Elizabethan Verse...* (1955)

49. Ibid.

50. Ibid.

51. Introduction to *An Elizabethan Song Book* (1955), p. xiv.

52. Ibid., p. xv.

53. Eric Walter White, *Benjamin Britten: A Sketch of his Life and Works* (rev. ed., London, 1954), p. 22.

54. Ibid., p. 23.

55. The piano-vocal score was published by Boosey and Hawkes, London.

56. There is a good analysis in Hoggart, op. cit., pp. 101-3. No one seems to have noticed that the end of the poem is a quotation from Lenin, who says that one must "go hungry, work illegally and be anonymous"; "The self must first learn to be indifferent." Auden quoted these passages in his 1934 essay on T. E. Lawrence, in which he drew a parallel between Lenin and Lawrence as examples of modern asceticism and selflessness "and to us, egotistical underlings, the most relevant accusation and hope."

57. The piano-vocal score, published by Boosey and Hawkes, London, is still available. The only complete recording—an excellent one made by Barbara Troxell, soprano, on WCFM-LP-15 in 1953—is unfortunately out of print and hard to find.

58. I am indebted here and in some other observations to the jacket notes on the Troxell recording.

59. Both these songs are included in the Troxell recording mentioned in the preceding notes; the jacket notes call "Willow" "one of the most charming of Britten's short vocal compositions."

60. Beach, pp. 191-202, discusses at great length the differences in the three versions of the poem: the original one of 1937 (reprinted unchanged in *Another Time*, 1940), the much shorter form in *Ballad of Heroes* (which was published by Boosey and Hawkes, 1939), and the final version in *Collected Poetry* (1945), which deletes only two unimportant stanzas from the original one. Beach assumes that Auden was responsible for deciding which parts of the poem Britten was to set and which were to be dropped; and he speculates elaborately on the political significance of such presumed decisions. There is, however, no evidence that Auden did anything of the sort, and it seems most unlikely; Britten presumably made the choices himself, and for reasons at least as much musical as political.

61. White, p. 40.

62. Published by Boosey and Hawkes, London, 1942; the score is dated "At sea...April 2nd 1942" and this would appear to mean that Britten composed it, or finished composing it, on shipboard returning to England.

63. "New Year Letter" eloquently describes her warmth, graciousness, musicianship and "learned peacefulness." She is presumably the same Elizabeth Mayer to whom Rilke wrote a letter in 1916, first published in Harry T. Moore's *Selected Letters of R. M. Rilke* (New York, 1960), pp. 197-8; Moore identifies her as "a friend of Hans Carossa" (1878-1956, Bavarian doctor and poet), and continues: [She] "was married to a psychiatrist; now a translator" (p. 198). She translated Britten's *Peter Grimes* into German in 1946 and recently collaborated with Auden in translating Goethe's *Italian Journey* (1962).

64. I am indebted to the interpretation of Ingeborg Hough in *The Explicator*, March 1960, though I disagree with it on several points. The

meter of the first section is the same as that of "The Groves of Blarney" (#167 in the *Oxford Book of Light Verse*)—an allusion which heightens the irony.

65. The first line of this section, "O ear whose creatures cannot wish to fall," probably recalls the penultimate stanza of Donne's "The Litanie"— a favorite passage of Auden's, quoted in the notes to "New Year Letter" (*Double Man*, p. 150), in his Swarthmore lecture of March 1950, and in the *Viking Book of Aphorisms* (1962), p. 88—which ends, "Heare us, weake ecchoes, O thou eare, and cry."

66. Jacket note by Gordon Stewart on Oiseau Lyre 5612.

67. According to Grove's *Dictionary*, Elisabeth Lutyens (English composer, b. 1906) set 1934-6 "Refugee Blues" and "As I Walked Out One Evening"; Luciano Berio (Italian composer, b. 1925) wrote in 1953 both an oratorio and a set of orchestral variations based on "Nones." These I have not heard nor seen, nor "We're Late," set by Lukas Foss as part of his "Time Cycle," 1961.

68. HMV DLP 1209. There are also good jacket notes by Andrew Porter. Berkeley (b. 1903) went to the same public school as Auden and was still at Oxford when Auden arrived.

69. See below, pp. 216-17. The best of these pieces now form the concluding section of *The Dyer's Hand* (1962), called "Homage to Igor Stravinsky."

70. The conventional statement that in lyric, which is at most chanted, the words are dominant, while in song the music imposes its own rhythm and melody upon the words, seems to me erroneous. The song should be a true marriage of words and music, in which the music makes of the words something other and vastly better than they could be alone; but for this to happen the words must be clearly established as legal head of the household and the music's function must be to make all it can of them. The song will be more "marriageable" if not too set in its ways, so to speak; a certain adaptability and flexibility is desirable, and other things are helpful: the more repetition and contrast the better, and conventional and emblematic images and an occasional excuse for imitative effects (storms, bells, galloping horses) are welcome. But the primary job of the poet writing a song to be set is to produce a good poem which will give the composer an experience that he can translate and interpret musically, re-create in musical terms.

71. In *Collected Poetry*, 1945 (p. 89), "mole" is misprinted "mote." Someone could write an essay on the role of the typographical error in Auden; see note 44 in the preceding section, and *Letters from Iceland*, p. 27.

72. *The Thirties*, p. 55.

73. Ibid., p. 61: the first printing was 2350 copies and a second printing of 2000 copies was called for within three months. For the earlier volumes, see above, note 1.

74. Much later, reviewing a biography of Byron (*The New Yorker*, April 26, 1958), Auden observes that Byron's satire is not that of the Insider, like Dryden or Pope, but of the Outsider, like Skelton or Lawrence. He does not, like the neo-classical satirist, speak for all sensible people and assume the eternal laws of the City of Man, but rejects the conventional laws and pieties and speaks for the uncorrupted individual. His weapon therefore is not the strict form of the heroic couplet, but satiric doggerel, anarchistic and childish in technique (as in Skelton and Lawrence), or comic verse as in Byron. In *The Dyer's Hand* (1962), pp. 294-5, 387-8, 394, Auden repeats and elaborates these distinctions, but revises his terminology to argue that Byron is not a satirist but a comic writer:

> Satire and comedy both make use of the comic contradiction, but their aims are different. Satire would arouse in readers the desire to act so that the contradictions disappear; comedy would persuade them to accept the contradictions with good humor as facts of life against which it is useless to rebel. (p. 388)

Auden's analysis (pp. 394-401) of the creative role of poetic form in *Don Juan* (i.e., the effect of the ottava rima stanza) is a very brilliant one, and casts much light on comic verse in general, including his own.

75. *The Descent of the Dove* was first published in London, 1939; a reprint with an introduction by Auden was published in New York, 1956. The passage in question occurs on p. 192 of the latter edition:

> "It is not possible," said Montaigne, "for a man to rise above himself and his humanity"; and again: "We are, I know not how, double in ourselves, so that what we believe we disbelieve, and cannot rid ourselves of what we condemn."
>
> The "double man" of Montaigne is not the same as the "double man" of the unknown Egyptian monk, . . .

In a note to 1.1600 of the poem (*The Double Man*, p. 153) Auden makes a general acknowledgment: "For this quotation, and for the source of many ideas in the poem, v. *The Descent of the Dove* by Charles Williams."

76. The allusions and historical background of the second stanza are explained by Phyllis Bartlett and John A. Pollard in *The Explicator*, Nov. 1955.

77. In "A Literary Transference," 1940, Auden says that Hardy first taught him something of the relations of Eros and Logos; in 1941 he calls his review of De Rougemont "Eros and Agape" (discussed below, pp. 189 ff.). The classic Protestant exposition of the radical distinction between Agape and Eros is Anders Nygren's *Agape and Eros*, London, 1932; the Roman Catholic position is that the two are united in *Caritas* (as in M. C. D'Arcy, S.J., *The Mind and Heart of Love*, London, 1945). Auden's attitude has always been Protestant in this respect.

In all of Auden's analyses of love, *The Divine Comedy* is in the background; in 1941 he described Dante as one of the three greatest influences on his work (see p. 21 above). *Purgatorio* haunts his imagination most, especially Virgil's explanation of the nature of love in Cantos XV and XVII (quoted, for instance, in *The Double Man*, pp. 158-60, *The Dyer's Hand*, pp. 139, 230, and, satirically, in "Address for a Prize-Day" in *The Orators*).

78. In *The Dyer's Hand*, p. 140, Auden remarks that he belongs to the characterological type of the punctual man "who cannot tell if he is hungry unless it first looks at the clock," and suggests a connection between Christianity and the notion of punctuality:

> I have heard it suggested that the first punctual people in history were the monks—at their office hours. It is certain at least that the first serious analysis of the human experience of time was undertaken by St. Augustine, and that the notion of punctuality, of action at an exact moment, depends on drawing a distinction between natural and historical time which Christianity encouraged if it did not invent.

79. "The Christian Tragic Hero," 1945; "K's Quest," 1946; "The Guilty Vicarage," 1948; introd. to *The Portable Greek Reader*, 1948; "The Ironic Hero: Some Reflections on *Don Quixote*," 1949; *The Enchafèd Flood*, 1950; introd. to *Tales of Grimm and Andersen*, 1952; review of *The Fellowship of the Ring*, 1954; "The Quest Hero," 1961; in *The Dyer's Hand*, 1962, especially "Genius and Apostle."

80. *The New Republic*, 1939.

81. The penultimate stanza, with its references to ape and tiger, recalls Tennyson's "In Memoriam," ll. 2495-6 (Section CXVIII): "Move upward, working out the beast, / And let the ape and tiger die"; Auden quoted this passage in his 1935 essay, "Psychology and Art Today," as an expression of doctrine proved false by psychology. In 1944 he edited a selection from Tennyson. The manuscript of "Crisis" is in the Lockwood Memorial Library of the University of Buffalo; it is reproduced in *Reading Poems*, ed. S. G. Brown and W. Thomas (New York, 1941), p. 630.

82. *Smith Alumnae Quarterly*, Aug. 1940, p. 357.

83. Ibid., p. 358. The influence of Groddeck is plain in this passage.

84. For example, "Criticism in a Mass Society," 1941. In 1943 Auden taught a seminar at Swarthmore called "Romantic Literature from Rousseau to Hitler."

85. *The Whispering Gallery* (London, 1955), p. 255.

86. Discussed by Hoggart, pp. 104-6.

87. Discussed by John Bayley, *The Romantic Survival* (London, 1957), pp. 164-6.

88. G. S. Fraser, in *The Modern Writer and his World* (London, 1953), pp. 241-2, has an excellent analysis of part of this poem.

89. Maurice Charney discusses a probable source (Sir Lewis Namier, *England in the Age of the American Revolution*, 1930) in *Philological Quarterly*, Jan. 1960, and R. M. Roth has a good analysis in "The Sophistication of W. H. Auden: A Sketch in Longinian Method," *Modern Philology*, Feb. 1951. Max Bluestone elucidates the iconographic sources in *Modern Language Notes*, April 1960.

90. Letter to M.K.S., July 21, 1962.

91. Revisions in the poems from *On This Island* are not extensive, and consist chiefly of the elimination of superfluous stanzas and minor verbal improvement: e.g., in "Out on the lawn...," four stanzas were dropped and lines 4-5, "Forests of green have done complete / The day's activity..." become "The congregated leaves complete / Their day's activity...." In many cases the changes merely carry further a process begun in *On This Island:* the version in that volume will have been much pruned from the original publication, and *Collected Poetry* will prune still more severely (e.g. "Now from my window-sill...").

92. Beach (pp. 49-52) discusses this question at length. His assumption is always that Auden's revisions are the result of changes in his ideas and convictions; he mentions the possibility of aesthetic considerations playing a part, but he does not seem to take this seriously. Thus he concludes that Auden's reasons for dropping this stanza are "inscrutable": "The only possible reason one can think of is that the statement is not made here in specifically and unmistakably religious terms" (p. 51).

93. The three set by Britten are: "Underneath the Abject Willow," "Autumn Song," and "Seascape"; the two popular ones are "O for doors to be open..." and "The Quarry."

1941-1947

<dl>
<dt>1941-42</dt>
<dd>Taught at the University of Michigan.</dd>

<dt>1941</dt>
<dd>

Paul Bunyan, a choral operetta, written with Benjamin Britten, produced in May. Both collaborators were dissatisfied with it and it has never been published.

The Double Man published by Random House in March; the Faber & Faber edition (May) was called *New Year Letter*. Dedicated to Elizabeth Mayer.

"Criticism in a Mass Society," in *The Intent of the Critic*, ed. D. A. Stauffer.

"The Role of Intellectuals in Political Affairs," in *Decision*, Jan. 1941.

"A Note on Order," in *The Nation*, Feb. 1, 1941.

"Opera on an American Legend," in the *New York Times*, May 4, 1941. (About *Paul Bunyan*.)

Reviews in *Decision* of *Where Do We Go From Here?*, by Harold Laski (Jan. 1941); *Towards a Philosophy of History*, by Ortega y Gasset ("The Masses Defined," May 1941).

Reviews in *The Nation* of *Christianity and Power Politics*, by Reinhold Niebuhr ("Tract for the Times," Jan. 4, 1941); *Love in the Western World*, by Denis de Rougemont ("Eros and Agape," June 28, 1941).

Reviews in *The New Republic* of translations of Kafka ("The Wandering Jew," Feb. 10, 1941); *Darwin, Marx and Freud*, by J. Barzun ("Ambiguous Answers," June 23, 1941); *The Nature and Destiny of Man*, by Reinhold Niebuhr ("The Means of Grace," June 2, 1941); *The Philosophy of Literary Form*, by Kenneth Burke ("A Grammar of Assent," July 14, 1941).
</dd>
</dl>

1942-45   Taught at Swarthmore College.
Concurrently teaching at Bryn Mawr College 1943-45.
Guggenheim fellowships 1942 and 1945.

1942   *Hymn to St. Cecilia*, Op. 27, by Benjamin Britten, with words by W. H. Auden, published by Boosey & Hawkes, Ltd., London.
Review of *Poems and New Poems*, by Louise Bogan, in *Partisan Review*, July-August 1942. ("The Rewards of Patience")
Review of *G.B.S., A Full Length Portrait*, by Hesketh Pearson, in *Commonweal*, Oct. 23, 1942. ("The Fabian Figaro")

1943   Review of *A Choice of Kipling's Verse*, by T. S. Eliot, in *The New Republic*, October 25, 1943 ("Poet of the Encirclement").
"Distrust of Language and Mathematics—Alarming Symptoms," in *Hispania*, October 1943.

1944   *For the Time Being* published by Random House (September) and by Faber & Faber, containing "The Sea and the Mirror," dedicated to James and Tania Stern, and "For the Time Being," dedicated to the memory of Auden's mother (d. 1941). "For the Time Being" has been translated into German by G. Fritsch: *Hier und Jetzt, ein Weihnachtsoratorium*, Salzburg, 1961.
Edited *A Selection of the Poems of Alfred Lord Tennyson* (New York: Doubleday).
Review of *The Jew in Our Day*, by Waldo Frank, in *The Nation*, Sept. 23, 1944.
Reviews in *The New Republic* of translation of Kierkegaard, *Either/Or* ("A Preface to Kierkegaard," May 15, 1944); *Gerard Manley Hopkins: A Life*, by Eleanor Ruggles ("A Knight of the Infinite," Aug. 21, 1944); *Christianity and Classical Culture*, by C. N. Cochrane ("Augustus to Augustine," Sept. 25, 1944).
Reviews in *The New York Times Book Review* of *The Portable Shakespeare* (Oct. 1, 1944); *Nevertheless*, by Marianne Moore (Oct. 15, 1944); *Grimms' Fairy Tales* ("In Praise of Brothers Grimm," Nov. 12, 1944).

1945   Sent overseas in April by the United States Air Force to
        investigate the effect of strategic bombing on German
        morale.

        Collected Poetry (dedicated to Christopher Isherwood
        and Chester Kallman) published by Random House in
        April.

        Reviews in *The New York Times Book Review* of *The
        Diaries of Tchaikovsky* (Dec. 2, 1945); *Moby Dick* ("The
        Christian Tragic Hero," Dec. 16, 1945).

1946   Became a United States citizen in April.

        Taught at Bennington College for one semester.

        Collaborated with Bertolt Brecht and H. R. Hays in
        adapting Webster's the *Duchess of Malfi;* starring Elisa-
        beth Bergner and Canada Lee, opened first in Boston and
        then in New York in October, at the Barrymore Theatre.

        "K's Quest," in *The Kafka Problem*, ed. A. Flores. (In-
        cluded in *The Dyer's Hand*, 1962).

        Review of *War and the Poet*, ed. R. Eberhart and S.
        Rodman, in *Commonweal*, Jan. 18, 1946 ("As Hateful
        Ares Bids").

1946-47 Taught at the New School for Social Research, New
        York.

        Taught concurrently at Barnard College second se-
        mester.

1947   *The Age of Anxiety: A Baroque Eclogue* published by
        Random House in October; published by Faber & Faber
        in 1949. Dedicated to John Betjeman. (A German trans-
        lation by Kurt Heinrich Hansen, with an introduction by
        Gottfried Benn, was published in Wiesbaden, apparently
        in 1947: *Das Zeitalter der Angst; ein barockes Hirten-
        gedicht.*)

        Edited *Slick but not Streamlined*, poems by John Bet-
        jeman. (New York: Doubleday.)

        Introduced and edited *The American Scene*, by Henry
        James (New York: Scribner's); introduction included in
        The Dyer's Hand (1962).

        Became Editor of Yale Series of Younger Poets and
        introduced Vol. 45, *Poems* by Joan Murray.

Introduction to Baudelaire, *Intimate Journals*, trans. Christopher Isherwood. (Hollywood: M. Rodd; pub. by Methuen: London, 1949, and in Boston as a Beacon Paperback, 1957.)

Review of *The Portable D. H. Lawrence*, ed. Diana Trilling, in *The Nation*, April 26, 1947.

Review of *The Portable Dante*, in *The New York Times Book Review*, June 29, 1947.

Essay, "I Like It Cold," *House and Garden*, Dec. 1947.

III

Religion and Longer Poems

Perhaps I always knew what they were saying:
Even the early messengers who walked
Into my life from books where they were staying,
Those beautiful machines that never talked
But let the small boy worship them and learn
All their long names whose hardness made him proud;
Love was the word they never said aloud
As something that a picture can't return.

And later when I hunted the Good Place,
Abandoned lead-mines let themselves be caught;
There was no pity in the adit's face,
The rusty winding-engine never taught
One obviously too apt, to say Too Late:
Their lack of shyness was a way of praising
Just what I didn't know, why I was gazing,
While all their lack of answer whispered "Wait,"
And taught me gradually without coercion,
And all the landscape round them pointed to
The calm with which they took complete desertion
As proof that you existed.

                         It was true.
For now I have the answer from the face
That never will go back into a book
But asks for all my life, and is the Place
Where all I touch is moved to an embrace,
And there is no such thing as a vain look.[1]

THE SHIFT IN PERSPECTIVE

Auden's religious position is not a denial but a fulfillment of
his earlier beliefs; the religious values do not contradict the

The notes are to be found at the end of the section, on page 242.

others, but clarify them and take them to another level. It is no accident nor effect of temporary intellectual fashions that his religious approach should be existential, for this type of religious philosophy starts from the same kind of psychological analysis that had formed the perduring basis of Auden's various attitudes and convictions. The ambiguity of *The Double Man* was not one of language but of belief, with liberal-humanist terms mixed with theological ones, so that the effect was frequently one of alternative descriptions and explanations of the same phenomena in two separate dimensions, according to two different systems of reference. In 1939-41 Auden was reading theology as well as political, sociological, and metaphysical analysis,[2] and was applying them all to elucidate the significance of the war. As we have seen, *The Double Man* expressed this transitional state of mind and unstable equilibrium. "New Year Letter" hesitates on the edge of belief, as in the concluding prayer to a deity who has been demonstrated to be a necessary cultural and philosophical presupposition and who is demonstrated in the prayer to be a fertile occasion of poetic metaphor. The "Epilogue," dated Autumn, 1940, seems fully committed to Christianity, and the evidence of reviews also would suggest that 1940 was the time of decisive change. Auden's return to Christianity was, however, a gradual process, and it would be misleading to try to fix it more precisely in time. Furthermore, the poem cannot be used as conclusive evidence as to the poet's beliefs; as Auden puts it, the poet "does not have to believe what he says, only entertain it as a possibility: e.g., if he writes a poem about the Crucifixion, there is no means of knowing from the poem whether he believes in it as a Christian must believe or is using it as a convenient myth for organizing the emotions his poem expresses, for in poetry dogma and myth are identical."[3] The poem quoted as epigraph to this section (published first in 1939) and numerous others, are examples of this entertaining of Christianity as a possibility without believing it fully. On the other hand, there are no poems written after 1940 in which the possibility that Christianity is *not* true is entertained.

So much nonsense has been written about Auden's "conversion," both by hostile critics who wish to unmask his ideology or reveal his psychological peculiarities and by the pious who wish to use him as an edifying example, that it seems advisable to present at some length Auden's own account of the matter. The book in which Auden's untitled essay appeared, *Modern Canterbury Pilgrims* (ed. James A. Pike, N.Y. 1956), is out of print, and Auden's essay is unfortunately omitted from the paperback reprint. Auden begins by describing the devout Anglo-Catholic atmosphere of his home, which had the advantage that his first religious memories were of "exciting magical rites"—at six he was a boat-boy—rather than of listening to sermons. On the other hand, he was accustomed to doctrinal and liturgical controversy from his earliest years, and thus grew up with a uniquely Anglican conception of the Church as "a community in which wide divergences of doctrine and rite can and do exist without leading necessarily to schism or excommunication." Soon after his confirmation, at thirteen, he gradually lost interest and therefore belief. One reason was the seeming irrelevance of the language and imagery of Christianity. "I sometimes wonder, for example, what would have happened if, when I was at school or the university, a godparent or friend had given me the works of Kierkegaard or Rudolf Kassner,[4] both of whom were, later in my life, destined to play a great part. The only theological writer I knew of at that time whom I found readable and disturbing to my complacency was Pascal." On the other hand, there were two continuing religious influences during these years: first, "I was lucky enough to be born in a period when every educated person was expected to know the Bible thoroughly and no undergraduate could take a degree without passing a Divinity examination"; second, he sang in his school choirs both as a pupil and, later, as a master. Hence, "however bored I might be at the very thought of God, I enjoyed services in His worship very much. . . ."

Of his beliefs from 1927 to 1937, Auden says:

> The various "kerygmas," of Blake, of Lawrence, of Freud, of Marx, to which, along with most middle-class intellectuals of my generation, I paid attention between twenty and thirty, had one thing in common. They were all Christian heresies; that is to say, one cannot imagine their coming into existence except in a civilization which claimed to be based, religiously, on the belief that the Word was made flesh and dwelt among us, and that, in consequence, matter, the natural order, is real and redeemable, not a shadowy appearance or the cause of evil, and historical time is real and significant, not meaningless or an endless series of cycles.
>
> They arose, as I suspect most heresies do, as a doctrinal protest against what one might call a heresy of behavior exhibited by the orthodox of their day. By a heretic in behavior, I mean not simply someone whose conduct or thinking on secular matters is inconsistent with his faith, but someone who is quite honestly unaware that there is any inconsistency and defends his actions as a Christian. . . .
>
> The doctrinal heretic perceives, usually more or less correctly, what doctrine is implied by the particular actions of which he more or less justly disapproves, and in protest propounds a doctrine equally one-sided in the opposite direction.
>
> My own experience convinces me of the folly of trying to protect people from heresy by censorship or repression. In all the figures I have mentioned, I have come to realize that what is true in what they say is implicit in the Christian doctrine of the nature of man, and that what is not Christian is not true; but each of them brought to some particular aspect of life that intensity of attention that is characteristic of one-sided geniuses (needless to say, they all contradicted each other), and such comprehension of Christian wisdom as I have, little though it be, would be very much less without them.

He goes on to describe the historical reasons for general loss of faith in liberal humanism:

> We assumed that there was only one outlook on life conceivable among civilized people, the liberal humanism in which all of us had been brought up, whether we came from Christian or agnostic homes (English liberalism had never been anti-clerical like its Continental brother).
>
> To this the theological question seemed irrelevant since such values as freedom of the person, equal justice for all, respect for the rights of others, etc., were self-evident truths. However, the liberal humanism of the past had failed to produce the universal peace and prosperity it promised, failed even to prevent a World War. What had it overlooked? The subconscious, said Freud; the means of production, said Marx. Liberalism was not to be superseded; it was to be made effective instead of self-defeating.
>
> Then the Nazis came to power in Germany. The Communists had said that one must hate and destroy some of one's neighbors now in order to create a world in which nobody would be able to help loving his neighbors tomorrow. They had attacked Christianity and all religions on the ground that, so long as people are taught to love a non-existent God, they will ignore the material obstacles to human brotherhood. The novelty and shock of the Nazis was that they made no pretense of believing in justice and liberty for all, and attacked Christianity on the grounds that to love one's neighbor as oneself was a command fit only for effeminate weaklings, not for the "healthy blood of the master race." Moreover, this utter denial of everything liberalism had ever stood for was arousing wild enthusiasm, not in some remote barbaric land outside the pale, but in one of the most highly educated countries in Europe, a country one knew well and where one had many friends. Confronted by such a phenomenon, it was impossible any longer to believe that the values of liberal humanism were self-evident. Unless one was prepared to take a relativist view that all values are

a matter of personal taste, one could hardly avoid asking the question: "If, as I am convinced, the Nazis are wrong and we are right, what is it that validates our values and invalidates theirs?"

Auden then proceeds to describe three personal experiences of 1937-40:

With this and similar questions whispering at the back of my mind, I visited Spain during the Civil War. On arriving in Barcelona, I found as I walked through the city that all the churches were closed and there was not a priest to be seen. To my astonishment, this discovery left me profoundly shocked and disturbed. The feeling was far too intense to be the result of a mere liberal dislike of intolerance, the notion that it is wrong to stop people from doing what they like, even if it is something silly like going to church. I could not escape acknowledging that, however I had consciously ignored and rejected the Church for sixteen years, the existence of churches and what went on in them had all the time been very important to me. If that was the case, what then?

Shortly afterwards, in a publisher's office, I met an Anglican layman, and for the first time in my life felt myself in the presence of personal sanctity. I had met many good people before who made me feel ashamed of my own shortcomings, but in the presence of this man— we never discussed anything but literary business—I did not feel ashamed. I felt transformed into a person who was incapable of doing or thinking anything base or unloving. (I later discovered that he had had a similar effect on many other people.)

So, presently, I started to read some theological works, Kierkegaard in particular, and began going, in a tentative and experimental sort of way, to church. And then, providentially—for the occupational disease of poets is frivolity—I was forced to know in person what it is like to feel oneself the prey of demonic powers, in both the Greek and the Christian sense, stripped of self-control and self-respect, behaving like a ham actor in a Strindberg play.

The "Anglican layman" was Charles Williams, as we know from Auden's introduction to the 1956 reprint of his *The Descent of the Dove,* which had a great influence on "New Year Letter" especially and which, since its appearance in 1939, has meant much to Auden.[5] Of Kierkegaard, whose influence is apparent in Auden's work far more often than that of any other writer, we shall have much to say. In the essay under discussion Auden makes two observations about him: first, that he "has the talent, invaluable in a preacher to the Greeks, of making Christianity sound bohemian," and second, that his great and characteristically Protestant limitation is that he is not interested in the body: "A planetary visitor might read through the whole of his voluminous works without discovering that human beings are not ghosts but have bodies of flesh and blood."

> As a spirit, a conscious person endowed with free will, every man has, through faith and grace, a unique "existential" relation to God, and few since St. Augustine have described this relation more profoundly than Kierkegaard. But every man has a second relation to God which is neither unique nor existential: as a creature composed of matter, as a biological organism, every man, in common with everything else in the universe, is related by necessity to the God who created that universe and saw that it was good, for the laws of nature to which, whether he likes it or not, he must conform are of divine origin.

Auden concludes his essay by observing that he wishes to say nothing about the question of why he should have "returned to Canterbury instead of proceeding to Rome," because the "scandal of Christian disunity is too serious."

Auden has always stressed the unifying factors among all Christians rather than the divisive ones; he is ecumenical, like Charles Williams and Reinhold Niebuhr. An Anglo-Catholic whose attitude is basically existentialist, he interprets the existential tradition with maximum catholicity:

> As a Christian, Kierkegaard belongs to the tradition of religious thinking ... represented by Augustine, Pascal, Newman, and Karl Barth, as distinct both from the Thomist tradition of official Catholicism and from the liberal Protestantism of men like Schleiermacher. As a secular dialectician, he is one of the great exponents of an approach, equally hostile to Cartesian mechanism and Hegelian idealism, to which the Germans have given the name Existential—though it is confined neither to Germans like Nietzsche, Jaspers, Scheler, Heidegger, but may be found, for instance, in Bergson and William James, nor to professional philosophers, for the same approach is typical of what is most valuable in Marx and Freud.[6]

The fundamental approach common to these apparently disparate modes of thought Auden thus describes:

> In contrast to those philosophers who begin by considering the *objects* of human knowledge, essences and relations, the existential philosopher begins with man's immediate experience as a *subject*, i.e., as a being in *need*, an *interested* being whose existence is at stake.

Cognition, for these thinkers, is always a historical act, accompanied by hope and fear; not something performed by a timeless, disinterested "I." Existentialism, says Auden, is not a surrender to relativism, but an attempt to begin the search for a common truth by being honest about this subjectivity. The relation of the theological, psychological, and political realms for the Christian existentialist he states thus:

> From this viewpoint, the basic human problem is man's anxiety in time; e.g., his present anxiety over himself in relation to his past and his parents (Freud), his present anxiety over himself in relation to his future and his neighbors (Marx), his present anxiety over himself in relation to eternity and God (Kierkegaard).

The last quotation is of special interest both as illuminating Auden's concept of the age of anxiety and as showing how this position transcends, without denying, the earlier Freudian and Marxist analyses. The anxiety viewed by Freud (or Homer Lane) as a disease, a maladjustment, is now seen as purposive, a concomitant of the choice confronting man in his dreadful freedom.

Auden adopted the existential position with his characteristic "touch of extravagance"; very early in 1941 we find him, reviewing a book by Reinhold Niebuhr, not sure that Niebuhr is "sufficiently ashamed," missing in him Kierkegaard's sense "of always being out alone over seventy thousand fathoms"; and he asks, "Does he believe that the contemplative life is the highest and most exhausting of vocations, that the church is saved by the saints, or doesn't he?" [7] Niebuhr (to whom Auden dedicated *Nones* in 1951), the leading representative in the United States of Protestant neo-orthodoxy and also vigorously liberal politically, is the theologian whose impact upon Auden would seem to be second only to Kierkegaard's. In the early 1940s the effect of Kafka, "the artist who comes nearest to bearing the same kind of relation to our age that Dante, Shakespeare and Goethe bore to theirs," [8] is also frequently apparent. In these years Auden deals constantly in Kierkegaardian paradoxes, and justifies the "absurdity" (according to human standards) of the divine; with the shocking patience of Kafka, he juxtaposes the incomprehensible divine and the reasonable human; he points out the theological heresies which have produced our political and social anarchy with the evangelical zeal and large historical generalizations of Niebuhr. These are the years when Auden was most vulnerable, for he conducted much of his religious education and spiritual exploration in public—even to the extent of writing poems containing passages closely parallel to his reviews or essays—and for this he has been sufficiently criticized.[9]

With the passage of time Auden has exhibited an increasing

awareness of the limitations of the existentialist approach. In 1950 he remarked that the typical modern heresy is "a Barthian exaggeration of God's transcendence which all too easily becomes an excuse for complacency about one's own sins and about the misfortunes of others," and commented that to the Christian "the existential is only one, admittedly very important, aspect of his situation." [10] We have seen his observations at the end of his *Modern Canterbury Pilgrims* essay on Kierkegaard's lack of interest in the body; along this same line he said in 1956:

> Like all polemical movements, existentialism is one-sided. In their laudable protest against systematic philosophers, like Hegel or Marx, who would reduce all historical existence to nature, the existentialists have invented an equally imaginary anthropology, from which all elements, like man's physical nature, or his reason, about which general statements can be made, are excluded.[11]

He continues, "the existentialist descriptions of choice, like Pascal's wager or Kierkegaard's leap, are interesting as dramatic literature, but are they true?" Remarking that in his own experience he has been unaware at the time of the importance of his decisive choices, he suggests: "In a reflective and anxious age, it is surely better, pedagogically, to minimise rather than to exaggerate the risks involved in a choice. . . ."

The influence of Kierkegaard has, however, been fundamental and pervasive in Auden's thought since 1940. His fullest discussion occurs in the long introduction to the volume of selections from Kierkegaard [12] that he edited in 1952; this whole volume is of great interest, not only intrinsically as a penetrating and well-balanced presentation of Kierkegaard, but as a useful background for studying Auden's later poetry. Auden draws a parallel between Kierkegaard and Cardinal Newman as the great preachers to a secularized society which was still officially Christian. Kierkegaard's polemic, he says, moves simultaneously in two directions: outwardly against the bourgeois Protestantism of the Denmark of his time, and inwardly against his own suffering.

> To the former he says, "You imagine that you are all Christians and contented because you have forgotten that each of you is an existing individual. When you remember that, you will be forced to realize that you are pagans and in despair." To himself he says, "As long as your suffering makes you defiant or despairing, as long as you identify your suffering with yourself as an existing individual, and are defiantly or despairingly the exception, you are not a Christian."   (p. 5)

Auden then describes Kierkegaard's three categories of the aesthetic, the ethical, and the religious, putting them in historical terms for the sake of clarity. The Greek gods exemplify the aesthetic religion, which glorifies passion and power; the gods are interested only in a few exceptional individuals, who are heroes, glorious but not responsible for their successes or failures. "The aesthetic either/or is not good or bad but strong or weak, fortunate or unfortunate."

> The facts on which the aesthetic religion is shattered and despairs, producing in its death agony Tragic Drama, are two: man's knowledge of good and evil, and his certainty that death comes to all men, i.e., that ultimately there is no either/or of strength or weakness, but even for the exceptional individual the doom of absolute weakness.
>   (p. 10)

The ethical religion is exemplified by the god of Greek philosophy. This is the worship of the universal, the First Cause which is self-sufficient. Its "either/or" is knowledge or ignorance of the eternal and universal truths of reason which cannot be known without being obeyed. Neither in this nor in the aesthetic category is time meaningful or temptation or choice real. Its premise, "Sin is ignorance; to know the good is to will it," cannot deal with the fact that the will to know must precede knowledge, nor that men do not in practice automatically will the good as soon as they know it. Finally, revealed religion (as in Judaism and Christianity) has a God Who is creator, but who is not present as an object of consciousness or knowable as an object. Since He is creator, there is no longer a question of establishing a relationship; the existence of the creature presupposes a relation, and the only question is whether it is the right one:

> ... if I try to banish it permanently from consciousness, I shall not get rid of it, but experience it negatively as guilt and despair. The wrath of God is not a description of God in a certain state of feeling, but of the way in which I experience God if I distort or deny my relation to him. The commands of God are neither the aesthetic fiat, "Do what you must" nor the ethical instruction, "These are the things which you may or must not do," but the call of duty, "Choose to do what at this moment in this context I am telling you to do."   (p. 16)

These three categories have been the basis of a great deal of Auden's thinking in the past two decades. (This is obvious in his various classifications of quests and heroes, and somewhat less so in his interpretations of tragedy and comedy.) [13] Finally, Auden quotes Newman on the absurdity of trying to argue non-believers into belief, for the "act of faith remains an act of choice which no one can do for another."

> Pascal's "wager" and Kierkegaard's "leap" are neither of them quite adequate descriptions, for the one suggests prudent calculation and the other perverse arbitrariness. Both, however, have some value: the first calls men's attention to the fact that in all other spheres of life they are constantly acting on faith and quite willingly, so that they have no right to expect religion to be an exception; the second reminds them that they cannot live without faith in something, and that when the faith which they have breaks down, when the ground crumbles under their feet, they *have to* leap even into uncertainty if they are to avoid certain destruction.   (pp. 17-18)

And he sums up Kierkegaard's notion of preaching to the non-believer:

> To show the non-believer that he is in despair because he cannot believe in *his* gods and then show him that Christ cannot be a man-made God because in every respect he is offensive to the natural man is for Kierkegaard the only true kind of Christian apologetics.   (p. 20)

It would be possible, and interesting, to quote at length from Auden's reviews in this period (1941-44) of spiritual clarification, but I shall confine myself to a brief indication of the political implications of his beliefs. "A Note on Order" (*The Nation*, Feb. 1, 1941) is an interesting combination of the "failure of metaphysics" analysis (based mainly on Collingwood) that we have seen earlier, with Trinitarian religious terminology (probably from Niebuhr). Here Auden argues that civilization is based upon two presuppositions: (1) that throughout the universe there is one set of laws according to which all events and movements happen; (2) that there are many different realms or societies, and that the peculiar laws of these several realms are modifications of the universal laws. He proceeds to identify the two corresponding heresies: (1) Dualism, "dividing the substance"—the denial of any relation between the universal and the particular. This produces either an other-worldliness which regards all attempts to establish a social order as vain, or a secularism which regards progress as inevitable; (2) Monism, "confounding the Persons"—the assumption that the laws peculiar to one of the realms are universal laws from which all the others derive. This produces either tyranny or violent revolution, and is manifest in the Marxist theory of history and in Freudian psychology. Since the Renaissance, a third heresy, really a modification of dualism, has arisen—an empiricism denying the necessity of metaphysics. This view, now dominant, is based on the scientific method of isolating the experimental field from the rest of nature; it assumes, by analogy, that this isolation is characteristic of

nature. Therefore it leads to an ignoring of the relations between different realms, and produces the atomistic view of
society typical of liberal capitalistic democracy. This "liberal"
view, being relativistic, provides no basis for stability except
force; and so has no ideological defense against fascism. True
civilization, Auden argues, must be based upon absolute and
religious sanctions, and he calls for recognition of the importance of metaphysics and theology.

Auden advocated no panacea, however, and had little faith
in programs; he was fond of expressing his attitude in the words
of Sydney Smith, "Trust in God and take short views." [14]
From the standpoint of the conditional, every sacrifice is in
vain, "for, to it, 'a live dog is always better than a dead lion' ";
we must become conscious of true necessity, which is internal
and absolute—so absolute that we obey it without worrying
about the future. [15] The Christian knows no distinction between
the personal and the political; all his relationships are both.
Neither an anarchist nor a non-political idiot, he acts in the
present, regarding neither past nor future; in theological language, he redeems the time. [16] Man cannot live without a sense
of the Unconditional; if he does not fear God, his unconscious
sees to it that he has something else, airplanes or secret police,
to fear. [17] When anxiety is not kept in its proper theological
place, it returns in realms—the moral and aesthetic—where it
should not be. Christian faith alone can make sense of man's
private and social experience. Following Niebuhr and Cochrane,
Auden observes that classical thought is unable to give meaning
to individuality and freedom—Platonic dualism and Stoic apathy
embodying the two heresies mentioned above—and that a
monolithic monotheism "is always a doctrine of God as either
manic-depressive Power or schizophrenic Truth." The Christian God of love is not self-sufficient; hence matter is not evil,
and there is no division into divine reason and mortal body.
Man is thus explained as image of God and as a fallen creature.
Everything man does is an act of religious worship: "Man always acts either self-loving, just for the hell of it, or God-

loving, just for the heaven of it; his reasons, his appetites, are secondary motivations." [18] A society is a group associated on the basis of the things the individuals in it love. For the Christian there is no one perfect form of society; the best is that in which at any historical moment love for one's neighbor can best express itself.

COLLECTED POETRY 1945

New Poems. The new poems, written mostly during the period 1940-44 and published in *Collected Poetry*, show the effect of the change in perspective very plainly. The attitude of foreboding, of impending doom, formerly based upon the Marxist concept of the death of a social order is now based upon the religious concept of man's generalized responsibility and insecurity when confronted by God and death. The crisis, the border situation, which men do not understand though they feel its effects, has been transposed from the political to the religious realm. Instead of the political choice, between issues the bourgeois does not understand, Auden now presents the existentialist choice, of which most men are unaware, and involving issues which no man can understand completely. Thus the religious point of view transcends, without denying, the earlier analyses. Auden's war images in the early verse were always too generalized and nebulous to fit Marxist terms, and the ultimate reference was always psychological and internal; the enemy, as Auden sees it, is always self-created, the result of our spiritual failures. As we have seen, Auden similarly interprets the real wars of our time in psychological terms, as resulting from our spiritual deficiencies: these "Nightmares that are intentional and real" arise from our sense of guilt; the unconscious has its revenge. (Cf. "Where do They come from? . . .," discussed above, p. 144, and "In War Time," with its bitter punning image of chaos in which Fortune rides off on her wheel as a bicycle: "Abruptly mounting her ramshackle wheel, / Fortune has pedalled furiously away; / The sobbing mess is on our hands today.") Thus the partly political reference of the early verse develops toward a more completely psychological reference. The bourgeois intellectual, unable to escape his class and cross the sociological frontier, or to escape his time and cross the chronological frontier, becomes Everyman, prevented by caution, by timid respectability, from confronting a choice no longer political or biological, but the ultimate religious choice between Eros and Agape. The satirical theme is unawareness, but the target has shifted from bourgeois respectability to the caution, timidity, and complacency which prevent men from realizing their anguished freedom and responsibility. "A Healthy Spot," for example, asks of the nice, well-intentioned, responsible people who "attend all the lectures on Post-War Problems, / For they do mind, they honestly want to help"; yet

> As they notice the earth in their morning papers,
> What sense do they make of its folly and horror
> Who have never, one is convinced, felt a sudden
> Desire to torture the cat or do a strip-tease
> In a public place? Have they ever, one wonders,
> Wanted so much to see a unicorn, even
> A dead one? Probably. But they won't say so,
> Ignoring by tacit consent our hunger
> For eternal life, that caged rebuked question . . .

The satiric norm in these poems is the Christian existentialist position already described: man's terrifying freedom, the necessity of choice, of redeeming the time in the present, of trusting in God and taking short views. A good example is "Leap Before You Look": "A solitude ten thousand fathoms deep / Sustains the bed on which we lie, my dear; / Although I love you, you will have to leap; / Our dream of safety has to disappear." "Under Which Lyre," though slightly later than the other poems we are considering (written 1946 and collected in

Nones), is the fullest version of this satirical attack on collectivism, uniformitarianism, and conformity. The poem contrasts the priggish, pompous, competent followers of Apollo who manage the world (described also in the "The Managers," 1948) and the erratic, unruly, individualistic followers of Hermes (of whom the poet is one). To strengthen the morale of his side Auden formulates a Hermetic Decalogue, beginning, "Thou shalt not do as the dean pleases" and ending:

> Thou shalt not be on friendly terms
> With guys in advertising firms,
>   Nor speak with such
> As read the Bible for its prose,
> Nor, above all, make love to those
>   Who wash too much.
>
> Thou shalt not live within thy means
> Nor on plain water and raw greens.
>   If thou must choose
> Between the chances, choose the odd;
> Read *The New Yorker*, trust in God;
>   And take short views.

Though these poems are not explicitly religious, their religious import is clear enough: the reasonable, respectable, responsible Managers exhibit a complacent secularism which prevents them and their subjects from being aware of religious issues; they believe in salvation through politics. The Hermetics, on the other hand, are the unpredictable, recalcitrant individuals for whom secularism can never satisfactorily account nor provide. "If he would leave the self alone, / Apollo's welcome to the throne," but the Apollonians aim at complete control of even education and art (through official art, or magic); the poet therefore advises the individual to remain nonconformist, to refuse to bow down before the secular political god and, trusting in God and aware of the true ultimate issues, to take short views.

Art versus Magic. In this period Auden was much concerned, under the pressures of the war, to resist any suggestion of a propaganda function for poetry, or official art:

> Art, as the late Professor R. G. Collingwood pointed out, is not Magic, i.e., a means by which the artist communicates or arouses his feelings in others, but a mirror in which they may become conscious of what their own feelings really are: its proper effect, in fact, is disenchanting. . . . By significant details it shows us that our present state is neither as virtuous nor as secure as we thought, and by the lucid pattern into which it unifies these details, its assertion that order is *possible*, it faces us with the command to make it *actual*. In so far as he is an artist, no one, not even Kipling, is intentionally a magician. On the other hand, no artist, not even Eliot, can prevent his work being used as magic, for that is what all of us, highbrow and lowbrow alike, secretly want Art to be.[19]

In his essay on "Henry James and the Artist in America" he notes that the subtlest temptation, the desire to do good by art, is powerful in our age of disintegration, in which the authorities turn to the artist and promise rewards "if he will forsake the artistic life and become an official magician, who uses his talents to arouse in the inert masses the passions which the authorities consider socially desirable and necessary." [20] But magic is not art, "for magic is a means of ruling children and all who cannot rule themselves, one kind of fraud and force, while art, like all kinds of truth, is one of the pleasures of free men." This is not to say that art is sacred; along with most human activities, it is in the ultimate and profound sense frivolous, for only one thing is serious: loving one's neighbor as one's self. As Auden puts it elsewhere, the nurse (government) begs the poet to make the patient fall in love with her; the patient wants to be made to feel happy and well; but the poet must refuse both, and "go on humming quietly to himself." [21] In "Music is International" (1947) he makes the same distinction, speaking of the art of music:

> For these halcyon structures are useful
> As structures go—though not to be confused
> With anything really important
> Like feeding strays or looking pleased when caught
> By a bore or a hideola;
> (*Nones*, p. 65)

And in his introduction to Cavafy's poems (1962) he defines the kind of truth a poem contains:

> One duty of a poem, among others, is to bear witness to the truth. A moral witness is one who gives true testimony to the best of his ability in order that the court (or the reader) shall be in a better position to judge the case justly; an immoral witness is one who tells half-truths or downright lies; but it is not a witness's business to pass verdict.   (p. ix)

Eros, Agape, Logos. Auden's distinctively Christian concepts of Eros, Agape, and Logos were evidently influenced by two books he reviewed during this period, Denis de Rougemont's *Love in the Western World* and Charles N. Cochrane's *Christianity and Classical Culture.* Reviewing De Rougemont (*The Nation*, June 1941), he states the book's thesis that, historically and metaphysically, the concept of romantic love is based upon Manicheism, holding matter and time to be evil, denying the flesh and the present, and seeking its perfection in death, when matter and time are transcended and the soul merges into the Logos. The great exemplar is Wagner's *Tristan.* This myth creates its negative mirror image; in Mozart's *Don Giovanni*, the flesh and the present are asserted, the spirit and the future denied; time is something to be aggressively destroyed. Opposed to both isotopes of Eros is the Christian concept of Agape; based on the Incarnation, it denies neither flesh nor spirit, and permits us to love human beings as individuals: to love God is to obey God, Who commanded us to love one another. De Rougemont is wrong, Auden says, in defining Eros as of sexual origin; Eros rather is the basic will to self-actualization without which no creature can exist (we have seen this concept in Auden's early poetry); Agape is Eros mutated by Grace, a conversion, not an addition; its symbol is not sex but eating, an act testifying to the dependence of all creatures on each other. The myth of romantic love is a false solution to the problem of enabling Eros to choose truly, an attempt to eliminate the possibility of wrong decisions through making one myth discharge the functions of religious faith, tradition, and other beliefs that once governed the conduct of life.

> It is only in the past hundred years that people have seriously tried to marry their mater-imagos or their lame shadows, and it is only quite recently that, dismayed at the failure of this attempt, they have denied the significance of personal relations altogether and returned to a collective and political myth of Eros.

Reviewing Cochrane's book in *The New Republic*, Sept. 1944, Auden remarks that he has read it many times since its appearance in 1940, "and my conviction of its importance to the understanding not only of the epoch with which it is concerned, but also of our own, has increased with each rereading." Summarizing Cochrane, Auden remarks upon the inability of classical thought to give positive value to freedom, to avoid the dualism of God and the world, mind and matter, time and eternity. Identifying the divine with the necessary or the legal, classical idealism cannot oppose tyranny on principle, cannot give meaning to individuality. As Augustine showed, only Christianity can make sense of both man's private and his social experience, the central doctrine being that of the Trinity, formulation of the belief that God is love—not Eros, the desire to possess something one lacks, but Agape, a reciprocal relation, dynamic free expression. If men love themselves, their society is an earthly city in which order is maintained by force; if they love God and their neighbors as themselves, a heavenly city in which order appears the natural consequence of freedom (i.e., through Agape, Eros and Logos are one). Like

Niebuhr and other neo-orthodox theologians, Cochrane thus shows the deficiencies of secular ethical and political thought and the relevance of Christian dogma to the problems; his influence on Auden is apparent not only in the present context but most of all in the symbol of the City, to be discussed presently.

After Auden's commitment to Christianity, the symbols of Eros, Agape, and Logos gain new distinctness and significance. The epilogue to *The Double Man* (called "Autumn 1940" in *Collected Poetry*) is the first clear expression. The ego, returning to the world of time after sleep, finds the present age particularly discouraging; the poet asks,

> Will the inflamed ego attempt as before
> To migrate again to her family place,
>   To the hanging gardens of Eros
>   And the moons of his magical summer?

The political myth of Eros is seductive; the prospects of anything else, any change of heart, are dim: "few have seen Jesus and so many / Judas the abyss." We do not understand the Logos: "who can / Tell what logic must and must not leave to fate, / Or what laws we are permitted to obey?" Predatory glaciers threaten; there seems little hope; we can only do "formal contrition / For whatever is going to happen." Auden closes with a deeply-felt prayer in praise of the Logos, part of which sounds so much like Eliot that it suggests that Eliot may have had some spiritual influence at this time.[22] "Christmas 1940" describes similarly the temptation to despair produced by our present predicament. The poet sketches the course of life on this planet leading to the right point of time (the "Kairos" of other poems) when "Flesh grew weaker, stronger grew the Word, / Until on earth the Great Exchange occurred." From that center of history, we have reversed the old equations, are returning to the "universe of pure extension"; now we are "reduced to our true nakedness" and confronted by an inescapable choice: "Either we serve the Unconditional /

Or some Hitlerian monster will supply / An iron convention to do evil by." Only the vision of "that holy centre," the Incarnation, can reconcile our rival errors, show how "The rich need not confound the Persons, nor / The Substance be divided by the poor." "It is the vision that objectifies," and only Christianity can resolve our difficulties; "only Love has weight" [23] in this "modern void"; but though only Agape can save us, it is an end, not a means.

"Kairos and Logos" (first published 1941) is a meditation on the significance of the incarnation. Logos here connotes the eternal, the timeless world of objective law and logic (as well as, of course, the Word); Kairos connotes the right point of time, the particular moment, the subjective world of the individual. Dreading death, obsessed by time, the Roman empire is dominated by "vast self-love"; Christ is "predestined love" which fell "like a daring meteor into time," bringing "certainty of love." Hence Christians do not condemn the world or hate time, but pray, in a favorite phrase of Auden's, "O Thou who lovest, set its love in order." [24] "In Sickness and in Health" is a good example of Auden's mature use of these symbols. Describing the dearth and perversion of love in our time, the poem shows how Eros produces its two isotopes, Tristan and Don Juan; "Nature by nature in unnature ends." Through the romantic myth we arrive at the political myth of Eros, and at war:

> The lovers of themselves collect,
> And Eros is politically adored:
> New Machiavellis flying through the air
> Express a metaphysical despair,
> Murder their last voluptuous sensation,
> All passion in one passionate negation.

Our loves are selfish, "we are always in the wrong [25] / Handling so clumsily our stupid lives"; yet Divine Love, though it appears to us as the Absurd, exists and works through us. We must "pray / That Love, to Whom necessity is play, / Do

what we must yet cannot do alone." The poet prays that
Agape, manifested in the Logos, will enable us, through Grace,
to avoid the perversions of love, preserve us "from presump-
tion and delay," and, paradoxically, "hold us to the voluntary
way."

For the Time Being, to be discussed fully in the next section,
employs the three symbols extensively. Eros, denying Agape,
caused the Fall: Eve, "in love with her own will, / Denied
the will of Love and fell," and the conflict between Eros and
Agape is put in historical terms: "the course of History is predictable in the degree to which all men love themselves, and
spontaneous in the degree to which each man loves God and
through Him his neighbour." Only the Incarnation explains
the relations of Time and Eternity, Necessity ("our freedom
to be tempted"), and Freedom ("our necessity to have faith");
only the Agape thus embodied unites Eros and Logos. The
metaphysical significance of the Incarnation as explained in
the doctrine of the Trinity is described by Simeon:

> Because in Him the Word is united to the Flesh without
> loss of perfection, Reason is redeemed from incestuous
> fixation on her own Logic, for the One and the Many are
> simultaneously revealed as real. So that we may no longer,
> with the Barbarians, deny the Unity, asserting that there
> are as many gods as there are creatures, nor, with the
> philosophers, deny the Multiplicity, asserting that God is
> One who has no need of friends and is indifferent to a
> World of Time and Quantity and Horror which He did
> not create, nor, with Israel, may we limit the co-inherence
> of the One and the Many to a special case . . .

The title indicates a central theme of the poetry from 1940 on:
to live in the present, "the Time Being to redeem / From insignificance," to refrain from seeking escape in the past or future
or some great suffering, and instead to try to manifest Agape
in the everyday world, is the most difficult task: "The Time
Being is, in a sense, the most trying time of all."

Although *Nones* (1951, containing poems written 1947-50) belongs properly to the next section, we may consider here the occurrence in it of these symbolic patterns. "The Love Feast" describes realistically the modern secular equivalent of the early Christian love feast (Agape):

> In an upper room at midnight
> See us gathered on behalf
> Of love according to the gospel
> Of the radio-phonograph.

The kinds of love exhibited at the party are contrasted throughout with Agape, as the "Love that rules the sun and stars / Permits what He forbids." The speaker is not, however, superior to the others; though he knows it is wrong, he has his erotic interest, and he concludes by echoing St. Augustine: "I am sorry I'm not sorry ... / Make me chaste, Lord, but not yet." This is, and is intended to be, a shocking poem, and some people have found it offensive; the question is not one of the propriety of juxtaposing the sacred and profane nor of the protagonist's candor, but rather of the tone: is he overly complacent about being a sinner?

The City. The dominant symbol in the volume is the City. Signifying civilization, man's social achievement, the City has always been a feature of Auden's moralized landscape, but it is given now a special connotation closely related to the symbols just discussed. The contrast of Eros and Agape and the meditations on the Logos lead naturally to a contrast of the earthly and heavenly cities (*civitas terrena* and *civitas Dei*), secular and Christian societies. Though the city symbol is universalized, the central image is usually that of ancient Rome fused with the present, for the state of our own civilization constitutes an inevitable parallel with that of collapsing Rome: both are naturalistic cultures rejecting, in the name of reason, the Absurd of Christianity, which alone can give meaning to history as well as to individual life. "The Fall of Rome" portrays our present bankrupt secularism in terms of that of decadent Rome. The reindeer at the end form an effective but elusive symbol:

> Altogether elsewhere, vast
> Herds of reindeer move across
> Miles and miles of golden moss
> Silently and very fast.

They suggest the "wholly other" realm of religion which man has left out of account, and also the purity of uncorrupted nature in contrast to what man has made of his world. "Under Sirius" presents Fortunatus in Rome in the dog-days of history, uncertain what to wish for. He hopes for a revelation, but his wish is ambivalent; perhaps he is part of the rotten fruit that must be shaken, not one of the reborn, but one of those "who refused their chance" and to whom the dull dog-days of secularism will seem in retrospect "golden with self-praise." He is, in short, the disillusioned naturalist, longing for yet fearing the supernatural; an Everyman reluctant to confront ultimate issues.

The notion of a secular hero who will save the city and perfect humanity has always seemed funny to Auden, as in Ode IV of *The Orators*, "Danse Macabre," "Stop all the clocks...," "Epitaph on a Tyrant." His versions of this theme —as indeed the whole image of the city—in *Nones* are obviously indebted to Cochrane's analysis of the philosophical defects of classical idealism which lead it always to impose order by coercion and to end in tyranny:

> The history of Graeco-Roman Christianity resolves itself largely into a criticism of that undertaking [Augustus's] and of the ideas upon which it rested; viz. that it was possible to attain a goal of permanent security, peace and freedom through political action, especially through submission to the 'virtue and fortune' of a political leader. This notion the Christians denounced with uniform vigour and consistency.
>
> (*Christianity and Classical Culture*, pp. v-vi)

"The Managers" contrasts our present secular saviors with those of the "bad old days": ours are managers, overworked, depersonalized bureaucrats, without glamor, heroics, or obvious pleasures—"Honours / Are not so physical or jolly now." But, though they think themselves altruists, dedicated to service, they are motivated by Eros—"The fact of belonging / To the very select indeed"—and deserve no pity: "No; no one is really sorry for their / Heavy gait and careworn / Look, nor would they thank you if you said you were."

"Memorial for the City" is Auden's most elaborate use of this symbol. The first section contrasts the naturalistic and Christian attitudes toward history and time. The world as it appears to animals or cameras is the naturalistic world of the Greeks in which time is the enemy and human events are without significance; only Nature "is seriously there" because she endures. But human beings, even "now, in this night / Among the ruins of the Post-Vergilian City / Where our past is a chaos of graves and the barbed-wire stretches ahead / Into our future till it is lost to sight," know, because of the Christian Revelation, that the "crime of life is not time," that our actions have significance, that we are not to pity ourselves nor to despair. The second section describes man's attempts to build a City. The Middle Ages achieved the Sane City, but it became corrupt; Luther denounced it as the Sinful City, pointed out a "grinning gap / No rite could cross" (i.e., between the human and the Divine) and the City became insecure and divided. In the Renaissance "poets acclaimed the raging herod of the will"; while art triumphed, glorifying man, the City was sundered by reason and treason. Later, reason and science (based upon the false belief that Nature "had no soul") brought civility and prosperity; the French Revolution aimed at the Rational City, based on natural goodness, seeking the prelapsarian man. In spite of all disasters, the same goal of the Glittering and Conscious City has been pursued ever since. The third section returns to the present: the end result of this secular progress is the "abolished City," in which civilization has broken down completely, leaving the barbed wire and ruins of war. The ultimate cause is that this secular ideal, ignoring religious faith, falsifies human nature, "the flesh we are but never would believe." Yet we must not despair, must hope that the "wire and the ruins are not the end"; "There is Adam, waiting for his City." The last section, "Let Our Weakness speak," personifies human weakness (timidity, gregariousness, stupidity, common sense, realism). This weakness, the despair of logicians and statesmen, is the irreducible core of individuality which protects man while it infuriates the social planners, the Apollonians ("As for Metropolis, that too-great city; her delusions are not mine"). The basis of humility, it is the reason man is no worse than he is, the one ground of hope. (A similar theme is developed in several other poems in the volume, e.g. "In Praise of Limestone," "Cattivo Tempo"–"Outwitting hell / With human obviousness," and "Under Which Lyre.")

Style. To return now to the new poems in *Collected Poetry*, the most striking development in style is the emergence of a kind of theological light verse. "Many Happy Returns," addressed to a boy on his seventh birthday, is a good example. It is written in the same stanza form as "Sharp and silent in the . . ." (1940): eight lines of trochaic trimeter, with the fourth and eighth lines catalectic and rhyming, and one other pair of lines rhyming unpredictably. In both poems, the contrast between the rapid uneven rhythm and the erudite content is effective; but the specific occasion and the clarification of ideas in this later poem make it vastly superior. The opportunity to offer advice to a very young man allows Auden to play lunatic clergyman by making the advice extravagant and shockingly unlike the worldly-wise observations that might be expected, but at the same time most seriously intended. (He is a "doubtful Fish," astrologically, because born under *Pisces.*) His first wish is for a sense of theater, recognition of the necessity of the mask; then of the need of accepting the human condition and resisting the uniquely human temptation to play at being God. Worldly success is not to be wished; nothing fails like success, and suffering is necessary; we must learn to "Love without desiring / All that you are not." And the final advice is against prudence and respectability: "Live beyond your income, / Travel for enjoyment, / Follow your own nose." This theme is very close to that of "Under Which Lyre": the dangers of conformity, of caution, of failing to keep in mind the difference between the values of Christianity and those of this world. Another child-poem is "Mundus et Infans," beginning, "Kicking his mother until she let go of his soul." [26] This describes the infant as tyrant, in amusing terms, and then draws a parallel between the speechless infant and the saint as the only humans who do not lie:

> He because he cannot
> Stop the vivid present to think, they by having got
> Past reflection into
> A passionate obedience in time. We have our Boy-
> Meets-Girl era of mirrors and muddle to work through,
> Without rest, without joy.

He is completely subjective, completely shameless: "Let him praise our Creator with the top of his voice, / Then, and the motions of his bowels. . . ." We ought to "be glad / When he bawls the house down" because he reminds us how we rightly expect each other to "go upstairs or for a walk if we must cry over / Spilt milk" such as our wish that "we had never learned to distinguish / Between hunger and love"—as he has not. There is a kind of mock-heroic effect in addressing the baby in terms of high-flown rhetoric, while at the same time the style remains colloquial. The same kind of mixed style—colloquial, but humorously inflated—is employed in "In Sickness and in Health," already discussed, and in part of the "Song for St. Cecilia's Day."

There are several exercises in complex virtuoso forms: "Kairos and Logos," already discussed, consists of four sestinas; "Canzone" is in five 12-line stanzas using only five end-words, repeated in a prescribed pattern and again in a five-line coda. Both these are, of course, theological, and in a style serious but not ironically elevated, capable of moving easily from the colloquial to the high: "The hot rampageous horses of my will, / Catching the scent of Heaven, whinny: Love / Gives no excuse to evil done for love...." And "Canzone" concludes with praise that "There must be sorrow if there can be love." The longer poems, to be discussed below, contain numerous examples of this virtuoso style and of all the other varieties discussed.

Finally, "At the Grave of Henry James" should be mentioned as a virtuoso exercise in sympathetic parody (like Caliban's speech in *The Sea and the Mirror*) and in humorously inflated style, which at the same time pays genuine tribute to James, finally invoking him as a saint: "Master of nuance and scruple, / Pray for me and for all writers living or dead...."

There are, in all, some 24 pieces in the *Collected Poetry* that had not previously appeared in book form, though more than half of these had been published in periodicals or anthologies. Most of them, of course, date from 1940-44; but one— "For what as easy"—goes back to 1932; Auden had not reprinted it in any collection since it appeared in *New Signatures* that year. In discussing Auden's earlier volumes, we have already considered how these were dealt with in *Collected Poetry*. We may now briefly review that volume as a whole.

The Collection as a Whole. Collected Poetry consists of nine sections. There is first a section of "Poems," arranged in alphabetical order of first lines, each supplied with a title—highly colloquial and often flip. Section II is "Letter to a Wound," from *The Orators*, and III is a section of 38 "Songs and Other Musical Pieces," arranged in alphabetical order of first lines but untitled. (Fifteen of the "Poems" and nine of the "Songs" had not previously been collected and are marked with aster-

isks.) Generally, the reason for segregating these from the
other poems is plain enough. There are, however, some perplexities. Some poems in the section of "Songs"— "The summer quickens all" from *Paid;* "What's in your mind..." from
Poems; "May with its light behaving" from *On This Island*—
do not seem distinctively musical in any obvious way. One is
tempted to conjecture that the distinction might be that Auden
had musical setting in mind in writing the poems in this section;
but this is made unlikely by the fact that he describes the composition of two of them without mentioning any such intention. And there are, in the section of "Poems," at least four
pieces that were actually set by Britten.[27] Clearly, then, neither
the intention nor the fact of musical setting was the criterion;
presumably Auden simply put poems in this section if he felt
they sounded enough like songs. Section IV is "Depravity:
A Sermon," from *The Dog Beneath the Skin.* One suspects that
the reason for sandwiching these two prose pieces (II and IV)
in after the two poetry sections was merely the obvious one
of contrast and relief—after all this verse, a little prose. There
is no discernible thematic relation, nor, when the poetry is
arranged alphabetically, could there possibly be. Section V is
"The Quest," the sonnet sequence from *The Double Man,* and
VI is "New Year Letter," from the same volume. Presumably
"New Year Letter" is put second so that it will separate the
two sonnet sequences, for VII is "In Time of War," from
Journey to a War. Last come the two long poems, "The Sea
and the Mirror" and "For the Time Being."

The arrangement of the shorter poems in alphabetical order
of first lines was an understandable gesture of protest against
those who would focus attention on the changes in Auden's
ideas and so imprison him in his own history. Auden's intention was presumably the reasonable one of presenting his
poems as poems rather than as historical or biographical docu-
ments; it is not necessary to assume, as some hostile critics
have done, that he was disowning the past. For most of the

"Songs and Other Musical Pieces" in Section III, this arrangement is unexceptionable. The trouble arises in the long first
section, which contains a considerable number of occasional
poems and a greater number that are otherwise intimately involved with history. Auden supplies titles consisting of or
including dates to many such poems, and plainly does not
mean to deny this aspect of them; but the arbitrary arrangement deprives the reader of any assistance from context, produces largely incongruous juxtapositions, and makes it a
laborious task to locate the poems of any particular time. Some
of the titles are illuminating, but many are deplorably facetious. The reader is left, then, with the poems as isolated and
discrete entities. If Auden were a relatively "pure" poet, primarily a love-lyricist, say, the arrangement would make little
difference; but he is exceedingly impure, frequently occasional,
full of direct references to historical events and characters and
an interpreter of the spirit of the times. Furthermore, his
poems are less autonomous and self-sufficient than those of
some other contemporary poets; a poem that, considered
alone, is impenetrably obscure will often reveal a meaning in
relation to his other poems of the same time, and awareness
of this context almost always adds significance to the poem.
This arrangement of the first section of *Collected Poetry*, then,
places unnecessary obstacles in the way of the reader who
wants more than the most casual acquaintance with the poetry,
and misrepresents the nature of the poetry. As a pedagogical
device, it is legitimate and useful to present poetry in complete
separation from biography and history (as I. A. Richards did
in his pioneering *Practical Criticism*, 1929); Auden and Garrett arranged their anthology, *The Poet's Tongue*, 1935, anon-
ymously and alphabetically. As a permanent arrangement, at
least for Auden's kind of poetry, it is extremely unsatisfactory.
Since he arranged the *Selected Poetry* of 1958 chronologically,
it appears that Auden has come to the same conclusion; and we
may hope that before too long he will publish a new *Collected*

Poetry in which, as in the collections of Yeats and Eliot, the poems to be preserved will be arranged as in the original volumes, unless strict chronology is preferred.

In *The Making of the Auden Canon* (Minneapolis, 1957) the late Professor J. W. Beach examined in detail Auden's procedures in selecting, arranging, and revising his poems for *Collected Poetry* 1945. The study contains a large amount of useful information about the publication of Auden's verse and the variations in its text, and many astute observations. It suffers, however, from two serious defects, aside from such unavoidable limitations as the fact that because he did not have access to *Poems* 1928 much of his discussion of the early verse is erroneous. In the first place, Beach seems to expect poems to be mystic unities which come into existence by inspiration at one time and have a single definitive meaning for the poet. Hence he is shocked by Auden's occasional radical revisions and use of the same passage in different contexts. Such practices are common, of course; Eliot and Yeats, to say nothing of poets like Pope, can be shown to have done the same kind of thing. In the second place, Beach is unsympathetic to Auden's religious convictions and in general to the ideas and attitudes characteristic of Auden since 1940. His own position is a secular liberal humanism, and therefore he tends to represent Auden's intellectual and spiritual development in the last two decades as a falling away from the truth and perhaps a succumbing to weakness and self-delusion. This is particularly serious because Beach reads the poetry very literally, as if it were primarily a statement of ideas; and he assumes that Auden's revisions and deletions are to be explained by the changes in his political and religious convictions. (It would be nearer the truth to say that Auden's criterion is usually aesthetic, though the two cannot be separated entirely because the weakest poems tend to be those that deal most explicitly in ideas or are closest to propaganda.) This lack of sympathy is perhaps responsible for Beach's tendency to condemn Auden both ways, because he does revise and because he does not. The two most striking cases he cites are the Commentary to "In Time of War" (beginning "Season inherits legally . . .") and "Depravity: A Sermon." His argument is that, in altering the final lines of the former to make them distinctively Christian, Auden is misrepresenting his original intention and disguising a secular poem as religious; while in not altering the latter from its appearance in *The Dog Beneath the Skin*, where it seemed anti-clerical, but rather attributing to it a Christian significance in *Collected Poetry*, Auden is being cynical or naïve. (The point is, of course, that the sermon was not primarily anti-clerical in *Dog*; it describes and exemplifies a type of spiritual corruption by no means peculiar to the clergy, as Auden points out in his note in *Collected Poetry*; in fact when it was first published in 1934 it was called "Sermon by an Armaments Manufacturer.") [28] Auden, then, is damned if he does revise and damned if he doesn't. The title of Beach's book is unfortunate, since the word "canon" is not usually applied to a poet's choice of his own poems and gives a wholly undeserved note of pretentiousness to Auden's procedure—a note which, in the light of the book's conclusions, turns out to be ironic. For all these reasons, Beach's book, though bibliographically indispensable (and I have acknowledged my considerable debt to it in the preface), seems to me unsatisfactory as interpretation. (Notes 11, 60, and 92 in the preceding section take issue with specific points in Beach.)

   Collected Shorter Poems 1930-1944 (published 1950) is the English equivalent of *Collected Poetry* except that it is limited, as its title indicates, to shorter poems and is therefore smaller (303 as against 466 pages). Thus it does not contain "For the Time Being" or "The Sea and the Mirror"; these, like the other longer works, are kept in print by the English publishers in their separate volumes. Naturally, it does not contain the prose pieces in *Collected Poetry*, "Letter to a Wound" and "Depravity: A Sermon." Up to this point the scope of the volume is logical; afterward there is an element of unpredictability. Thus "New Year Letter" is excluded, reasonably; but so are "The Quest" and all the shorter pieces in *The Double Man* (presumably because they would all be purchased in this separate volume). On the other hand, *Paid on Both Sides* is included complete (and this means, of course, that the poems excerpted from it in *Collected Poetry* are not to be found in *Collected Shorter Poems* as separate poems). The volume consists of four sections: Poems, *Paid on Both Sides*, Songs and Other Musical Pieces, and "In Time of War." As in *Collected Poetry*, the Poems and Songs are arranged alphabetically; Beach, after a thorough comparison, found that the texts were exactly the same: in fact, it continued to use the same asterisks designating poems not previously published in book form, though obviously all the poems had been published in *Collected Poetry*. There are two notable improvements over *Collected Poetry:* first, an index of first lines is added, and second, the titles of about a dozen poems are altered, in every case for the better; the new titles are never objectionable and are sometimes helpful. The most interesting change, however, is that Auden included in the volume four poems that he had rejected for *Collected Poetry*. Three of these were from *On This Island*: "August for the people . . . ," "Here on the cropped grass . . . ," and "The chimneys are smoking. . . ." The reasons for rejecting these have already been discussed; presumably, with the passage of time, the reasons simply ceased to appear compelling to Auden. In only one case is there any revision: in "Here on the cropped grass . . ." 22 lines are omitted. This is a speech by the "bones of war," explaining that our civilization collapsed because of a "distortion in the human plastic by luxury produced," which led us to hate instead of love. It is easy to see why Auden would want to eliminate this preposterously simple diagnosis of what went wrong. The fourth poem is "You who return tonight . . ." from *The Dog Beneath the Skin*, which is given the title "Prothalamion." This is an amusing satirical piece, a burlesque prothalamion, celebrating in the play the union of the hero and the dummy, and embodying the pathos and absurdity of love under capitalism.

FOR THE TIME BEING

Auden's mother, who was devout and to whom he had been very close,[29] died in 1941. *For the Time Being,* dedicated to her memory, was written in 1941-2.[30] The subtitle is "A Christmas Oratorio"; it is of course too long to be set in its entirety, but an abridgement of it was set by the American composer, Melvin Levy, and performed in New York a few years ago. It follows the oratorio form faithfully, except that musical setting is not essential: i.e. it is an oratorio to be spoken or read. In many respects, the oratorio form enables Auden to achieve effects he sought in the plays: there is no dramatic illusion, no identification, and no dramatic characterization. There is, so to speak, a built-in alienation effect, since in the oratorio singers use only their voices to represent their roles, without acting, and the audience is aware continuously of the singers as singers as well as participants in the drama; hence the characters move in two dimensions, as, simultaneously, the unique historical characters and the moderns who are representing them. The oratorio differs from the plays in presenting a story both historical and thoroughly familiar, so that the traditional Christmas pageant or tableau can be suggested, as well as the miracle play, and the lighter elements of popular song and contemporary language can more effectively surprise the reader who expects a wholly solemn, elevated work. The verse is an equivalent for the kind of distancing produced by musical setting, and in variety of forms and meters it succeeds in producing many of the effects of music. The chorus expresses collective feelings and attitudes in a formal, often exalted manner, while the narrator, voluble, articulate, and thoroughly modern, expresses the other side of the contemporary consciousness. Together, they mediate between the audience and the action more effectively than any of Auden's previous choruses or announcers.

From the religious point of view, the form of the Christmas

oratorio immediately suggests three kinds of meaning: (1) the unique Incarnation; (2) by association with Christmas and with other Christmas oratorios, plays, pageants, and the like, the annual attempt in Christendom to apprehend and experience the event as the center of the Christian year; (3) the constant attempt of Christians to understand, make viable, and in some sense repeat the Incarnation in their daily lives. *For the Time Being* generally succeeds in keeping the reader simultaneously aware of all three of these meanings. The piece is the fullest and most balanced expression of Auden's religious attitudes; the ideas and dominant images that have been seen partially and transitionally in other poems here may be seen in their final place as part of an ordered whole. Much could be said of the religious background of the piece (the respective influences of Kierkegaard, Niebuhr, Williams, Cochrane, and Eliot) and of the relation of the ideas in it to those Auden had been expounding both in prose and verse; but I shall forego this kind of discussion in favor of what will, I hope, be more immediately useful—an interpretative commentary keeping close to the work itself.

The first section, "Advent," represents in the historical sense the exhaustion and despair of the ancient world on the eve of Christ's birth. (As we have seen, Auden had been much concerned in his prose writings with defining the philosophical impasse of the classical world and the parallel with the present.) But two other levels are constantly present: the perennial situation of man without Christ, and, as the title indicates, the annual Church season of preparation for Christmas—the Incarnation, that is, is presented as a recurring as well as a unique event. The opening chorus is trimeter, iambic but with one anapaest to the line; it is probably modeled (as earlier critics have suggested) on the final chorus of Dryden's "Secular Masque," but has a very different effect, suggesting plodding weariness and monotony. The semi-chorus interrupts twice, in very irregular trimeter, to describe the loss of hope of a secular savior; great Hercules is not only unable to reinvigorate the empire but is, himself, utterly lost. The chorus plods on in the original meter: "Darkness and snow descend," and "The evil and armed draw near." Into their lamentations breaks the rational, mundane voice of the narrator. He complains that an outrageous novelty has been introduced, so that "nothing / We learnt before It was there is now of the slightest use"; as if the room had "changed places / With the room behind the mirror over the fireplace." What has happened, he says, is that the locus of reality has shifted: "the world of space where events re-occur is still there, / Only now it's no longer real; the real one is nowhere / Where time never moves and nothing can ever happen." (This central theme of the relation of Time to Reality, of the entry of the Eternal into the world of Time as the center of history, and of the resentment and resistance with which the "outrageous novelty" is greeted by human beings is inevitably rendered sometimes in tones and images recalling its great modern master, Eliot.) In this first speech the narrator continues to explain the consequences to man's sense of identity and relation to the self: "although there's a person we know all about / Still bearing our name and loving himself as before, / That person has become a fiction. . . ." The chorus chants in despair, "Alone, alone, about a dreadful wood / Of conscious evil runs a lost mankind" [31] and concludes, "We who must die demand a miracle," since "Nothing can save us that is possible." The section ends with a recitative and chorus; the former explores the paradoxical nature of religious truth in long, six-stress lines that are precise and restrained in diction ("The Real is what will strike you as really absurd") and introducing the garden and desert symbols ("For the garden is the only place there is, but you will not find it / Until you have looked for it everywhere and found nowhere that is not a desert"); the Chorus, written in elegiacs (alternating dactylic hexameter and pentameter) and elevated in diction, and hence reminiscent of Greek poetry, describes man's condition and his peculiar temptations and difficulties as compared to the other creatures.

Alas, his genius is wholly for envy; alas,
The vegetative sadness of lakes, the locomotive beauty
  Of choleric beasts of prey, are nearer than he
To the dreams that deprive him of sleep, the powers that compel
    him to idle,
  To his amorous nymphs and his sanguine athletic gods.

How can his knowledge protect his desire for truth from illusion?
  How can he wait without idols to worship . . .

The second section, "The Annunciation," begins with the
four faculties—intuition, feeling, sensation, thought—that were
once one but were dissociated by the Fall. They identify themselves in the manner of abstractions (e.g. the Seven Deadly
Sins) in medieval drama, and the dimeter quatrain they employ
at first recalls Goethe's *Faust;* their second speeches are in dramatic blank verse. They are the "Ambiguous causes / Of all
temptation" and "lure men either / To death or salvation";
their function here is to report what happens in the Garden.
The Annunciation proper is expressed in a series of beautiful
metaphysical lyrics, majestic and complex for Gabriel and exalted and intense for Mary. Gabriel makes explicit the parallel
with Eve in her earlier Garden: she, "in love with her own
will / Denied the will of Love and fell"; but "What her negation wounded, may / Your affirmation heal today":

> Love's will requires your own, that in
> The flesh whose love you do not know,
> Love's knowledge into flesh may grow.

Mary rejoices that God, as a pledge of his love for the world,
"Should ask to wear me, / From now to their wedding day, /
For an engagement ring." The conceit is brilliant and precise,
but the tone of the last image seems to me incongruous and
anticlimactic. This fault, if real, is no more than the result of
the risk inherent in this metaphysical style. More unfortunate
is the refrain in the final part of the section, in which the chorus
rejoices because *"There's a Way. There's a Voice."* For American readers at least, this suggests both the Glory Road of the

revivalist and the American, or democratic, Way of Life of the propagandist. Auden may have been misled by the musical analogy here. As a sung choral refrain, the line would probably be unobjectionable, but italicized on the page, it stands out, and the contractions with their suggestion of informality are incongruous with the capitalized abstractions.

The third section, "The Temptation of St. Joseph," begins audaciously in the vein of the music hall or popular song. Joseph is made very much the average man trying to have faith in spite of appearances; he asks for one reason for believing in divine justice, "one / Important and elegant proof / That what my Love had done / Was really at your will / And that your will is Love." But Gabriel answers only, "No, you must believe; / Be silent, and sit still" [32]—thus defining the nature of faith. The narrator comments amusingly on the relations between the sexes, concluding by observing that Joseph and Mary must be man and wife as if nothing had occurred; for faith abolishes the distinction between the usual and the exceptional: "To choose what is difficult all one's days / As if it were easy, that is faith. Joseph, praise." The section closes with a brilliant semi-chorus in which Joseph and Mary are invoked to pray for various types of sinners: first, the romantic lovers "Misled by moonlight and the rose" who hope to regain innocence through knowledge of the flesh, believe "Simultaneous passions make / One eternal chastity"; then the "independent embryos" (i.e., presumably, children in the womb) who exhibit the original sin in "every definite decision / To improve"—even in the "germ-cell's primary division"; [33] finally, the bourgeoisie, the "proper and conventional," with their "indolent fidelity" and their habit-forming "Domestic hatred," their willed disease. Auden still describes this type with special acerbity:

> O pray for our salvation
> Who take the prudent way,
> Believing we shall be exempted
> From the general condemnation
> Because our self-respect is tempted
> To incest not adultery ...

Finally, as types of the "common ungifted" human being and of marriage, Joseph and Mary are invoked to "Redeem for the dull the / Average Way."

Section four, "The Summons," forms the dramatic climax, in which mere human wisdom is contrasted with the Christian revelation. Historically, the Magi reveal the inadequacy of classical speculative philosophy, while the Fugal-Chorus in ironic praise of Caesar reveals the inadequacy of ancient state-craft or political philosophy; but the parallel between the years one and 1941 is explicit, and the terms more modern than ancient. In this section Auden has the special problem of avoiding both the powerful influence of Eliot's "Journey of the Magi" and the clichés of Christmas pageants. He manages this by divesting the Magi of their customary solemn impressiveness and transferring it to the Star, which begins by pronouncing the "doom of orthodox sophrosyne," of the classical wisdom of moderation; the faith which replaces it offers no security, but is like the fairy-tale "Glassy Mountain where are no / Footholds for logic" or a "Bridge of Dread / Where knowledge but increases vertigo." [34] The Wise Men speak in stanzas characterized by internal rhyme and a rollicking anapaestic beat, but breaking down into formless prose in the latter part of the stanza to represent frustration and confusion. The first one is a natural scientist: "With rack and screw I put Nature through / A thorough inquisition"; but her reaction to the investigator (or torturer) made her unreliable; so he follows the Star "to discover how to be truthful now." The second Wise Man has put his faith in the constant flow of Time, but has discovered that the Present disappears under analysis: "With envy, terror, rage, regret, / We anticipate or remember but never are." He follows the star "to discover how to be living *now*" (my italics). The third has been a kind of social scientist, hoping to make passion philanthropic by introducing the concept "Ought"; [35] but calculating the greatest good for the greatest number "left no time for affection," and he follows the star "to discover how to be loving now." The three of them together sing that after their journey "At least we know for certain that we are three old sinners" and together they seek "To discover how to be human now." The star tells them they must endure terror and tribulation, but if they keep faith all will be well.

In strong contrast comes the voice of the secular state, Caesar's proclamation, followed by a Fugal-Chorus in ironic praise of him. The state is more our own than that of Augustus, and the Seven Kingdoms Caesar has conquered are the boasted achievements of our civilization: Abstract Idea includes everything from language to philosophy, and is the basis of the rest; Natural Cause is obviously the natural sciences (considered as a substitute religion); Infinite Number is mathematics; Credit Exchange is the monetary system and finance capitalism; Inorganic Giants are clearly machines; Organic Dwarfs seem to be drugs, which can not only control disease, pain, and worry but stimulate emotions; the last, Popular Soul, is of course propaganda and the techniques of mass psychology. In style, the repetition of formulas and patterns does produce a fugal effect, and the musical analogy is amusing. This is followed by the narrator's news broadcast, fusing modern and ancient, and concluding once more with the secular boast, "Our great Empire shall be secure for a thousand years." But this is followed immediately by the confession that "no one is taken in, at least not all of the time":

> In our bath, or the subway, or the middle of the night,
> We know very well we are not unlucky but evil,
> That the dream of a Perfect State or No State at all,
> To which we fly for refuge, is a part of our punishment.

And he points out, in orthodox fashion, that societies and epochs are transient details, important only as transmitting "an everlasting opportunity / That the Kingdom of Heaven may come, not in our present / And not in our future, but in the Fullness of Time." The section ends with a prayer in chorale form, recalling in meter and diction the traditional hymn (and providing an interesting contrast with the parody hymn "Not, Father, further . . ." in *The Orators*).

"The Vision of the Shepherds," the next section, interprets the shepherds in traditional fashion as the poor, though they are modern mass-men rather than pastoral types: they keep the mechanism going. This section alone would be enough to confute those who say Auden lacks understanding of or sympathy with the common man; it is shrewd, amusing, and without condescension. The shepherds observe that those who sentimentalize poverty and ignorance have "done pretty well for themselves," while those who insist that the poor are important and should stand up for their rights also insist that the individual doesn't matter. But, they say, what is real about us all "is that each of us is waiting" for the Good News. The Chorus of Angels then announces to them the "ingression of Love" and the consequent Gospel: the old "Authoritarian / Constraint is replaced / By his Covenant, / And a city based / On love and consent / Suggested to men. . . ." The chorus adds that "after today / The children of men / May be certain that / The Father Abyss / Is affectionate / To all Its creatures, / All, all, all of them. . . ."

"At the Manger" presents the traditional tableau with Wise Men and Shepherds. Mary sings a tender lullaby in modified sepphics (five instead of three eleven-syllable lines, followed by a short line of four instead of the customary five syllables), reflecting that her human flesh and maternal care can only bring the Child anxiety, tears, sorrow, and death. The Wise Men and Shepherds characterize their former selves contrastingly, the death-wish ("arrogant longing to attain the tomb") versus regression ("sullen wish to go back to the womb"), "Exceptional conceit" with "average fear," as they bring, instead of the traditional gifts, their bodies and minds to the Child. The Wise Men have discovered that "Love is more serious than Philosophy / Who sees no humour in her observation / That Truth is knowing that we know we lie." Repeating (in a virtuosic display) the same rhymes eight times, they explain why human identity and personality is valuable: "Love's possibilities of realisation / Require an Otherness that can say *I*" and what the true reality of space and time is: "Space is the Whom our loves are needed by, / Time is our choice of How to love and Why."

"The Meditation of Simeon," in contrast to the stress on Love in the preceding section, emphasizes the philosophical meaning of the Incarnation. Since Simeon is the type of the convert, this is appropriate. As has often been observed, it is probably the best brief exposition of Auden's religious position, or at least of its intellectual aspect. It is in prose—the first time prose has been used in the oratorio—interspersed with one-line alliterative comments by the chorus, which render emotionally what Simeon has been saying in prose. Simeon's style is eloquent, without any particular mask or characterization; his language is that of the modern intellectual. (There is no resemblance whatever to Eliot's "Song for Simeon.") He explains first that before the Incarnation could take place, it was necessary that the nature and effects of the Fall become clear, that man understand his original sin and the failure of remedy or escape: "The Word could not be made Flesh until men had reached a state of absolute contradiction between clarity and despair in which they would have no choice but either to accept absolutely or to reject absolutely...." But now "that which hitherto we could only passively fear as the incomprehensible I AM, henceforth we may actively love with comprehension that THOU ART." Simeon then proceeds to spell out the intellectual consequences. First, since "He is in no sense a symbol," this existence gives value to all others. The distinction between sin and temptation is clarified, "for in Him we become fully conscious of Necessity as our freedom to be tempted, and of Freedom as our necessity to have faith." The meaning of Time is illuminated, for "the course of History is predictable in the degree to which all men love themselves, and spontaneous in the degree to which each man loves God and through Him his neighbour." (This passage has been cited earlier in the discussion of Love in the shorter poems of this period, as has the one about the elimination of the distinction between the Average and the Exceptional, the Common Man and the Hero: "disaster is not the impact of a curse upon a few great families, but issues continually from the hubris of every tainted will. Every invalid is Roland . . . , every stenographer Brunnhilde. . . .") A further aesthetic consequence is that the Ridiculous is no longer confined to the Ugly; since "of themselves all men are without merit, all are ironically assisted to their comic bewilderment by the Grace of God"; hence the logic of fairy tales represents spiritual truth: "Every Cabinet Minister is the woodcutter's simple-minded son to whom the fishes and the crows are always whispering the whereabouts of the Dancing Water. . . ." Similarly, every situation is now essentially as interesting as any other: "Every tea-table is a battlefield littered with old catastrophes . . . every martyrdom an occasion for flip cracks and sententious oratory." Finally, in a passage we have already quoted (above, p. 193), Simeon explains the metaphysical value of the Trinity: since the Word is united to the Flesh, the One and the Many are simultaneously revealed as real, so that neither can be denied. Truth is One, but "the possibilities of real knowledge are as many as are the creatures in the very real and most exciting universe that God creates with and for His love. . . ." Simeon concludes by praying that "we may depart from our anxiety into His peace."

As Simeon is the type of the Christian convert and intellectual, Herod, in the next section, "The Massacre of the Innocents," is the type of the liberal intellectual, the Manager and Apollonian we have seen in the shorter poems, dedicated to service, progress, and the advancement of reason, now confronted with the Irrational. His speech, which counterbalances Simeon's as the only other one in prose, is a deft fusion of ancient and modern: Herod is both the historical character and the liberal of the late 1930s, trying to cope with the threats of war and fascism.[36] His speech is witty, amusing, and highly persuasive on its own premises: his long struggle to establish law and order and push back superstition is doomed by this irruption of the Irrational. In terms sometimes recalling Yeats's play, "The Resurrection," and sometimes recalling Nietzsche, he gloomily predicts the consequences—Reason will be replaced by Revelation, Idealism by Materialism, Justice by Pity. "Naturally this cannot be allowed to happen," and he concludes reluctantly that he must send for the military to prevent it. Petulantly, he complains, "Why can't people be sensible? I don't want to be horrid. Why can't they see that the notion of a finite God is absurd?" It is unreasonable that a decision as to the existence of God should be up to Herod: "How dare He allow me to decide?" (In other words, he refuses to go beyond the secular and rejects the existentialist Choice.) He concludes uneasily and self-pityingly, "I've tried to be good. I brush my teeth every night. I haven't had sex for a month. I object. I'm a liberal. I want everyone to be happy. I wish I had never been born."

The Soldiers speak next, their callous brutality and cynical humor embodying the perennial cruelty and evil of human nature; their speech comes after Herod's with massive irony, reminding us that the end in practice of Herod's plausible speech has been the decision to massacre the Innocents. The fantasy and exaggeration of the Soldiers' speech and its ironic tall-story "good fellowship" prevents any effect of striving for pathos, which is merely indicated by the presentation at the end of the section of Rachel weeping for her children in a speech of great power and restraint.

The last section, "The Flight into Egypt," presents Joseph and Mary being tempted by Voices of the Desert as they pursue their journey through the looking-glass, i.e. the journey of faith. These Voices seem to represent the temptations of the "normal" and particularly modern world; [37] they tempt with nonsense songs that sound like advertising commercials gone mad. (*The Age of Anxiety* employs this style extensively.) Joseph and Mary observe that insecurity is the condition natural to humanity: "Safe in Egypt we shall sigh / For lost insecurity...." Then follows a fine recitative interpreting the Flight as a redemption of the past: "Fly, Holy Family, from our immediate rage, / That our future may be freed from our past...." [38] The narrator's long speech modulating back to the present of Christmas trees and everyday life is both amusing and profound. The atmosphere of Christmas as it is for most of us is evoked with great precision, and contrasted with its religious meaning: "Once again / As in previous years we have seen the actual Vision and failed / To do more than entertain it as an agreeable / Possibility, once again we have sent Him away...." We think of the future, of the coming of Lent and Good Friday; "But, for the time being, here we all are, / Back in the moderate Aristotelian city," the everyday world. And to deal properly with this world and the present time is most difficult: "To those who have seen / The Child, however dimly, however incredulously, / The Time Being is, in a sense, the most trying time of all." To escape our guilt and inhibit our self-reflection, we are tempted to pray for temptation and suffering. They will come,[39] but "In the meantime / There are bills to be paid, machines to keep in repair, / Irregular verbs to learn, the Time Being to redeem / From insignificance." In a metaphor developed later in "Nones" and in the rest of "Horae Canonicae," Auden says, "The happy morning is over, / The night of agony still to come; the time is noon..."; and the soul knows that "God will cheat no one, not even the world of its triumph." [40] This magnificent conclusion is followed by a rather weak and anticlimactic chorus, perhaps necessary to carry out the musical analogy, but seeming flat on the page.

For the Time Being has enjoyed a good deal of popularity: as we have seen, an abridged version of it was set to music by Melvin Levy and performed in New York in 1959, and it is reprinted entire in *Modern Poetry*, edited by Maynard Mack, Leonard Dean, and William Frost (New York, 1950)—a widely used textbook—and in *Religious Drama 1*, edited by M. Halverson (New York, 1957); it is performed rather frequently by religious groups. Probably the fact that Eliot's *Four Quar-*

tets, which embody many of the same themes (though in a very different way), happened to appear shortly before it has had much to do with the failure of the oratorio to impress the critics profoundly; comparison with Eliot's towering achievement is inevitable and the result is a foregone conclusion. The oratorio has also suffered from the equally inevitable comparison with the other work that originally appeared in the same volume with it, *The Sea and the Mirror*, which has seemed to most critics more brilliant, novel, and provocative, and therefore has the lion's share of their attention. Considered on its own terms, and at this distance in time, the work may be seen as a unique and remarkable success both formally and as a whole. The traditional forms of the Christmas pageant and oratorio are transformed and deepened to embody the apprehension by the modern consciousness of the central event in history, understood psychologically, emotionally, and intellectually, by constant parallels with contemporary life; the various characters represent various types and also aspects of each of us, and the different episodes represent different aspects of the religious life of the individual, as well as the historical events. There is thus a great range and variety implicit in the scope of the piece, shown most obviously in the formal variety of verse and prose. Throughout, there is a triple consciousness at three levels: first, the unique historical event of the Incarnation; second, the collective, seasonal aspect of Christmas in its place in the Christian year, with its annual attempt to make it possible for Christ to be re-born, so to speak; and finally, the moment-to-moment effort of the individual to redeem everyday life from insignificance, to manifest the Incarnation in himself, to be a Christian. There are, as always in Auden, flaws and unevenness; but the central problem of rendering these three kinds of consciousness simultaneously is solved with brilliant success, and provides an adequate unifying principle for the enormous scope and variety of the piece. The oratorio does not seem dated or topical, nor does the religious attitude expressed seem in any way eccentric or extravagant. Auden placed the oratorio last both in *For the Time Being*, 1944, and in *Collected Poetry*, 1945, presumably because he felt, with justice, that it provided a very suitable conclusion for a volume.

THE SEA AND THE MIRROR

The Sea and the Mirror was written after *For the Time Being*, between 1942 and 1944.[41] Obviously, the religious commitment with its basic shift in perspective would require a new aesthetic formulation; and that is essentially what *The Sea and the Mirror* is: a definition and exploration of the relations between the Mirror of Art and the Sea of Life, or Reality. Appropriately, the piece is a virtuoso display of Auden's technical accomplishment: each character speaks in a different form, and many of them are very complicated indeed—ballade, villanelle, sestina, sapphics, elegiacs, terza rima, syllabic verse, and the prose style of the later James. But there is also a great variety of songs in Auden's best vein.

The Sea and the Mirror has no such definite form to follow as *For the Time Being*, its subtitle being "A Commentary on Shakespeare's *The Tempest*." There is the implicit setting of a theater, after a performance of *The Tempest;* the Stage Manager addresses the Critics in the Preface, and the Prompter echoes the last speech. In the first scene, Prospero, packing up to leave the Island, bids farewell to Ariel; in the second, the rest of the cast, on a ship taking them back to Italy from the Island, speak *sotto voce* to each other and to the audience. They are all still in the world of the play, but at the same time are sufficiently detached from it to comment on its meaning and on their future lives; in some sense they are leaving the Enchanted Island of the art work and emerging into "real" life. The last of them, Caliban, addresses the audience directly and develops explicitly the speculations about the relation between Art and Life suggested both by the play and by the dual roles the other characters have just been playing. It is all done with mirrors: an exercise in illusion, in *trompe-l'oeil* reversals in which mirrors turn out to be paintings and paintings are revealed as windows. In this theme, and in the whole notion of a closet drama which is also a philosophical commentary on itself and on the nature of art, there is some resemblance to Goethe's *Faust*. There is, however, nothing to control the form, no musical analogy and no dramatic action. This becomes clearest in Caliban's address to the audience, which, though very brilliant indeed, is inordinately long (about half the total length) and inordinately subtle for any dramatic analogy, and proliferates into a baroque profusion of distinctions and elaborations. The imagination boggles at the thought of actually staging it. This is not necessarily a defect; it is clearly intended as closet drama, and full advantage is taken of its impracticability for the stage. (The divisions that I have called scenes are called "chapters" in the first printing.) Just as there is one verse form not even Auden would be audacious enough to attempt here—Shakespearian blank verse—so he must make it very clear that he is not attempting drama in Shakespearian terms, that he is not writing a sequel to *The Tempest*.

In the Preface the Stage Manager discourses to the Critics on the limits of art and its difference from life. Beginning with audience psychology, he argues that it is the predictability, the lack of surprise, that make it enjoyable. Art moves us, but does not affect the will; it does not help us to satisfy "Between Shall-I and I-Will, / The lion's mouth whose hunger / No metaphors can fill." (This is parallel to Auden's formulations in prose—see below, pp. 335-6—of the ultimate frivolity of art.) Finally, he suggests that the "real" world, the other side of the footlights, is also illusory, and concludes in a beautiful pastiche of Shakespeare:

> All the rest is silence
> On the other side of the wall;
> And the silence ripeness,
> And the ripeness all.

The meter is the same as that of the opening chorus of *For the Time Being*, but its effect in this witty and elegantly colloquial lyric is quite different. The first scene (or chapter) introduces Prospero saying farewell to Ariel as he packs to leave the island; appropriately, he speaks in elegiacs. The symbolism is basically traditional: Prospero is the writer giving up his art, setting free Ariel (imagination), and leaving the enchanted island (the world of art) to return to the real world. In Kierke-gaardian terms, he is renouncing the aesthetic for the religious; or in more general terms he is discovering that art is not a sub-stitute for religion even for the artist, whose art gives him no special privileges from the religious standpoint. Prospero com-ments that he is glad he has freed Ariel, under whose influence death is inconceivable, for now he can "really believe I shall die." He recalls his motives for first resorting to magic in childhood as escape and compensation, and defines magic as "the power to enchant / That comes from disillusion." Once we have learned "to sit still and give no orders" Ariel offers his echo and mirror; "We have only to believe you, then you dare not lie." As Prospero bids him farewell, he reflects that Ariel has corrupted him through his own weaknesses and hence he has broken "Both of the promises I made as an appren-tice;– / To hate nothing and to ask nothing for its love"–the first by tempting Antonio into treason, the second in wishing for Caliban's absolute devotion. He describes the other charac-ters; all have been "soundly hunted / By their own devils into their human selves" and are pardoned. As he thinks of the prob-able difficulties of Ferdinand and Miranda, he reflects that he is glad to be through with youth and all its problems–and the longings of youth are embodied ironically in the fine song "Sing first that green remote Cockagne," which, like the other two songs in this chapter, Prospero sings to Ariel. Finally, he says, now that the partnership with Ariel is dissolved, that is, now that he has abandoned art and is a man like any other, it is as if he had dreamed all his life about an imaginary journey, "And now, in my old age, I wake, and this journey really exists, / And I have actually to take it, inch by inch. . . ." His journey, or quest, is the religious one in which he will no longer be interesting, but will appear perfectly ordinary, yet will be (in Kierkegaard's phrase) "Sailing alone, out over seventy thousand fathoms"; he will not be able to speak, but must "learn to suffer / Without saying something ironic or funny / On suffering." If he is lucky, he may learn before he dies "The difference between moonshine and daylight." The final song contrasts Ariel's unconcern with the human condition: he is an "unfeeling god," "unanxious one" who can therefore sing brilliantly, lightly "Of separation, / Of bodies and death. . . ."

The second scene presents the supporting cast on the ship going home, as they look back to the island and reflect on their experiences. (They have all been introduced and characterized in Prospero's speech.) Antonio, villain of the play, the wicked usurping brother, is the only character who is unchanged, and he dominates the section. In his terza rima speech he takes an ironic view of the other characters, the metamorphoses and the happy ending: it is all an illusion, a product of Prospero's art— "What a lot a little music can do." But Antonio makes it impossible for him to renounce his magic by refusing to submit to it: "as long as I choose / To wear my fashion, whatever you wear / Is a magic robe; while I stand outside / Your circle, the will to charm is still there." And this is his revenge, to prevent Prospero's return to innocence. After his own speech, and after each of the other characters speaks, Antonio sings a song addressed ironically to Prospero, comparing himself to the character in question. This reiterated opposition gives a certain dramatic tension to the section.

Ferdinand, in a sonnet (with dodecasyllabic lines) addressed to Miranda, celebrates their love and the mystery of their union in reverent terms. Stephano, the drunken butler, in contrast sings a love song to his belly: it is a ballade, and pathetic rather than humorous, with its refrain, "A lost thing looks for a lost name."

Gonzalo, the good old man, defines (in trochaic tetrameter

with catalexis) what has happened as they leave the "island where / All our loves were altered." He has explained too much, been too fond of his own eloquence, he says; instead he should have "trusted the Absurd" and reproduced the song (the reference is to Ariel's warning in *Tempest* II, i); but through "Doubt and insufficient love" he has frozen "Vision into an idea" and "made the song / Sound ridiculous and wrong." Now, however, he can be "a bell" ready to express the divine will. Adrian and Francisco, the lightweight courtiers, have an amusing couplet suggesting that they have learned that fashionable chit-chat cannot cover up the ultimate issues: "it's madly ungay when the goldfish die." [42]

Alonso then makes a long speech, the most substantial and profound as well as the richest poetically in the whole scene. The verse is syllabic (lines of nine syllables) [43] and the stanzas consist of twelve lines in a complex pattern: first two couplets, then a modified envelope quatrain, then a modified alternate quatrain (aabbcddefefc). Alonso begins by advising Ferdinand on the familiar Renaissance theme of the proper behavior for a prince. The two symbols in the first stanza come naturally from *The Tempest*, in which the sea and sea-changes, and yellow sands, have been prominent. At first they are used merely for a contrast between the human and the non-human: the sea and the desert and their creatures regard sceptres, crowns, and kings themselves as no more than physical objects. In the first two stanzas this powerful but essentially simple contrast is used as a warning against pride, a reminder of mortality and of human limitations. But then in the next two stanzas the symbols are developed further as the two extremes between which the "Way of Justice is a tightrope." [44] The fears they represent are described as, respectively, sinking in the sea "entangled in rich robes" or standing undressed in the desert exposed to ridicule. The corresponding temptations are, from the sea, "a night / Where all flesh had peace" and from the desert, "a brilliant void / Where his mind could be perfectly clear / And all his limitations destroyed." But to succumb to either of

these extremes means "To join all the unjust kings." Alonso
goes on to warn Ferdinand of the difficulty of holding to the
way of justice, avoiding both the "watery vagueness" and the
"triviality of the sand," steering between "loose craving" and
"sharp aversion," "aimless jelly" and "paralysed bone," remem-
bering "that the fire and the ice / Are never more than one
step away / From the temperate city." The dying Alonso concludes by advising Ferdinand that if, like him, he should lose
his kingdom, he should "praise the scorching rocks / For their
desiccation of your lust" and "Thank the bitter treatment of
the tide / For its dissolution of your pride" so that the "whirl-
wind may arrange your will / And the deluge release it." He
may then find the "spring in the desert, the fruitful / Island in
the sea, where flesh and mind / Are delivered from mistrust."

These are subtle and rich symbols, not to be violated by
crude paraphrase; but we may suggest that the sea is associated
with the flesh, the senses, potentiality, and subjectivity; the
desert with mind, abstraction, the temptation to ignore the
limitations of the human creature. Only through balancing one
against the other, and allowing each to purge the characteristic
vice of the other—the desert drying up lust, the sea dissolving
pride—can the two be reconciled and the oasis in the desert or
island in the sea be found. (There is a general resemblance to
Kierkegaard's Aesthetic/Ethical categories, though the meaning of the symbols is ultimately very different.) [45]

The song of the master and boatswain, "At Dirty Dick's and
Sloppy Joe's" (based on Stephano's song in The Tempest, II,
ii), makes a fine contrast to the exalted seriousness of Alonso,
who has concluded by expressing his readiness "to welcome /
Death, but rejoicing in a new love, / A new peace, having
heard the solemn / Music strike and seen the statue move / To
forgive our illusion." [46] Their song is remarkable in combining
pathos with the convivial song so that, while the tone remains
earthy and humorous, the sailors' loneliness and hopelessness
appear movingly underneath. Sebastian, the wicked brother
who had tried to kill Alonso, but been prevented by Ariel, next

makes his confession and rejoices in his defeat and exposure ("my proof / Of mercy that I wake without a crown"); the form is that of the sestina. Trinculo, the jester, then sings a sad song about his isolation, and Miranda concludes the section with a very beautiful villanelle. Appropriately, it draws its imagery from the world of childhood (fairy tales, nursery rhymes, and the like). Some critics have complained that the first line ("My Dear One is mine as mirrors are lonely") lacks precise meaning; but this seems to me to ignore the context. Miranda is saying that her love is as true and unquestionable as three natural and unquestionable truths—unquestionable, of course, only to an innocent, sheltered, and trusting nature. Mirrors are, to such a nature, lonely of course because there is nobody there; they want somebody to reflect.[47] This is her mode of understanding reality—limited, vulnerable, and probably highly temporary; she still believes fairy-tale happy endings and her understanding of politics is limited to the conviction that good kings are always concerned for the poor. We are meant to keep in mind Prospero's earlier forebodings about the course of her and Ferdinand's love when they are married and out in the everyday world. All this adds overtones of pathos to her villanelle, which expresses a unique innocence and purity as she emerges from childhood into happy love.

Finally, the third scene, almost half of the whole, consists of "Caliban to the Audience."[48] Caliban explains that he is appearing instead of Shakespeare to take the curtain call because he is himself "the begged question you would speak to him *about*." Speaking in a mild and sympathetic parody of the style of the later James, Caliban in rapid succession puts on three different masks, each time addressing a different group upon a different topic. In the first section, Caliban, speaking for the audience, addresses Shakespeare about the nature of art and its difference from life. The Jamesian tone is highly appropriate, since the English Muse is represented as a society matron whom Shakespeare has offended by the *faux pas* of introducing Caliban (Life, Reality, Nature). The audience wishes to preserve the distinction between Art and Life and Caliban, in a tone of injured complaint, points out to Shakespeare his offense against decorum. The world of Art, the salon of the Muse, is one of freedom without anxiety, of "the perfectly tidiable case of disorder, the beautiful and serious problem exquisitely set without a single superfluous datum and insoluble with less"; to introduce the symbol of Reality into this world is unforgivable. The audience feels an intentional insult:

> Are we not bound to conclude then, that, whatever snub to the poetic you may have intended incidentally to administer, your profounder motive in so introducing Him to them among whom, because He doesn't belong, He couldn't appear as anything but His distorted parody, a deformed and savage slave, was to deal a mortal face-slapping insult to us among whom he does . . . ?

In life Caliban and Sycorax appear as Cupid and Venus: "the nude august elated archer of our heaven, the darling single son of Her who, in her right milieu, is certainly no witch but the most sensible of all the gods . . . our great white Queen of Love herself." This confusion of the realms may lead, the spectators think, to worse consequences:

> Is it possible that, not content with inveigling Caliban into Ariel's kingdom, you have also let loose Ariel in Caliban's? . . . For if the intrusion of the real has disconcerted and incommoded the poetic, that is a mere bagatelle compared to the damage which the poetic would inflict if it ever succeeded in intruding upon the real. We want no Ariel here, breaking down our picket fences in the name of fraternity, seducing our wives in the name of romance, and robbing us of our sacred pecuniary deposits in the name of justice.

After a brief transition, Caliban speaks for Shakespeare: he delivers "a special message from our late author" to prospective poets ("any gay apprentice in the magical art") on the topic of the poet as citizen, the effect of poetry upon the poet.

The partnership with Ariel, magician and familiar, is at first a brilliant success; but when, tiring, the artist wishes to dismiss him, Ariel becomes a "gibbering fist-clenched creature"—Caliban, "not a dream amenable to magic but the all too solid flesh you must acknowledge as your own." Ignoring the ethical, the artist neglects his quotidian self, and when his charms crack, he is left alone with the dark thing he could never abide to be with. The outlook for the future, Caliban comments, is not bright: "the only chance ... of my getting a tolerably new master and you a tolerably new man, lies in our both learning ... to forgive and forget the past, and to keep our respective hopes for the future within moderate, very moderate, limits."

Caliban's final transition is to the religious level, where he speaks for himself and Ariel to the audience on the nature of reality. Life is a journey made up of long waits between the "three or four decisive instants of transportation"; everyday life is the "Grandly Average Place from which at odd hours the expresses leave seriously and sombrely for Somewhere":

> But once you leave, no matter in which direction, your next stop will be far outside this land of habit that so democratically stands up for your right to stagestruck hope, and well inside one of those, all equally foreign, uncomfortable and despotic, certainties of failure or success. Here at least I, and Ariel too, are free to warn you not, should we meet again there, to speak to either of us, not to engage either of us as your guide, but there we shall no longer be able to refuse you ... Here ... I can at least warn you what will happen if at our next meeting you should insist ... on putting one of us in charge.

The consequences of putting either Caliban or Ariel in charge are vividly portrayed in symbolic fantasies that are fascinating, infinitely suggestive, and impossible to paraphrase. There is an obvious but elusive relation to the sea and desert symbols we have discussed as they appear in "Alonso to Ferdinand"; in general, Caliban's realm is that of the sea (pure deed, sensation, etc.) while Ariel's corresponds to the desert (pure word, abstraction, etc.); but the correspondence is not exact.[49] Those who take Caliban as guide do so in the hope of recovering the lost Eden of childhood, of which alternative versions are brilliantly evoked:

> Carry me back, Master, to the cathedral town where the canons run through the water meadows with butterfly nets and the old women keep sweet-shops in the cobbled side streets, ... Pity me, Captain, ... let me see that harbour once again just as it was before I learned the bad words. Patriarchs wiser than Abraham mended their nets on the modest wharf; white and wonderful beings undressed on the sand-dunes; sunset glittered on the plate-glass windows of the Marine Biological Station ... Look, Uncle, look. They have broken my glasses and I have lost my silver whistle. Pick me up, Uncle, let little Johnny ride away on your massive shoulders to recover his green kingdom ... O Cupid, Cupid, howls the whole dim chorus, take us home. We have never felt really well in this climate of distinct ideas ...

(We remember that Caliban appears as Cupid in the "real" world.) But, says Caliban, he cannot transport them to any such Eden "which your memory necessarily but falsely conceives of as the ultimately liberal condition," but only to that state as it really is, a desolate and indifferent scene "where Liberty stands with her hands behind her back, not caring, not minding *anything*." Here, he concludes in terms that parody those of atheistic existentialism, "your existence is indeed free at last to choose its own meaning, that is, to plunge headlong into despair and fall through silence fathomless and dry, all fact your single drop, all value your pure alas."

The fate of those who put "my more spiritual colleague," Ariel, in charge is no happier. These are idealists, Managers, responsible and respectable people (whereas the followers of

Caliban have been Hermetics, common, all-too-human men);
they surrender to Ariel in the hope of escaping the mess of life:

> Deliver us, dear Spirit, from the tantrums of our tele-
> phones and the whispers of our secretaries conspiring
> against Man; deliver us from these helpless agglomera-
> tions of dishevelled creatures with their bed-wetting,
> vomiting, weeping bodies, their giggling, fugitive, dis-
> appointing hearts, and scrawling, blotted, misspelt minds,
> to whom we have so foolishly tried to bring the light
> they did not want; deliver us from all the litter of *billets-
> doux*, empty beer bottles, laundry lists, directives, prom-
> issory notes and broken toys, the terrible mess that this
> particularised life, which we have so futilely attempted to
> tidy, sullenly insists on leaving behind it; translate us,
> bright Angel, from this hell of inert and ailing matter . . .

Ariel leads them into a "nightmare which has all the wealth of
exciting action and all the emotional poverty of an adventure
story for boys" to fulfill their desire for unconditional freedom. In this realm there is a "state of perpetual emergency and
everlasting improvisation"; all voluntary movements are possible, but "any sense of direction, any knowledge of where on
earth one has come from or where on earth one is going to is
completely absent." Other selves exist, but no one knows who
are his friends or enemies, what is going on, what his own
role is:

> Everything, in short, suggests Mind but, surrounded by
> an infinite extension of the adolescent difficulty, a rising
> of the subjective and subjunctive to ever steeper, stormier
> heights, the panting frozen expressive gift has collapsed . . .

From this "nightmare of public solitude" there is no escape;
the inevitable end is "a serious despair, the love nothing, the
fear all." These, Caliban concludes, are "the alternative routes,
the facile glad-handed highway or the virtuous averted track,
by which the human effort to make its own fortune arrives all
eager at its abruptly dreadful end."

In the final section Caliban returns to the plight of the artist, discussing it now in ultimate terms, and concerned not with art versus life but with both versus the Divine. The artist is in a "serio-comic embarrassment" since he cannot represent both divine truth and the human condition of estrangement from the truth: the more truthfully he paints the condition, the less clearly can he indicate the truth from which it is estranged, the brighter his revelation of the truth in its order, its justice, its joy, the fainter shows his picture of your actual condition in all its drabness and sham...." His ultimate aim must be to "make you unforgettably conscious of the ungarnished offended gap between what you so unquestionably are and what you are commanded without any question to become...." Yet the final danger is that the more he succeeds in doing this "the more he must strengthen your delusion that an awareness of the gap is in itself a bridge, your interest in your imprisonment a release"; instead of leading to contrition and surrender, "the regarding of your defects in his mirror" becomes a game, the most interesting of all games. Hence the artist, caught in these dilemmas, must hope "that some unforeseen mishap will intervene to ruin his effect"; that his art will fail. The final image is the venerable one of the world as stage, but rendered as mock-heroic: life as "the greatest grand opera rendered by a very provincial touring company indeed." All of us, as actors, hope for, not applause, but the "real Word which is our only *raison d'être*." The mirror and proscenium represent the gulf which separates all life from that "Wholly Other Life," yet we can rejoice in the perfected Work which is not ours.

I have tried to indicate only the main outlines of this extremely complex speech, which is full of amusing and fascinating detail. Within the light framework the argument is, of course, intensely serious; but Auden needs the complicated system of masks, the double irony, to enable him to speak seriously.[50] His innovation consists in preparing the reader for ironic argument by creating a faintly ridiculous style and fantastic masks, and then making the argument *not* ironic; the technique is what William Empson might term "the Fool speaks truth."

The "Postscript" is a song addressed to Caliban by Ariel, with echo by the Prompter. It would be rash indeed after Caliban's speech to say in a word what Ariel and Caliban represent here, but the primary meaning would seem to be the traditional one: Ariel is Art with its inhuman perfection and Caliban is Life with all its imperfection. Ariel is a "shadow cast / By your lameness" partly because art is compensation for the artist's defects (as Freud argued), and partly because art arises from and deals with human imperfection and suffering (this is the theme of Yeats's "Vacillation": "Homer is my example and his unchristened heart"). Hence Ariel is "Helplessly in love with you, / Elegance, art, fascination, / Fascinated by / Drab mortality." They must forever remain separate but complementary.

What can one say, finally, of *The Sea and the Mirror* as a whole? It is brilliant, infinitely suggestive, and often obscure. It is baroque in the proliferation and complication of its form: full of double and triple ironies as it deals with the relation of Art and Life in the guise of an art work commenting on another art work, shifting back and forth over imaginary footlights with sleight-of-hand rapidity. It is more uneven and less coherent than *For the Time Being*, but perhaps more audacious and varied; and it contains some of Auden's finest poetry. In terms of Auden's career, it is a definitive renunciation of art as magic, a clear distinction between the roles of man and poet, and an extensive definition of the boundaries between life and art.

THE AGE OF ANXIETY

A substantial part of *The Age of Anxiety: A Baroque Eclogue* was written by 1944, and at least half by 1945;[51] the whole was published in October 1947. The subtitle suggests the extravagance of form through which Auden attains distance and indirection. The trappings of the eclogue are there: the slight dramatic form, with dialogue; the singing contest; an elegy; love-songs and laments, with courtship of a shepherdess; a dirge; formal, "artificial" diction and meter. But this idyll takes place in a Third Avenue bar, and the pastoral imagery is either symbolic or ironic. The Nordic mask is used for the first time since the early 1930s, but with very different effect. Old English meter, with its four heavy stresses and constant alliteration, is imitated rather than, as in the early verse, merely suggested. The style is now a rhetoric consciously assumed, deliberately incongruous with what is said; its effect is therefore mock-heroic or distancing, rather than intensifying and heightening as in, for example, "Doom is dark. . . ." "Baroque" indicates the packed, extravagant quality of the piece, full of violent contrasts and incongruities, reflecting the stresses of a baroque age.

The poem may be described as a sympathetic satire on the attempts of human beings to escape, through their own efforts, the anxiety of our age. The anxiety with which the poem deals is, in Auden's view, essentially a religious phenomenon (see above, pp. 178-9, 214), man's "guilt the insoluble / Final fact, infusing his private / Nexus of needs, his noted aims with / Incomprehensible comprehensive dread / At not being what he knows that before / This world was he was willed to become" (p. 24). Though felt by all men in all times, anxiety is intensified in our civilization with its failure of tradition and belief, its atomism which leaves the individual isolated, without aid or support in his terrifying responsibility for his own ultimate destiny. This condition is further heightened in wartime, when "everybody is reduced to the anxious status of a shady character or a displaced person, when even the most prudent become worshippers of chance" (p. 4). The scene is a bar, which offers "an unprejudiced space in which nothing particular ever happens, and a choice of physiological aids to the imagination whereby each may appropriate it for his or her private world of repentant felicitous forms, heavy expensive objects or avenging flames and floods. . . ." The time is All Hallows Eve, and the characters are, metaphorically, souls in purgatory, each dreaming in his own way of escape, but aware (except for Malin) of no recourse beyond the human level. The poem deals with the imaginary worlds they create and through which they reveal themselves. The tone of the poem is mock-heroic: this space in which time is unreal is a parody of the religious "moment out of time," as their alcoholically-induced visions are parodies of religious visions. The genre is the Quest, in which everyman seeks spiritual knowledge. There is a generalized parallel with Dante's *Purgatorio* in the sevenfold division of ages and stages and in the vision of innocence as goal, of which the archetype is the Eden regained in Dante's twenty-eighth canto. This, however, is "negative knowledge" (p. 136); the piece is a mock-pastoral because it is a quest for innocence, but the anxiety from which the characters imagine escape through a variously attained innocence can be overcome only by faith. Their myth is of regaining the lost Eden of childhood, the happy pre-lapsarian place where Eros is unconfined because Logos is unknown; but only the Christian Agape can make Eros and Logos one, can make, that is, Love become Law; only faith can enable man to take "short views" and "redeem the time."

The four characters are sharply distinguished; each bears a different relation to the main symbolic patterns of the poem and each moves through his own private world of symbols. The parallels and contrasts among them are contrapuntal in abundance and intricacy. Malin, the Canadian airman and Medical Intelligence officer, is the most intelligent and perceptive of them, and functions as guide and commentator; he disclaims having faith (pp. 135-6), but his viewpoint is distinctively Christian, and he is certainly aware of the true problem—as the others are not. Rosetta, the Jewish department-store buyer, has achieved material success, but her race makes her a special case of homelessness and spiritual insecurity; she moves through a dream-world dominated by the Innocent Landscape of the detective story,[52] upon which reality intrudes in images of isolation and persecution. Since she is the only one who

changes, discarding her illusory and accepting her real childhood with all its implications, she is, in a sense, the protagonist.
Quant, the aging Irish widower, is outwardly a failure, his
intelligence much superior to his position as clerk; he denies,
humorously or bitterly, any meaning in life, and his typical
imagery is that of classical mythology. Perhaps he represents
Kierkegaard's "despair of weakness." Emble, the handsome
young American sailor, is insecure youth seeking a vocation
and success; his images are of the Quest, the sea (potentiality,
belief), mountains (difficult action, choice). Physically he is
exceptional, the potential Aesthetic Hero, but unable to find a
Quest; in contrast, Quant is no hero, Malin perhaps the potential Ethical Hero, that is, possessing superior knowledge, but
not absolutely committed as is the Religious Hero.

At the beginning of the poem, the characters are introduced
in their private reveries, each a variation on the central theme
of guilt and innocence. A newscast recalls them to the present,
and the War symbolism becomes dominant. The effect of the
Nordic mask is to take away the specificity of World War II
by merging it with all wars, to extend the situation from the
topical and contemporary to the universal. Unable to agree
on the significance of the war (their interpretations reveal their
philosophies),[53] the characters agree to discuss, not the past or
the future, but the "incessant Now of / The traveller through
time." Malin states the subject: man's perennial attempt to become reconciled to himself, to escape guilt, anxiety, and dread.

Part II, "The Seven Ages," puts Shakespeare's seven ages
into psychological terms. Every infant repeats the Fall: "that
ban tempts him; / He jumps and is judged: he joins mankind, /
The fallen families, freedom lost, / Love become Law." Eros
and Logos henceforth conflict; the will is corrupt. In the Second Age, realizing he "has laid his life-bet with a lying self /
Who wins or welches," the child becomes self-conscious and
divided, lives isolated in dreams and self-pitying fantasies. In the
Third Age, "learning to love, at length he is taught / To know he
does not"; sexual love, being still narcissism, ends in disillusion:

Quant's surrealist description of the sightseeing voyage to Venus Island puts this vividly. The Fourth Age presents Everyman emerging from the domination of Eros (abandoning his fantasies of being exceptional, loved for himself alone) into the real world of "theology and horses." Rosetta, persisting in her regression, protests, "Too soon we embrace that / Impermanent appetitive flux . . . which adults fear / Is real and right"; Emble remarks that this "real" world is full of perversions of Eros: "a dean sits / Making bedroom eyes at a beef steak / As wholly oral as the avid creatures / Of the celibate sea," financiers lust for money, while average married people, losing interest in sex, long for change, the Absolute Instant. Quant replies that the Unexpected is always present, any stability illusory: "We are mocked by unmeaning." In the Fifth Age, Malin goes on, he obtains worldly approval and success. Emble describes the youthful fear of never attaining this:

> . . . To be young means
> To be all on edge, to be held waiting in
> A packed lounge for a Personal Call
> From Long Distance, for the low voice that
> Defines one's future . . . It is getting late.
> Shall we ever be asked for? Are we simply
> Not wanted at all?

Quant describes failure to obtain success; Rosetta argues that it is meaningless in our time, and Quant replies that all times are the same, history has no meaning. The Sixth Age shows Everyman aging, unhappy, longing for the innocence of childhood. Again, each character interprets in his own terms: Quant portrays the aging failure, who has abandoned the Quest after one glimpse of the "glaciers guarding the Good Place," and who returns with a consciousness of his own evil; Rosetta describes the innocent dolls running down, the paternal landscape fading, the illusion lost; Emble remembers the garden to which he has lost the key; the desert is now his home. In the Seventh Age, Everyman's "last illusions have lost patience / With the human enterprise," and at death he is "modest at last." Ironically, each character then returns to his illusions, unaffected by the analysis: Rosetta thinks of the deaths of lovable eccentrics in her Innocent Landscape; Emble compares himself with the Average ("Must I end like that?"); Quant, describing odd deaths, takes refuge in humor and cynicism.

Part III, "The Seven Stages," is based on the pattern of the Quest. This journey homeward to the center of time, the Quiet Kingdom, follows the "Regressive road to Grandmother's House": i.e. it is a parody-Quest for an unrecoverable Innocence consisting in being non-human like a doll, or ignorant of the Logos like a child. Rosetta, appropriately, serves as guide; but the members of the group have achieved an alcoholic rapport which allows them to "function as a single organism." Since they seek "that state of prehistoric happiness which, by human beings, can only be imagined in terms of a landscape bearing a symbolic resemblance to the human body," the landscape is all moralized (cf. the earlier discussion of this technique, pp. 141ff.). Because the complex symbolism of each stage is interpreted differently, in an intricate counterpointing, by each character, an adequate commentary on this section would run to inordinate length; I can therefore give only the briefest of outlines. Isolated at the beginning, each character finds enough water (belief, hope) to motivate his Quest. Climbing the mountains (action, choice) they arrive at a watershed in the "high heartland" (in terms of the body, the heart as seat of the will and emotions). Thence they proceed in the second stage to the maritime plains, where each reacts characteristically: Rosetta sees the ports as disorderly, Emble in military terms; Malin sees in the ocean a metaphysical and religious "border," and Quant is overwhelmed by its immensity: the desperate spirit is "a speck drowning / In those wanton mansions where the whales take / Their huge fruitions." The third stage takes them inland to the Metropolis (civilization; in terms of the body, the brain), on which they comment in the fourth stage. The City is a "facetious culture," outwardly planned and orderly, but ignoring ultimate questions; the planners have taken care of everything but the anxiety and evil of individuals. In the Big House, the fifth stage, Rosetta finds only her imaginary childhood environment turned sour, its innocence corrupted, "mating and malice of men and beasts." As they race away, each makes a typical comment; Malin fears that failure will indicate sin; Quant believes the average is safest; Emble rejoices in his superiority but tries to look modest; Rosetta says, "I can't hope to be first / So let me be last." The Graveyard at the end of this stage represents the end of secular planning for the individual, the fact that it omits. The sixth stage takes them to the Hermetic Gardens (in the symbolic body, the genitals); on the journey each feels sexual attraction. The implication is that sexual love is narcissistic, the object self-created: Malin's impulse is really towards a son created in his own image, Quant's toward a daughter-wife. The beauty of the gardens, recalling their sins of love, afflicts them with psychosomatic disease, and the seventh stage takes them alone into the forest, despairing of love. At the edge they encounter the Desert, "lands beyond love," i.e. the place of trial; confronted by this, all feel self-doubt. Thus they refuse to attempt the only true Quest, to become aware of the religious Choice; and "their fears are confirmed, their hopes denied. For the world from which their journey has been one long flight rises up before them now. . . ." All feel guilt and see visions of terror; then they return to themselves and the present.

Part IV, "The Dirge," is dominated by the City symbol. Discouraged by the apparent meaninglessness of nature and the hopeless situation of man, the characters think of some "semidivine stranger with superhuman powers, some Gilgamesh or Napoleon, some Solon or Sherlock Holmes" who promises to rescue man and nature, but who always dies or disappears. This is, of course, the False Messiah, the Secular Savior to whom, without Christianity, mankind will always look for relief from anxiety and guilt. This dirge is therefore a parody: the Lawgiver they ironically lament is the Hero of all Quests, the Lucky Son, the Grail Knight, Caesar and any dictator—the universal Exceptional Man in whom the Average, to escape responsibility, put their faith. In psychological terms, he is the Father-image, "Our lost dad, / Our colossal father." The characters cannot, however, take this solution seriously.

Part V, "The Masque," resumes the Quest pattern: the theme now is sexual love, the Erotic Quest of Emble and Rosetta, perennial Prince and Princess. Auden comments that in wartime "even the crudest kind of positive affection between persons seems extraordinarily beautiful, a noble symbol of the peace and forgiveness of which the whole world stands so desperately in need." So Malin invokes "Heavenly Venus" as a quasi-Platonic symbol of universal love, in contrast to Quant's previous bitter picture of Venus Island. Emble woos in his characteristic Quest images; Rosetta replies in her Innocent Landscape. Though aware that sexual love is regressive and narcissistic, Malin and Quant tolerantly urge them to cherish their illusions. The Vision of Innocence they all participate in is the crowning illusion, the climax of the whole poem as a parody Dream Quest: each describes in his own terms the triumph of Eros and Innocence (the false goal they pursue throughout the poem). But all the illusions fail, Emble passes out, and Rosetta renounces her dream of "the Innocent Place where / His law can't look," of "a home like theirs." Abandoning her Innocent Landscape, she accepts her real childhood ("the semi-detached / Brick villa in Laburnum Crescent, / The poky parlor . . ."), her "poor fat father," and the fact of her race which he symbolizes: "Time is our trade, to be tense our gift / Whose woe is our weight; for we are His Chosen." For her there is no escape from evil, insecurity, the hard fate of her race; accepting these realities, she concludes by reciting the Jewish Creed in Hebrew.

Part VI, "Epilogue," consists of Malin's meditations on the nature of love and time (the first time in the poem that the Christian concepts of Agape and Logos have been introduced other than by negative implication), counterpointed by Quant's meditations on the Heraclitan flux of time and the meaningless cycles of history: there is always a war and a peace-treaty, bringing hopes for a better world which are always doomed to disappointment. Malin reflects that we do not learn from the past, that the future looks bleak:

> Yet the noble despair of the poets
> Is nothing of the sort; it is silly
> To refuse the tasks of time
> And, overlooking our lives,
> Cry—'Miserable wicked me,
> How interesting I am.'
> We would rather be ruined than changed,
> We would rather die in our dread
> Than climb the cross of the moment
> And let our illusions die.

But after this passage—which, if any, is the "message" of the poem—he returns to his negative knowledge: we cannot understand the relation between time and eternity, the "clock we are bound to obey / And the miracle we must not despair of"; we cannot conceive of Agape, of how the "raging lion is to lime / With the yearning unicorn." Neither reason nor imagination can enable us to comprehend these matters; the meaning is "reserved / For the eyes of faith to find," and our own efforts, without Grace, cannot achieve faith. Eros is corrupt; our passions pray to "primitive totems"; science or no science, our dreams are of "Bacchus or the Great Boyg or Baal-Peor, / Fortune's Ferris-wheel or the physical sound / Of our own names"; our worship is mostly "so much galimatias to get out of / Knowing our neighbor." Thus "in choosing how many / And how much they will love, our minds insist on / Their own disorder as their own punishment." Yet "His love observes / His appalling promise," and Divine Grace, Agape, is vouchsafed us, "His Good ingressant on our gross occasions," in our "mad unbelief" as we "wait unawares for His World to come."

The Age of Anxiety was received rather coolly by the critics, most of whom thought it too artificial and rhetorical, lacking in dramatic quality—all the characters aspects of Auden, saying the same thing—and, as a war poem or a tract for the times, unrealistic and superficial. As usual, the most damning comment was made by Randall Jarrell:

> *The Age of Anxiety* is the worst thing Auden has written since "The Dance of Death"; it is the equivalent of Wordsworth's "Ecclesiastical Sonnets." The man who, during the thirties, was one of the five or six best poets in the world has gradually turned into a rhetoric mill grinding away at the bottom of Limbo, into an automaton that keeps making little jokes, little plays on words, little rhetorical engines, as compulsively and unendingly and uneasily as a neurotic washes his hands.
>
> (*The Nation*, Oct. 18, 1947)

On the other hand, Leonard Bernstein was inspired by the poem, which he called "fascinating and hair-raising," to write "The Age of Anxiety (Symphony No. 2 for Piano and Orchestra) (After W. H. Auden)," completed in 1949, which is interesting as an attempt to produce a musical equivalent, rather than a setting of any part of the work. Bernstein divides the poem into two parts, following it section by section but without pause between the three sections of each part. The prologue consists of a "lonely improvisation" by two clarinets and echotone, and is followed by "a long descending scale which acts as a bridge into the realm of the unconscious, where most of the poem takes place." [54] The Seven Ages and Seven Stages are both variation movements. Part II begins with The Dirge, which employs a twelve-tone row; The Masque "is a kind of scherzo for piano and percussion alone ... in which a kind of fantastic piano-jazz is employed"; to represent the anticlimactic end "the piano protagonist is traumatized by the intervention of the orchestra for four bars of hectic jazz. When the orchestra stops, ... a *pianino* in the orchestra is continuing the Masque, repetitiously and with waning energy, as the Epilogue begins." The piano-protagonist does not take part in the Epilogue, but observes it; the orchestra is a mirror in which he sees himself. But he does toward the end contribute to the orchestra's declaration of faith "one eager chord of confirmation."

John Bayley, in *The Romantic Survival* (1957), goes so far as to call *Age* Auden's "greatest achievement to date, and the one which best shows the true nature of his scope and talent" (p. 185). He likes the modesty and sympathy of tone, the effects of tenderness and pathos—"the poetry of Rosetta is perhaps the most moving he has written"—and most of all the fact that here Auden can give free rein to his characteristic "exuberance of particularity," which Bayley considers to link Auden both to the Romantics and to the novel, especially Dickens. I have expressed my admiration for, and debt to, Mr. Bayley's book, which seems to me to contain the most perceptive criticism of Auden that has appeared in recent years. I am dubious, however, about Mr. Bayley's thesis as a whole (see above, p. 65), and I suspect that he over-rates the *Age* because of the neatness with which it fits his argument. The mere presence of the "exuberance of particularity" or the "trivia of the consciousness" does not necessarily make *Age*, or any other poem, good; one must point out, with pedagogical obviousness, that what matters is how they are used, what kind of coherence and unity they form.

My own view is that *Age* is almost as far from being Auden's best as it is from being his worst poem. It is full of provocative and fascinating ideas, many of which do not quite come off—like the Seven Ages and the landscape-body analogy in the Seven Stages. It is, like all the other long poems, uneven; but it contains more flats than the others perhaps because of the use of the single meter for most of the poem, and because some of the ideas seem to be carried on too long. The Seven Stages is the best part, because (for one thing) it contains more variety in form—all the lyrics published separately (except the Dirge) and those preserved in *Selected Poetry* are from this section. It is not as rich nor varied nor profound as either "For the Time Being" or "The Sea and the Mirror," as I see it. But it is a brilliant and moving and impressive performance, and one we would not willingly be without.

The three long works we have considered in this section complement each other in certain interesting respects, and together they constitute a unity. The beliefs and attitudes that are basic to all of Auden's writing after 1940 are defined in them in a manner that seems, retrospectively, almost programmatic: religious in *For the Time Being*, aesthetic in *The Sea and the Mirror* (in which the central ideas of *The Dyer's Hand*, 1962, are already implicit), and social-psychological in *The Age of Anxiety*. In technique, *For the Time Being* is external and objective, *The Age of Anxiety* internal and subjective, with *The Sea and the Mirror* intermediate. Auden has written no long poems since, and certainly one reason is that the three works together make a kind of triptych, a completed achievement.

Aesthetically, perhaps the central weakness of *Age* is that the Quest is largely internal: the social-psychological diagnosis of contemporary anxiety, isolation, and anonymous solitude is represented in subjective terms, with all the action psychic and no real interaction among the characters. In terms of the pendulum-swing that I have tried to avoid suggesting as a metaphor, this is a swing in the direction of fantasy, in contrast to the diagnosis-swing described at the end of the last section. But the longer works to be considered in the next section—opera libretti and sequences of companion poems—exhibit a kind of compensating countermovement. Operas, though dream-literature, have a dramatic objectivity; they are embodied in music, and performed; and the companion poems have an external framework, of canonical hours or moralized landscape. In the later poems the Island of fantasy, which has figured in the earlier poetry as amorous escape or selfish isolation, in *The Sea and the Mirror* as Art, and in *The Age of Anxiety* as one form of the false alcoholic Eden sought by all the characters, is located definitively outside the realm of Clio and identified either with Eden (timeless and supernatural) or with the dominion of Dame Kind.

1. First published Autumn 1939, entitled "The Prophets." I am indebted to Hoggart (op. cit., pp. 142-3), who uses this poem similarly as an epigraph.

2. See above, p. 123. The Oxford philosopher and historian, R. G. Collingwood (1889-1943), profoundly influenced Auden. He quotes Collingwood's *Essay on Metaphysics* (Oxford, 1940) in the notes to "New Year Letter" (*The Double Man*, p. 112), in his Smith College address of 1940, and elsewhere. For the influence of Collingwood's *The Principles of Art* (Oxford, 1938), see above, p. 188; the pervasive idea of art as bringing emotions to consciousness and of the artist as creating a world of language seems to derive from Collingwood, e.g., *Principles*, p. 291:

> Theoretically, the artist is a person who comes to know himself, to know his own emotion. This is also knowing his world, that is, the sights and sounds and so forth which together make up his total imaginative experience. The two knowledges are to him one knowledge, because these sights and sounds are to him steeped in the emotion with which he contemplates them: they are the language in which that emotion utters itself to his consciousness. His world is his language. What it says to him it says about himself; his imaginative vision of it is his self-knowledge. But this knowing of himself is a making of himself ... The coming to know his own emotions is the coming to dominate them, to assert himself as their master.... Moreover, his knowing of this new world is also the making of the new world which he is coming to know. The world he has come to know is a world consisting of language ... In so far as this world is thus expressive or significant, it is he that has made it so.

3. Contribution to symposium, "Religion and the Intellectuals," *Partisan Review*, Feb. 1950.

4. For Kassner, see below, pp. 244a-b.

5. Charles Williams (1886-1945) worked for the Oxford University Press all his life, in London 1908-39 and in Oxford 1939-45. Many others besides Auden have testified to the effect of his personal goodness as well as the impressiveness of his thought—most notably T. S. Eliot, C. S. Lewis, and Dorothy Sayers. In his introduction to *The Descent of the Dove* Auden remarks that when he met Williams (perhaps in connection with the editing of the *Oxford Book of Light Verse*, 1938) he had read none of his books; when he read them he realized that their basic theme of exchange and substitution was also Williams's way of life and ex-

plained why "in his company one felt twice as intelligent and infinitely nicer than, out of it, one knew oneself to be"; he "gave himself completely to the company that he was in" (p. v), so that any conversation with him was a genuine dialogue. Auden considers the *Descent of the Dove* to be his masterpiece, and comments that after reading and re-reading it for some sixteen years he finds it "a source of intellectual delight and spiritual nourishment which remains inexhaustible" (p. xii). I have noted above (p. 134 and n.75) the influence of this book on *The Double Man*, which is even greater than would appear from Auden's notes; it seems virtually certain, for example, that the following quotations come not from the original sources given in the notes but from *Dove*, in which they figure prominently: *D.M.*, p. 133, "Postremum Sanctus Spiritus effudit" from *Dove*, pp. 132-3; *D.M.*, p. 158, "Quando non fuerit, non est" from *Dove*, p. 39; "O da quod jubes, Domine" from *Dove*, p. 65, and "Our life and death are with our neighbour" from *Dove*, p. 46. Auden made a general acknowledgment that *Dove* was "the source of many ideas in the poem" (*D.M.*, p. 153). Auden quotes *Dove* on the "scandal of Christian disunity" at the end of his essay in *Modern Canterbury Pilgrims*. He considers Williams's novels his least satisfactory writings; after *Dove* he admires most the critical books (he calls *The Figure of Beatrice* "magnificent") and theological essays, and he admires the poetry with reservations. In *The Dyer's Hand* (1962) he quotes a long passage from Williams's poetry (pp. 236-7) and a passage from his *Witchcraft* (1941), p. 55; in the *Viking Book of Aphorisms* he quotes numerous passages from Williams. Williams's influence can be seen generally in the symbols of the City and of Eros-Agape-Logos.

6. Review of *Either/Or*, *The New Republic*, 1941.

7. Review of *Christianity and Power Politics*, *The Nation*, 1941. In the same year Auden reviewed Niebuhr's major work, *The Nature and Destiny of Man*, in *The New Republic*.

8. Review of translations of Kafka in *The New Republic*, 1941.

9. Aside from "New Year Letter," perhaps the most striking example is "Christmas 1940," in which some passages from Auden's reviews of Niebuhr and "Note on Order" (all published in 1941) are put into verse —or, conceivably, vice versa.

10. "Religion and the Intellectuals" in *Partisan Review*.

11. "Hic et Ille," in *Encounter*, 1956; reprinted in *The Dyer's Hand* (1962), pp. 152-3. Reviewing a book on Luther (*The Mid-Century* #13, June 1960), Auden suggests that the Protestant Era, with its emphasis on the unique and private will rather than the universal body and reason, its denial of the Mother and the Flesh (Faith, not Works), is over now and that we have entered a Catholic Era in which a catholic theology must be dominant with a protestant ideology as restraining and critical opposi-

tion. The Protestant approach cannot solve our difficulties because it is precisely this approach that has caused them; Newman's conversion in 1845, he suggests, is the beginning of this new era. Our danger is lack of belief in and acceptance of the existence of others; our need is for a catholic community.

12. *The Living Thoughts of Kierkegaard*, Presented by W. H. Auden (New York, 1952). A paperback reprint has been announced for 1963 (Indiana University Press).

13. For Quests, see note 79 in the preceding section.

14. Review of Barzun, *The New Republic*, 1941. In his introduction to Sydney Smith's *Selected Writings* (1956) Auden observes that Smith's Whig tradition is today under a cloud:

> Yet, unattractive and shallow as one may feel so many liberals to be, how rarely on any concrete social issue does one find the liberal position the wrong one. Again, how often, alas, do those very philosophers and writers who have most astounded us by their profound insights into the human heart and human existence, dismay us by the folly and worse of their judgments on the issues of everyday life.   (p. xix)

And he concludes by suggesting a parallel between Smith and Kierkegaard.

15. Review of Laski in *Decision*, 1941. A spiritual revolution (i.e., change of heart) must precede a material one, Auden argues; not, as Marx thought, the other way around.

16. Review of Cochrane in *The New Republic*, 1944. Eliot expresses a very similar attitude in the Krishna-Arjuna passage of "The Dry Salvages."

17. Review of Niebuhr in *The Nation*, 1941.

18. Review of Cochrane in *The New Republic*, 1944.

19. Review of Eliot's *A Choice of Kipling's Verse*, *The New Republic*, 1943. The reference is to Collingwood's *Principles of Art*, 1938.

20. *Harpers*, July 1948.

21. "Squares and Oblongs," 1948. See pp. 303-4 below.

22. The poem has been discussed as a whole above, p. 172. The last three stanzas are particularly Eliotic: "Time remembered bear witness to time required, / The positive and negative ways through time / Embrace and encourage each other / In a brief moment of intersection;..."

23. In *The Viking Book of Aphorisms*, p. 82, "My love is my weight" is quoted from St. Augustine.

24. According to his note to line 56 of "New Year Letter," Auden picked it up from E. M. Forster's quotation (from Jacopone da Todi) in

I Believe (ed. C. Fadiman, 1940), to which Auden also contributed. In another note (*Double Man*, p. 131-2) Auden quotes Paul Tillich on the relation of Kairos and Logos; another passage from the same work of Tillich's (*The Interpretation of History*, New York, 1936, p. 129) illuminates the meaning of the terms: "We call this fulfilled moment, the moment of time approaching us as fate and decision, *Kairos*." Kairos, Tillich continues, is opposed to the thinking in the timeless and abstract Logos. Pure theory is asceticism toward Kairos, Eros toward Logos; it regards the world as a system of eternal forms. Pure practice is asceticism toward the Logos and Eros toward Kairos—this is the practical man's attitude. (This passage also casts light on the Caliban-Ariel contrasts in *The Sea and the Mirror*.) In *The Dyer's Hand* (p. 140n.) Auden speaks, in a different context, of "The Greek notion of *Kairos*, the propitious moment for doing something. . . ."

25. Kierkegaard, *Either/Or*, ed. H. A. Johnson (New York, 1959, vol. II, p. 343), "The edification implied in the thought that as against God we are always in the wrong." The whole poem is pervaded by Kierkegaard, perhaps more so than any other poem of Auden's. The poem is dedicated to Maurice Mandelbaum, who was then teaching philosophy at Swarthmore, and his wife; they were Auden's close friends and, for a time, landlords.

26. Auden probably took the title from de la Mare's *Come Hither!*, in which an extract from the play, *Mundus et Infans* (*c.* 1500) is given on p. 28 and discussed p. 516. The poem is dedicated to Auden's particular friends at the University of Michigan, Mr. and Mrs. Albert K. Stevens (Auden mistakenly gives the Christian name as "Arthur"); the occasion was the birth of their son, Auden Stevens, in 1943. (I am much indebted to R. H. Super of the University of Michigan for providing me with this and other information about Auden's stay at Michigan.)

27. See above, p. 106 and notes 37, 38, in which the pieces in question are listed.

28. See p. 100, above. This was first pointed out by Edward Callan in his "Annotated Checklist of the Works of W. H. Auden," *Twentieth Century Literature*, April-July 1958 (also available as a book from Alan Swallow, Denver, Colorado). Beach was not aware of it; his whole argument is based on Auden's presumed *intention* in writing the piece as part of *Dog*.

29. *Letters from Iceland*, p. 239: "The Church of Saint Aidan at Smallheath to my mother / Where she may pray for this poor world and me"; p. 204, "We imitate our loves: well, neighbours say / I grow more like my mother every day." In "A Literary Transference" (1940) Auden says that Hardy "looked like my father: that broad unpampered moustache,

bald forehead and deeply lined sympathetic face belonged to the other world of feeling and sensation (for I, like my mother, was a thinking-intuitive)."

30. It was "begun in Ann Arbor and finished before I came to Swarthmore" (letter to M.K.S., March 21, 1962). Several portions were published in periodicals: "At the Manger" in *Commonweal*, Dec. 25, 1942; "Herod Considers the Massacre of the Innocents" in *Harpers*, Dec. 1943; "After Christmas" (the Narrator's final speech) in *Harpers*, Jan. 1944.

31. There is an obvious allusion to the beginning of the *Divine Comedy*.

32. Cf. Psalm 46:10 and the "Prayer for Quiet Confidence" in the *Book of Common Prayer*.

33. See above, pp. 189-90, for Auden's definition of Eros as the basic will to self-actualization without which no creature can exist; but in a note to "New Year Letter" (*Double Man*, p. 107) Auden distinguishes between doing evil and sinning: "To do evil is to act contrary to self-interest. It is possible for all living creatures to do this because their knowledge of their self-interest is false or inadequate. Thus the animals whose evolution is complete, whose knowledge of their relations to the rest of creation is fixed, can do evil, but they cannot sin."

34. Cf. Auden's volume of selections from Kierkegaard, p. 30: "Christianity is certainly not melancholy, it is, on the contrary, glad tidings—for the melancholy; to the frivolous it is certainly not glad tidings, for it wishes first of all to make them serious. That is the road we all have to take—over the Bridge of Sighs into eternity."

35. The image is a brilliant one that perhaps needs paraphrase: observing that the Venus of the Soma (i.e., the biological Eros of note 33, above) is myopic, he hopes that his moral imperative will rectify the optical errors (lens-flare and lens-coma) that mislead the sensual eye.

36. Randall Jarrell, in his brilliant but inimical essay, "Freud to Paul: The Stages of Auden's Ideology," *Partisan Review*, Fall 1945, complains that Auden chose Herod rather than Pilate to represent the typical Liberal: "We are so *used* to rejecting Herod as a particularly bogey-ish Churchill that Auden can count on our going right on rejecting him when he is presented as Sir Stafford Cripps" (p. 442). One wonders whether Jarrell can actually have thought Auden was free to replace Herod by Pilate, as if they were both fictional characters.

37. Auden explains the symbolism of the Desert in *The Enchafèd Flood* (1950): it is the abode of those who reject or are rejected by the City, with the modern connotations of spiritual drouth, triviality, mechanization, and level uniformity. In "The Shield of Achilles" and "Plains" the Desert is the symbol of modern life at its worst.

38. The manuscript of this is in the Lockwood Memorial Library at the University of Buffalo, in the *Sea and the Mirror* notebook.

39. Cf. the epigraph: "Shall we continue in sin, that grace may abound? God forbid."

40. In his review of translations of Kafka, *The New Republic*, 1941, Auden quotes Kafka's aphorism, "One must cheat no one, not even the world of its triumph." (It is included in the *Viking Book of Aphorisms*, p. 92.)

41. Letter from Auden referred to in note 30, above. Only two portions appeared in periodicals: "Preface" in *The Atlantic Monthly* for Aug. 1944 and "Alonzo to Ferdinand" in *Partisan Review*, Oct. 1943.

The piece is dedicated to James and Tania Stern, who collaborated with Auden in translating Brecht's *Caucasion Chalk Circle* (see note 18 to the preceding section) and translated *Grimm's Fairy Tales* (New York, 1944; Auden reviewed the translation) and Kafka's *Letters to Milena* (London and New York, 1953).

The Lockwood Memorial Library at the University of Buffalo has the notebook Auden used in writing "The Sea and the Mirror," consisting of more than 100 pages containing everything from first tentative lists of characters and verse forms to much of the finished work. This manuscript would provide rich material for a study of the process of composition; it effectively gives the lie to any notion that Auden is a careless writer who never blots a line, for it shows him both revising painstakingly and minutely and often completely rewriting passages in a different form or style. Perhaps I should note that I deliberately refrained from consulting the manuscript until after I had written my interpretation of "The Sea and the Mirror," because I did not want to risk confusing what Auden intended (as revealed by the manuscript) with what is actually in the finished work; obviously, the two are not necessarily the same, particularly in a long work written over a considerable period of time. I then used it as a negative check, to make sure I had not gone astray or missed any major significance. A diagram Auden gives toward the end is worth reproducing as an indication of the polarities in terms of which he was thinking (manuscript p. 105):

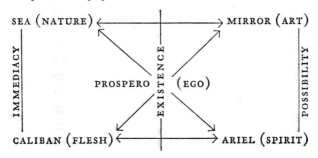

42. "Gay" is New York slang for homosexual, and very likely this connotation is relevant.

43. According to G. S. Fraser (*The Modern Writer and his World*, London, 1953, p. 245) this is Auden's first use of syllabic meter, and it probably owes something to Marianne Moore's example. Fraser seems to me right on both counts. (It is worth noting that Auden reviewed a volume of Miss Moore's verse in 1944.) Hoggart (pp. 106-10) analyzes part of the speech. The Buffalo manuscript indicates that Auden took more pains with this than with any other speech; there are at least six or eight different versions of it, occupying manuscript pp. 44-70, in different meters and styles.

44. Cf. "Many Happy Returns" (*Collected Poetry*, p. 71): "Tao is a tightrope..." This poem is in many respects a lighter parallel to *The Sea and the Mirror* (see p. 197 above).

45. While he was writing *The Sea and the Mirror* Auden was teaching at Swarthmore a course called "Romanticism from Rousseau to Hitler," and he used in it a diagram which is interesting because it shows the polarities in terms of which his mind was working and the associations various symbols had for him. Since it casts some light upon Caliban's description of his and Ariel's kingdoms, as well as upon the passage now in question, a brief description of it may be worthwhile.

Beginning with the Fall from Paradise (Eden) into This World (or from Essential into Existential Being), the chart tabulates in the center column the characteristics of Dualism of Experience or Knowledge of Good and Evil in This World. An arrow to the left-hand column indicates the search for salvation by finding refuge in nature, leading to the Hell of the Pure Deed, of Power without Purpose; and the left-hand column tabulates the characteristics of this state. The right-hand column describes the Hell of the Pure Word, of Knowledge without Power, arrived at through the search for salvation by finding release from nature. Down the left side of the chart runs a series of categories, each carried across the three columns. For example, the first category is Primary Symbol: in the center of the page, this is City; verging to the left, still in the center column describing This World, is Forest; in the left-hand Hell (of Pure Deed) it is Common Night and at extreme left, Sea. Verging to the right in the center column it is Mountain; in the right-hand Hell (of Pure Word) it is Private Light and, still farther, Desert. A few other examples may be given, though in less detail. In the category of Metaphysical Condition, the center column gives Actualization of the Possible, with Growth as alternative description; Art verges to the left and Science to the right; the left-hand Hell is Pure Aesthetic Immediacy with Pure Ethical Potentiality, and the right-hand one is Aesthetic Nonentity with Pure Ethical Actuality. For the category of Order the center is Differentiated Unity or Civilization, with Rivers and Country verging left to the Hell of Monist Unity (water) and Barbaric Vagueness, while Roads and Towns verge right to the Hell of Dissociated Multiplicity and Decadent Triviality. In the category, Sin, the central condition is Anxiety with Criminals and Bohemians verging left to the Hell of Sensuality, while Police and Bourgeois Pharisees verge right to the Hell of Pride. Finally, the last category, The Quest, indicates the alternative methods of attaining Forgiveness (Purgatory) through, on the left, "The voluntary journey of the corrupt mind through the sea. Purgation of pride by Dissolution" and, on the right, "The voluntary passing of the corrupt body through the desert. Purgation of lust by Desiccation." (Arrows indicate that each condition must pass through the other to achieve the goal.) On the left of the center column the descriptions are Fertilizing the Waste Land and The Island; on the right, Draining the Swamp and The Oasis.

Kenneth Lewars, a member of Auden's seminar in Romanticism at Swarthmore, preserved the original of this chart and reproduced it in his M.A. thesis, "The Quest in Auden's Poems and Plays" (Columbia, 1947). I am indebted to Samuel Hynes for calling the chart to my attention and giving me a copy of it, and to Mr. Lewars as well as Mr. Auden for allowing me to quote from it. Mr. Lewars intends to publish shortly a thorough study of the chart (which is a lengthy document covering three typescript pages) together with a complete reproduction; this should be an article of unusual interest. Many of the ideas tabulated in the chart—especially those dealing with archetypal symbols—were worked out by Auden in *The Enchafèd Flood*, 1950.

46. As Hoggart points out, the reference is to the end of *The Winter's Tale*. There is also a possible allusion by contrast to the end of *Don Giovanni*, this statue not punishing but forgiving.

47. In relation to the basic symbolism of the whole piece, there is a further ironic meaning: the mirror of art is indeed always lonely.

48. In the Buffalo MS., there are several drafts of the beginning of Caliban's speech. The first is in verse (MS., p. 97): "Ladies and gentlemen, please keep your seats. / An unidentified plane is reported / Approaching the city. Probably only a false alarm / But naturally, we cannot afford / To take any chances. So all our lights are out / And we must sit in the dark. I can guess / What you are thinking: How odd this feels: to be sitting / In a theatre when the final curtain has fallen / On a dream that ended agreeably with wedding bells / Substantial rewards for the good, and for the bad / Nothing worse than a ducking...." This is revised (still in verse), and then a prose version begun on p. 103, but with no trace of the Henry James style of the final version.

49. There is also a relation to the Logos-Kairos symbolism discussed

above in note 24, and to Kierkegaard's Aesthetic/Ethical categories (pp. 181-2 above). The philosophy of A. N. Whitehead is definitely in the background here and elsewhere in the poem, most explicitly in the triviality/vagueness antithesis (cf. *Process and Reality*, New York, 1929, pp. 170-72). Auden quotes *Process and Reality* in the notes to "New Year Letter" (*The Double Man*, p. 153) and shows Whitehead's influence in other poems 1939-44; Whitehead appears frequently in the *Viking Book of Aphorisms* (1962), and the analysis of various types of "societies" in *The Dyer's Hand* owes something to him.

50. Like other ironists, Auden has paid the penalty of being taken literally. He has been accused of snobbery (by Bayley, p. 145) because Caliban refers to "collarless herds who eat blancmange and have never said anything witty" (p. 379); but Caliban here is parodying the naïve snobbery of the audience (in the snobbish accents of James). Similarly, Auden has been accused (by Harry Levin, in an otherwise very brilliant review of *For the Time Being* in *The New Republic*, Sept. 18, 1944) of remoteness from common life because Caliban says "there is probably no one whose real name is Brown" (p. 398); but Caliban is here parodying adolescent romanticism, "an infinite extension of the adolescent difficulty, a rising of the subjective and subjunctive to ever steeper, stormier heights" (p. 398). Both passages are about as far from statements by Auden in his own person as they could possibly be.

51. Letter W.H.A. to M.K.S., March 21, 1962. Reviews of *For the Time Being* in Sept. 1944 reported *The Age of Anxiety* as in progress. Two excerpts were published in American magazines: "Spinster's Song" (*Age*, p. 80) in *The New Yorker*, Sept. 28, 1946, and "Metropolis" (*Age*, p. 75) in *Commonweal*, Dec. 20, 1946. In England "Lament for a Lawgiver" (*Age*, p. 104) was published in *Horizon*, March 1948.

The poem was dedicated to John Betjeman, for whose volume *Slick but not Streamlined* Auden wrote an introduction in the same year.

52. See "The Guilty Vicarage: Notes on the Detective Story by an Addict," 1948; including in *The Dyer's Hand* (1962). This analysis of the detective story as a form of magic, not art, whose function is to indulge the fantasy of escape from guilt, casts much light upon the central theme of *Age* as well as upon Rosetta's fantasy-world.

53. Emble justifies the war in simple and popular terms: Rome fell through softness, "Better this than barbarian misrule"; Malin replies that the new barbarian was born here, inside the City, and we share the blame ("A crime has occurred, accusing all"); Quant sees no meaning beyond a temporary "defense of friends against foes' hate"; Rosetta thinks the war will change nothing and its end will see a return to the "lies and lethargies" of peace.

54. From Bernstein's own description on the jacket of Col. ML 4325.

1948-1962

1948   Awarded Pulitzer Prize in May.

Began spending the spring and summer of each year on the Italian island of Ischia.

Edited *The Portable Greek Reader* (New York: Viking).

Edited *A Beginning*, by Robert Horan (Vol. 46 of Yale Series of Younger Poets).

"Squares and Oblongs," in *Poets at Work*, ed. Charles D. Abbot (New York: Harcourt, Brace; partially included in *The Dyer's Hand*, 1962).

"Yeats as an Example," in *Kenyon Review*, Spring 1948.

"The Guilty Vicarage: Notes on the Detective Story by an Addict," in *Harper's*, May 1948 (included in *The Dyer's Hand*, 1962).

"Henry James and the Artist in America," in *Harper's*, July 1948.

"Opera Addict," *Vogue*, July 1948.

1949   Edited *The Grasshopper's Man*, by Rosalie Moore (Vol. 47 of Yale Series of Younger Poets).

"The Heresy of our Time," *Renascence*, Spring 1949.

"The Question of Ezra Pound," *Partisan Review*, May 1949.

"A Note on Graham Greene," *The Wind and the Rain*, Summer 1949.

"The Ironic Hero: Some Reflections on Don Quixote," *Horizon*, Aug. 1949.

Review of *Notes Towards a Definition of Culture*, by T. S. Eliot, in *The New Yorker*, April 23, 1949 ("Port and Nuts with the Eliots").

Review of *A Writer's Notebook*, by Somerset Maugham, in *The New York Times Book Review*, October 23, 1949.

1950   *Collected Shorter Poems 1930-1944* published by Faber
        & Faber.

   *The Enchafèd Flood: the Romantic Iconography of the
Sea* published by Random House; by Faber & Faber 1951.
Dedicated to Alan Ansen.

   Edited, with Norman Holmes Pearson, *Poets of the
English Language*, 5 vols. (New York: Viking).

   Edited *Edgar Allan Poe: Selected Poetry and Prose*
(New York: Rinehart).

   Introduction to *Red Ribbon on a White Horse* by Ania
Yesiersko (New York: Scribner's; included in *The Dyer's
Hand*, 1962).

   "Nature, History, and Poetry," in *Thought*, Sept. 1950.
(Included in *The Dyer's Hand*, 1962.)

   Review of *The Recollections of A. de Tocqueville*, in
The Nation, April 8, 1950 ("A Guide-book for All Good
Counter-Revolutionaries").

   Review of *The Paradox of Oscar Wilde*, by G. Wood-
cock, in *Partisan Review*, April 1950 ("A Playboy of the
Western World: St. Oscar, the Homintern Martyr").

   Review of *Boswell's London Journal* in *The New
Yorker*, Nov. 25, 1950.

1951   With Lionel Trilling and Jacques Barzun, founded the
        Reader's Subscription book club, and wrote occasionally
        for its periodical, *The Griffin*, until 1958.

   The Rake's Progress, by Igor Stravinsky, with libretto
by Auden and Chester Kallman, performed in Venice on
September 11th. (The libretto was written in 1947-48.)

   Nones (dedicated to Reinhold and Ursula Niebuhr)
published by Random House and Faber & Faber.

   Edited *A Change of World*, by Adrienne Rich (Vol. 48
of Yale Series of Younger Poets).

   "Some Reflections on Opera as a Medium," *Tempo*
(London), Summer 1951 (reprinted in *Partisan Review*,
Jan. 1952; included in *The Dyer's Hand*, 1962).

   "The World that Books Have Made," *The New York
Times Book Review*, Dec. 2, 1951.

   Review of *Short Novels of Colette* in *The Griffin*,

Vol. I, #2, Dec. 1951. (Reprinted in *Perspectives U.S.A.* #3, Spring 1953.)

Review of *Old Friends and New Music,* by N. Nablov, in *The New York Times Book Review,* Feb. 4, 1951.

Review of Virgil's *Aeneid,* trans. Rolfe Humphries, *The Nation,* March 10, 1951.

1952   Edited *The Living Thoughts of Kierkegaard* (New York: David McKay; London: Cassell, 1953).

Italian translation of poems: *Poesie.* Introduzione, versione e note di Carlo Izzo (Parma).

Edited *A Mask for Janus,* by W. S. Merwin (Yale Series of Younger Poets, Vol. 49).

Introduction to *Tales of Grimm and Andersen* (New York: Random House).

"Sigmund Freud," in *The New Republic,* Oct. 6, 1952.

"Notes on the Comic," *Thought,* Spring 1952. (Included in *The Dyer's Hand,* 1962.)

Review of *Rome and a Villa,* by Eleanor Clark, in *The Griffin,* Vol. I, #5, April 1952 ("Our Italy").

"Portrait of a Whig," in *English Miscellany,* III, ed. M. Praz, Rome. (On Sydney Smith.)

Review of *Henry Irving,* by L. Irving, in *The New Yorker,* July 12, 1952.

Review of *A Composer's World,* by Paul Hindemith, in *New York Times Book Review,* Feb. 24, 1952.

1953   W. A. Neilson Research Professor at Smith College for second semester.

"Delia or a Masque of Night: Libretto for a one-act Opera," published in *Botteghe Oscure,* Rome. (Written with Chester Kallman; suggested by Peele's *Old Wives' Tale.*)

Edited *Various Jangling Keys,* by Edgar Bogardus (Yale Series of Younger Poets, Vol. 50).

"The Mythical Sex," in *Woman Today,* ed. Elizabeth Bragdon (Indianapolis: Bobbs, Merrill).

"Two Sides to a Thorny Problem: Exploring below the Surface of Shakespeare's 'Merchant'," *The New York Times,* March 1, 1953.

"Huck and Oliver," *The Listener*, Oct. 1, 1953.

Jacket notes for recording (RCA Victor LM 6106) of Mascagni, *Cavalleria Rusticana* and Leoncavallo, *I Pagliacci*. (Included in *The Dyer's Hand*, 1962.)

Reviews in *The Griffin* of T. S. Eliot, *Complete Poems and Plays* (Vol. 2, #3, March 1953); G. Verga, *The House by the Medlar Tree* (Vol. 2, #7, July 1953); T. S. Eliot, *Selected Essays* (Vol. 2, #9, Oct. 1953).

Review of *Freud: Life and Works*, Vol. I, by Ernest Jones, *The Listener*, Oct. 8, 1953 ("The Greatness of Freud").

Review of *My Host the World*, by G. Santayana, *The New Yorker*, May 2, 1953 ("Through the Collarbone of a Hare").

Review of *The Translations of Ezra Pound* in *Encounter*, Dec. 1953.

1954   In January, awarded Bollingen Prize for 1953.

Elected to American Academy of Arts and Letters.

Mountains published as an Ariel poem by Faber & Faber.

Translation of Cocteau, *Les Chevaliers de la Table Ronde*, broadcast on B.B.C. Third Programme.

Recording: Caedmon TC 1019, *W. H. Auden Reading his Poems;* recorded Dec. 12, 1953.

Edited *An Armada of Thirty Whales*, by Daniel G. Hoffman (Yale Series of Younger Poets, Vol. 51).

Introduction to *The Visionary Novels of George Macdonald*, ed. Anne Fremantle (New York: Noonday).

"Ballet's Present Eden: Example of *The Nutcracker*," *Center*, Feb. 1954 (reprinted in booklet accompanying Westminster recording of Tchaikovsky's *The Nutcracker*, #1205).

"Fog in the Mediterranean," *The Christian Scholar*, Dec. 1954 (on Camus).

"The Word and the Machine," *Encounter*, April 1954.

"Balaam and the Ass: The Master-Servant Relationship in Literature," *Thought*, Summer 1954. (Also in *Encounter*, July 1954; included in *The Dyer's Hand*, 1962.)

"How Cruel is April?", London *Times Literary Supplement*, Sept. 17, 1954.

Reviews in *The New Yorker* of *The Notebooks of Virginia Woolf*, March 6, 1954; *The Hedgehog and the Fox*, by Isaiah Berlin, Sept. 25, 1954; *The Private Diaries of Stendhal*, Dec. 18, 1954 ("The Pool of Narcissus").

Reviews in *Encounter* of *Rhythm and Tempo: a Study in Music History*, by C. Sachs, Jan. 1954 ("Words and Music"); *The Anathemata*, by David Jones, Jan. 1954 ("A Contemporary Epic"); *The Fellowship of the Ring*, by J. R. R. Tolkien, Nov. 1954 ("A World Imaginary but Real").

Reviews in *The Griffin* of *The Century of Total War*, by R. Aron, Vol. 3 #4, April 1954; the *Freud-Fleiss Letters*, Vol. 3 #6, June 1954; the *Private Diaries of Stendhal*, Vol. 3 #11, Nov. 1954.

Reviews in *The New York Times Book Review* of *The Diaries of Lewis Carroll*, Feb. 28, 1954; *The Fellowship of the Ring*, by J. R. R. Tolkien, Oct. 31, 1954 ("The Hero is a Hobbit").

1955   *The Shield of Achilles* published by Random House (February) and by Faber & Faber. Dedicated to Lincoln and Fidelma Kirstein.

Edited, with Chester Kallman and Noah Greenberg, *An Elizabethan Song Book* (New York: Doubleday).

Recording: (with New York Pro Musica Antiqua, directed by Noah Greenberg) *An Evening of Elizabethan Verse and its Music*, Columbia ML 5051.

Essay (untitled) in *Modern Canterbury Pilgrims*, ed. James A. Pike (New York: Morehouse-Gorham).

"The Anglo-American Difference," *The Anchor Review*, #1 (New York: Doubleday).

"The Dyer's Hand," "The Poetic Process," "Writing Poetry Today," *The Listener*, June 16, 23, 30, 1955 (reprinted in *The Anchor Review*, #2 1957, as "The Dyer's Hand." (Partially included in *The Dyer's Hand*, 1962.)

Reviews in *The Griffin* of *An End to Innocence*, by Leslie Fiedler, Vol. 4 #3, March 1955 ("Authority in America"); *The Fellowship of the Ring*, by J. R. R.

Tolkien (same issue); *Young Sam Johnson*, by James L. Clifford, Vol. 4 #4, April 1955; *The Life and Work of Freud*, Vol. 2, by E. Jones, Vol. 4 # 11, Nov. 1955.

Review of *The Letters of W. B. Yeats*, ed. A. Wade, *The New Yorker*, March 19, 1955.

1956-61   Professor of Poetry, Oxford University.

1956   *Making, Knowing, and Judging*, inaugural lecture given June 11, 1956, published by Clarendon Press, Oxford, and in 1957 by Oxford University Press, New York. (Included in *The Dyer's Hand*, 1962.)

In February, National Book Award for *The Shield of Achilles*.

With Chester Kallman, made an English version of *The Magic Flute* for the Mozart bicentenary; performed on NBC-TV and published by Random House.

The Old Man's Road published by Voyages Press, New York (limited edition of 750 copies).

Edited *Selected Writings of Sydney Smith* (New York: Farrar, Straus & Cudahy).

Edited *The Faber Book of Modern American Verse* (London: Faber & Faber); in United States called *The Criterion Book of Modern American Verse* (New York: Criterion Books). (Introduction included in *The Dyer's Hand*, 1962.)

Edited *Some Trees*, by John Ashbery (Yale Series of Younger Poets, Vol. 52).

Introduction to *The Descent of the Dove*, by Charles Williams (New York: Meridian Books; also published in *The Christian Century*, May 2, 1956).

"Putting it in English: a Translator Discusses the Problems of Changing Opera's Language," *The New York Times*, Jan. 8, 1956.

"An Eye for Mystery," *Harper's Bazaar*, July 1956 (about children).

"Hic et Ille," *Encounter*, April 1956. (Included in *The Dyer's Hand*, 1962.)

Reviews in *The Griffin* of *English Literature in the Sixteenth Century*, by C. S. Lewis, Vol. 5 #3, March 1956;

Evenings with the Orchestra, by H. Berlioz, Vol. 5 #5, May 1956; *D. H. Lawrence: Selected Literary Criticism,* ed. A. Beal, and *D. H. Lawrence: Novelist,* by F. R. Leavis, Vol. 5 #9, Sept. 1956; Dostoevsky, *Memoirs from the House of the Dead,* Vol. 5 #12, Nov. 1956.

Review of *Njál's Saga,* trans. C. Bayerschmidt and L. Hollander, *New Statesman,* Nov. 3, 1956 ("Concrete and Fastidious").

Review of *The Great Captains,* by Henry Treece, *Encounter,* Sept. 1956.

1957   Awarded Feltrinelli Prize (Rome).

Bought farmhouse in Kirchstetten, Lower Austria, and began spending spring and summer there.

Edited *The Green Wall,* by James Wright (Yale Series of Younger Poets, Vol. 53).

"Music in Shakespeare," *Encounter,* Dec. 1957. (Included in *The Dyer's Hand,* 1962.)

"Verismo Opera," in *World Treasury of Grand Opera,* ed. G. R. Marek (New York: Harper).

"Squares and Oblongs," in *Language: An Inquiry into its Meaning and Function,* ed. R. N. Anshen (New York: Harper). (This is not the same as the 1948 essay of identical title.)

Reviews in *The Griffin* of Vol. II, Pts. 1 & 2, of *Oxford History of English Literature,* Vol. 6 #3, April 1957; *Complete Works of Nathanael West,* Vol. 6 #4, May 1957 (included in *The Dyer's Hand,* 1962); *The Disinherited Mind,* by Erich Heller, Vol. 6 #9, Oct. 1957.

Review of *The Stones of Troy,* by C. A. Trypanis, *Encounter,* March 1957.

Reviews in *The New Yorker* of *The Borzoi Book of French Folk Tales,* March 16, 1957 (included in *The Dyer's Hand,* 1962); *My Dear Dorothea,* by G. B. Shaw, Sept. 7, 1957; *Sainte-Beuve,* by H. Nicholson, and *Gogol: a Life,* by D. Margarshack, Nov. 30, 1957 ("Talent, Genius and Unhappiness").

Review of *A. E. Housman: a Divided Life,* by G. L. Watson, *New Statesman,* May 18, 1957.

1958   *Selected Poetry* published in England by Penguin Books; published in New York in 1959 (Random House: The Modern Library).

Preface to *Jean Sans Terre*, by Yvan Goll (New York: T. Yoseloff).

"Commentary on the Poetry and Tragedy of 'Romeo and Juliet,' " in *Romeo and Juliet*, ed. Francis Fergusson (The Laurel Shakespeare, New York: Dell).

Reviews in *The Griffin* of *Paideia*, by Werner Jaeger, Vol. 7 #3, March 1958; *The Art of Eating*, by M. S. K. Fisher, Vol. 7 #6, June 1958; *The Human Condition*, by Hannah Arendt, Vol. 7 #10, Sept. 1958 ("Thinking What We Are Doing").

Review of anthology of polar exploration in *New Statesman*, July 19, 1958 ("Sacred Cold").

Reviews in *The New Yorker* of Aubrey's *Brief Lives*, ed. O. L. Dick, Feb. 15, 1958; *Byron: A Biography*, by L. A. Marchand, April 26, 1958 ("The Life of a That-There Poet").

1959   With Jacques Barzun and Lionel Trilling, established Mid-Century Book Society and wrote occasionally for its periodical, *The Mid-Century*, until 1963, when all three editors resigned.

With Chester Kallman, made English version of Brecht-Weill ballet cantata *The Seven Deadly Sins;* performed at New York City Center. (Published in *Tulane Drama Review* for Autumn 1961.)

The Play of Daniel, a Thirteenth Century Musical Drama, ed. Noah Greenberg, with Narration by Auden, published by Oxford University Press.

"The Fallen City," *Encounter*, Nov. 1959 (on Shakespeare's *Henry IV*; included in *The Dyer's Hand*, 1962).

"The Creation of Music and Poetry," *The Mid-Century* #2, Aug. 1959 (based on R. Craft, *Conversations with Stravinsky* and P. Valéry, *Art of Poetry*).

"The Private Life of a Public Man," *The Mid-Century* #4, Oct. 1959 (based on W. B. Yeats, *Mythologies*).

Reviews in *The Mid-Century of Collected Poems* by John Betjeman and recording, *A Golden Treasury of*

John Betjeman ("Mr. Betjeman's Poetic Universe"), #1, July 1959; *O To Be a Dragon*, by Marianne Moore ("Miss Marianne Moore, Bless Her!"), #5, Fall 1959.

Reviews in *Encounter* of *The Human Condition*, by Hannah Arendt, Jan. 1939 ("Thinking What We Are Doing"); *The Complete Letters of V. Van Gogh*, April 1959 ("Calm Even in the Catastrophe").

1960   *Homage to Clio* published by Random House (May) and by Faber & Faber. (Dedicated to E. R. and A. E. Dodds.)

Recording: *W. H. Auden Reads a Selection of His Poems*, Spoken Arts 780 (Nov.).

Foreword to *Times Three*, by Phyllis McGinley (New York: Viking).

Review in *The New Yorker* of *Queen Mary*, by James Pope-Hennessy, May 21, 1960.

Reviews in *The Mid-Century* of Faulkner, *The Mansion* ("The Magician from Mississippi") and *A Treasure Chest of Tales* (for children), #8, Jan. 1960; *Apologies to the Iroquois*, by Edmund Wilson, #9, Feb. 1960; *The Anger of Achilles*, by Robert Graves ("An Unclassical Classic"), #10, March 1960; *Young Man Luther*, by E. Erikson ("Greatness Finding Itself"), #13, June 1960; Kafka, *The Great Wall of China* and *Kafka*, by Max Brod ("K"—included in *The Dyer's Hand*, 1962), #17, Fall 1960; *The Less Deceived*, by P. Larkin and *For the Unfallen*, by G. Hill ("Two Ways of Poetry"), #18, Oct. 1960; *From Rococo to Cubism in Art and Literature*, by W. Sypher ("The Problem of Nowness"), #19, Nov. 1960.

1961   The opera *Elegy for Young Lovers*, by Hans Werner Henze, with libretto by Auden and Chester Kallman, performed at Schwetzingen in May, then at Zurich and Munich, and in English at Glyndebourne. Libretto published in Mainz (B. Schott's Söhne).

English version of *Don Giovanni* (with Chester Kallman) published by G. Schirmer, New York (commissioned by and performed on NBC-TV).

Edited *Van Gogh: A Self-Portrait* (selected letters; New York Graphic Society).

Introduction to *The Complete Poems of Cavafy* (New York: Harcourt, Brace & World).

"The Quest Hero," *The Texas Quarterly*, Winter 1961.

"The Alienated City," *Encounter*, Aug. 1961 (on Shakespeare's *Othello;* included in *The Dyer's Hand*, 1962).

"Dag Hammarskjöld," *Encounter*, Nov. 1961.

Review of *The Letters of Beethoven*, ed. E. Anderson, *The Spectator*, Nov. 10, 1961.

Memorandum on the New Arden Shakespeare, *The Mid-Century*, #21, Jan. 1961.

Reviews in *The Mid-Century* of Ford, *Parade's End* ("Il Faut Payer"), #22, Feb. 1962; *Phaedra and Figaro* translated by R. Lowell and J. Barzun, #24, April 1961; *The Delights of Detection*, ed. J. Barzun ("The Case is Curious"), #26, June 1961; Robert Graves, *Collected Poems* ("A Poet of Honor"), #28, July 1961; *The Genius of Leonardo da Vinci*, by A. Chastel ("A Universal Eccentric"), #33, Christmas 1961; *The Burning Brand: Diaries 1935-50*, by Cesare Pavese ("The Conscience of an Artist"), #34, Dec. 1961.

1962   Elected an Honorary Student (i.e. Fellow) of Christ Church College, Oxford University.

The Dyer's Hand and Other Essays (new and selected criticism) published by Random House (November) and by Faber & Faber (April 1963). Dedicated to Nevill Coghill.

Translated (with Elizabeth Mayer) Goethe, *Italian Journey* (London: Collins; New York: Pantheon). (The introduction was published in *Encounter*, Nov. 1962.)

Edited (with Louis Kronenberger) *The Viking Book of Aphorisms* (New York: Viking).

"Anger" (No. 7 in series on Seven Deadly Sins), London *Sunday Times*, Jan. 21, 1962. (Reprinted in *The Seven Deadly Sins*, New York: Morrow.)

"The Poet and the City," *The Massachusetts Review*, Spring 1962 (included in *The Dyer's Hand*).

"Today's Poet," *Mademoiselle*, April 1962.

"Today's 'Wonder-world' Needs Alice," *The New York Times Magazine*, July 1, 1962.

"Mirror: a Set of Notes," *Vogue*, Dec. 1962 (included in *The Dyer's Hand*).

"Do You Know Too Much?," *Esquire*, Dec. 1962.

Review in *Encounter* of *The Strangled Cry*, by John Strachey, Oct. 1962.

Reviews in *The Mid-Century* of *The Drug Experience*, ed. D. Ebin ("The Chemical Life"), #35, Jan. 1962; *A Marianne Moore Reader*, #36, Feb. 1962; *A Working Friendship* (Strauss-von Hofmannsthal correspondence: "A Marriage of True Minds"), #37, March 1962; *A Muriel Spark Trio* and *In Parenthesis*, by David Jones, #39, May 1962; *The Senses of Animals and Men*, by Lorus J. and Margery Milne, #42, Midsummer 1962 ("The Justice of Dame Kind").

IV

Operas, Criticism, and Rites of Homage

All the others translate: the painter sketches
A visible world to love or reject;
Rummaging into his living, the poet fetches
The images out that hurt and connect

From Life to Art by painstaking adaption,
Relying on us to cover the rift;
Only your notes are pure contraption,
Only your song is an absolute gift.

Pour out your presence, O delight, cascading
The falls of the knee and the weirs of the spine,
Our climate of silence and doubt invading;

You alone, alone, O imaginary song,
Are unable to say an existence is wrong,
And pour out your forgiveness like a wine.[1]

OPERAS

Auden is, in every possible sense, a musical poet. As painting is the "other art," appearing constantly as metaphor and analogy and inspiration in Yeats and Wallace Stevens, so music is for Auden. His imagination is, like Eliot's but to a greater degree, more auditory than visual. But Auden's relation to the sister art has been more important and extensive than that of any of the poets mentioned. In his Oxford inaugural lecture of 1956, he remarked:

> I know ... that through listening to music I have learned
> much about how to organize a poem, how to obtain

The notes are to be found at the end of the section, on page 340.

262

variety and contrast through changes of tone, tempo, and rhythm, though I could not say just how. Man is an analogy-drawing animal; that is his great good fortune. His danger is of treating analogies as identities, of saying, for instance, "Poetry should be as much like music as possible." I suspect that the people who are most likely to say this are the tone-deaf. The more one loves another art, the less likely it is that one will wish to trespass upon its domain.   (*The Dyer's Hand*, pp. 51-2)

We have discussed Auden's earlier collaborations with Benjamin Britten, and the songs and other musical pieces that he has, fortunately, never ceased to write. Since 1940, however, his writing for music has largely taken the specialized form of writing opera libretti; and since *The Age of Anxiety* such libretti have been his only long works (except the groups of companion-poems, to be discussed later).

Apparently Auden came rather late to his passion for opera, though he had, as we have seen, loved other forms of vocal music from an early age. He has remarked that he was fortunate in never having heard Italian opera until after 1937, when he was old enough to appreciate a "world so beautiful and so challenging to my own cultural heritage." [2] Mozart and Wagner, and the contrast between them, are discussed in "New Year Letter" and other writings of 1940-41, but chiefly in moral-theological terms owing a good deal to Nietzsche, De Rougemont, and Kierkegaard.[3] *Paul Bunyan* (1941), Auden's first attempt at opera, is described as a "choral operetta" and has really little resemblance to grand opera; as we shall see in a moment, it is closer to Brechtian epic drama. But by 1948 Auden can describe himself as an opera addict, and include Bellini, Donizetti, and Verdi in his pantheon; [4] Spender, seeing him at intervals 1947-49, observes that his main interests seem to be theology and Italian opera.[5] By 1948 he had also written the libretto of *The Rake's Progress*, which provides conclusive evidence of his love and mastery of the form.

During the last decade Auden has written a number of exceptionally interesting critical and speculative pieces dealing with music. Music, he suggests, imitates or is about *choice:* "a successful melody is a self-determined history; it is freely what it intends to be, yet is a meaningful whole not an arbitrary succession of notes." [6] In a later statement he says that music "presents a virtual image of our experience of living as temporal, with its double aspect of recurrence and becoming." [7] He continues: "If music in general is an imitation of history, opera in particular is an imitation of human willfulness"; the great operatic roles are all passionate and willful states of being (that in real life would all be bores) and the crowning glory of opera is the big ensemble, which presents them in immediate and simultaneous relation to each other (p. 470). Comparing the libretto with the play, he observes that in some respects the librettist is more limited than the dramatist: "The dramatist, for instance, procures some of his finest effects from showing how people deceive themselves. Self-deception is impossible in opera because music is immediate not reflective; whatever is sung is the case. At most self-deception can be suggested by having the orchestral accompaniment at variance with the singer. . . ." While in drama the discovery of the mistake (upon which, says Auden, all drama is based) can be a slow process, in the libretto it must be abrupt, "for music cannot exist in an atmosphere of uncertainty; song cannot walk, it can only jump." On the other hand, the librettist has the great advantage of not needing to worry about probability: "No good opera plot can be sensible for people do not sing when they are feeling sensible." A good libretto is melodramatic; it "offers as many opportunities as possible for the characters to be swept off their feet by placing them in situations which are too tragic or too fantastic for 'words' " (pp. 471-2). Finally, Auden makes a sharp distinction between the libretto and the lyric: in the libretto the verses are really a private letter to the composer; their purpose is to suggest a melody to him, after which they are expendable. They cannot and should not be poetry; one trouble with the *Rosenkavalier*, for instance, is that it is too close to real poetry. (Like many other distinctions in this essay, this one seems too black and white, too absolutely antithetical; but it makes clear Auden's conviction that the libretto must be emphatically subordinate to the musical necessities of the opera.) As the discussion of probability has indicated, the operas are, in a sense, a fulfillment of Auden's impulse towards fantasy; they provide an opportunity and justification for transcending the limits of the "normal," common-sense world and representing instead the world of myth, fairy-tale, magic, the supernatural—the inner world that has always fascinated Auden, in which the shapes of things are bent to the desires of the mind.[8] This is plain in Auden's first experiment in writing a libretto, though *Paul Bunyan* is in most other respects different from the later operas.

Paul Bunyan, a choral operetta, with libretto by Auden and music by Benjamin Britten, was performed in Brander Matthews Hall, Columbia University, for a week's run beginning May 5, 1941, by the Columbia Theater Associates, with the cooperation of the Department of Music and a chorus from the New York Schola Cantorum. There seems to have been unanimous agreement that the work was unsuccessful: it has never been performed again or published, and the copies of the libretto and score possessed by the Columbia University Library are, by request of the authors, not allowed to circulate. (According to Daniel G. Hoffman, to whom I am indebted for most of my information about the operetta, so many changes were made in both words and music during the run that in fact no definitive version exists even in manuscript.) Neither Auden nor Britten had had any previous experience with the medium of opera; neither had ever before tried to write anything "suitable for high schools," as the publishers, Boosey and Hawkes, had specified that this work should be; and neither had been in this country long enough to have a very extensive foundation for interpreting the American mind and soul.

The failure is, however, an interesting one, worth discussing for the light it throws on some of the problems of opera-writing in our day and for what it shows, by comparison with his later work, of Auden's progress in learning the craft of the librettist. Auden placed his intentions fully on record.[9] America, he said, was unique in being the only country to create myths after the industrial revolution, and he described the legend of Paul Bunyan as "a projection of the collective state of mind of a people whose tasks were primarily the physical mastery of nature." The operetta was intended to present "in a compressed fairy-story form the development of the continent from a virgin forest before the birth of Paul Bunyan to settlement and cultivation when Paul Bunyan says goodbye because he is no longer needed." Auden cited three principal difficulties in putting the legend on the stage, which he attempted to surmount in ways consistent with the didactic style of epic drama advocated by Brecht. First, Bunyan's "size and general mythical characteristics prevent his physical appearance on the stage," and so he is presented only as a speaking (not singing) voice. (Similarly, Babe, the Blue Ox, who represents Paul's *anima*, cannot appear as a character.) Some other character must therefore play the chief dramatic role, and Inkslinger was chosen because, says Auden, he came closest to satisfying Henry James's plea for a fine lucid intelligence as a compositional center; in fact, he is the only person capable of understanding who Paul Bunyan really is, and in a sense the operetta is an account of his process of discovery. Second, most of Paul's exploits are not susceptible of stage presentation, and so are related by narrative ballads between the scenes, which are in this respect the equivalent of a solo Greek chorus. Third, female voices are needed in an opera, but there are no women in the Bunyan legend. Hence a Camp Dog and two Camp Cats were introduced, to be sung by a coloratura and two mezzo-sopranos.

Hoffman summarizes the action thus:

> Paul Bunyan gathers a crew to tame the continent. Hel Helson is his foreman, Johnny Inkslinger his book-

keeper. Tiny, his daughter by an unhappy marriage, arrives after her mother's death and falls in love with Slim, the camp cook. The men taunt Helson into rebelling against Paul; he is beaten in fair fight and is reconciled with Bunyan again. As the wilderness is cleared, some of the men turn from logging to the occupations of civilized life. John Shears leads the farming contingent, who take to the soil with Paul's blessing. At last Babe, the Blue Ox, tells Paul that his work is done. The gang has a farewell Christmas party. Helson becomes a builder of high-tension power lines; Slim and Tiny go to New York to run a big hotel; Inkslinger is called to Hollywood. And Paul moves on to other deserts where his spirit is still needed to subdue the wilderness.

Thus there is one main plot (conquering the wilderness) and two sub-plots (Slim and Tiny's courtship, and Helson's revolt). In addition, there is yet another element running through the play. Auden satirizes reactionary politics, the vulgarities of advertising, and the vacuity of the glamorized dream life presented by Hollywood and the slick magazines. These realities of the present, some of which appear as Paul Bunyan's prophetic dreams, are contrasted to the happy state of natural man in which the action takes place.[10]

According to Hoffman, who saw the performance and later made a thorough study of the script, the fundamental trouble is that Auden "seems never to have decided . . . exactly what sort of a play he had set out to write. It is by turns an epic, a romance, and a satire; consequently, the total effect is confusing" (p. 146). The satire, Hoffman suggests, contradicts the epic; "Paul is a Promethean hero who brings men to a civilization he himself cannot enjoy. Like Moses, another Promethean pioneer with a similar dream, he does not suffer except in being excluded from the life that is to come. But in Auden's play, that life is compounded of such hypocrisy, tinsel, and shallowness that Paul Bunyan's exile to a fresher wilderness is only to be envied" (p. 151). "In *Paul Bunyan* we can see his ambivalence toward America: half celebration, half disenchantment" (p. 153).

"The Glamour Boys and Girls Have Grievances Too," a song published in *The New Yorker*, August 24, 1940 (and the date is significant in showing that at least part of the operetta was written this early), provides a sample of the satire described by Hoffman. It begins with a "Chorus of Movie Starlets and Juveniles":

> You've no idea how dull it is
> Just being perfect nullities
>   The idols of a democratic nation,
> The heroes of the multitude
> Their dreams of female pulchritude;
>   We're very, very tired of admiration.

Starlets, juveniles, male and female Powers models ("The Hercules of underwear, / The Venus of cosmetics"), and male and female athletes sing in turn and together, complaining that they are bored with being glamourous and amorous, with being shown "To all the world's inhibited / As representative Americana"; they "never want to die again, / Or throw a custard pie again, / To give the decent citizen / Vicarious satisfaction."

Robert A. Simon, reviewing *Paul Bunyan* in *The New Yorker* for May 17, 1941, observed that the expectations aroused by the eminence of its authors and the timeliness of the subject matter, together with such unconventional theatrical devices as wild geese, a Western Union messenger on a bicycle, a moon that turned blue, and a duet on the relative merits of soup and beans, were disappointed. "In the theater . . . *Paul Bunyan* didn't jell"; there were no interesting characters and the show failed to build.

The reasons for the failure of this attempt to fuse American folklore, contemporary satire, Jungian psychology, and the techniques of Henry James and Bertolt Brecht are plain enough and need no further comment. There are, however, three songs from the operetta that Auden has preserved in *Collected Poetry*.

"Carry her over the water," a humorous prothalamium with a strong American folk element, we have mentioned earlier as having been set very effectively by Lennox Berkeley. The humor consists in a lightly ironic exaggeration of the importance of the occasion, and produces no complexity or ambiguity. " 'Gold in the North,' came the blizzard to say," is Paul's "dream of defeat, which he holds as a warning to the pioneers about to enter the wilderness" (Hoffman, p. 149). In the refrain, the diction, and the stanza with its triply repeated rhyme, there is an obvious resemblance both to the older ballads and to American ballads and blues. The theme is "America can break your heart," and American idiom and folk motifs are used effectively. The third song is "The single creature leads a partial life." This is sung by the coloratura and two mezzo-sopranos, representing Fido the dog and Moppet and Poppet the cats (Hoffman, p. 188); it deals with the relation between man and animals, not with the contrast (as is usual in Auden) but rather with the similarity, the mutual need.

The Rake's Progress. It is perhaps not impertinent to speculate that one of the numerous difficulties under which *Paul Bunyan* labored was this: the librettist should be subordinate to the composer of an opera, but Auden was older, much more famous, and no doubt a more dominant personality than Britten. No such problem could arise in Auden's collaboration with Stravinsky.

The story of the genesis of *The Rake's Progress* is told in full in *Memories and Commentaries*, by Igor Stravinsky and Robert Craft (New York, 1960), in which Auden's letters to Stravinsky and their first scenario for the opera are also printed. As the intimate record of a collaboration, the material is of exceptional interest. To summarize the essentials briefly, the idea of basing an opera on Hogarth's *Rake's Progress* occurred to Stravinsky in 1947. He chose Auden as librettist on the recommendation of Aldous Huxley, knowing of his work only the commentary for the documentary film, "Night Mail." In

October Auden accepted the invitation, making his position clear immediately: "it is the librettist's job to satisfy the composer, not the other way round..." (p. 145). In November 1947 he visited Stravinsky in California; they agreed on a "Mozart-Italian" type of opera, embodying a moral fable, and together they worked out a complete scenario. Stravinsky says,

> Mother Goose and the Ugly Duchess [i.e., Baba] were Auden's contributions, of course, but the plot and the scheme of action were worked out by the two of us together, step by step. We also tried to co-ordinate the plan of action with a provisional plan of musical pieces, arias, ensembles, and choruses.   (p. 146)

After returning to New York Auden began work on the libretto, and on January 16 wrote to Stravinsky that he had taken as collaborator Chester Kallman, "an old friend of mine in whose talents I have the greatest confidence," and had finished Act I. Act II was finished by January 28, and the whole by March 31, when Auden and Stravinsky spent a day working together in Washington. Stravinsky then composed the music, taking about a year for each act, and finishing early in 1951; he conducted, and Auden and Kallman were present for, the premiere at Teatro La Fenice, Venice, in September 1951. Auden had expressed the wish that he and Kallman might advise during rehearsals, and presumably they did so. This first production was unfortunately not a very good one, according to report (several competent critics feel that the best of all the numerous productions the work has had in Europe was that directed by Ingmar Bergman in Stockholm in the summer of 1961). Of some 200 performances of the work in the first two years, only seven were in the United States; [11] the Metropolitan Opera's production in 1953 was dropped from the repertory the next year.

Since Chester Kallman was Auden's collaborator not only in the *Rake* but in the two later libretti, as well as in the "Englishings" of *The Magic Flute, Don Giovanni,* and Brecht's *Seven Deadly Sins,* and in the editing of the *Elizabethan Song Book,* we should consider his function as collaborator before proceeding with the discussion of the *Rake.* The friendship is of long standing: Auden dedicated *Another Time* to him in 1940 and the *Collected Poetry* of 1945 to him and Isherwood. Kallman was born in Brooklyn in 1921 and educated at Brooklyn College and the University of Michigan. In addition to the collaborations with Auden, he wrote the libretto for *The Tuscan Players,* an opera by the Mexican composer Carlos Chavez, and has translated the libretti of several operas, among them Verdi's *Falstaff,* Monteverdi's *Coronation of Poppea,* and Bartók's *Bluebeard's Castle.* In 1945-46 he reviewed the opera season for *Commonweal.* He has published one book of poems, *Storm at Castelfranco* (New York: Grove Press, 1956); a second, *Absent and Present,* is to appear in 1963. Kallman, Auden has said, "was the person who was responsible for arousing my interest in opera, about which previously, as you can see from *Paul Bunyan,* I knew little or nothing. . . ." [12]

Apparently Kallman does his full share in all the collaborations. We know specifically which parts of the *Rake* he wrote; [13] they constitute a good half, and include some of the most admired passages. Auden has ascribed the larger share of their latest opera, *Elegy for Young Lovers,* to Kallman. [14] Since the whole point of a successful collaboration is that it is more than and different from what each collaborator could do separately, there seems little point in trying to disentangle their respective contributions. It is interesting, however, to consider what special qualities Kallman would seem to have brought to the joint work. Judging by his single brief volume (61 pages), Kallman's poetry is much like Auden's and sometimes bears the mark of obvious derivation; this is to be expected, and in the circumstances the remarkable thing is that Kallman's poetry is as individual as it is. In general, his verse has a more open texture than Auden's; there is in this respect a much stronger resemblance to Kallman's verse than to Auden's in the joint libretti. Much of his poetry deals with music ("Night Music," "Aria for an Emperor") or uses such musical devices as refrains and repetition; much of it is written as if for musical setting (Song: "I tiptoed naked down the unlit hall"). In technique, Kallman is a virtuoso comparable to Auden in skill and variety. There is a deep religious concern ("Prayer in the Form of a Debate"), but also wit, polish, and true lightness ("Two Epigrams," "Nightmare of a Cook"). Many of the poems are richly allusive, with constant reference to painting, music, myth, history; but this weight is carried easily and unobtrusively because of the characteristics already described. The most ambitious, and possibly the best, poem in the volume is the title one, "Storm at Castelfranco."

The Rake's Progress is subtitled, "A Fable"; it follows Hogarth's tableaux only partially and generally,[15] transposing the story into modern religious and psychological terms, while brilliantly maintaining the "period" quality. Three primary myths are employed: Eden (with variant forms: the Golden Age, pastoral innocence, and the location of evil in economic problems), Venus and Adonis, and Faust-Mephistopheles; from the world of fairy tale and nursery rhyme there are the three wishes, the Ugly Duchess, and a depraved Mother Goose. To show how these are reinterpreted and fused together, a brief analysis of the libretto will be necessary.[16]

The opening duet of the lovers, Anne Trulove and Tom Rakewell, at Trulove's home in the country, suggests the first two of these myths immediately. They describe spring in ritual terms, "this festival of May," when the "pious earth observes the solemn year," and refer to it as the work of the "Cyprian Queen." Through love, they say, the lost innocence and joy of Eden is restored: in neoclassical terms, "swains their nymphs in fervent arms enfold / And with a kiss restore the Age of Gold." Trulove, in contrast, voices "a father's prudent fears," justified immediately by Tom's refusal to work; instead, he will trust to Fortune, saying "Come, wishes, be horses; / This beggar shall ride." When he makes his first wish, for money, Nick Shadow promptly appears to tell him of a legacy and take him to London. (Nick is both Mephistopheles, to be paid in a year and a day and, psychologically, "your shadow," given power by Tom's wishes.) Scene Two, set in Mother Goose's brothel in London, presents the whores and roaring boys celebrating the rites of Venus and of Mars. Tom recites the catechism that Shadow, as godfather, has taught him: to do his duty to himself and "follow Nature as my teacher." But he balks at the word "love," and in his cavatina "Renews the vow he did not keep, / Weeping, weeping, / He kneels before thy wounded shade." (The second stanza directly prepares for the ending, as Tom prays "Though thou daily be forgot, / Goddess, O forget me not"; and asks her to "be nigh / In my darkest hour that I, / Dying, dying, / May call upon thy sacred name.") He is then initiated by Mother Goose herself, in the long Lanterloo chorus that is a sinister parody of nursery rhymes and children's games; it begins:

> The sun is bright, the grass is green:
>   *Lanterloo, lanterloo.*
> The King is courting his young Queen.
>   *Lanterloo, my lady.*

At the end, the question "What will he do when they lie in bed?" is answered, "Draw his sword and chop off her head." And Shadow toasts Tom ironically, "Sweet dreams, my master. Dreams may lie, / But dream. For when you wake, you die." A brief third scene shows Anne deciding to go to London; she knows that Tom needs her help. "Love hears, Love knows, / Love answers him across the silent miles, and goes."

Act Two presents Tom in his London house, bored with following Nature ("O Nature, green unnatural mother, how I have followed where you led") and disgusted with pleasure. He makes his second wish, "I wish I were happy." Shadow appears and proposes that he demonstrate his freedom by marrying the bearded Baba the Turk, precisely because there is no reason to do so: true freedom is to ignore the twin tyrants of pleasure and duty, appetite and conscience, passion and reason: "he alone is free / Who chooses what to will, and wills / His choice as destiny / ... Whom neither Passion may compel / Nor Reason can restrain." Tom laughs (for the proposal is absurd) and agrees. (In a letter to Stravinsky Auden calls Baba "L'acte gratuit," and this notion, so prominent in Gide and later in Camus and other French writers of atheist-existentialist tendency, is clearly what is represented here: it is one form of freedom and one form of the absurd.) Scene Two shows Anne in front of Tom's house, where she confronts him as he brings Baba home after marrying her. She has sung, foreshadowing the denouement, "A love that is sworn before Thee can plunder Hell of its prey" as she waits for Tom. To Tom's protestations of unworthiness she has said, "Let worthiness, / So you still love, reside in that"; but upon discovering the marriage she leaves, after she and Tom have recalled in their parting songs the springtime Venus-Adonis imagery of the first scene, now transformed to winter as Adonis goes to the underworld. "O bury the heart," Tom sings, "And should it, dreaming love, ask —When / Shall I awaken once again? / Say—Never, never, never; / We shall this wint'ry promise keep— / Obey thy exile, honour sleep / Forever." In Scene Three Baba and Tom are revealed at home, Tom bored and sulking, Baba prattling in her patter aria, then appealing in her song, then furious; Tom finally cuts her off by plopping a wig on her head backwards, which reduces her to a state of suspended animation. Shadow appears while Tom sleeps and in pantomime demonstrates a fake machine for converting stones into bread; Tom, awaking, says he has dreamed of the machine and makes his third wish, "I wish it were true." When Shadow shows him the machine he hopes that it will enable him to regain Anne through his own merit: "O may I not, forgiven all my past / For one good deed, deserve dear Anne at last?" The machine, abolishing need, will make earth "an Eden of good will":

> Thanks to this excellent device
> Man shall re-enter Paradise
>   From which he once was driven.
> Secure from want, the cause of crime,
> The world shall for the second time
>   Be similar to heaven.

Shadow, in ironic counterpoint to Tom's rejoicing, comments on how easy it is to swindle people, and urges the "men of sense" to invest and make money. (In his letter to Stravinsky, Auden interpreted the incident: "Il désire devenir Dieu.")

Act Three begins with the same scene, with everything, including Baba, covered with cobwebs and dust; citizens are examining Tom's goods which are to be sold at auction, now that the swindle has been exposed. Sellem auctions off Baba as an "unknown object"; when he snatches the wig off her head she comes back to life and finishes her interrupted speech. Tom and Shadow sing off-stage, "Old wives for sale." Anne and Baba sing a duet in which Baba tells Anne that Tom still loves her and urges her to go to him; Baba will go back to the stage. Tom and Shadow are again heard singing off-stage, and Anne rushes after them. In Scene Two Tom and Shadow are seen in a churchyard, where Shadow claims his wages after serving Tom for a year and a day. He tells Tom to look in his eyes "and recognize / Whom—Fool! you chose to hire"; Tom's soul is forfeit, and he must kill himself on the stroke of twelve. As the clock is striking, however, Nick suspends it and offers Tom escape if he can name three cards; he explains to the audience that this adds to the sport: "To win at once in love or cards is dull." Tom guesses two, and Shadow tricks him by repeating the first card, the Queen of Hearts, for the third, commenting:

> The simpler the trick, the simpler the deceit;
> That there is no return, I've taught him well,
>   And repetition palls him:
> The Queen of Hearts again shall be for him the Queen of Hell.

But Tom, hearing Anne sing off-stage her arioso from II. ii, "A love / That is sworn before Thee can plunder hell of its prey," chooses the Queen of Hearts again, however "absurd" this may appear. (This is the true Absurd, as against the false Absurd of the *acte gratuit;* it is an act of faith, the Pascalian "wager" or Kierkegaardian "leap.") Shadow, balked of his prey, makes Tom insane, and the scene closes with Tom sitting on the grave in spring once more, believing he is Adonis. The final scene reveals Tom in Bedlam as Adonis (to be mad is to be simultaneously on earth and in hell, rather than alternately as in the classical myth), with Anne visiting him as Venus. He repents, begs forgiveness, and she says, "Thy ravishing penitence / Blesses me, dear heart, and brightens all the past. / Kiss me Adonis: the wild boar is vanquished." In a duet they rejoice in their love, then Anne sings him to sleep in a lullaby (the only lyric Auden preserved separately from this libretto; it is called "Barcarolle" in *The Shield of Achilles*), describing Eden, "paradise regained." Trulove appears to take Anne home; she tells Tom, "In this earthly city we / Shall not meet again, love, yet / Never think that I forget." After they leave, Tom wakes, seeks Venus, and dies, while the chorus sings "Mourn for Adonis. . . ." In the epilogue, the characters each draw a moral: Anne says, "Not every rake is rescued / At the last by Love and Beauty; / Not every man / Is given an Anne / To take the place of Duty." Baba warns that all men are mad; "All they say or do is theatre"; Tom warns young men "who fancy / You are Virgil or Julius Caesar" lest they find they are only rakes; Shadow laments that he "Must do as he is bidden"; "Many insist / I do not exist. / At times I wish I didn't." Together, they sing that the Devil finds work for idle hands "And hearts and minds" to do.

The epilogue has been criticized as an overly abrupt return to the mood of Hogarthian comedy and moral platitude, and as nervously mocking the moral tale. But it seems plain enough that, though the obvious meaning of the proverb is certainly not denied, the "idle hands" for which the Devil finds work are those of seekers after freedom in the atheist-existentialist sense, followers of the false absurd, shown in Tom's *acte gratuit* of marrying Baba, rather than of the true absurd, shown in his act of faith in the card game, when he chooses Anne's card for the second time in defiance of reason and common sense. Similarly, the ending has been criticized as ineffectively rendering the theme of redemption since Tom, being mad, dies without understanding. But Tom's crucial act of faith has already shown the fullest understanding and most complete surrender to love ("I wish for nothing else. / Love, first and last, assume eternal reign; / Renew my life, O Queen of Hearts, again"), and his madness merely translates him to literal acceptance of the role of Adonis, in which he repents and regains innocence, Eden, before he dies. This state, being out of time, may well be represented by madness. Anne is a kind of Venus Urania, Heavenly Aphrodite, symbol and bearer of divine grace—like Dante's Beatrice; without her aid, Tom could not have been saved. In human terms, she embodies Agape, unselfish love; it is not Tom's merits but his need that sends her to his rescue. As the epilogue gives a deeper meaning to one familiar proverb, so it might be said that the role of Anne rehabilitates and makes significant the sentimental platitude about the redeeming influence of the love of a good woman.[17]

Perhaps the other chief criticism of the opera has been that the character of Baba is implausible in human terms. In defense one may say that in addition to her symbolic usefulness, she functions dramatically in effectively hindering the reunion of Tom and Anne, and in befriending and encouraging Anne. Her peculiar character aids the plausibility of her actions. She is also amusing as a caricature: "It is hard to know what is more dreadful, her chatter, her tantrum, or her saccharine little love song." [18] Most of the humor is associated with her, and the revelation that she has a heart of gold, as well as dignity and authority in her last appearance, makes her, in spite of her freakish exterior, sympathetic as well as amusing.

Kerman calls the *Rake* "the most genuine and the most delightful work for the theatre in years, to say nothing of its being an operatic masterpiece on almost any terms"; the librettists' contribution he describes as "only slightly less brilliant than Stravinsky's," and he says that the work "offers a unique delight to the combined musical and poetic sensibilities. ... It is faintest praise to observe that no other opera has been written in English with anything like the same effect." And he goes so far as to wonder "whether there ever has been an opera with so elegant-sounding a libretto." [19]

Delia. Delia or A Masque of Night, "Libretto for a one-act Opera, (Suggested by George Peele's play, *The Old Wives' Tale*)," was published in *Botteghe Oscure* (Rome) in 1953 (XII, 164-210).[20] The relation of the Auden-Kallman libretto to Peele's play is little closer than that of the *Rake* to Hogarth's pictures; they take the general situation and the characters of Sacrapant, Delia, and Xantippe from Peele, but the plot is original and so are such major characters as Orlando and Bungay (though brilliantly in keeping with the period and the atmosphere of Peele). There is hardly any verbal indebtedness to *The Old Wives' Tale,* which is mostly in prose. As with the *Rake,* however, the device of invoking and transforming an earlier work provides a décor—costumes, settings, and manners —and justifies a period style that are both attractive in themselves and means of achieving distance and detachment. For, like the *Rake,* this libretto deals with a fantasy-world that must be distanced to be credible: a world of magic, fairy-tale, and allegory, but with a folklore element (one of the great attractions of Peele's play) rather more important than the proverbial element in the *Rake.* A brief summary will make this clear.

Orlando, a knight, appears in quest of Delia, of whom he has dreamed; she is held captive by Sacrapant, a sorcerer. Orlando encounters a Crone; when he treats her kindly and gives her money, she follows fairy-tale custom and gives him a magic willow to enable him to find Delia. In the comic subplot Bungay is ordered by his shrewish wife Xantippe not to seek instruction in sorcery from Sacrapant; but he disobeys her and Sacrapant transforms him into a bear and assigns him to Delia's service. Orlando, however, helps Bungay by giving him the willow so that he can find Xantippe (in a comic counterpoint to the principal quest). By this time it has appeared that the Crone is Sacrapant's opponent. After Orlando has lost Delia through drawing his sword in her defense (thereby breaking a vow), the Crone offers to free Delia if Orlando will marry her; willing to renounce Delia in order to save her, Orlando agrees, and when he kisses the Crone she is revealed as Queen of Night and Elfland, "Whom some Diana, some Dame Nature call, / To all that live wise Mother original." With her help, Orlando conquers Sacrapant, who has felt secure in the prophecy that only "a son born motherless" can defeat him; but it develops that Orlando's mother died just before his birth. In the climactic scene, Delia must choose between Orlando, who represents Day, and Sacrapant, who represents Night, after an allegorical pageant in which Time, Mutability, Toil, Age, Death, and Pain have appeared (like the Seven Deadly Sins in a morality play). She chooses Day—the human condition—in spite of all its drawbacks; and Bungay is restored from bear to human form.

The final chorus is the same as the poem Auden printed (with some revision) as "Lauds" in *The Shield of Achilles;* in the opera the refrain is "Day breaks for joy and sorrow" and there is one verse not in the later version:

> Of good, and ill all men are capable,
> God bless the Queen, God bless the people.
> *Day breaks for joy and sorrow.*

Day is dawning because Sacrapant is vanquished, magic has been rejected, animals have been transformed back into men; the human condition has been accepted by Delia. The Crone intersperses lines indicating that Sacrapant and she will soon re-begin their nightly wars; she kisses him and thus relights his magic light.

As far as I know, *Delia* has not yet been set to music. This seems a pity, because—although a far slighter piece in every respect than the two major operas—it is remarkably attractive and full of varied musical opportunities. In the quest to rescue a maiden from the powers of Night, the allegory of the eternal conflict between Day and Night, the contrasted noble and rustic lovers, and some other points, *Delia* resembles *The Magic Flute*, which Auden and Kallman translated and rearranged a few years later (in my opinion making more sense of the allegory than had ever been made before). Their next libretto, however, leaves the fantasy-worlds of *Rake* and *Delia* for one very much closer to "normal" experience.

Elegy for Young Lovers. Hans Werner Henze (b. 1926, described by Grove as being in the front rank of present German composers, advanced in technique and influenced by Schoenberg and Stravinsky, but strikingly original and individual in style; composer of three symphonies, several ballets, and as early as 1952 of the opera *Boulevard Solitude*) was commissioned by the Suddeutscher Rundfunk (Stuttgart) to do an opera, and invited Auden and Kallman to do the libretto. The resulting opera, *Elegy for Young Lovers,* had its premiere at Schwetzingen in May 1961; it was then performed at the Zurich festival in June and, with the composer directing and conducting and the lead sung by Dietrich Fischer-Dieskau, at Munich; later in the summer it was sung in English at Glyndebourne. So far it has not been performed in the United States. My comments are based on the libretto alone, published by B. Schott's Söhne, Mainz; the music is not accessible and no recording has yet been made. According to a reviewer, the orchestra consists of five strings, bass and winds, an electric guitar, and various exotic percussion instruments which tend to dominate it; each character is represented by an instrument, so that the orchestra can counterpoint the action.[21]

In a remarkably interesting afterword, "Genesis of a Libretto," Auden and Kallman describe the process of composition and the reasons behind the various choices they made. They began with the composer's requirements: this was to be a "chamber" opera for a small cast with no chorus, and for a small subtle orchestra; the composer wanted a subject and situation which "would call for tender, beautiful noises."

> The notion that these conditions suggested to us was of five or six persons, each of whom suffered from a different obsession so that, while all inhabiting a common world, each would interpret that world and the actions of the others in a completely different way.

The first obsession they conceived was one with the past, as in Dickens's Miss Havisham; this idea survives in the character of Hilda Mack, the old lady who has visions. For a young heroine they thought of a lady's maid masquerading as a great lady. For pathos, she was to have an incurable disease, a situation which required a doctor, whose son could be the maid's lover. Although eventually the lady's maid was dropped, while the doctor and his son stayed in, she was responsible for the choice of setting: a mountain resort out of season would make such a masquerade possible, and would also provide romantic scenery. To make a triangle, they gave the young man a mature, worldly, and cynical rival; to conform with the theme, he would have to have an obsession, and at first they made him an actor. But this did not work, and the pattern of relations refused to come clear. "The break-through came when we realized that the older rival, whoever he might be, must be the principal character in the libretto, the figure to whom all the other characters would already be related before the curtain rose." They then asked themselves two questions: what kind of person can dominate an opera both dramatically and vocally, and what kind of mature man can be involved simultaneously with a mad old lady, a young girl, and a doctor. They also kept it in mind that the most successful operatic characters, however individualized, embody some myth: singing masters what is otherwise a pure instrument of egotism, the human voice; hence operatic characters seem to be singing on behalf of the whole human race, and the singing itself produces an effect of triumph. The answer they arrived at was: "the artist-genius of the nineteenth and early twentieth century."

> This is a genuine myth because the lack of identity be-tween Goodness and Beauty, between the character of man and the character of his creations, is a permanent aspect of the human condition. The Theme of *Elegy for Young Lovers* is summed up in two lines by Yeats:
>
>> *The intellect of man is forced to choose*
>> *Perfection of the life or of the work.*

Aesthetically speaking, the personal existence of the artist is accidental; the important thing is his work. As the nineteenth century conceived him, the artist-genius "made this aesthetic presupposition an ethical absolute, that is to say, he claimed to represent the highest, most authentic, mode of human exist-ence." If this claim is accepted, "it follows that the artist-genius is morally bound as a sacred duty to exploit others whenever such exploitation will benefit his work and to sacrifice them whenever their existence is a hindrance to his production." The artist-genius's various reasons for needing others provided a pattern of relationships and the basis for a plot.

> Our ambition in writing the libretto has been to see how much psychological drama and character interest we could make compatible with the conventions of the operatic medium, and the Great Ancestors whose blessing we continually found ourselves invoking were Ibsen and Hofmannsthal.

(*Elegy* is dedicated by its "three makers" to "the memory of Hugo von Hofmannsthal, Austrian, European and Master Li-brettist.") One difficulty, they observe, in the dramatic por-trayal of an artist-genius is in giving the audience convincing samples of his work. Mittenhofer has been working on a poem throughout the opera; "in order to complete it successfully, he (morally) murders two people and breaks the spirit of a third." Unless the audience at the end is convinced that the poem is a very good one, the whole point of the opera is lost. The best way of achieving this conviction, the librettists believe, is "by having the poem represented in another artistic medium—as a man, Mittenhofer sings words; as a poet he is dumb, and his poem is represented by orchestral sound and pure vocalisation." They conclude by pointing out that, though they have made Mittenhofer Viennese, they certainly do not "think his outrageous behavior an Austrian characteristic"; the myth is a European one.

The scene of the opera is an inn in the Austrian Alps; the time, 1910. The short first scene presents Hilda Mack, who has tried to arrest time since her bridegroom was lost on the mountain the day after their wedding, forty years ago, still waiting for his return. Mittenhofer, the poet, uses the mad old lady's visions as material. The second scene, called "The Order of the Day" (each act and scene has an old-fashioned title which makes the symbolism perfectly clear), is an amusing one in which Mittenhofer is seen through the eyes of his secretary, Carolina—her last name is "von Kirchstetten," Auden's little joke: this is the Austrian village in which he owns a farmhouse—and his doctor; they describe the work of "The Servants of the Servant of the Muse," and he appears as a vain, tyrannical, but impressive figure. The Doctor's son, Toni, arrives; when he and Elizabeth, Mittenhofer's young mistress, join hands for the first time, Hilda has a vision of snow and a pair of lovers sacrificed on a white altar; "Briefly their Eden / Blooms in the falling / Snow . . ." Mittenhofer furiously takes notes and is delighted with this material: "Exactly what I hoped for. / The note that I had vainly groped for, / Of magic, tenderness and warning. / Even the form is now in sight." He then goes on to abuse his contemporary rivals—George, Rilke, and Hofmannsthal—in an amusing passage, and after cruelly insulting Carolina, goes happily through the ritual of finding the money she hides for him daily. The body of Hilda's fiance is found, preserved in the glacier for forty years; when Hilda is told, she warns Elizabeth to flee, in a last vision, and ends her "sworn to-day of waiting" as "Time unlocks the tears / That in my crystal burned." Toni, watching Mittenhofer and Elizabeth go off, has a vision like Hilda's, "but his journey from the present is backwards" to his dying mother (because of whom he hates his father). In the last scene, "To-morrow: Two Follies Cross," Hilda emerges from her long obsession ("Mine is the now you deliver me into, ... *Vale*, my hero! The crystal is broken! / What a nice day it is! More are to come!") while Toni expresses his hope of escaping his obsession with his dead mother through Elizabeth ("In her love I would begin to / Live and would myself become"). The act is called "The Emergence of the Bridegroom," and the meaning of the title is now plain: both Hilda's long-expected and Elizabeth's future one have emerged.

Act II, "The Emergence of the Bride," begins with Elizabeth and Toni, some days later, rejoicing in their love. Carolina and the Doctor discover them and attempt to persuade them to be sensible (it emerges in this scene that Elizabeth has loved Mittenhofer as a father-substitute, her obsession with her father paralleling Toni's with his mother); Elizabeth is furious, but Toni begins to be reconciled to his father. Mittenhofer enters, and when Carolina tries to tell him, reveals that he already knows about Elizabeth and Toni. (This is a scene of striking technical virtuosity, the speeches of the five characters interweaving to form regular couplets.) Mittenhofer has been angry with Elizabeth for telling Hilda about the recovery of her bridegroom's body (in restoring her to sanity, this has destroyed her value as source of poetic material); he explains that he was not merely being selfish, but acting for the sake of his poetry. But he apologizes to Elizabeth, in a long and amusing description of "what it is like / To be a poet, / Of what it means / Never, never, / To feel, to think, to see, to hear, / Without reflecting: 'Now, / Could I use that somehow?' "—and after calling her his "Lovely Muse" he offers her her freedom. At the end of this speech he sounds much like Prospero in *The Sea and the Mirror:* "But there I go / Performing again. / Shall I never learn to stop it? / Elizabeth, my dear, / Forgive me!" Elizabeth, brought back under his spell, reproaches herself and decides to stay. Trying to explain to Toni, she puts the situation in fairy-tale terms, with herself as goose-girl who won her prince, but hasn't lived happily ever after. Toni replies that Mittenhofer is no prince but an old sorcerer who has had her under a spell, and he is a shepherd boy who loves the princess. Toni insists on a showdown, and he and Mittenhofer both ask Elizabeth to choose, though the latter says the choice is "to fulfil / The woman, or remain the Muse." Hilda, now very sane but slightly tipsy, enters at the height of this dramatic scene and reduces it momentarily to comedy; Elizabeth decides to marry Toni later on and for the immediate future accepts Hilda's invitation to go with her on holiday. Mittenhofer persuades the Doctor to join him in giving his blessing to the match, because of "that prophecy / Their love fulfils for us." He recites part of his poem, "The Young Lovers":

> Out of Eden, bringing Eden
> With them, the young lovers come
> Hand in hand to the cold lands.
> The snow falls. There is no welcome.
> Their singleness reproaches our mingled
> Isolations, their love our songless
> Ice-altars; we refuse the rose
> Of Heaven's children. Nevertheless,
> One who dare break the barrier . . .
> His own . . . who only will turn, will move to
> Reach for and bless their happiness,
> Shall heedlessly enter Eden too.
> They bring us a gift from afar:
> A fragile, an eternal flower.

Mittenhofer then asks the lovers to remain one more day so that they can bring him some edelweiss from the mountain, "a visionary 'aid' " to help him complete his poem in time for his sixtieth birthday a few days hence. They readily agree. In the next scene each expresses his "vision of to-morrow"; the guide, Mauer, offers to get the edelweiss, but Mittenhofer refuses, making it clear that it isn't the flower he is after. In the last scene of the act, Mittenhofer reveals his complete contempt for all the other characters and his boundless egotism, his grotesque and grimly humorous speech ending, "Why don't they just blow up and disappear! / Why don't they all DIE?" In a neat counterpoint, the now-sane Hilda sees him at the height of his tantrum and laughs.

As the third act, "Man and Wife," begins, Toni and Elizabeth are starting up the mountain singing a folk-song. Hilda, preparing to leave, says "Farewell to-day / To more than half my life: / A fool's romantic hell / Of being always interesting," and regrets having made a god of her dead lover; the Doctor, speaking, like her, to himself, expresses his guilt and sorrow ("What have I done to Toni? Am I vile?") as he too prepares to leave; all the while Mittenhofer is audibly writing and complaining, while Carolina ministers to him. After Hilda has tried unsuccessfully to make Carolina perceive the resemblance between them and thereby awaken her from her obsession (showing her an enormous scarf: "Laugh at this monster baby I have knit / For forty years, and as you laugh, admit / Your own dear monster laughable a bit"), she and the Doctor make their farewells and depart. The guide Mauer comes in and warns of an impending blizzard; there would be just time, he says, to bring back anyone on the mountain. Mittenhofer, supported by Carolina, deliberately refrains from telling him about Toni and Elizabeth. Carolina retreats further into her obsession of mothering and worshipping Mittenhofer, even accepting Hilda's symbolic scarf; there is an effective allusion to *Dr. Faustus* when her escape to a false Eden is put in the terms of Mephistopheles' explanation of Hell: "Why this is Eden, nor were we ever out / Of it. How warm it is. I am with you still. . . ." The scene changes to the lovers in the blizzard, exhausted and knowing they are to die. He says, "What a funny kind of fairy tale / We've gotten into, where Godmother sends / Wild weather on the wedding night"; and she, "Now that no choice can change what is, / Without hope, in innocent play, / We may dream of a world that won't be." They pretend to be an old couple looking back over forty years of marriage; recognizing finally that their love is an illusion, they say, "Now we know. Now we are free / To die together and with good will / Say farewell to a real world." Having unlearned their lies, they can "come to death with clean hearts"; they give thanks for Grace, ask forgiveness, and confront death with faith: "Grant us Thy peace. / Light with Thy Love our lives' end." The final scene shows Mittenhofer on his birthday, first adoring himself in the mirror, then reading his "Elegy for Young Lovers" (dedicated to Toni and Elizabeth) in a Vienna theater, against a backdrop representing Mount Parnassus, the Muses crowning a poet, Apollo with lyre and cherubim—all the romantic properties. As he reads (wordlessly), "from behind him come one by one until they are all together, the voices of all who contributed to the writing of the poem: Hilda with her visions, Carolina with her money and management, Doctor Reischmann with his medicines, Toni and Elizabeth with their illusory but rhymable love."

Incredible as it may seem, some critics of the opera have thought that Mittenhofer was being presented as an admirable character, and thereby have missed the whole point. An anonymous reviewer in the London *Times Literary Supplement*, August 1961, says that Mittenhofer seems a caricature but is intended to be taken seriously, and observes that the opera exhibits the same kind of uncertainty of tone and attitude as the Vicar's Sermon in *The Dog Beneath the Skin*.[22] The reviewer, Martin Bernheimer, in the *Musical Quarterly* for January 1962 seems to imply a similar interpretation in describing the libretto as "basically romantic, frequently preposterous, and none-too-operatic." It is hard to see how the librettists could have made it any clearer that Mittenhofer is both a follower of a false religion and himself a false god; the contrast between his religion of art and the true religious perception of the young lovers is made very sharp. The theme of obsession, escape, illusion, is developed fully in terms of the Eden myth, as Hilda, Elizabeth and Toni, and the Doctor abandon their false Edens for a true awareness of reality; while Carolina and Mittenhofer remain the prisoners of their Eden-Hells.

Reprise: Words and Music. Finally, let us recur briefly to the question of the quality *as poetry* of the opera libretti which have been Auden's only long works (except for the groups of companion-poems) in recent years. We have considered their merits as libretti, and we have seen that Auden says flatly that the libretto must not only be subordinate to the musical demands of the opera, but that it should not be poetry. Let us consider the beginning of *The Rake's Progress*, where Anne sings.

> The woods are green and bird and beast at play
> For all things keep this festival of May;
> With fragrant odours and with notes of cheer
> The pious earth observes the solemn year.

Rakewell answers,

> Now is the season when the Cyprian Queen
> With genial charm translates our mortal scene,
> When swains their nymphs in fervent arms enfold
> And with a kiss restore the Age of Gold.

This is pleasant, admirably calculated for singing, sufficiently but not artificaly "period" in diction, and full of simple conventional properties for the composer to work with. It introduces the opera's central themes: the quest for lost innocence, Eden; Venus-Adonis, both as the universal power of love in the biological sense of Venus, and the redeeming and transforming effect of Christian love as Anne will embody it. But the texture is strikingly different from that of Auden's non-operatic songs, much thinner and more open and much more conventional. To say, as Auden suggests, that it is not poetry [23] is to make the distinction too black-and-white, too nearly absolute; it is perhaps better to say that this is a highly specialized form of poetry—like that of Eliot's later plays, and for similar reasons. Its interest is, considered simply as verse, very limited; it is not intended to stand alone, but exists as framework or vehicle for the music, is a deflated balloon until the music blows it up. Or we may say that it is poetry with most of the irony, ambiguity, tension, and other elements of inherent verbal interest carefully removed, so that the words will not call attention to themselves as words, but be absorbed into the music. It is probably significant that Auden preserved three songs from *Paul Bunyan*, written before he had mastered the art of the libretto, in *Collected Poetry;* but in later volumes he has thought only one lyric from *Delia* and one from *The Rake's Progress* ("Lauds" and "Barcarolle," respectively) worth collecting. To recapitulate, we may say that Auden writes three distinct varieties of verse for music. The first is the opera libretto, in which the verbal texture is subordinate to larger musical and dramatic necessities, so that the libretto is an extremely important but inseparable element in a unified whole, not to be judged independently. The second is the song, which is a genuine poem that also, by intention or chance, fits the composer's requirements or desiderata. Even when songs are written with the intention of being suitable for musical setting, they are written to be the dominant partner; or so I should argue. The third type is the self-sufficient or literary song, that is, the song which produces the illusion that it can be set, but which, in fact, has its own built-in verbal rhythm too complex and powerful to be adaptable to music. "Look, stranger" is a good example.

About the musical aspect of Auden's achievement we may say, against the condescending reviewer who called him the "Da Ponte of our time," that he has rehabilitated the art of the libretto, that he has in his critical writings clarified some of the perennial questions about the relation of music and poetry, and that he has written a large number and variety of great songs.

The Reluctant Critic. Auden once wrote that he was "suspicious of criticism as the literary genre which, more than any other, recruits epigones, pedants without insight, intellectuals without love" (in a letter praising James Agee's film criticism as an exception, *The Nation*, Nov. 18, 1944). In his daydream College for Bards the "library would contain no books of literary criticism, and the only critical exercise required of students would be the writing of parodies" (*The Dyer's Hand*, p. 77). Attacking bad books is "not only a waste of time but bad for the character"; "One cannot review a bad book without showing off" (ibid., pp. 10-11). He describes four types of bad critic: the prig, "for whom no actual poem is good enough since the only one that would be is the poem he would like to write himself but cannot"; the critic's critic, whose analysis "is so much more complicated and difficult than the work itself as to deprive someone who has not yet read it of all wish to do so"; the romantic novelist, who deals in the private lives of authors, and the maniac (ibid., pp. 48-9). Auden has written a great deal of criticism, but until very recently had published only one critical volume, *The Enchafèd Flood* (1950). This was a somewhat specialized analysis of the attitudes toward society, nature, the hero, and God implied by the Romantics. It may be summarized thus:

> Instead of the traditional symbol of evil and danger, the sea becomes for the Romantics desirable as the place of freedom, solitude, and decisive events; voyaging becomes, instead of a necessary evil, the symbol of man's true condition. Abandoning the image of the Just City (the civilized true community, as distinguished from society) because they no longer believe in its possibility, the Romantics symbolize modern civilization as a desert, level and mechanized, which destroys individuality. "Urban society is, like the desert, a place without limits. The city walls of tradition, mythos and cultus have crumbled."

(p. 37) Surviving real individuals, outcasts (Ishmaels) from the desert, flee therefore to the sea, though with little hope; their only goal is the Garden or Happy Island, representing traditionally the concept of innocence, the earthly paradise where Eros and Logos, desire and duty, are one. But this happy Prelapsarian Place inevitably proves illusive, for the Romantics can identify it only with childhood.[24]

The moral Auden draws is as follows:

We live in a new age in which the artist neither can have such a unique heroic importance nor believes in the Art-God enough to desire it, an age, for instance, when the necessity of dogma is once more recognized, not as the contradiction of reason and feeling but as their ground and foundation, in which the heroic image is not the nomad wandering through the desert or over the ocean, but the less exciting figure of the builder, who renews the ruined walls of the city. Our temptations are not theirs. We are less likely to be tempted by solitude into Promethean pride: we are far more likely to become cowards in the face of the tyrant who would compel us to lie in the service of the False City. It is not madness we need to flee but prostitution.   (p. 153)

Perhaps reluctant to join the ranks of self-confessed critics, he has been slow to collect his criticism, and in the foreword to *The Dyer's Hand* (1962) remarks defensively that these pieces were all commissioned and "I wrote them because I needed the money." *The Dyer's Hand*, however, shows both self-knowledge and scrupulous care. Auden observes that systematic criticism seems to him "lifeless, even false," and he prefers a critic's notebooks to his treatises; hence he has, whenever possible, reduced his own critical pieces to "sets of notes." He is, in short, essentially an aphorist, writing best in short, provocative passages, often personal and deliberately unsystematic. *The Viking Book of Aphorisms*, edited by Auden and Louis Kronenberger and published almost simultaneously with *The*

Dyer's Hand, provides a convenient definition. An epigram need be true only of a single case, while an aphorism claims universal truth; an epigram must be amusing and brief, while an aphorism has more latitude in both respects. The genre is essentially an aristocratic one: "The aphorist does not argue or explain, he asserts." Like most aphorists, Auden is essentially a moralist, and the critic in him cannot be separated from the sage and teacher. He has written profoundly and well on moral subjects, from his essay "Gossip" (1938) to his latest one, "Anger" (1962). Although little of this kind of writing appears directly in *The Dyer's Hand*, it contributes implicitly to the depth and solidity of the point of view expressed. Auden has many brilliant passages of technical analysis, but his central interest is in the larger questions of the nature of poetry, its relation to society, its effect on the writer and the reader, and its religious significance. In this kind of discussion he has a range and depth, as well as a provocative wit, unmatched by any other critic of our time.

Although Auden, in presenting himself as an aphorist and breaking up many of his earlier pieces into aphorisms, deprecates any appearance of system, *The Dyer's Hand* is in fact composed and arranged with great care to develop certain themes. One such theme is the nature of poetry, seen in a new light.

Rites of Homage. In "Making, Knowing, and Judging," his inaugural lecture (1956) as Professor of Poetry at Oxford, Auden said, "The impulse to create a work of art is felt when, in certain persons, the passive awe provoked by sacred beings or events is transformed into a desire to express that awe in a rite of worship or homage...." The rite is neither magic, idolatry, nor devotion; rather it "is verbal; it pays homage by naming." Poetry is rooted in imaginative awe; it "must praise all it can for being as for happening." In concluding, he quotes Hardy's "Afterwards" as an example of a "rite of homage

to sacred objects which are neither gods nor objects of desire. . . ." [25]

In a sense, this definition explains and justifies the magical
aspect of poetry (discussed above, pp. 188-9): art is not sacred,
but as far as the psychology of composition is concerned, it
originates in encounters with the sacred. What Auden means
by "sacred" is clarified by his further comment:

> The impression made by a sacred event is of an over-
> whelming but undefinable significance. In his book
> *Witchcraft*, Mr. Charles Williams has described it thus:
> "One is aware that a phenomenon, being wholly itself,
> is laden with universal meaning. A hand lighting a ciga-
> rette is the explanation of everything; a foot stepping
> from the train is the rock of all existence. . . . Two light
> dancing steps by a girl appear to be what all the School-
> men were trying to express . . . but two quiet steps by an
> old man seem like the very speech of hell. Or the other
> way round." The response of the imagination to such a
> presence or significance is a passion of awe.
>
> (*The Dyer's Hand*, p. 55)

In another context, he considers the two possible interpretations a Christian can make of the fact that certain objects,
beings, and events arouse in his imagination a feeling of sacred
awe, while others do not:

> Either he can say, leaning towards Neoplatonism: "That
> which arouses in me a feeling of sacred awe is a channel
> through which, to me as an individual and as a member
> of a certain culture, the sacred which I cannot perceive
> directly is revealed to me." Or he can say, leaning to-
> wards pantheism: "All objects, beings and events are
> sacred but, because of my individual and cultural limita-
> tions, my imagination can only recognize these ones."
> Speaking for myself, I would rather, if I must be a heretic,
> be condemned as a pantheist than as a Neoplatonist.
>
> (Ibid., pp. 459-60)

Any such definition by a poet is, as Auden observes, more a description of the kind of poetry he wants to write, a "guess-work map of the future," than an attempt at an objective description of all poetry. As such, this one is strikingly different in emphasis from Auden's earlier definitions of poetry as a game of knowledge, or a kind of psychotherapy whose function is to bring emotions to consciousness, or as the "mirror" that reveals man to himself as he really is. A more recent statement makes the difference even plainer:

> The concern of the poet in A.D. 1962 is no different from what it was in 1962 B.C.; that is to say, he is *not* interested in personalities or psychology or progress or news—the extreme opposite of poetry is the daily paper. What moves him to write are his encounters with the sacred in nature, in human beings, nothing else.
>
> By the sacred I do not, of course, mean only the good. The sacred can arouse horror and despair as well as awe, wonder, and gratitude. La belle Dame sans merci is no less a sacred figure than Beatrice. Nor is the sacred confined to the romantically mysterious, to "faery lands forlorn." Indeed, every set of verses, whatever their subject matter may be, are by their formal nature a hymn to Natural Law and a gesture of astonishment at the greatest of all mysteries, the order of the universe. Nothing and no one become sacred through their own efforts; it is rather the sacred that chooses them as vehicles through which to manifest itself. Nor can a poet feel the presence of the sacred simply by wishing or trying to. To say that poetry must be inspired does not mean that it is written in a state of trance like automatic writing; it means that the stimulus to a good poem must be given the poet—he cannot simply think one up.
>
> ("Today's Poet," *Mademoiselle*, April 1962)

This new definition of poetry, as it has emerged in the last decade, is one aspect of the theme of cosmic acceptance that is implicit in all of Auden's Christian poetry, from the "absurd command—Rejoice" ("In Sickness and in Health," 1945) to

"That singular command / I do not understand, / *Bless what there is for being,* / Which has to be obeyed..." ("Precious Five," 1951) and the title and central myth of the latest volume, *Homage to Clio* (1960), with its celebration of both the human and the natural.

> One of the principal functions of poetry... is the preservation and renewal of natural piety toward every kind of created excellence, toward the great creatures like the sun, moon, and earth on which our lives depend, toward the brave warrior, the wise man, the beautiful woman.[26]

Acceptance of the universe as ultimately good does not mean acceptance of the existing order in politics, morality, religion, or anything else; there is no inconsistency in a satirist's affirming that "whatever is, is right" while also pointing out how wrong many things and people are—though hostile critics of Auden as of Pope have delighted to confound the two kinds of acceptance. Auden's verbal rites are anything but pious or solemn, and the homage they pay is often ironic and severely limited. Satire is by no means renounced, but it becomes more generalized, dealing not with one man or some men, but with the poet as Everyman or all men, with the human condition itself. The tone is more compassionate than it used to be, with emphasis on the paradox that human weakness is also the source of hope for salvation. The dominant myth is at first that of the City; then the new myth of Clio and Dame Kind emerges, dramatizing the relationship between history and nature, especially within human nature. But these matters, as they appear in the poetry, will be discussed later; we are concerned here with the critical theory.

Nature and History, Numbers and Faces. In *The Dyer's Hand*,[27] Auden's central theme is the description of the realms of Nature and History and their relations to each other, and the definition of poetry in relation to these polarities. After an aphoristic prologue and the lecture, "Making, Knowing and

Judging," which we have just discussed, Auden places "The Virgin & the Dynamo," based chiefly on "Nature, History and Poetry" from *Thought*, 1950 (with some material from "The Dyer's Hand," *The Listener*, 1955, and other pieces) but much revised. This essay sets up, concisely, systematically, and rather abstractly, the definitions and classifications that underlie the rest of the book. Borrowing (and changing) Henry Adams's terms, Auden thus describes the two real worlds:

> 1) The Natural World of the Dynamo, the world of masses, identical relations and recurrent events, describable, not in words but in terms of numbers, or rather, in algebraic terms. In this world, Freedom is the consciousness of Necessity and Justice and equality of all before the natural law. (*Hard cases make bad law.*)
> 2) The Historical World of the Virgin, the world of faces, analogical relations and singular events, describable only in terms of speech. In this world, Necessity is the consciousness of Freedom and Justice the love of my neighbor as a unique and irreplaceable being. (*One law for the ox and the ass is oppression.*)   (pp. 61-2)

There are also two chimerical worlds:

> 1) The magical polytheistic nature created by the aesthetic illusion which would regard the world of masses as if it were a world of faces. The aesthetic religion says prayers to the Dynamo.
> 2) The mechanized history created by the scientific illusion which would regard the world of faces as if it were a world of masses. The scientific religion treats the Virgin as a statistic. "Scientific politics is animism stood on its head."
>
> Without Art, we could have no notion of Liberty; without Science no notion of Equality; without either, therefore, no notion of Justice.
>
> Without Art, we should have no notion of the sacred; without Science, we should always worship false gods.[28]
>   (p. 62)

Auden then distinguishes between crowds, societies, and communities. Crowds are united only arithmetically. Societies are united by self-love and by definite size and structure. Communities consist of rational beings, united by common love for something other than themselves, and indefinite in number. In the perfect order, a community would be completely embodied in a society expressing the love which is its *raison d'être;* but this is the case only in Paradise, where "love is the fulfilling of the law." In historical societies, order, like love, is always imperfect. Applying these definitions to poetry, Auden says that a poem is the transformation of a crowd of historical occasions of feeling ("among which the most important are recollections of encounters with sacred beings or events") into a community, through embodying it in a verbal society. The poem is a natural organism, not an inorganic thing. In it, meaning and being are identical. "A poem might be called a pseudo-person. Like a person, it is unique and addresses the reader personally. On the other hand, like a natural being and unlike a historical person, it cannot lie" (p. 68). The poem is the result of a struggle between the feelings and the verbal system; it may fail through either excluding too much and resulting in banality, or excluding too little and trying to embody more than one community at a time, resulting in disorder. Pseudo-poets often seek not creation but self-perpetuation, not analogy but identity, like parents who do not really wish to beget new persons analogous to themselves, but to prolong their existence in time; the true poet must be willing to sacrifice his feelings to the poem. "Every poem, therefore, is an attempt to present an analogy to that paradisal state in which Freedom and Law, System and Order are united in harmony." But the harmony is possible and verbal only, and it is an analogy, not an imitation. Since the poem reconciles contradictory feelings, it also presents an analogy to the forgiveness of sins.

> The effect of beauty, therefore, is good to the degree
> that, through its analogies, the goodness of created exist-

> ence, the historical fall into unfreedom and disorder, and
> the possibility of regaining Paradise through repentance
> and forgiveness are recognized. Its effect is evil to the
> degree that beauty is taken, not as analogous to, but
> identical with goodness, so that the artist regards himself
> or is regarded by others as God, the pleasure of beauty
> taken for the joy of Paradise, and the conclusion drawn
> that, since all is well in the work of art, all is well in
> history. But all is not well there.   (p. 71)

In other pieces, not collected in *The Dyer's Hand,* Auden
discusses a wide range of subjects in terms of these ideas. Thus
he defines Freud's achievement by means of the nature-history
polarity: Freud

> made real knowledge of the psyche possible by regarding
> mental events, not as natural events, but as historical
> events to be approached by the methods of the historian.
> In the historical order every event is unique and related
> to others by the principle of analogy ... which means
> that they are not quantitatively measurable ... further,
> while change is reversible in the inorganic order and
> cyclical in the organic, historical change is irreversible
> yet every new event changes all past events; lastly, while
> in the natural order what is real must necessarily be true,
> in history a deliberate lie, a mistaken notion, are as real
> and important as the truth.[29]

"It has not been the priests who have been most shocked by
psychoanalysis; it has been, and still is, the neurologists." Causation in the life of the mind is historical, not natural: A provides B with a motive for occurring, but does not mean that
B has to occur.[30]

In another context, Auden argues that poetry is the mother
of science, in that the presupposition of order in nature could
scarcely have occurred to men unless they were previously
acquainted with worlds in which law and order are immediately manifest. They had first to learn that order can exist: "By
taking as their material the disorder of sensory experience and
creating out of it imaginary worlds in which that disorder was

transformed into something far more orderly than either nature or human society exhibited, the poets proved that it could." [31] In our age, however, when many people think the kind of truth sought by science is the only kind, "the most important educational role of poetry and the other arts is to assert that the verb 'to know' can be used in another sense than that in which the experimental scientist uses it," as in "Then Adam knew his wife, Eve." This is the only possible way in which persons can be known. In the scientific sense to know means ultimately to have power over; this is fully valid only for things, partially valid for living organisms, and for persons not only invalid but immoral to attempt: "To the degree that it is possible to know a person in the scientific sense, he is not a person, that is to say, a freeman, but a slave, and our moral duty is to try to educate him to the point where such knowledge is no longer possible." [32] Thus propaganda, commercial or political, and much psychology and education are immoral, because they try to keep people on, or reduce them to, a sub-personal level at which they can be scientifically controlled, at which it is no longer possible to know them in the poetic sense.

A recent article, "Do You Know Too Much?" (1962), is of interest as presenting Auden's latest meditations on the nature and responsibilities of knowledge and on the relations of man and the non-human world of nature. He observes the modern tendency to acquire irrelevant and useless knowledge through social conformity or laziness or worse motives. Auden points out our moral blind spot which prevents us from recognizing that curiosity, when indulged without control, is not good. "The scholar who looks down his nose at the multitude reading their newspaper reports of crimes and personal disasters is proud of having unearthed and edited and published the intimate papers of a dead writer, and his scientific colleague, who thinks much literary curiosity frivolous, sees nothing questionable in his own attempts to discover a nerve gas against which no defense is possible." Man always desires knowledge for a purpose, and the kinds of knowledge sought by an individual or a culture betray that purpose. "To know" originally meant a relation between persons, as in the Biblical use to mean sexual intercourse. "Knowledge in this sense is mutual; I cannot know anyone well without being equally well-known by him, and, moreover, the better we get to know each other, the better we get to know ourselves. So we behave towards those whom we regard as 'brothers.' In relation to those we regard as 'others,' we desire but one thing, to be stronger than they...." About the "others," in short, we want only the kind of knowledge that gives power. We know, says Auden, that most of the universe is composed of things about which we can acquire knowledge but which cannot know us, and that we can therefore manipulate them as we wish; but we have not drawn the "obvious moral, namely, that if nothing in creation is responsible for our existence then we are responsible for all created things." While the best individual scientists "are contemplatives who rejoice in their discoveries, not for the practical value they may have, but because it is a joy and wonder to know that things are as they are," they are enslaved by "that faceless fabulously wealthy Leviathan called Science which has no concern whatever for the right of anything or anyone to exist except its anonymous power that acknowledges no limits, and that has a scarcely disguised contempt for those whom it employs." Auden suggests that we must, unless we wish to commit suicide by bombs or by exhausting essential natural resources, change our conception of science by accepting three presuppositions:

> 1) Not only everything that "lives" is holy, but everything that exists, from human beings to electrons. An electron has as much right to exist as we have.
>
> 2) Though it is good that everything exists, the way in which a particular thing exists may be evil or, at least, not as good as it could be.
>
> 3) So far as we know, we are the only created beings who, by their own conscious efforts, can make themselves better or worse, or ask questions about the nature of other beings.

If these are accepted, then teleology will find its place again in scientific thinking; and Auden suggests that "it is up to man to enable other created beings to realize goals which are proper to them but which they can only realize with his help, that his authority over nature should be that of a father, not an irresponsible despot." As we increase our knowledge, we increase also our power and hence our duty to educate: "What, unknown to itself, does an electron want to become? We don't know and perhaps never shall, but to know that should be the ultimate aim of science."

I have quoted this essay at some length because it seems to me to demonstrate simultaneously several points: Auden's originality and penetration as moralist, his continuing interest in science, the depth and importance of his meditations on the relation of Clio and Dame Kind, and the way his religious convictions are related to all these matters.

The Poet and the City. To return to *The Dyer's Hand,* the third and last essay in the title section, "The Poet & the City," presents Auden's latest reflections on the relation between art and society. The artist ("and in our age, almost nobody else") is still his own master, personally responsible for what he makes; and this fact explains the fascination of the artistic vocation for the untalented. There are, Auden suggests, actually four principal reasons why the poet's vocation is more difficult in the modern world than it used to be. First, the older picture of an everlasting and unchanging universe has been replaced by the scientific picture of nature as a "process in which nothing is now what it was or what it will be." "It is difficult for a modern artist to believe he can make an enduring object when he has no model of endurance to go by; he is more tempted than his predecessors to abandon the search for perfection as a waste of time and be content with sketches and improvisations" (p. 78). Second, there has been a progressive loss of belief in the significance and reality of sensory phenomena since Luther and Descartes. The older conception of the external world was one of sacramental analogies: "that which the senses perceived was an outward and visible sign of the inward and invisible, but both were believed to be real and valuable." Modern science, in destroying our belief that we can know what the physical universe is really like, has also destroyed the traditional conception of art as *mimesis*, "for there is no longer a nature 'out there' to be truly or falsely imitated; all an artist can be *true* to are his subjective sensations and feelings." Third, technology, "with its ever accelerating transformation of man's way of living, has made it impossible for us to imagine what life will be like even twenty years from now." Archaeology and anthropology have also made us aware of the tremendous variety of human behavior. "The artist, therefore, no longer has any assurance, when he makes something, that even the next generation will find it enjoyable or comprehensible. He cannot help desiring an immediate success, with all the danger to his integrity which that implies." Further, "tradition" no longer means a way of working handed down from one generation to the next, but a consciousness of the whole of the past as present. "Originality no longer means a slight modification in the style of one's immediate predecessors; it means a capacity to find in any work of any date or place a clue to finding one's authentic voice. The burden of choice and selection is put squarely upon the shoulders of each individual poet and it is a heavy one." Finally, the modern attitude toward the distinction between private and public life reverses the Greek attitude, and regards public life as the impersonal sphere of necessity and private life as the place a man is free to be his personal self. In consequence, the arts have lost their traditional chief human subject, the man of action, the doer of public deeds. The machine has also destroyed the direct relation between a man's intention and his deed, so that the good or evil done by public figures depends more on the amount of impersonal force they command than on their characters and intentions. This makes it very hard to write poetry about them. "The true men of action in our time, those who transform the world, are not the politicians and statesmen, but the scientists," and poetry cannot celebrate them because their deeds are concerned with things, not with persons.

In the relation of the poet to the city, one of the most damaging modern developments has been the emergence of what Kierkegaard called "the public," created by the growth in size of societies and the development of mass media of communication. Passive, uncommitted, abstract, the public is a kind of crowd—and Auden uses the term in the sense he has previously defined in distinguishing crowds, societies, and communities—unknown to earlier times. Before the public appeared, there was naïve art and sophisticated art, folk poetry and court poetry, different from each other "but only in the way that two brothers are different." But the "appearance of the Public and the mass media which cater to it have destroyed naive popular art." The "highbrow" artist survives, because his audience is too small to interest the mass media. "But the audience of the popular artist is the majority and this the mass media must steal from him if they are not to go bankrupt." This they do by offering "not popular art, but entertainment which is intended to be consumed like food, forgotten, and replaced by a new dish. This is bad for everyone; the majority lose all genuine taste of their own, and the minority become cultural snobs."

> The characteristic style of 'Modern' poetry is an intimate tone of voice, the speech of one person addressing one person, not a large audience; whenever a modern poet raises his voice he sounds phony. And its characteristic hero is not the 'Great Man' nor the romantic rebel, both doers of extraordinary deeds, but the man or woman in any walk of life who, despite all the impersonal pressures of modern society, manages to acquire and preserve a face of his own.   (p. 84)

The good poem, as we have seen, is an analogue to Utopia or Eden, not to a historical society. The poet aims at completeness and unchanging permanence: a "poetic city would always contain exactly the same number of inhabitants doing exactly the same jobs forever."

> A society which was really like a good poem, embodying the aesthetic virtues of beauty, order, economy and sub-ordination of detail to the whole, would be a nightmare of horror for, given the historical reality of actual men, such a society could only come into being through se-lective breeding, extermination of the physically and mentally unfit, absolute obedience to its Director, and a large slave class kept out of sight in cellars.
>
> Vice versa, a poem which was really like a political democracy—examples, unfortunately, exist—would be formless, windy, banal and utterly boring.   (p. 85)

Poets are "singularly ill-equipped to understand politics or eco-nomics," which are concerned with large numbers of people and with impersonal, largely involuntary relations; poets are naturally interested in singular individuals and personal rela-tions. If embittered, poets are likely to "combine aggressive phantasies about the annihilation of the present order with im-practical day-dreams of Utopia. Societies have always to be-ware of the utopias being planned by artists *manqués* over cafeteria tables late at night" (p. 84).

On the other hand, in our age "the mere making of a work of art is itself a political act." The existence of functioning art-ists reminds "the Management of something managers need to be reminded of, namely, that the managed are people with faces, not anonymous numbers, that *Homo Laborans* is also *Homo Ludens*." And poet and peasant, whatever their differ-ences, agree in suspicion of officialdom; "both sniff in any offi-cial world the smell of an unreality in which persons are treated as statistics" (p. 88).

Eden. The myth of Eden has been prominent in Auden's recent work; we have seen the part it plays in *The Age of Anxiety* and in the operas, and will shortly consider its place in the postwar poetry.[33] In *The Dyer's Hand* it is extremely important. Near the beginning, Auden gives a description of his own dream of Eden, in answer to an imaginary questionnaire (which all critics, he says, should be obliged to answer, so that readers will be in a position to judge their judgments). It covers everything from landscape ("Limestone uplands . . . with at least one extinct volcano. A precipitous and indented sea-coast") to religion ("Roman Catholic in an easy-going mediterranean sort of way"), government ("Absolute Monarchy, elected for life by lot"), public entertainments ("Religious Processions, Brassbands, Opera, Classical Ballet. No movies, radio or television") and sources of public information ("Gossip . . . no newspapers"). Eden is the realm of wishes, of fantasy; it is timeless, perfect, without suffering and evil. The dream of a lost Eden or the wish-game of the fairy-tale are harmless if recognized for what they are, but dangerous if the wishes are not recognized as fantastic, if they are located in a future New Jerusalem on earth, or if they lead to a rejection of the self and an abandonment of all desire ("West's Disease"). The essay, "Dingley Dell & the Fleet" contrasts Eden and New Jerusalem and the Arcadian and Utopian dreamers at length, and proceeds to discuss the four great experts on Eden: Dickens, Wilde, Firbank, and Wodehouse. (It is notable that these are all English and are all comic writers.) Eden enters variously into many of the essays: for example, the analysis of the detective story in "The Guilty Vicarage" as "the fantasy of being restored to the Garden of Eden, to a state of innocence, where he may know love as love and not as the law" (p. 158), or the description of the worst features of the American scene which leads us to "understand by contrast the nature of the Good Place" (p. 323).

Most significantly, Eden figures in the suggestive generalizations in the essay on Frost: all poems may be described as collaborations between Ariel, inhabitant of a timeless, perfect, innocent Eden of pure play, and Prospero, who is concerned with the pain and disorder of temporal life and tries, through revealing what life is really like, to free the reader from self-enchantment and deception. Ariel is concerned with beauty, Prospero with truth, in the conventional formulation. Ariel's glory and limitation is that he has no passions; "The earthly paradise is a beautiful place but nothing of serious importance can occur in it": "Ariel's other name is Narcissus" (p. 340). The Prospero-dominated poet (e.g. Frost or, obviously, Auden) is concerned with two basic questions:

> 1) *Who am I?* What is the difference between man and all other creatures? What relations are possible between them? What is man's status in the universe? What are the conditions of his existence which he must accept as his fate which no wishing can alter?
>
> 2) *Whom ought I to become?* What are the characteristics of the hero, the authentic man whom everybody should admire and try to become? Vice versa, what are the characteristics of the churl, the unauthentic man whom everybody should try to avoid becoming?
>
> (pp. 344-5)

Prospero and Ariel. I have attempted to do justice only to the theory of poetry enunciated in the section called "The Dyer's Hand"; to do more than glance at the rest of this immensely rich and stimulating book would take disproportionate space.[34] The section called "The Well of Narcissus" deals with the relation of the ego and self: "Hic et Ille" (recalling Yeats's poem) is a collection of aphorisms; "Balaam and his Ass" deals with the master-servant relation, which is the mode of expression in literature of the ego-self relation, and may be a parable of Agape; "The Guilty Vicarage" analyzes the dialectic of innocence and guilt in the detective story, which is a form of magic, not art, based on the fantasy of recovering Eden; "The I Without a Self" deals with Kafka and quest works that are in some respects detective stories in reverse.

"The Shakespearian City" is a group of essays concerned with the relation of the temporal or natural realm and the supernatural or fantastic realm in Shakespeare, with two interludes dealing with the nature of fantasy (in fairy stories and in

Nathanael West's novels). Falstaff is essentially an operatic character, inhabitant of a timeless Eden, and a comic symbol for the supernatural order of Charity as contrasted to the temporal order of Justice. In *The Merchant of Venice* the fairy-tale world of Belmont is contrasted to the historical world of Venice, but with an effect opposite to that of the similar contrast in *Henry IV*. The analysis of *Othello* is based on the definition of the practical joke, which demonstrates that "the distinction between seriousness and play is not a law of nature but a social convention which can be broken"; Iago exhibits "a self lacking in authentic feelings and desires of its own" and treats Othello "as an analyst treats a patient except that, of course, his intention is to kill not to cure"; for us, he is a parabolic figure for the autonomous pursuit of scientific knowledge, the reduction of human beings to the status of things.

The essays on Lawrence and Marianne Moore in the section called "Two Bestiaries" deal explicitly with the relation between man and animals, among many other things. "The Shield of Perseus" defines the comic as basically a contradiction between man as natural creature and as historical person, and explores various kinds of comedy and satire, together with the question of representing sanctity or blessedness in art, the Christian hero. Agape speaks in the comic mode on earth, as in *Pickwick Papers* and, especially, in *Don Quixote*, the only successful indirect portrayal of the Knight of Faith.

The final section, on music and opera, defines music as being about "Our experience of Time in its twofold aspect, natural or organic repetition, and historical novelty created by choice. And the full development of music as an art depends upon a recognition that these two aspects are different and that choice, being an experience confined to man, is more significant than repetition" (p. 465). The question of naturalism ("verismo") in opera is explored, and the point made that it has little to do with the success of *Cavalleria Rusticana*, which depends on the interplay of rite and personal action, and *Pagliacci*, which is based on the psychological question of identity. The work of art, Auden concludes, "is not *about* this or that kind of life; it *has* life, drawn, certainly, from human experience but transmuted, as a tree transmutes water and sunlight into treehood, into its own unique being. Every encounter with a work of art is a personal encounter; what it *says* is not information but a revelation of itself which js simultaneously a revelation of ourselves" (p. 482).

It is remarkable that in *The Dyer's Hand* Auden is constantly able to do two things at once: to develop an argument about a literary subject which casts light on it and on literature in general, and simultaneously to develop a general moral or religious argument, with a particular relevance to the contemporary world. This is plainest in the section on Shakespeare, but I hope that my inadequate summary has indicated that it is characteristic of the whole book. In addition to their intrinsic interest and value, these larger themes and moral arguments supply the context within which various of Auden's aphorisms and statements that have been puzzling or curious in some earlier form now are thoroughly intelligible. It becomes clear that he does not divorce poetry from truth and seriousness, as he has sometimes been accused of doing, and his emphasis on play, frivolity, the comic, and the fantastic takes on its full significance. The book offers a magnificent example of a mature and powerful intelligence, aware of its nature and limitations, casting fresh light upon individual works and writers, upon the perennial problems of criticism, and upon the nature of man.

The volume closes with a discussion of the musical aspect of *The Tempest,* and, specifically, of Prospero's farewell at the end. As we have seen, Auden suggests that Ariel represents beauty, the perfect, timeless, and inhuman world of art, while Prospero represents truth, morality, the "real" world with its ugliness and disorder, and that all poetry may be regarded as a tension and collaboration between the two. The application to Auden's own poetry is inevitable, and the terms we have used earlier may be combined with these if we consider Ariel as equivalent to the impulse toward fantasy and magic and Prospero equivalent to the impulse toward disenchantment and diagnosis. Auden is a Prospero-dominated poet, one of those whose aim is to "show us what life is really like and free us from self-enchantment and deception" (*The Dyer's Hand*, p. 338), but Ariel never leaves him, however often he is set free, nor does Prospero get completely away from the Enchanted Island. The Island must be known for what it is and renounced in this life; but as prelapsarian innocent Eden, earthly paradise where Love becomes Law, supernatural realm of Agape, and land of dream, fantasy, and magic, it remains very much in view in the poetry. Shakespeare's Prospero, Auden suggests, "has the coldness of someone who has come to the conclusion that human nature is not worth much, that human relations are, at their best, pretty sorry affairs" (ibid., p. 129); at the end of the play he seems to long only for silence. But Auden-Prospero is not like this at all. A central theme of his later poetry is acceptance, rites of homage, and this protopoetic function of celebrating the sacred is a kind of equivalent of magic, which otherwise is to be used only to disenchant. Human nature is regarded compassionately but realistically, and the tone is one of hard-bitten cheerfulness.

NONES AND THE SHIELD OF ACHILLES

Nones (1951) is a transitional volume that broaches themes which are developed and begins patterns which are completed in *The Shield of Achilles* (1955) and *Homage to Clio* (1960). Thus the title poem, "Nones," together with "Prime," is reprinted in *Shield* as part of the sequence "Horae Canonicae," and both are best considered in that context. "In Praise of Limestone" is very close in theme and technique to the "Bucolics" in *Shield*, and may be regarded as a kind of prelude to them.[35] The City symbolism that dominates the volume has already been discussed (pp. 194-7, above); the Nature-History polarity suggested by it leads into the further development of this theme in *Clio*. "Their Lonely Betters" introduces the contrast between the human and the natural that is fundamental to *Clio*, and "Precious Five" (already quoted) introduces the other major theme of that volume, homage to existence and to the Earthly Muse. *Nones* contains some brilliant songs (for example, "Deftly, admiral, cast your fly")[36] and some fine light verse (such as "Under Which Lyre"). The dominant style is the colloquial, used with great success in lyrics; the kind of low-keyed, informal, often amusing poem that results depends on an attractive and viable *persona*. The last poem in the volume, "A Walk After Dark," is a good example, in which the romantic subject of the stars on a cloudless night is dealt with informally and candidly: the "clockwork spectacle" is impressive, but in a "slightly boring / Eighteenth-century way"; the poet recalls that it "soothed adolescence a lot" to see the stars still there in spite of his shocking deeds, and "Now, unready to die / But already at the stage / When one starts to dislike the young," he is glad the stars can also be called middle-aged, for

> It's cosier thinking of night
> As more an Old People's Home
> Then a shed for a faultless machine,
> That the red pre-Cambrian light
> Is gone like Imperial Rome
> Or myself at seventeen.

But the poet will not be led by these meditations into Stoic detachment or the "lacrimae rerum note"; man is responsible for his own destiny:

> For the present stalks abroad
> Like the past and its wronged again
> Whimper and are ignored,
> And the truth cannot be hid;
> Somebody chose their pain,
> What needn't have happened did.

Here, again, one must say that the two succeeding volumes develop this tendency further and contain numerous colloquial lyrics. Since *Nones* thus has no independent principle of organization, it needs little discussion; poems relevant to the later work will be discussed in that context. G. S. Fraser is probably right in suggesting that the title is intended to suggest "nonce"—i.e., this is poetry for the nonce, for the time being. Certainly it recalls the end of *For the Time Being:* "The happy morning is over, / The night of agony still to come; the time is noon"; and both allusions indicate awareness of this volume as transitional, as marking time. The dedicatory poem to Reinhold and Ursula Niebuhr is one of Auden's most revealing and impressive comments on his relation to his audience. He would like to express joy and wholeness and wisdom, sing "in the old grand manner" from "a resonant heart." But all "sane affirmative speech" has been debased and profaned by the mass media and the "promiscuous crowd," so that "No civil style survived / That pandaemonium / But the wry, the sotto-voce, / Ironic and monochrome." The only shelter left is the "suburb of dissent."

The Shield of Achilles,[37] in contrast to *Nones*, is the most elaborately organized of all Auden's volumes. It begins with a set of seven "Bucolics" (all written before December 12, 1953, when Auden recorded them). These are not pastorals in the conventional sense, having nothing to do with shepherds or rural life; but they are concerned with the relation of man to nature in one particular mode. Each deals with a natural force or object and the human qualities and attitudes it suggests. The whole section is thus an explicit development of the myth of psychic geography, *paysage moralisé*. "In Praise of Limestone" in *Nones* is a good introduction to the series, as we have suggested. Its symbol is the limestone country previously used in the same way in "New Year Letter" (see above, pp. 142-3): "If it form the one landscape that we the inconstant ones / Are consistently homesick for, this is chiefly / Because it dissolves in water." The "best and worst" seek other soils: granite, completely unresponsive, attracts future saints; clay and gravel, completely responsive, attract secular saviors, "intendant Caesars"; the oceanic solitudes attract the "really reckless." The limestone landscape, varied, responsive but unpredictable, represents human nature as seen by the child innocently dominated by Eros; more important, it symbolizes the weakness and individuality of common human nature. It is "not the sweet home that it looks / Nor its peace the historical calm of a site / Where something was settled once and for all"; yet it "calls into question / All the Great Powers assume." This weakness and individuality challenge the secular saviors, protect man from the extremists; they are the ultimate basis of humility and faith. It is only in terms of this landscape, the poet says, that he can imagine "a faultless love / Or the life to come."

To return to the "Bucolics": they display all Auden's technical exuberance and virtuosity, for each is in a different meter and stanza and several produce striking effects through the use of special kinds of diction. The first, "Winds," is dedicated to Alexis Léger (St.-John Perse) and begins as a kind of irreverent commentary on his *Vents* (1946): the style and tone form a deliberate contrast to Perse's solemn, noble, enigmatic and allusive periods. Like "Limestone," it is written in unrimed syllabic verse, alternating six- and seven-syllable lines (with the order reversed in the second part).[38] Wind suggests first the original—and arbitrary—divine choice of the human over the other species to inspire, so that man could say, "I am loved, therefore I am" (correcting the Cartesian *cogito*). (The poet comments, "And well by now might the lion / Be lying down with the kid, / Had he stuck to that logic.") This choice is associated with the uncertainty and unpredictability of weather and the wind that bloweth where it listeth. The image of "our Authentic City" is that of amateurs trying anxiously to predict the weather, with uncertain instruments. The second part of the poem is a mock-invocation of the "Goddess of winds and wisdom" (deftly associated with the White Goddess, witches, the Unconscious) [39] to inspire the poet,

> That every verbal rite
>   May be fittingly done,
> And done in anamnesis
>   Of what is excellent
> Yet a visible creature,
>   Earth, Sky, a few dear names.

These lines are, of course, a version of the definition of poetry that we discussed in the preceding section, and it is possible that Perse, both by precept and by example, had some influence in forming the concept of poetry as essentially ceremonial praise.[40]

The second poem, "Woods," is written in six-line rimed stanzas of regular iambic pentameter. A flavor of eighteenth-century poetic diction in the first two stanzas fits the exposition of the old idea of sylvan nature as savage and licentious. The truth, the poet argues, is opposite; the innocence and calm of plant life make the public "Bridle its skirt-and-bargain-chasing eye," and trees are an index to a country's soul and probable future: "A culture is no better than its woods." After this exercise in maximum regularity, the next poem, "Mountains" (separately published in 1954 as a Faber Ariel Poem), employs an audacious balancing of maximum irregularity against just enough regular pattern to maintain the principle of order. The meter is syllabic, with lines of the following numbers of syllables in each stanza: 11, 7, 11, 7, 11, 13, 13, 9, 5, 11, 5; the two short pairs (7 and 5) rime. In other words, the stanza consists of two quatrains of alternating long and short lines with the short lines riming, separated by three unrimed long lines; the riming short lines produce a fine effect of bringing the long lines back under control. The tone is relaxed and easily personal. The basic contrast is between the exceptional and isolated (and also unsociable and monstrous) types who love mountains and the normal and ordinary people who don't. The poet likes the scenery and the freedom and individualism it fosters; but feels that the isolation is both dangerous and boring: "For an uncatlike / Creature who has gone wrong, / Five minutes on even the nicest mountain / Is awfully long."

"Lakes," in unrimed iambic hexameter alternating with pentameter, is the slightest of these poems, contrasting the humanity and cosiness of lakes with the estranging and alien quality of oceans and rivers, and suggesting that they are usually false Edens, too regressive and "comfy." "Islands" ("What is cosier than the shore / Of a lake turned inside out?") is a light and broad satire on the egocentric isolation that islands always suggest in Auden; it is witty, allusive, and amusing.

> How fascinating is that class
>> Whose only member is Me!
> Sappho, Tiberius and I
>> Hold forth beside the sea.

"Plains," one of the best, is in unrimed eleven-syllable lines, personal in tone. The poet expresses his horror of plains as dead-level equality, uniformity, a ground for warriors and totalitarian governments ("it is here they chamber with Clio"); instead of Cupid, "that old grim She" (Dame Kind) presides over their love-lives. The poet concludes, "I've reason to be frightened / Not of plains, of course, but of me," and confesses:

> I wish I weren't so silly. Though I can't pretend
>> To think these flats poetic, it's as well at times
> To be reminded that nothing is lovely,
>> Not even in poetry, which is not the case.

Finally, "Streams" describes the psychic landscape that Auden loves best (complementing "In Praise of Limestone"), dominated by water, "Pure being, perfect in music and movement": unpredictable, innocent, musical, varied, telling of another world, an ideal city. It is in regular unrimed quatrains: in each, the first two lines have twelve syllables and masculine endings, the third nine and a feminine ending, the fourth ten; a syllable within line one rimes with a syllable in line three; the final syllable of line two rimes with the penultimate syllable of line four, and the penultimate syllable of line three rimes with a syllable within line four. The rhythm is largely dactylic and could be called rippling. The poem concludes with a dream-vision appropriate to this landscape of prelapsarian innocence, playfulness, and joy, a kind of lightly mock-heroic version of the procession Dante encountered in Paradise.[41]

The second section, "In Sunshine and in Shade," begins with the title poem, "The Shield of Achilles," in which, as in the *Iliad*, the shield symbolizes art, image of the human condition. Auden's version, however, is mock-heroic, contrasting the Homeric description to the life the modern artist must represent. In the shield of art Hephaestos (the artist) shows Thetis (the audience) not the classical city but the plain of modern life on which multitudes are ordered about by totalitarian rulers (a faceless voice reciting statistics through a loudspeaker). Instead of the "ritual pieties," we have barbed wire enclosing an "arbitrary spot" where there is a travesty of the Crucifixion being performed by bored bureaucrats while "ordinary decent folk" watch, in which helpless individuals are shamefully deprived of human dignity before death. Instead of dancing and games, we have on the vacant plain a juvenile delinquent who knows nothing but violence, hardness, and selfishness.

The rest of this section is, as the title suggests, highly varied in tone, subject, and technique. "Fleet Visit" follows "Shield" naturally because it begins with a similar mock-heroic reference, comparing the American sailors to the Homeric Greeks. "The Willow-wren and the Stare" uses the device of the medieval bird-*débat* (as in *The Owl and the Nightingale*) to render the ambiguity of sexual love. In contrast to the more rigorous view expressed in Auden's earlier versions of the Eros-Agape-Logos myth, the suggestion here is that Eros may possibly lead to Agape, and the tone is one of tolerant, humorous, wistful acceptance. "The Proof" is based on the ordeal scene of *The Magic Flute*, interpreting the fire and water through which Tamino and Pamina pass to mean the twin dangers of love: rage and spite. Clearly, one reason *The Magic Flute* has had a particular interest for Auden (and the poem is presumably a by-product of his work with Kallman in translating the libretto) is that it deals with a Quest, and that Papageno and the Queen of the Night both represent aspects of the natural in man. "The Truest Poetry is the Most Feigning" is in Auden's best vein of light light verse: a defense of lying and exaggeration in love-poetry, with Dante's treatment of Beatrice as the grand example. (The title comes from *As You Like It*.) In elegant heroic couplets, Auden maintains that such a love-poem has the advantage that it can easily be converted, if necessary, to a panegyric on the "new pot-bellied Generalissimo." Man is the only creature that can lie; neither love nor truth is natural to him; only tall tales and verbal playing can trick him into saying that "love, or truth in any serious sense, / Like orthodoxy, is a reticence." "A Permanent Way" is a kind of anti-existentialist celebration of the virtues of dogmas as permanent ways, like railways, which relieve one of the responsibility of further choice but leave him free to dream: "And what could be greater fun, / Once one has chosen and paid, / Than the inexpensive delight / Of a choice one might have made." "Ode to Gaea" meditates upon earth, the mother, as seen from the air and known more completely than ever before. We hope for victory in the perennial battle, for things to change for the better. "But who on Cupid's Coming would care to bet?" Earth "till the end, will be herself," whatever our hopes of Utopia or dreams of Eden: ". . . what, / To her, the real one, can our good landscapes be but lies, / Those woods where tigers chum with deer and no root dies, / That tideless bay where children / Play bishop on a golden shore."

The final section, "Horae Canonicae," consists of seven poems, each in a different meter and style, on the canonical hours and the church offices associated with them. These offices celebrate historical events, all relating to the Crucifixion, and at the same time form a cycle repeated daily; they therefore suggest varied treatments of the relations of nature and history. The first, "Prime" (6 A.M.), reflects upon the moment of waking and assuming human nature, of re-entering history. When identity, volition, and memory are assumed, paradise is lost, but the human task is begun again, the "lying self-made city" is again our responsibility. The poem's movement is slow and meditative; nine-syllable and seven-syllable lines alternate in sixteen-line stanzas with internal rime counterpointing occassional end rime. The meter is syllabic, but strongly rhythmical. In its dramatic rendering of the daily transition from sleep into time, guilt, the human condition, and "our living task, the dying / Which the coming day will ask," the poem forms a quiet but effective beginning for the series.

In 1950 Auden discussed this poem in a lecture at Swarthmore,[42] supplying some interesting background and describing, in part, the process of composition. The plan of "Horae Canonicae" was conceived in the summer of 1947; they were all to deal with the relation of nature and history, a theme that had interested Auden for many years. "Prime," first of the series to be written, was done in August 1949, in Italy. Auden had been interested in the possibilities of syllabic meters for some time, and had been reading Marianne Moore, Horace, and French verse; he had also been reading some of Valéry's prose meditations dealing with the significance of waking. The original beginning of the poem was as follows:

> Simultaneously as at the instant
> Word of the light the gates of the body,
> The eyes and the ears open
> Into its world beyond,
> The gates of the mind, the horn gate, the ivory gate,
> Swing to, shut off
> The nocturnal rummage of its angry fronde,
> Crippled and second-rate,
> Still suffering from some historical mistake.

But this was too free; a more rigorous form was needed. Auden found this partly in following the syllabic principle strictly, alternating nine- and seven-syllable lines (with full elision, i.e., eliding contiguous vowels and *h*), and partly in employing an elaborate pattern of rimes, with both end rimes and internal rimes irregularly placed, so that the line stop and the rime stop do not coincide regularly but are counterpointed. The process of finding these rimes was a help in making the diction of the poem more precise and more evocative; and Auden gave several examples of how the need for rime helped to suggest the right word. Thus the third line first read "knock of the dawn"; "vaunt," with its vivid image, was suggested by the need for rime both with "dawn" and with "horn" in line six. In the last stanza, the sixth line first read "level sea"; "steady" was suggested as a rime for "ready" in line ten.

The end of the poem originally read:

> No honest companion but my accomplice
>   For now, my assassin to be:
> Once more I claim in my name, and yours
>   Stands, my beloved, for that care
> Which can neither pretend to be love
>   Nor stop me wishing it were.

But this was too personal, out of key with the rest of the poem. The second version was:

> No honest companion but my accomplice
>   For now, my assassin to be and
> My name stands for that pride which because
>   It cannot choose its choice, for
> The joy it hopes for is already there
>   Refuses not to despair.

And from this the final version was produced, partly through elaborating the rime-patterns.

"Terce" presents man at 9 A.M., in his private and domestic capacity, when the hangman is kind and playful with his dog, before entering the world and starting the machinery that makes every day a Good Friday. "Sext" (noon) celebrates the sense of vocation, of self-forgetfulness in work, that leads man to "ignore the appetitive goddesses" and makes civilization possible: without it, we should still be "slaves of Dame Kind, lacking / All notion of a city." In slow unrimed couplets, deliberately prosaic, the poem develops the paradox that the same qualities that are responsible for human civilization are also responsible for human guilt as typified in the Crucifixion; in both respects, man goes beyond nature, and both his achievement and his capacity for sin are uniquely human. The end of the poem recalls Auden's prose discussions (above, pp. 297, 303), of the difference between crowds and other kinds of pluralities: "Few people accept each other and most / will never do anything properly, / but the crowd rejects no one, joining the crowd / is the only thing all men can do. / Only because of that can we say / all men are our brothers," and therefore we are superior to the ants—the poem concludes with a fine irony—who would never stop work "to worship / The Prince of this world like us, / at this noon, on this hill, / in the occasion of this dying."

"Nones," the best of the series, follows immediately in context: the Crucifixion, the archetypal sin, has taken place, and we, the crowd, though trying to evade responsibility, "are left alone with our feat." Now we can no longer believe ourselves innocent; we must see that evil will have its sway. The poem gains much dramatic effect from being set in the siesta hour (3 P.M.) of sleepy after-dinner stillness, after the act but before the consequences. It is well, the poet suggests, with realism and humility, for our minds to try to escape, though they escape into nightmare,—and here Auden has a stanza of fine romantic ominousness—while our bodies restore themselves, while our "wronged flesh" restores its own natural order. The poem closes with an effective contrast between human guilt and the innocence and limitations of natural creatures, "The bug whose view is balked by grass, / Or the deer who shyly from afar /

Peer through chinks in the forest." "Vespers" is not a poem at all, but a prose contrast of two types (on a somewhat deeper level than the similar contrast in "Under Which Lyre") at sunset, "this hour of civil twilight" when "all must wear their own faces" in the City. The poet is an Arcadian, whose goal is Eden; his anti-type is a Utopian, whose goal is the New Jerusalem. (Cf. *The Dyer's Hand*, p. 409.) But in spite of all their opposition they are united in guilt for the innocent victim "on whose immolation (call him Abel, Remus, whom you will, it is one Sin Offering) arcadias, utopias, our dear old bag of a democracy, are alike founded." "Compline" (9 P.M.) presents the body returning to sleep, the mind forgetting its guilt but meditating on forgiveness, humbly and humorously asking to be spared.

> That we, too, may come to the picnic
>   With nothing to hide, join the dance
> As it moves in perichoresis,
>   Turns about the abiding tree.

The stanza-form is the same as that of "Nones" and "Prime" (i.e., 16 lines of alternating nine- and seven-syllable lines, with irregular rime), so that these three poems form a sequence within the series. The last poem, "Lauds," is a lyric with refrain, medieval in tone, simple and innocent in feeling, returning to dawn and the moment of waking. (As we have seen, it was used as the final chorus of the opera *Delia* in 1953, and it has been set to music by Lennox Berkeley.) The form is the medieval Spanish *cossante*, close to folk poetry and to music. Gerald Brenan, who quotes a thirteenth-century aubade in this form, describes it thus:

> In the *cossante* the lines are grouped in assonanced distiches or couplets, the odd couplets having an *i* assonance and the even an assonance in *a*. In between each couplet there is a single-lined refrain which does not change. . . . But the *cossante* has also a sense pattern, which conflicts with the rhyme pattern. According to

this the even couplets repeat the sense of the odd couplets, whilst every odd couplet except the first begins by repeating the *second* line of the preceding odd couplet and then introduces a new line to rhyme with it. . . . By this device, known as the *leixa-pren (laisser prendre)*, a term taken from the dance, a slow, gradually uncoiling movement is set up which is capable of giving effects of remarkable beauty.

(*The Literature of the Spanish People*,
Cambridge 1951, p. 54)

The concern is no longer with individual guilt, but with others: communion is restored.

> Men of their neighbours become sensible;
> God bless the Realm, God bless the People:
> *In solitude, for company*.

HOMAGE TO CLIO

Homage to Clio (1960), though not as tightly organized as *Shield*, is more unified and sequential than it at first appears to be. The title poem states the central theme of the volume, which is developed variously in the following poems. This theme is the contrast between the realm of Clio, Muse of time and history, and therefore of the distinctively human, and the realm of Artemis and Aphrodite (called the "appetitive goddesses" in "Sext"), who govern plant and animal life. Auden's Clio does not stand for History in the conventional sense; *Clio* is, in fact, remarkably detached from contemporary history, the only topical reference being in the dedication,[43] with its cheerful resolve to make the best of a dry time: "Against odds, / Methods of dry farming may still produce grain." Two poems in *Nones* state aspects of the theme developed more fully in "Homage to Clio": "Their Lonely Betters" contrasts the garden noises of vegetables and birds with human language, awareness of self and time: "Let them leave language to their lonely betters / Who count some days and long for certain letters; / We, too, make noises when we laugh or weep, / Words are for those with promises to keep." "Precious Five" celebrates the "Earthly Muse," with her "revolving wheel / Of appetite and season"; she presides over the appetites and senses, and though freed from her, we re-enter her domain "At any drink or meal." The immediately preceding group of poems, "Horae Canonicae," in distinguishing History from Nature had emphasized human guilt; and in this context *Clio* is a counterbalancing defense of and paradoxical homage to the human world of unique persons in unique moments of time, capable of guilt and forgiveness, as against the innocent, merciless, and perfect world of Nature. Reversing the customary definition of speech as the distinctive human attribute, Auden describes Clio as characterized by silence. The realm of Nature is characterized by noise, and humans, too, make noises when under the sway of Nature; but Clio, "Madonna of silences," is able to be silent and is, therefore, merciful and forgiving. The children of Artemis, kings and warriors, make noise ("superfluous screams"), and Aphrodite is unforgiving; but lives that obey Clio "move like music, / Becoming now what they only can be once, / Making of silence decisive sound." (We remember here Auden's definition of music as an imitation of choice.) The poet begs Clio to "forgive our noises / And teach us our recollections"—i.e. forgive our subjection to Nature, and instruct us through anamnesis (a favorite term of Auden's in this period, meaning, technically, a psychiatric case history; it is part of the human experience of time, as the epigraph to Part I of *Clio* puts it: "Between those happenings that prefigure it / And those that happen in its anamnesis / Occurs the Event . . ."). Clio is, ultimately, the Madonna.

"Reflections in a Forest" contrasts the stability, unity, and innocence of trees with human deceit, divisiveness, and concealment, and defends the latter. "Hands," considering the distinctive physical attribute of man, celebrates the fact that each hand and its handwriting is physically unique. "The Sabbath" is a kind of cheerful version of Armageddon: the natural creatures rejoice that "Ruins and metallic rubbish" is all that is left of man, and they go on with their existences, "Beautiful, happy, perfectly pointless. . . ." But then man reappears, and is both "More bloody-minded than they remembered" and "More god-like than they thought." "On Installing an American Kitchen in Lower Austria" celebrates the modern kitchen as the highest achievement of our civilization: clean, democratic, unlaborious, fostering a distinctively human pleasure. The tone is mildly ironic, but with a realistic and humorous acceptance of the human animal; it is a kind of minimal and wholly unpretentious defense of "our City," which will at least provide us with a good dinner before we march to Thermopylae. This poem is notably superior to any of the preceding ones except "Homage" and "Hands," perhaps because it is occasional: when provided with an occasion which enables him to imagine a particular audience, Auden responds with unflagging wit and precise control of tone. Three sonnets follow, rather abstract and involved, and each containing an element of obscurity. "Objects" contrasts the wordless and tearless creatures of nature with the human world of persons who can feel loss. "Words" defines the relation between the world of language and the world of "our fate," the curious power of "verbal chance" over our lives (the prose interlude deals with the same subject, as do some of the essays discussed earlier, where the point is made that the poem, as a natural creature, cannot lie). The third, "The Song," describes a rebellious bird (presumably, in the traditional symbolism, the poet) which intends to gain immortality and "make amends / For whiteness drabbed for glory said away" but who, because the morning is so large and unreproachful, ends by "Denying what it started up to say." "Makers of History" observes that the kings and warriors who ceaselessly assert their self-importance meet with poetic justice: they are absorbed into legend and myth and forgotten as persons, while the true makers of history "who bred them better horses, / Found answers to their questions, made their things" or even wrote poetry are remembered as individuals.

"T the Great" gives an example: T, once the terror of the world, soon declines to nursery bogeyman, and survives now only as an obscure name in crossword puzzles, in anagrams such as "a nubile tram" (to which one solution is, of course, "Tamburlaine").[44] "Secondary Epic" and "The Epigoni" deal not only with the collapse of classical civilization with its tradition of celebrating warriors and kings, but also with the role of the poet. "Secondary Epic" is a witty and amusing criticism of Virgil for the scene at the end of Book VIII (paralleling the Shield of Achilles in the *Iliad*) in which the shield Vulcan makes for Aeneas has on it scenes representing the future history of Rome up to the victory of Augustus over Antony. Auden imagines a Gothic poet continuing the book to describe the victory of the Goths ("Alaric has avenged Turnus..."), and proceeds to point out that no account of the future could be plausible if it failed to note the astonishing proof of providence in the name of the last Roman emperor (Romulus Augustus, deposed A.D. 476 by Odovacer). The rimed anapaestic meter is most effective for dealing ironically with Virgil's gravity and self-importance, and contrasts beautifully with the imitation of Virgil in the imaginary Gothic continuation. "The Epigoni" praises the poets of the dying Roman empire for not lamenting or dramatizing their fate but concerning themselves instead with linguistic and metrical experiments that would be "Called shallow by a mechanized generation to whom / Haphazard oracular grunts are profound wisdom." Obviously, a modern parallel and perhaps apologia is intended; but it is a gross exaggeration to say, as have some reviewers, that Auden now characteristically adopts the *persona* of an epigone. The rimed couplets perfectly maintain the lightly ironic tone. "The More Loving One" is an anti-poetic meditation that is also a kind of parody love-poem, and employs a prosaic colloquial style that is highly effective; it is related to the theme of the volume insofar as it implies a witty reversal of the romantic view of man's relation to external nature. "Looking up at the stars, I know quite well / That, for all they care, I can go to hell, . . ."

The prose interlude, "Dichtung und Wahrheit (An Unwritten Poem)", continues in the vein of "Words" and of "The Truest Poetry is the Most Feigning" in *Shield*, and forms a transition to Part II. The subject is the relation of poetry and truth, or the verbal world and the "real" world, and the role of the poet as exponent of language, the distinctive human characteristic. It concludes with the reflection that the love-poem which would be true and adequate to the actual situation cannot be written, and invokes, ironically, Dame Kind as the one who will probably preside over the actual meeting of the lovers.

Part II begins with "Dame Kind," a tour de force employing baroque contrasts in diction, from the racily colloquial and bawdy to the technical and archaic. Dame Kind is roughly equivalent to the "appetitive goddesses," Artemis and Aphrodite, in other poems, and presides over the same physical and "natural" aspects of humanity; but she is more specialized and cruder: she rules specifically over sex. "She mayn't be all She might be but / She is our Mum." At least she is better than the "hypochondriac / Blue-stocking from Provence," pseudo-spiritual romantic love; and through her "dirty work," "sheer bloody misrule," she finds counterparts for even anomalous lovers. Insofar as Part II is unified, it is by Dame Kind and by a defense, seriously meant if also ironic, of her earthy part in human life. "First Things First" is an anti-romantic love poem in long dactylic lines, informed by a realistic and humorous acceptance of the human condition, which concludes with the recognition that "Thousands have lived without love, not one without water." "An Island Cemetery" is a deliberately prosaic celebration of the skeleton over the other parts of man, rather like Housman's "The Immortal Part" without the defiant ironies and the poetic intoxication. "The Old Man's Road" and "Walks" deal with an abstract subject—the way or path or road through life—but in a realistic and undramatic way. "The Old Man's Road" (title poem of the 1956 pamphlet which included six other poems) deals with the relation of God and history, divine and human.[45] The Old Man I take to be God, and his road crosses the "Great Schism" between Catholic and Protestant and ignores church authorities on both sides ("God's Vicar," the Pope; "God's Ape," the Protestant attempt at individual imitation). The Old Man's Road is not suspected, not predictable by humans—"Unlookable for, by logic, by guess: / Yet some strike it, and are struck fearless." It offers the only true freedom from the state and from history: "Assuming a freedom its Powers deny, / Denying its Powers, they pass freely." "Walks" is a much more limited poem, in restrained tetrameter quatrains; though utterly different in style, it is like Frost's "The Road Not Taken" in its manipulation of natural symbols into abstractions. But Auden's version is far more generalized, without any such particular dramatic situation as Frost's. In a sense, the poem is anti-existentialist, since it is a justification of avoiding choice, or of decreasing its importance: by taking circular walks, the poet avoids having to choose the point at which he would have to reverse his steps. "The History of Truth" contrasts the past world of lasting objects modeled on absolute truth to the present world of paper dishes and untruth as an anti-model. The rhetorical device used is ellipsis which shifts the parts of speech: "In that ago when being was believing" (modifying Berkeley's *esse est percipi*). "The History of Science" imagines a fourth fairy-tale brother who rejects all advice and who, instead of finding the sought-after goal, blunders into a different but equally wonderful one; thus the role of error, unpredictability, wrongheadedness in scientific discovery suggests that these qualities have values "sound Authority" dare not confess. (This is another version of the theme, recurrent in the volume, of the justification of human fallibility.) Then comes a limerick called "History of the Boudoir," apparently intended as a humorous parallel to the two preceding "Histories" but actually rather silly; and then the most amusing and immediately attractive poem in the volume, the "Metalogue to *The Magic Flute*." This was written for the Mozart Bicentenary, to be spoken between acts of the NBC television production for which Auden and Kallman translated the libretto. When Auden is provided with a suitable occasion and a mask like this one, his tone never wavers into falseness and his invention never falters; the "Metalogue" is both a brilliant pastiche, in elegantly "period" heroic couplets, and a witty and profound poem in its own right. It is related to the theme of the volume in being an unpretentious meditation on history—1756, 1956, 2156, with the predictions about the latter date limited to one: "Whether they live in air-borne nylon cubes, / Practice group-marriage or are fed through tubes," they will still love Mozart, who "did no harm to our poor earth" and "Created masterpieces by the dozen."

After a limerick in doubtful taste comes "Limbo Culture," describing an imaginary tribe completely incapable of either unselfish love or exactness, in contrast to the human capacity (however limited) for both: "Could it be / A Limbo tribesman only loves himself? / For that, we know, cannot be done exactly." "There Will Be No Peace" is a somewhat uncharacteristic and puzzling poem: the second-person address, the war images, and the moralized landscape at the beginning are so close to self-parody as to lead some critics to take the whole poem as just that (Thom Gunn, reviewing *Clio* in *The Yale Review*, opined that this was the worst poem Auden had ever published in a book). The language and rhythm are indeed prosaic, the verse much freer than Auden usually writes. Auden observed in a public reading that the poem "seems to be about paranoia," [46] and certainly the person described is convinced of motiveless persecution and hostility. It is not, however, merely a clinical rendering of this disorder, but a use of it to symbolize the ultimate isolation, beyond any such use of these images in Auden's earlier verse. "Friday's Child" is in memory of Dietrich Bonhoeffer, the pastor and theologian who was hanged by the Nazis on Good Friday in 1945. It is a kind of post-existentialist meditation on how dreadfully complete man's freedom is, in a tone of chastened puzzlement and shock, tempered by colloquial diction and sardonic wit. The volume closes with "Good-bye to the Mezzogiorno," a light, amusing, and wittily personal commentary on national characteristics (Gothic North and classical South) and on the Anglo-Saxon in Italy; it is dedicated to Carlo Izzo, who translated a selection of Auden's poems into Italian in 1953. The "Academic Graffiti" printed as an addendum consist of a series of clerihews [47] which are sometimes trivial and sometimes witty—they are, of course, a special form of academic humor—with mildly amusing limericks on Eliot and Yeats, and finally lines "addressed to Dr. Claude Jenkins, Canon of Christ Church, Oxford, on the occasion of his Eightieth Birthday"—graceful and amusing, but mere pastiche and, as such, a profound contrast to the "Metalogue" which they superficially resemble.

As the reviewers were quick to point out, *Clio* is a much less impressive volume than *Shield*. This is, in part, merely a predictable cycle; like all poets who write copiously, Auden is uneven; and after a particularly fine collection like *Shield* it was to be expected that the next one would be inferior, particularly in contrast. Some of the failures and peculiarities of *Clio* seem to derive from an uncertainty of rapport with the audience. The limericks and graffiti may be attempts to return to Oxford undergraduate humor, inspired by Auden's professorship at Oxford; and perhaps also reactions against American earnestness. (In his introduction to the *Faber Book of Modern American Verse* Auden observed that in American poetry "the easy-going tone of a man talking to a group of his peers is rare" and "for a 'serious' poet to write light verse is frowned on.") Perhaps, too, the specialization and fragmentation of the reading public in the United States has a cumulative effect (in this respect the cost of transplantation is greater when a writer moves in the reverse direction from James and Eliot—especially one like Auden, who depends upon his sense of an audience for an essential element of control). The latter half of the fifties was a bad time for poetry generally; there was little of the atmosphere of crisis to which Auden responds so magnificently, and the complacencies and anti-intellectualisms of the Eisenhower era provided no stimulus. But these considerations must not be exaggerated: the two most distinctive achievements of *Clio* depend on rapport with an audience, and show a highly developed and successful sense of it. These are the colloquial lyric (low-keyed, urbane, candid, displaying an attractive *persona*), as in "Hands," "The More Loving One," and "First Things First," and light verse in a period or localized style, as in "American Kitchen," "Secondary Epic," "Metalogue," and "Goodbye to the Mezzogiorno." No volume containing such triumphs and delights as these needs any apology or justifies any condescension.

From 1952 to 1962 Auden was associated with Lionel Trilling and Jacques Barzun in the direction of a high-level book club (The Reader's Subscription until 1959, The Mid-Century thereafter), and in this capacity was jointly responsible for choosing books and reviewed some of them in the club's periodical. Clearly, one of the compensations of this work has been the sense of participation in a joint intellectual enterprise and the sense of relation to a considerable public. Auden remarked, in reviewing Yeats's *Mythologies* (*The Mid-Century* #4, Oct. 1959), "A writer can neither love nor hate the public; either he must be obsessed by it, as a speculator is obsessed by the stock market, or he must not think about it at all." On the other hand, his recent tendency in style, as we have seen (above, p. 303), is certainly in part a reaction to his sense of the public: "Those who believe as I do that what any poem says should be true and that, in our noisy, overcrowded age, a quiet and intimate poetic speech is the only genuine way of saying it," will find what they are looking for in Marianne Moore, he suggests.[48] The comment reveals also his own conscious direction.

CONCLUSION (FOR THE TIME BEING)

The first general observation to make about Auden is that, though he has been a famous poet for more than thirty years, he is still comparatively young, by the standards of this age of long-lived and green-aged poets. He is still capable of major surprises, and therefore not yet to be pigeonholed; any generalizations about him must be tentative and provisional. I am not likely to forget this, for during the closing months of 1962, as I tried to put this book into final form, Auden erupted into furious activity in both prose and verse (see Chronology). If the attempt to take account of these latest publications has left me with the sensation of running to keep up, it has also left me feeling that my exertions were amply rewarded; and it has, I trust, eradicated any unconscious tendency to write as if Auden's career were over and his work a *corpus* to be laid out.

For a closing survey of Auden's work as it appears at present, perhaps the most useful perspective will be obtained by returning to the basic indictment brought against him by critics throughout his career. This is the charge of radical frivolity and irresponsibility: in F. R. Leavis's words, his "uncertainty as to the degree of seriousness he intended," [49] his allegedly irresponsible revisions as discussed by Beach, his changes of "ideology" as discussed by Jarrell, and, finally, his definitions of art as a game or a form of play. Sometimes these criticisms have an obvious political or religious motive. The Left naturally regarded Auden as a lost leader, gone over to the forces of reaction and frivolity. As we have seen, this view rests on a misconception of Auden's early poetry and, probably, of all poetry; it also ignores the fact that he has remained a liberal (in the American sense) and has never ceased to be concerned with political and social problems.[50] To this misconception was often added the grievance that Auden had abandoned politics for religion, that he had settled smugly and selfishly for private salvation. To what has already been said one point may be added in Auden's defense: that time has at least given evidence of the depth and sincerity of his religious commitment; nothing could be further from the faddish or superficial or temporary.

I do not mean to suggest, however, that the indictments were always completely without grounds. The phenomena the critics pointed to were partly, no doubt, the result of Auden's temperamental limitations and liabilities: facility and copiousness that sometimes became carelessness (but a glance at the manuscript of "The Sea and the Mirror" would dispel any notion that Auden never takes pains), a powerful impulse to the internal and private that sometimes led to obscurity, and a love of wit and clowning even when not wholly appropriate. For "private joking in a panelled room," for the "fair notion fatally injured," Auden has apologized; as he confessed his faults in "New Year Letter,"

> Time and again have slubbered through
> With slip and slapdash what I do,
> Adopting what I would disown
> The preacher's loose immodest tone . . .

Partly these faults were the result of principle, expressing the right to frivolity and play and irreverent humor that protects the individual against the state, the Hermetic against the Apollonian, the artist against the Managers: a part of the distinctive humanity of Faces as against Numbers. Much of the apparent frivolity may also be explained as bait (sometimes badly chosen) to attract a larger audience, or as resulting from an uncertain sense of relation to an audience. Auden is incorrigibly didactic as well as a born entertainer, and he needs a large audience to amuse and instruct; the difficulty of establishing and maintaining such a rapport in our time is apparent throughout his career.

The volume of Auden's poetry published in England in 1958 as one of the Penguin Poets (selected by the author) and in the United States the next year in the Modern Library as *Selected Poetry* (identical in every respect except title to the English edition) is a gratifying contrast to the *Collected Poetry* of 1945.

It manifests a confident and responsible attitude toward the reading public. Appearing in these two series, the volume is intended to represent Auden's work to a very wide audience in both countries; Auden obviously prepared it with great care, and it is thus of special interest as showing his sense of the meaning of his own work. In a prefatory note dated 1957, Auden states that the poems are arranged "more or less in the chronological order of their writing," the first from 1927, the last 1954, and that he has revised some "in the interests of euphony or sense or both." As far as one can tell by checking publication dates, departures from strict chronology are few and slight, and there are no detectable errors. In contrast to those in *Collected Poetry*, the titles are never facetious; they are always sensible and sometimes illuminating. As further evidence of real consideration for the reader's convenience, there are indexes of titles and first lines. The revisions are generally minor—alterations of punctuation and of individual words and phrases, often with an obvious gain in clarity or significance.[51] There are some further deletions from the early poems: two stanzas are dropped from "Taller To-day" and three more from "The Watchers" (as compared to the *Collected Poetry* versions, reprinted also in *Collected Shorter Poems*), in both cases to the improvement of the poems. In general, however, the revision does not consist of large-scale deletion, as it did in *Collected Poetry*, but of careful improvement in matters of detail.

We have discussed earlier (pp. 59-60, 155) the selections from the volumes through *The Double Man* (1941). Seven of the twenty-four shorter poems first brought together in *Collected Poetry* 1945 are included: songs, a villanelle, "Mundus et Infans" as example of theological light verse, a colloquial lyric, and perhaps the finest of all Auden's dream love-poems, "The Lesson." There is only one selection from *For the Time Being*, the "Song of the Old Soldier"; but from *The Sea and the Mirror* there are most of the shorter songs, "Alonso to Ferdinand," and the complete speech of Caliban. No doubt the fact that *For the Time Being* contains fewer songs and speeches that are self-sufficient when detached played a part in Auden's decision; but the inference seems inescapable that he agrees with most critics that the *Commentary* is superior to the *Oratorio*. From *The Age of Anxiety* there are only "Three Dreams," those of Malin, Quant, and Emble as they embark on the first of the "Seven Stages." *Selected Poetry* contains twelve of the twenty-eight poems in *Nones* (including all those I have discussed as related to the later volumes); on the other hand, *Shield* is included almost complete: only five poems, all from the middle section, are omitted. Aside from a poet's understandable partiality for his latest work, this seems a realistic representation of the relative merits of the two volumes. The selections from *Shield* are rearranged to put the title poem first, followed by the others from the middle section; this is an improvement, since it allows "Shield" to follow "Precious Five" and puts the two sequences ("Bucolics" and "Horae Canonicae") together. Since 1954 is the terminal date, nothing later than *Shield* is included. In broad terms (and computing from the American edition) there are seventeen pages from 1927-34, ninety-six pages from 1935-45, and sixty-two pages from 1947-54. This seems a reasonable proportion—at least for all but those who maintain that Auden's career has been one of steady decline since the early thirties.

Auden's reading of his own verse, as exhibited on his Spoken Arts recording (1960) and in his recent public readings, seems to me to have improved enormously since his 1954 recording. He has always been potentially an excellent reader: his rendering of the Elizabethan songs on the 1955 recording with the New York Pro Musica, for instance, could hardly be bettered; but in reading his own poems on the 1954 and earlier recordings he had been afflicted by a brittle self-consciousness and nervous stridency. The complete absence of such qualities in the recent readings, the ability to let go and bring out the musical and emotional aspects of the poems (without departing from his natural mode of understatement), would seem to indicate, like the handling of *Selected Poetry*, a more dependable sense of the audience and a more confident relation to it.

The poems Auden has published since *Clio* [52] reinforce this impression, for they are all light in the best sense: easily and unselfconsciously personal and, at the same time, public and colloquial. The most amusing of them is "Encomium Balnei," which marks the complete abandonment of Auden's long campaign against those "who wash too much," and sets up the bathroom beside the kitchen as a supreme achievement of our civilization. In this, as in the rest of the group, there is a kind of humility, a humorous acceptance, though with full awareness of limitations and imperfections, of the present and the self. The best of them seems to me to be "Whitsunday in Kirchstetten," which is a different kind of religious poem from any Auden has written before. Even in "Horae Canonicae," Auden has been on the whole an impersonal religious poet: instead of dealing explicitly with personal experience, like Hopkins or Eliot, he has usually begun with a traditional and objective framework and allowed the personal experience to appear only in the way these matters of common humanity are rendered. The epigraph to Part II of *Clio* put the case with humorous exaggeration: "Although you be, as I am, one of those / Who feel a Christian ought to write in Prose, / For Poetry is Magic—born in sin, you / May read it to exorcise the Gentile in you." In *The Dyer's Hand* he remarks, "Poems, like many of Donne's and Hopkins', which express a poet's personal feelings of religious devotion or penitence, make me uneasy. . . . Is there not something a little odd, to say the least, about making an admirable public object out of one's feelings of guilt and penitence before God?" (p. 458). But "Whitsunday in Kirchstetten" is very personal indeed, presenting the poet's meditations on a specific occasion as he attends Mass at the Roman Catholic church in the Austrian village where he has his summer home. Even the people are named: "*Komm Schöpfer Geist* I bellow as Herr Bayer / picks up our slim offerings and Pfarrer Lustkandl / quietly gets on with the Sacrifice / as

Rome does it. . . ." And the poet mentions his "own little anglo-american / musico-literary set" as contributing one to the variety of Pentecostal accents heard. It is true that there is still no attempt to render directly the poet's spiritual experience in itself; instead there is objective description: "An altar bell makes a noise / as the body of the Second Adam / is shown to some of his torturers. . . ." The basic theme is, in a sense, political: an answer to the question of how we should face the threat of nuclear war. There is, first, the Christian gospel of hope: "whether the world has improved / is doubtful, but we believe it could / and the divine Tiberius didn't. . . ." Beyond that there is, to calm hysteria about "Crimtartary" and other international tensions, the acceptance of mystery, trust in God —for what seems to us catastrophe may be the operation of Grace (Pentecostal fire); and following the epigraph ("Grace dances. I would pipe. Dance ye all") the poet concludes, "if there when Grace dances, I should dance." The syllabic meter, with alternating lines of eleven and nine syllables, controls the tone perfectly. Nothing could be further from histrionic despair than this calm and understated affirmation; nothing could be at once more personal and more impersonal.

Finally, *The Dyer's Hand* (1962) testifies massively to Auden's seriousness and responsibility. We have noted the care with which the pieces in it are revised and arranged, and the self-knowledge Auden has shown in emphasizing the aphoristic aspect of his prose. Like other aphorists, Auden has often stated one aspect of truth as if it were the whole truth; and if taken literally, his formulations have seemed to reduce complex questions to impossibly simple dichotomies. But seen in the large, in a generous collection like *The Dyer's Hand*, his criticism supplies its own correctives and one aphorism counters but does not cancel another, thereby revealing complementary aspects of the truth. Thus the definition of art as a game, as essentially frivolous, is understandable in the context (p. 432): the *only* serious occupations are those calling for no particular natural gifts, unskilled labor and the priesthood; all others "are only serious in so far that they are the means by which those who practice them earn their bread and are not parasites on the labor of others, and to the degree that they permit or encourage the love of God and neighbor." In this ultimate sense, for the Christian "both art and science are secular activities, that is to say, small beer" (p. 456). Those who make a religion of art (consciously or unconsciously) will of course be offended by this clearcut distinction; but the frivolity attributed to art here is very different from the kind normally connoted by the word; and the point is that art has precisely as much seriousness as anything whatever except the two occupations specified. This is further clarified by other aphorisms on the relation between genius and apostle, the ordinary and the exceptional man, art and religion. "There can no more be an art about the common man than there can be a medicine about the uncommon man" (p. 477); and in this dichotomy religion belongs with medicine, not with art. The genius is called to his vocation by his gift; the apostle on no basis apparent to men; "one cannot speak of a talent for being an Apostle or of the apostolic temperament" (p. 443). But the apostle cannot be portrayed in art, because he cannot be made dramatically interesting (Ibsen's *Brand*); the only great example of an indirect portrayal is *Don Quixote*.

The distinction of poetry from magic is repeated:

> Poetry is not magic. In so far as poetry, or any other of the arts, can be said to have an ulterior purpose, it is, by telling the truth, to disenchant and disintoxicate. (p. 27)

On the other hand, the opposite heresy to this of art as propaganda is "to endow the gratuitous with a magic utility of its own, so that the poet comes to think of himself as the god who creates his subjective universe out of nothing" (p. 76), as did Mallarmé and Rilke. But this emphasis in dealing with the *effects* of art is counterbalanced by the emphasis, with regard to the creative process, on the origin of art in encounters with the sacred. The supernatural, the numinous, is thus put in its proper place; its importance is not denied, but its realm is the protopoetic, the private relation between artist and subject or inspiration, not the public realm of the relation between the work of art and the audience.

A few comparisons—still keeping in mind the charges of frivolity and irresponsibility—may be suggested as points of reference. Consider, for example, another expatriate of great gifts and reputation for precocity, interested in both science and religion, possessing wit, facility, and a special talent for satire. I mean, of course, Aldous Huxley, whose career as artist and thinker seems to me to provide a striking contrast to Auden's. His work and ideas show none of the responsible and disciplined growth that marks Auden's: the doctrine of *Karezza*, a kind of spiritualized free love with built-in contraceptive technique, is his latest universal nostrum, presumably to be incorporated in the perennial philosophy. Again, critics have sometimes suggested that Auden is the same kind of poet as John Betjeman (whose *Slick but not Streamlined* Auden introduced and to whom he dedicated *The Age of Anxiety*). Certainly there are resemblances: metrical virtuosity, fondness for period styles and exaggerated poses, gifts for mimicry and pastiche, and perhaps most of all, loving attention to the surfaces of everyday objects, places and people. But the resemblance to Betjeman is little closer than that to Phyllis McGinley, whose *Times Three* Auden also introduced; he admires and probably envies them both, for he would like to entertain as large an audience. Auden is, in this respect, not "modern," for he has always been unblushingly dedicated in the old-fashioned manner to the instruction and improvement of the largest possible audience. In this intention, in professional skill, in conscious awareness of his role and of his heritage, Auden is a thoroughly traditional poet.

He is more like Dryden, for example, than like most modern poets: he is a kind of maverick and extremely unofficial Anglo-American laureate, and, appropriately, writes much occasional verse. Like Dryden, he was much reproached for changes of faith and allegiance, and like him outmoded such reproaches by the tenacity and obvious sincerity of his convictions. Auden, too, has genuine modesty with regard to his own gifts, developing them with conscientious craftsmanship but employing them prodigally and hence unevenly, so that high-minded critics accuse him of insufficient respect for his art. The work of both exhibits a superb virtuosity in all the techniques of poetry. Auden, like Dryden, writes much for music, collaborates frequently, and spends a good deal of time in translating and adapting; he is a major critic as well as poet. If one superimposes on the figure of Dryden that of Lord Byron, to contribute audacity, rebelliousness, comic vigor and cosmopolitan sophistication; and then adds the spectre of Coleridge to bring in magic and the supernatural, an affinity with Germany and a concern for abstruse questions of aesthetics and theology, the composite image is close to Auden. Though this quadruple portrait is more than faintly absurd, it does at least suggest Auden's continuity with the tradition, his deep sense of his relation to the whole of English literature.

Among modern poets, Yeats and Eliot are the two who are most like Auden and with whom he can most profitably be compared. The fact that Auden was proclaimed as their successor prematurely and on the wrong grounds—he was to lead us out of the Waste Land—should not prevent us from seeing that he belongs in their company. In Yeats and Eliot there is a similar tension between the private and the public, the personal and the impersonal (though the terms in each case are, of course, very different); in both the great achievement has been finally to attain a situation in which the poet can speak freely and fully in his own person, with his whole career and his unique and peculiar vision in the poem, and yet be confident that he speaks for many. ("Among School Children," "The Tower," "The Circus Animals' Desertion," and numerous other poems of Yeats's great period are examples; and from Eliot, of course, we have the *Four Quartets*.) In Auden, as we have seen, an equilibrium is achieved in the poems of the latter thirties, but in a topical and temporary mode; a new line of development begins after the move to America and the shift in religious perspective. In the "Bucolics" and "Horae Canonicae," some of the poems in *Clio*, and most clearly in such new poems as "Whitsunday in Kirchstetten," a complex synthesis may be seen of the personal, the public, and the religious, all expressed in a tone moving easily from the light to the deeply serious. And the development is, fortunately, by no means at an end.

Like Yeats and Eliot, Auden has been an excellent influence on younger poets, both by example and by critical precept. His emphasis on technique, the variety of his own work, and the candor of his advice have all been extremely healthy. One repeatedly encounters acknowledgments by other poets of his beneficent influence, and it is a rare poet (as opposed to critics) who does not speak of him with admiration.

In two studies published in 1951 [53] I argued that Auden was essentially a satirist. I have avoided using the term in this book; in fact I have refrained from propounding any single thesis, on the ground that it would be restrictive if not misleading. I should prefer now to emphasize most of all the variety of his poetry, its range and scope and capacity for surprise. A religious poet who is also a clown, a virtuoso who is incorrigibly didactic, a satirist who is also a musician and lyricist, is likely to perplex and annoy critics. But we have had enough critical condescension toward Auden; instead of quibbling about whether he quite deserves the title of major poet or whether any of his poems is really quite satisfactory, we would do better to be grateful both for his skill and wisdom and for the fact that he is not yet classified or predictable. Let us hope that he will create more enchanted islands of opera, while continuing to cast his spells against magic and all forms of deception and intoxication. Light, candidly personal, ever more rigorously devoted to the naked truth, these are disenchantments that we deeply need.

1. "The Composer," first published 1939. Auden remarks: "In my musical and aesthetic education I owe an enormous debt to Walter Greatorex, the music master (and my piano-teacher) at Gresham's School, Holt. He was a first-rate musician and also the first schoolmaster to treat me as an equal human being" (letter to M.K.S., May 11, 1963).

2. *The Dyer's Hand*, p. 40.

3. *The Double Man*, pp. 141-4. Nietzsche and De Rougemont contribute chiefly to the analysis of Wagner's *Tristan;* Kierkegaard to the analysis of *Don Giovanni.* (The most recent version of the contrast is that in *The Dyer's Hand*, pp. 118-123.) In his review of *Either/Or* (*New Republic*, 1944) Auden observed that Kierkegaard provided the "only illuminating suggestion for a musical aesthetic that I have seen"; and in his own essays Auden has worked out some of Kierkegaard's suggestions: the contrast, for instance, between the immediacy of music and the reflective quality of language and therefore of poetry is developed in *The Dyer's Hand*, pp. 466, 472, and elsewhere. See Auden's volume of selections from Kierkegaard, p. 66.

4. "Opera Addict," in *Vogue*, July 1948.

5. *World Within World*, p. 271.

6. *The Dyer's Hand*, p. 466; originally published in *Tempo*, 1951, as "Some Reflections on Opera as a Medium."

7. *Ibid.*, p. 504; originally published in *Encounter*, 1957.

8. In his introduction to *Visionary Novels of George Macdonald* (1954) he includes opera libretti in the category of Dream Literature.

9. In his program notes and his article in the *New York Times* ("Opera on an American Legend," May 4, 1941). Both these are summarized in Eric Walter White, *Benjamin Britten, A Sketch of His Life and Works* (London, 1954), pp. 85-9; my account is based on White, and the quotations are from Auden.

10. Daniel G. Hoffman, *Paul Bunyan: Last of the Frontier Demigods* (Philadelphia, 1952), pp. 144-5.

11. Joseph Kerman, in *Hudson Review*, Summer 1954 (pp. 436-44), reviewing the Columbia recording of the *Rake*.

12. Letter to M.K.S., April 10, 1963.

13. Alan Ansen, who was Auden's secretary 1948-53 (*The Enchafèd Flood*, 1950, is dedicated to him), and who has recently published a book of poems, *Disorderly Houses*, Wesleyan University Press, 1962, gave this information in a letter to the *Hudson Review* (Summer 1956, p. 319), as an authorized corrective to critics who ignored Kallman's contribution. Kallman wrote, he says, the second half of I,i, all of I,iii, the

first half of II,i, and all of II,ii, all of III,i, and the middle part of III,ii (including the recitativo secco). Stravinsky and Craft (op. cit., p. 150n.) also specify Kallman's contribution: they attribute to him the second rather than the third scene of I and only the first aria in II,i. Since they quote a letter from Auden revising part of I,ii (p. 152) and their statement about II,i looks confused as it covers only one aria but seems intended to cover more, while Ansen states specifically that Kallman wrote the next passage ("O Nature, green unnatural mother"), it appears that Ansen's account is the more reliable. It is easy to see how Stravinsky could be confused on such points since the order of scenes was changed in the process of composition.

14. Letter to M.K.S., Feb. 19, 1962: "about 75% is by Mr. Kallman."

15. The only scenes that bear much resemblance to Hogarth are the brothel, the auction, and Bedlam. Anne is very different from, but probably suggested by, the milkmaid in Hogarth who, seduced and deserted, nevertheless repeatedly tries to save the Rake; but there is little resemblance between Baba and Hogarth's rich old maid. There is, of course, no suggestion of any mythical level in Hogarth.

16. I am much indebted to Joseph Kerman's excellent analysis, published in the *Hudson Review*, 1954, and then included in his *Opera as Drama* (New York, 1956). I have taken some points also from George Mac-Fadden's interpretation in the *Hudson Review*, Spring 1955, and from Robert Craft's annotations to the Columbia recording.

17. My interpretation of the epilogue owes much to MacFadden (see the preceding note); but I have freely changed and revised his suggestions.

18. Kerman, *Opera as Drama*, p. 240.

19. Kerman in the *Hudson Review*, 1954; Kerman does not include these comments in *Opera as Drama*, but he calls *Wozzeck* and the *Rake* the "major operas of this century" (p. 247) and suggests that "in dramatic conception *The Rake* is finer and more meaningful than *Wozzeck*, even though it fails at the end" (p. 248). The libretto, he says, "is indeed unusually subtle for an opera book—though I should certainly not say unduly subtle" (p. 240).

20. Unfortunately, a page is missing in the *Botteghe Oscure* printing: the reprise of the big quintet. The text contains two acrostics, on the first names of Stravinsky and his wife (Igor and Vera). (Letter W.H.A. to M.K.S., July 21, 1962.)

21. Martin Bernheimer in *Musical Quarterly*, Jan. 1962, pp. 118-20.

22. This reviewer may have been reading Beach's *Making of the Auden Canon*. I have argued above (p. 203) that the Vicar's sermon does not in fact show any such uncertainty, and have explained my reasons for rejecting Beach's thesis. One is obliged to point out, also, (a) that the

libretto is a collaboration, and (b) that to be taken seriously does not necessarily mean to be taken as a pattern for emulation.

23. I did say this at the English Institute meeting in New York in September 1962 and provoked much indignation from the audience—with which, on further reflection, I found myself in agreement.

24. From the review by M.K.S. in *Poetry*, August 1950, p. 293. The book's title comes from *Othello*, II.i.17.

25. *The Dyer's Hand*, pp. 57-60; the reference to and quotation from Hardy are omitted in the book version.

26. Introduction to *An Armada of Thirty Whales*, by Daniel G. Hoffman, 1954.

27. The title comes from Shakespeare's Sonnet CXI; Auden had used it twice before, in a review of 1939 and an essay of 1955.

28. The central theme of *The Dyer's Hand* undoubtedly owes much to the influence of Rudolf Kassner, who is quoted only once in the volume (p. 459) but to whom Auden has elsewhere acknowledged a profound debt. He cited him together with Kierkegaard as playing a great part in his religious development (above, p. 173). In his contribution to the Festschrift for Kassner's eightieth birthday in 1953 (ed. A. C. Kensik and D. Bodmer, Winterthur, Switzerland) Auden said that Kassner's *Zahl und Gesicht* (1919, rev. 1925 and 1956) was one of those few books that had so conditioned his vision of life that he could not imagine who he was before he read them; hence "discussion is not called for, only gratitude and homage" (p. 58). Kassner, though apparently little known in the English-speaking world, was an astonishing figure. A Viennese of incredibly varied gifts, he wrote about physiognomy, mathematics, and psychology, as well as painting and music, translated numerous works from four or five languages, and produced several volumes of memoirs and essays. He was essentially, however, a religious philosopher. He was a friend of Rilke and Hofmannsthal, and knew D. H. Lawrence. Auden quotes him as early as 1939 ("Rilke in English," in *The New Republic*), translates two passages from *Zahl und Gesicht* in his volume of selections from Kierkegaard, 1952 (pp. 19, 180), and quotes *Die Geburt Christi* (1951) in *The Dyer's Hand*. Kassner is a difficult, oblique, and profound writer, not to be summed up briefly; but it may be said that *Zahl und Gesicht* deals with the distinction between the realm of number and that of faces, the distinctively human attribute. Unlike "scientific" physiognomists, Kassner insists on the uniqueness of each human face, on human freedom; he meditates on the nature of identity, appearance and reality, and similar themes, distinguishing man from animals, objects, and machines. (The passage in *The Age of Anxiety*, p. 8, beginning, "The faceless machine / Lacks a surround..." is based on *Zahl und Gesicht*, p. 98): "Die Maschine ist ohne diese Umwelt;...Die Maschine ist ohne Gesicht. Wo Umwelt ist, dort ist Gesicht.")

Another Viennese writer, perhaps slightly better known because of Erich Heller's chapter on him in *The Disinherited Mind* (1957), is the satirist and poet Karl Kraus (1874-1936), whom Auden quotes (pp. 15, 23) as an example of the critic's proper concern with language. As to other influences, these are varied and eclectic. The continuing emphasis on the difference between art and magic reflects Collingwood (and has often been misinterpreted by critics who have not read Collingwood). Kierkegaard is quoted frequently, as is Nietzsche, and Valéry more often than either. (These are, of course, all aphorists; and the number of quotations from them and other aphorists such as Goethe and Thoreau is not unrelated to Auden's work in compiling the *Viking Book of Aphorisms*.) Hannah Arendt, whose *The Human Condition* Auden reviewed enthusiastically in 1958, describes the artist as "the only 'worker' left in a laboring society" and "present-day labor theories, which almost unanimously define labor as the opposite of play ... and every activity which is not necessary either for the life of the individual or for the life process of society is subsumed under playfulness" (p. 127). Hence art is dissolved into play and loses its worldly meaning, and play becomes the realm of freedom. Auden develops these and related ideas most explicitly in "The Poet & the City."

29. Review of the Freud-Fliess letters, *The Griffin*, June 1954.

30. Review of E. Jones, *Life and Work of Freud*, *The Griffin*, Nov. 1955.

31. Review of W. Jaeger, *Paideia*, *The Griffin*, March 1958.

32. Ibid. The argument is repeated and expanded at the end of the essay on *Othello* in *The Dyer's Hand*, pp. 270-2, and in "Do You Know Too Much?" in *Esquire*, 1962.

33. In "Ballet's Present Eden" (1954) Auden defines ballet in terms of this myth. Ballet time "is a continuous present; every experience which depends on historical time lies outside its capacities." It cannot express memory, but it "expresses, as no other medium can, the joy of being alive. Death is omnipresent as the force of gravity over which the dancers triumph; everything at rest is either a thing, or it is asleep, enchanted or dead. If it moves, it comes to life.... The more energy implied by an emotion, the more danceable it is. Thus defiance can be danced but despair is impossible, and joy is the most danceable of all.

"Since suffering, as human beings understand it, depends on memory and anticipation which are alien to the medium, it may be said that nobody suffers in ballet: if they did, their movement would become unbalanced and ugly ... all real ballets take place in Eden, in the world of pure being without becoming and the suffering implied by becoming, a world where things, beasts and men are equally alive, a world without history and without seriousness.... It is not an accident that so many of the most successful ballets are based on fairy stories."

34. Roughly half of the book consists of previously unpublished material; the other half is selected from Auden's criticism of the last 15 years or so (I have noticed only a few brief passages from earlier work), with very effective revision and rearrangement. Some of the published material had appeared only in book-club periodicals or on record jackets and had thus not been generally available. The choice seems to me excellent: some unfortunate pieces, e.g., the 1959 introduction to *Romeo and Juliet* and the poet-historian contrast from the 1955 "Dyer's Hand," are excluded; partially successful ones are cut and revised, or survive only as aphorisms; the unqualified triumphs are preserved complete. The new material—a brilliantly suggestive and close-packed exploration of the nature of Shakespeare's drama, an essay on the *Merchant of Venice*, long essays on Lawrence, Marianne Moore, and Frost, studies of *Don Juan*, *Pickwick Papers*, *Brand*, and *Peer Gynt*, to name only the most notable— is, if anything, better than the old.

35. Auden so called it in the jacket notes to the 1954 Caedmon recording. Francis Berry, in *Poetry and the Physical Voice* (New York, 1962, p. 186) discusses a recording of Auden reading "Easily, my dear..." on Jan. 27, 1936 (B.B.C. Record #2160, library #1497c). The Harvard Film Service made a record in 1941 of Auden reading "The Traveller," sonnets XVII, XXI, XXVII from "In Time of War," "Song," and "Spring in Wartime." The Library of Congress recorded in 1949 Auden reading "Alonzo to Ferdinand," "Musée des Beaux Arts," and "Refugee Blues" (record P3 in Record Lab album P1).

36. Bayley, op. cit. pp. 37-9, has a good analysis of this poem, which he calls a "sung short story," and of "Secrets," with its "long linked succession of subordinate clauses kept perfectly in control until the main verb descends with precision in the sixteenth line" (p. 174). He speaks of the "lucid, musing urbanity" of these poems in contrast to the earlier "exuberant dread" (p. 175).

37. Dedicated to Lincoln and Fidelma Kirstein. Kirstein is General Director of the New York City Ballet, a dance critic and novelist. (See n.33 above for Auden's interest in ballet.)

38. Auden describes the meter and other formal aspects of this and the other poems included in his Caedmon recording, 1954, in the jacket notes. In *The Dyer's Hand*, p. 25, Auden mentions and quotes Perse.

39. "The wind is always a force which the conscious will cannot cause or control" (*The Enchafèd Flood*, p. 78). In his Introduction to Hoffman's *Armada of Thirty Whales* (1954) Auden recommends Graves's *The White Goddess*.

40. Robert Graves may have had some influence, for his notion of poetry has always been, in a highly specialized sense, religious: "The function of poetry is religious invocation of the Muse; its use is the experience of mixed exaltation and horror that her presence excites" (Foreword to *The White Goddess*). Paul Valéry, whom Auden quotes frequently in *The Dyer's Hand* and *The Viking Book of Aphorisms*, may have contributed to it: "Un poème doit être une fête de l'Intellect. . . . Fête: c'est un jeu, mais solennel, mais réglé, mais significatif; image de ce qu'on n'est pas d'ordinaire, de l'état ou les efforts sont rythmés, rachetés. On célèbre quelque chose en l'accomplissant ou la representant dans son plus pur et bel état" (*Morceaux Choisis*, Paris 1930, p. 167). But there is no end to the citing of such parallels, and no need to speculate on any particular source; this is one permanent aspect of poetry, from Homer through Blake and Lawrence. In "The Creation of Music and Poetry" (1959) Auden draws an exceptionally interesting parallel between Valéry and Stravinsky: "Both prefer the formal to the happy-go-lucky, an art which disintoxicates to an art which would bewitch, both have a horror of the pseudo-grandiloquent."

41. Cf. the passages quoted from *The Dyer's Hand*, p. 249 above, and the epigraph from Nietzsche: "We have Art in order that we may not perish from Truth." Cf. also Thomas Mann's definition of art as a "serious jest" (commentary on *The Magic Mountain*).

42. I am indebted to Daniel G. Hoffman for lending me a tape of this lecture, given March 9, 1950; to Dean Susan Cobbs for giving me a copy of the transcription of the original version of "Prime" that Auden distributed to the audience; and to Mr. Auden for permitting me to quote from this original version and from his lecture.

43. E. R. Dodds, Regius Professor of Greek at Oxford, is perhaps best known for *The Greeks and the Irrational* (Berkeley and Los Angeles, 1951). In *Letters from Iceland* MacNeice hopes Professor Dodds will "forgive my academic slips." Auden dedicated the *Oxford Book of Light Verse* (1938) to Professor Dodds, and made a special acknowledgment to Mrs. Dodds, "to whose industry, scholarship, and taste he owes more than he finds it comfortable to admit." (Mrs. Dodds is the author of *The Romantic Theory of Poetry*, 1926.)

44. This solution was pointed out to me by Leo Braudy at Swarthmore.

45. In England, country people often attribute an ancient artifact to *The Old Man*, meaning some prehistoric race about whom nothing is remembered.

46. YM-YWHA, Philadelphia, Feb. 13, 1962.

47. See *Letters from Iceland*, p. 113, for early examples of the clerihew.

48. *The Mid-Century* #5, Fall 1959. Another writer of syllabic verse,

William Carlos Williams, has significantly influenced Auden's most recent poetry, beginning with *Clio*.

49. F. R. Leavis, *New Bearings in English Poetry* (new edition, 1950), p. 227. Leavis adds that Auden "has hardly come nearer to essential maturity since, though he made a rapid advance in sophistication."

50. See note 14 to section III and *The Dyer's Hand*, pp. 87-8. In an interview published in *The Listener*, May 5, 1960, Auden, when asked about his early poetry, observed that he and his friends didn't know enough and were often motivated by vanity, but that he did not think their political views were wrong.

51. For example, the "nude young male who lounges / Against a rock displaying his dildo" in the original version of "In Praise of Limestone" becomes "the flirtatious male who lounges / Against a rock in the sunlight, never doubting / That for all his faults he is loved ..."

52. "A Change of Air," *Encounter*, Jan. 1962 ("Corns, heartburn, sinus headache, and such minor afflictions")

"You," *Saturday Evening Post*, March 3, 1962 ("Really, must you")

"Hammerfest," *The London Magazine*, March 1962 ("For over forty years I'd paid it atlas-homage")

"Encomium Balnei," *Encounter*, Aug. 1962 ("It is odd that the English")

"After Reading a Child's Guide to Modern Physics," *The New Yorker*, Nov. 17, 1962 ("If all a top physicist knows")

"Whitsunday in Kirchstetten (For H. A. Reinhold)," *The Reporter*, Dec. 6, 1962 ("*Komm Schöpfer Geist* I bellow as Herr Bayer")

(Dedicatory verses, which I have not yet seen, to *English and Medieval Studies* presented to J. R. R. Tolkien on the occasion of his seventieth birthday, ed. N. Davis and C. L. Wrenn. Oxford, 1962.)

53. "Late Auden: the Satirist as Lunatic Clergyman" and "The Dominant Symbols of Auden's Poetry," both in *The Sewanee Review*, 1951. A third article, "Auden in the Fifties: Rites of Homage" (*The Sewanee Review*, 1961), is completely superseded by the present book; the earlier two might conceivably still be of some interest.

Appendix

NOTE: These indexes include all of Auden's published poetry. (The title index is intended to be used only for cross-reference to the other.) In the first-line index, titles are not repeated if they remain the same in later printings; it is to be understood that only changes are noted. For example, "A shilling life will give you all the facts" was untitled when published in *On This Island* as No. XIII; it remained untitled in *Selected Poems* and *Some Poems*, was given the title, "Who's Who" in *Collected Poetry*, and retained the same title in *Collected Shorter Poems*. The following abbreviations are used:

Age	The Age of Anxiety, N.Y. 1947
AT	Another Time, N.Y. 1940
Clio	Homage to Clio, N.Y. 1960
CP	Collected Poetry, N.Y. 1945
CSP	Collected Shorter Poems 1930-1944, L. 1950
Dog	The Dog Beneath the Skin, N.Y. 1935
DM	The Double Man, N.Y. 1941 (New Year Letter, L. 1941)
Frontier	On the Frontier, N.Y. 1938
F6	The Ascent of F6, N.Y. 1937 (L. 1936)
FTB	For the Time Being, L. 1944
1934	Poems, N.Y. 1934
1938 SP	Selected Poems, L. 1938
Journey	Journey to a War, N.Y. 1939
Letters	Letters from Iceland, N.Y. 1937
MS. Buffalo	Manuscript in Lockwood Memorial Library at the University of Buffalo
Nones	Nones, L. 1951
Orators	The Orators, L. 1932; in P 1934
OTI	On This Island, N.Y. 1937 (Look, Stranger!, L. 1936)
P	Poems: Oxford 1928, L. 1930, L. 1933; N.Y. 1934
Paid	Paid on Both Sides, in The Criterion, Jan. 1930; in P 1930, 1933, 1934
Road	The Old Man's Road, N.Y. 1956 (unpaginated)
Shield	The Shield of Achilles, L. 1955
Some P	Some Poems, L. 1940
SP	W. H. Auden: A Selection by the Author, L. 1958 (Selected Poetry, N.Y. 1959)

Alfred. Alfred, Come along. Come along. (Prose)
  New Writing, II, Autumn 1936: "Alfred" (A Cabaret Sketch. For
  Therese Giehse.)
All fables of adventure stress
  New Statesman, June 9, 1956: "The History of Science"; Road;
  Clio, 66
All had been ordered weeks before the start
  New Republic, Nov. 25, 1940: "The Preparations" (The Quest No.
  2); DM, 166; CP, 251; SP, 72:I
All that which lies outside our sort of why,
  Encounter, Jan. 1957: "Objects"; Clio, 19
All the others translate: the painter sketches
  New Writing, Spring 1939: "The Composer"; AT, 35; CP, 5; CSP, 21
All winter long the huge sad lady
  Kenyon Review, Summer 1947: "The Duet"; Nones, 54
Almost happy now, he looked at his estate.
  The Listener, March 9, 1939: "Voltaire at Ferney"; Poetry, June, 1939;
  AT, 28; CP, 6; CSP, 22
Although you be, as I am, one of those
  Epigraph to Part II of Clio
Always far from the centre of our names,
  Journey, 284 (In Time of War, XXVI); CP, 333; CSP, 285
Always the following wind of history
  Paid (1934, 68); Modern British Poetry (ed. L. Untermeyer), 1936 ed.
Amoeba in the running water
  P 1928, I.g
Among the leaves the small birds sing;
  Shield, 80: "Lauds" (Horae Canonicae, 7); SP, 194. (Based on final
  chorus of "Delia": Botteghe Oscure, XII (1953)) Musical setting by
  Lennox Berkeley
And the age ended, and the last deliverer died
  New Verse, June-July 1936: The Economic Man; Journey, 270
  (In Time of War, XII); Some P, 78; CP, 325; CSP, 277; SP, 55: A
  New Age (So an ... its ...)
And the traveller hopes: "Let me be far from any
  The Listener, Oct. 7, 1936: "Journey to Iceland": A Letter to Christo-
  pher Isherwood, Esq.; Poetry, Jan. 1937; Letters, 25; 1938 SP, 123;
  Some P, 74; CP, 7; CSP, 23
Anthropos apteros for days
  DM, 154 (notes to NYL) CP, 9: "The Labyrinth"
Appearing unannounced, the moon
  Shield, 50: "Nocturne I"
Ares at last has quit the field
  Harpers, June 1947: "Under Which Lyre"; Modern British Poetry
  (ed. L. Untermeyer), 1950 ed.; Nones, 57
Around them boomed the rhetoric of time,
  Southern Rev., Spring 1941: "Kairos and Logos"; CP, 11; CSP, 25

As a young child the wisest could adore him;
    Journey, 268 (In Time of War, X); CP, 324; CSP, 276
As evening fell the day's oppression lifted;
    variant of:
    But in the evening the oppression lifted;
As I listened from a beach-chair in the shade
    Nones, 15: "Their Lonely Betters"; SP, 133
As I walked out one evening,
    New Statesman, Jan. 15, 1938: "Song"; AT, 42 (People and Places
    XXVI); CP, 197 (Songs I); CSP, 227; SP, 33: "One Evening." Musical
    setting 1954-6 by Elizabeth Lutyens.
As it is, plenty;
    OTI, 32 (XII); CP, 17: "His Excellency"; CSP, 31. Musical setting
    1937 by B. Britten.
As the poets have mournfully sung,
    Clio, 74: "The Aesthetic Point of View"
Ashamed to be the darling of his grief
    New Republic, Nov. 25, 1940: "The First Temptation" (The Quest
    No. 6); DM, 170; CP, 254
At Dirty Dick's and Sloppy Joe's
    FTB; CP, 369 (Sea & Mirror); SP, 101: "Song of the Master and
    Boatswain"
At last the secret is out, as it always must come in the end,
    F6, 116; CP, 199 (Songs II); CSP, 229
At peace under this mandarin sleep, Lucina,
    Shield, 53: "In Memoriam L.K.A. 1950-1952"; SP, 160
At the far end of the enormous room
    New Verse, Oct. 1933: III of Five Poems
August for the people and their favourite islands
    New Verse, Oct.-Nov. 1935, 7: "To a Writer on His Birthday";
    OTI, 63 (XXX, To Christopher Isherwood); 1938 SP, 114; Some P,
    70; CSP, 32: "Birthday Poem" (To Christopher Isherwood). MS.
    Buffalo.

Be patient, solemn nose
    Harpers, Oct. 1950: "Precious Five"; Nones, 67; SP, 148
Because I am bewildered, because I must decide, (Prose)
    Harpers, Dec. 1943: "Herod Considers the Massacre of the Innocents";
    CP, 454 (FTB); Selden Rodman (ed.), 100 Modern Poems (1951),
    135: "Herod" (from FTB)
Because sap fell away
    P 1928, IX
Before this loved one
    P 1930, XVIII; 1934, 34; CP, 19: "This One"; CSP, 36; SP, 16
Begot like other children, he
    Clio, 24: "The Great"

Commemoration. Commemoration. What does it mean? (Prose)
    Criterion, XI (Oct. 1931), 60: "Speech for a Prize-Day"; Orators,
    sec. I (P 1934, 93): "Address for a Prize-Day"

Comrades who when the sirens roar
    variant of:
    Brothers, who when the sirens roar

Consider if you will how lovers stand
    Oxford Poetry, 1927: "Extract" ("... lovers lie"); P 1928, I.f; Quoted
    by Isherwood in New Verse, Nov. 1937, 6

Consider this and in our time
    P 1930, XXIX; 1934, 53; CP, 27: "Consider"; CSP, 43

Control of the passes was, he saw, the key
    P 1928, XV; 1930, XV; 1934, 26; CP, 29: "The Secret Agent"; CSP, 44

Corns, heartburn, sinus headache, and such minor afflictions
    Encounter, Jan. 1962: "A Change of Air"

Darkness and snow descend
    FTB; CP, 407: "For the Time Being"

Dear, all benevolence of fingering lips
    CP, 29: "In Sickness and in Health" (For Maurice and Gwen Mandel-
    baum); CSP, 45

Dear Son, when the warm multitudes cry,
    Partisan Review, Sept.-Oct. 1943: "Alonzo to Ferdinand"; FTB; CP,
    366 (Sea & Mirror); SP, 98

Dear, though the night is gone,
    New Verse, April-May 1936: "The Dream"; OTI, 61 (XXVIII); CP,
    200 (Songs IV); CSP, 230; SP, 30: "A Dream"; MS. Buffalo

Dear water, clear water, playful in all your streams,
    Atlantic, May 1955: "Streams"; Shield, 30; "Streams" (Bucolics, 7);
    SP, 174

Death like his is rich and splendid
    F6, 88; 1938 SP, 80

Deep below our violences,
    Shield, 15: "Winds" (Bucolics, 1); SP, 161

Deftly, admiral, cast your fly
    Horizon, Nov. 1948: "Songs"; Nones, 17; SP, 134

Did it once issue from the carver's hand
    Journey, 19: "The Sphinx"; Some P, 77; CP, 33; CSP, 49; SP, 58

Doom is dark and deeper than any sea-dingle.
    New Signatures, 1932: "Chorus from a Play"; P 1933, II; 1934, 9;
    1938 SP, 41; Some P, 19; CP, 34: "Something is Bound to Happen";
    CSP, 49: "The Wanderer"; SP, 17: "Chorus"

Driver, drive faster and make a good run
    AT, 78: "Calypso" (4th of Four Cabaret Songs for Miss Hedli
    Anderson)

Each lover has some theory of his own
    CP, 35: "Are You There?"; CSP, 50: "Alone"

From bad lands where eggs are small and dear
　　Dedicatory poem on t-p of Shield: For Lincoln and Fidelma Kirstein;
　　SP, t-p, no dedication
From scars where kestrels hover,
　　P 1930, XXIV; 1934, 44; CP, 43: "Missing"; CSP, 58
From the very first coming down
　　P 1928, XI; 1930, V; 1934, 13; CP, 44: "The Love Letter"; CSP, 60;
　　SP, 9: The Letter
From this new culture of the air we finally see,
　　The Listener, Dec. 16, 1954: "Ode to Gaea"; Shield, 55

Generally, reading palms or handwriting or face
　　Swarthmore Dodo, Feb. 1943: "To the Model"; CP, 45: The Model;
　　CSP, 61; SP, 85
Gently, little boat,
　　The Rake's Progress, 1951: "Barcarolle"; Shield, 49 (Aria from the
　　Rake's Progress)
Get there if you can and see the land you once were proud to own
　　P 1930, XXII; 1934, 39
Ghosts whom Honour never paid,
　　F6, dedicatory poem: To John Bicknell Auden
"Gold in the North," came the blizzard to say,
　　(Paul Bunyan, 1941); CP, 202 (Songs VII); CSP, 232
Great is Caesar: He has conquered Seven Kingdoms
　　FTB; CP, 432; A Little Treasury of Modern Poetry, ed. O. Williams
　　(1946): "Fugal-Chorus from FTB"
Guard, Civility, with guns
　　Epigraph to "In Sunshine and in Shade" in Shield

Hail, future friend, whose present I
　　Road: "c. 500 A.D."; Clio, 60: "Bathtub Thoughts"
Happy the hare at morning, for she cannot read
　　Dog, 21 (paperback, 57); CP, 46: "The Cultural Presupposition";
　　CSP, 62: "Culture"
Having abdicated with comparative ease
　　Cambridge Left, Summer 1933: "Interview"
Having finished the Blue-plate Special
　　New Yorker, Feb. 12, 1949: "In Schrafft's"; Nones, 27
He disappeared in the dead of winter:
　　New Republic, March 8, 1939: "In Memory of W. B. Yeats" (d.
　　Jan. 1939); London Mercury, April, 1939; AT, 93; CP, 48; CSP, 64;
　　SP, 66
He looked in all His wisdom from the throne
　　Journey, 269 (In Time of War, XI); Some P, 77; CP, 324; CSP, 276;
　　SP, 54: "Ganymede"
He parried every question that they hurled:
　　New Republic, Nov. 25, 1940: "The Hero" (The Quest No. 16);
　　DM, 180; CP, 259

In that ago when being was believing,
    Clio, 65: "The History of Truth"
In the bad old days it was not so bad:
    Horizon, Nov. 1948: "The Managers"; Nones, 31; SP, 139
In villages from which their childhoods came
    New Republic, Nov. 25, 1940: "The City" (The Quest No. 5);
    DM, 169; CP, 253
Incredulous, he stared at the amused
    New Republic, Nov. 25, 1940: "Vocation" (The Quest No. 12);
    DM, 176; CP, 257; SP, 74: IV
Inexorable Rembrandt rays, which stab
    Oxford Poetry, 1926: "Thomas Epilogizes"
It is a lovely sight and good
    Public Schools Verse, 1923-4, ed. Martin Gilkes, Richard Hughes &
    P. H. B. Lyon (1924); name misprinted as W. H. Anden
It is odd that the English
    Encounter, Aug. 1962: "Encomium Balnei"
It was Easter as I walked in the public gardens
    P 1930, XVI; 1934, 27; Some P, 22; CP, 62: "1929"; CSP, 79
It was quiet in there after the crushing
    Isherwood, Lions & Shadows (1947 ed.), 186: "The Engine House"
Its days are over now; no farmyard airs
    Isherwood, Lions & Shadows (1947 ed.), 186: "The Traction Engine"
It's farewell to the drawing-room's civilised cry,
    The Listener, Feb. 17, 1937, 304: "Song for the New Year"; AT, 13
    (People and Places, VIII); CP, 59: "Danse Macabre"; CSP, 77.
    Musical setting by B. Britten, 1939
Its leading characters are wise and witty;
    Journey, 23; CP, 62: "Hongkong 1938"; CSP, 79
It's no use raising a shout
    P 1933, IX; 1934, 18; O. Williams (ed.), A Little Treasury of Modern
    Poetry (1946), 566

James Honeyman was a silent child
    AT, 63: "James Honeyman" (2nd of Three Ballads)
Johnny, since today is
    CP, 68: "Many Happy Returns" (For John Rettger); CSP, 84
Jumbled in the common box
    The Nation, March 29, 1941: "Song"; CP, 206 (Songs IX); CSP, 235;
    SP, 89: "Doomsday Song" ("...one common...")
Just as his dream foretold, he met them all:
    OTI, 31 (XI); CP, 72: "Nobody Understands Me"; CSP, 88

Kicking his mother until she let go of his soul
    Commonweal, Oct. 30, 1942: "Mundus et Infans"; New Poems 1943,
    ed. Oscar Williams (1943), 15; CP, 72: "Mundus et Infans" (For
    Arthur and Angelyn Stevens); CSP, 89; SP, 91

Roar Gloucestershire, do yourself proud
    Orators, Ode IV; 1934, 166
Round the three actors in any Blessed Event
    DM, 159 (notes to NYL); CP, 103: "Blessed Event"

Say this city has ten million souls,
    New Writing, Autumn 1939; AT, 85: "Refugee Blues"; CP, 227
    (Songs XXVIII); CSP, 256. Musical setting 1934-6 by Elizabeth
    Lutyens
Season inherits legally from dying season;
    Journey, 289: Commentary (to In Time of War); CP, 337; CSP, 286
Seen when night is silent,
    Dog, 58 (Song of 1st Mad Lady); CP, 228 (Songs XXIX); CSP, 258
Self-drivers may curse their luck,
    Shield, 48: "A Permanent Way"; SP, 158
Sentries against inner and outer,
    P 1930, XIV; 1934, 25; CP, 104: "Shut Your Eyes and Open Your
    Mouth"; CSP, 114
Serious historians care for coins and weapons,
    Road: "Makers of History"; Clio, 22
Sharp and silent in the
    AT, 55 (Lighter Poems, I); CP, 105: "Heavy Date"; CSP, 115
She looked over his shoulder
    Poetry, Oct. 1952: "The Shield of Achilles"; Shield, 35; SP, 152
Should the shade of Plato
    New Yorker, March 7, 1959: "On Installing an American Kitchen in
    Lower Austria"; Clio, 15
Simple like all dream wishes, they employ
    Journey, 280 (In Time of War, XXII); CP, 331; CSP, 283
Simultaneously, as soundlessly,
    Nones, 9: "Prime" (Horae Canonicae, 1); Shield, 61; SP, 177
Since the external disorder, and extravagant lies,
    OTI, dedicatory poem to Erika Mann
Since you are going to begin today
    P 1930, III; 1934, 10; 1938 SP, 43; CP, 109: "Venus Will Now Say
    a Few Words"; CSP, 118
Sing, Ariel, sing,
    FTB; CP, 359 (Sea & Mirror); SP, 95: "Invocation to Ariel"
Sir, no man's enemy, forgiving all
    P 1930, XXX; 1934, 55; Some P, 29; CP, 110: "Petition"; CSP, 120
Sirocco brings the minor devils:
    Horizon, Oct. 1949: "Cattivo Tempo"; Nones, 43
Sixty odd years of poaching and drink
    Quoted by Isherwood in New Verse, Nov. 1937: "The Carter's
    Funeral"
Sleep on beside me though I wake for you
    New Verse, Oct. 1933: I of Five Poems; (Privately printed, Christ-
    mas, 1934)

So an age ended, and its last deliverer died
    variant of:
    And the age ended, and the last deliverer died
So from the years the gifts were showered; each
    Journey, 259 (In Time of War, I); CP, 319; CSP, 271
So large a morning so itself to lean
    Clio, 21: "The Song"
Sob, heavy world,
    Horizon, March 1948: "Lament for a Lawgiver"; Age, 104
Some say that handsome raider still at large
    P 1928, XIX; Paid (1934, 80)
Some say that Love's a little boy
    AT, 76: "O Tell Me the Truth About Love" (2nd of 4 Cabaret
    Songs for Miss Hedli Anderson)
Sometimes we see astonishingly clearly
    Nones, 14: "One Circumlocution"; SP, 132
Spinning upon their central thirst like tops,
    New Republic, Nov. 25, 1940: "The Adventurers" (The Quest No.
    18); DM, 182; CP, 261
Steatopygous, sow-dugged and owl-headed,
    Encounter, May 1960: "Dame Kind"; Clio, 53
Steep roads, a tunnel through the downs are the approaches;
    New Verse, Nov. 1937: "Dover"; AT, 46; CP, 111: "Dover 1937";
    CSP, 121
Stop all the clocks, cut off the telephone,
    F6, 112 (1st 2 st.; ff. by 3 different st.); AT, 78: "Funeral Blues"
    (3rd of 4 Cabaret Songs for Miss Hedli Anderson); CP, 228 (Songs
    XXX); CSP, 258; SP, 41: (1st of) Two Songs for Hedli Anderson
Suppose he'd listened to the erudite committee,
    New Republic, Nov. 25, 1940: "The Lucky" (The Quest No. 15);
    DM, 179; CP, 259; SP, 75: VI
Suppose they met, the inevitable procedure
    P 1928, IV; P 1930, XXV
Sylvan meant savage in those primal woods
    New Poems by American Poets, ed. Rolfe Humphries (1953), 8;
    Shield, 18: "Woods" (Bucolics, 2); SP, 163

Taller today, we remember similar evenings,
    P 1928, XVI; P 1930, XXVI; 1934, 48; CP, 113: "As Well as Can Be
    Expected"; CSP, 122: "Taller To-day"; SP, 10
That night when joy began
    OTI, 59 (XXVI); CP, 229 (Songs XXXI); CSP, 259
That we are always glad
    Ladies' Home Journal, Aug. 1950: "Secrets"; Nones, 46
The aged catch their breath,
    Atlantic Monthly, Aug. 1944: "Preface"; FTB; CP, 351: The Sea
    and the Mirror; O. Williams (ed.), A Little Treasury of American
    Poetry (1952), 702

New Republic, Dec. 7, 1938 (var.: Man does not die and never is completed); Journey, 279 (In Time of War, XXI); CP, 330; CSP, 282

The lips so apt for deed of passion
L. A. G. Strong, ed. The Best Poems of 1926 (N.Y., 1926), 9: "Portrait"

The maid has just cleared away tea (Prose)
Orators, I.iv; 1934, 111; CP, 191: "Letter to a Wound"

The mind to body spoke the whole night through
P 1928, X

The Mother had wanted
The Adelphi, June 1931: "Case-Histories, I."

The nights, the railway-arches, the bad sky,
New Writing, Spring 1939: "Rimbaud"; AT, 18; CP, 121; CSP, 133; SP, 63

The over-logical fell for the witch
New Republic, Nov. 25, 1940: "The Useful" (The Quest No. 13); DM, 177; CP, 258; SP, 74; V

The piers are pummelled by the waves;
Nation, June 14, 1947: "The Fall of Rome"; Nones, 28; "The Fall of Rome" (For Cyril Connolly); SP, 138

The sailors come ashore
Shield, 38: "Fleet Visit"; SP, 154

The scene has all the signs of a facetious culture,
Commonweal, Dec. 20, 1946: "Metropolis"; Age, 75 (Malin speaks)

The sense of danger must not disappear:
CP, 123: "Leap Before You Look"; CSP, 135

The shining neutral summer has no voice
New Writing, Autumn 1939: "In Memory of Ernst Toller (d. 1939)"; AT, 97; CP, 124; CSP, 136

The silly fool, the silly fool
P 1930, XIX; 1934, 35; CP, 125: "Happy Ending"; CSP, 137

The single creature leads a partial life,
(Paul Bunyan, 1941); CP, 230 (Songs XXXII); CSP, 259

The smelting-mill stack is crumbling, no smoke is alive there,
Quoted by Isherwood, New Verse, Nov. 1937: "Allendale"

The snow, less intransigeant than their marble,
Partisan Review, July-Aug. 1941: "At the Grave of Henry James"; CP, 126; CSP, 137

The soldier loves his rifle
F6, 96 (in part); New Verse, April-May, 1936: "Foxtrot from a Play"; O. Williams, ed., A Little Treasury of Modern Poetry (1946), 570; MS. Buffalo

The spring unsettles sleeping partnerships,
Paid (1934, 69); Louis Untermeyer, ed., Modern British Poetry, 1936; CP, 131: "It's Too Much"

The spring will come
P 1928, XVII; Paid (1934, 82)

Index

383